George Stevens

The Films of a Hollywood Giant

NEIL SINYARD

McFarland & Company, Inc., Publishers

Jefferson, North Carolina

Library of Congress Cataloguing-in-Publication Data

Names: Sinyard, Neil, author.
Title: George Stevens : the films of a Hollywood giant / Neil Sinyard.
Description: Jefferson, North Carolina : McFarland & Company, Inc.,
Publishers, 2019 | Includes bibliographical references and index.
Identifiers: LCCN 2019012517 | ISBN 9780786477753
(paperback : acid free paper) ∞
Subjects: LCSH: Stevens, George, 1904–1975—Criticism and interpretation. |
Motion picture producers and directors—United States—Biography. |
Motion pictures—United States—History—20th century.
Classification: LCC PN1998.3.S738 S56 2019 | DDC 791.4302/32092—dc23
LC record available at https://lccn.loc.gov/2019012517

British Library cataloguing data are available

ISBN (print) 978-0-7864-7775-3
ISBN (ebook) 978-1-4766-3660-3

Front cover: George Stevens, 1952 (Photofest)

Printed in the United States of America

*McFarland & Company, Inc., Publishers
Box 611, Jefferson, North Carolina 28640
www.mcfarlandpub.com*

To
George Stevens, Jr.

Table of Contents

Acknowledgments

This book is dedicated to George Stevens, Jr., in gratitude for his friendship, encouragement and support over many years. I first met George in 1984 when he appeared at a retrospective of his father's films at the National Film Theatre in London. He was there to introduce a screening of his outstanding documentary, *George Stevens: A Filmmaker's Journey*, which included unique color footage of the D-Day landings and rare interviews with some of Stevens' associates, including Fred Astaire, Ginger Rogers, Katharine Hepburn, Warren Beatty, Elizabeth Taylor, Charlton Heston, Fred Zinnemann, Frank Capra, John Huston, Rouben Mamoulian and Max von Sydow. In an act of typical generosity, while I was writing this book, he supplied me with transcriptions of all the interviews he conducted in the making of the documentary and gave his permission for me to quote from them when required; I am deeply grateful.

I had written the program notes for the NFT Stevens season and had been overjoyed to receive a letter of appreciation from George. We stayed in touch; and it had long been an ambition of mine to repay his kindness with a book that did justice to his father's remarkable career. It has been a long time coming, but I hope it proves worth the wait. Needless to say, he has in no way interfered with my work or attempted to influence my judgment. All errors of fact and imperfections of judgment are entirely my responsibility.

Additional special thanks should go the David Lean Foundation Trust, who supported my research on *The Greatest Story Ever Told*; to Brian Hoyle, for tracking down some valuable documents and articles on my behalf; to Susan Smith for sending me her book on Elizabeth Taylor, which has a first-rate chapter on *Giant*; to Francois Gallix and Michel Ciment for their kindness in supplying me with a copy of *Positif* (February 2017 issue), which contains a fascinating dossier on Stevens; and to Ian Payne and David Miller, director and programmer respectively, of the Keswick Film Festival, for allowing me to share my enthusiasm for Stevens at their 2018 festival.

I have benefited enormously from consulting the work of a number of critics on the work of Stevens, particularly (in alphabetical order): Gilbert Adair, Eugene Archer, Nicholas Bartlett, Ben Brewster, Mark Harris, Penelope Houston, Joseph McBride, Douglas McVay, Ivan Moffat, Donald Richie and Andrew Sarris. A special mention is owed to Marilyn Ann Moss, whose critical biography of Stevens is a valuable source of information and stimulation.

There are a number of people whose friendship has sustained me during the writing of this book and to whom I owe the deepest thanks (in alphabetical order); Lesley Brill, Judith Buchanan, Jonathan Coe, Peter Evans, Tom Leitch, Brian McFarlane, David Rolinson, Adrian Turner and Melanie Williams. I would like also to mention three dear friends, now deceased, who were infallible sources of guidance and encouragement and whose memory I cherish: David Shipman, Peter Walsh and Gilian West.

Many thanks also to David Alff and all at McFarland & Company who have not only been unfailingly courteous and supportive of the whole enterprise but also patient and understanding when circumstances delayed the book's completion.

Above all, none of this would be possible without the strength and confidence I gain from the love of my wonderful family: my daughters, Nathalie and Jessica, my son, Joel, and my wife, Lesley, who has been my Woman of the Year for the last 45 years, and always.

Chronology

1904: Born 18 December in Oakland, California, son of Lander Stevens, actor and stage manager, and Georgie Cooper, stage actress daughter of legendary classical actress Georgia Woodthorpe, who was said to be the toast of San Francisco during the Gold Rush. His uncle, Ashton Stevens, is an esteemed drama critic in Chicago and, according to Orson Welles, the model for the character of Jed Leland, played by Joseph Cotten, in *Citizen Kane*.

1921: the family moves to Los Angeles, where Lander works as an actor, Georgia as a bit player in silent movies.

1924: joins Hal Roach studios as an assistant cameraman, studying with Floyd Jackman.

1927: cameraman on Laurel and Hardy two-reeler comedies. He will photograph some of their most famous shorts, including *Battle of the Century, Another Fine Mess* and *Big Business*. (Coincidentally, some of Laurel and Hardy's greatest shorts of the early sound era, such as *Laughing Gravy, Our Wife, Beau Chumps, One Good Turn*, all made in 1931, will be directed by Stevens' cousin, James Horne.)

1930: writer and director on Hal Roach's *Boy Friends* short films, such as *Call a Cop!* and *The Kick-Off*. Marries Yvonne Sherlin, a Mack Sennett employee who has been introduced to Stevens by her friend, Oliver Hardy.

1932: moves to Universal Studios and works as scriptwriter, then director, for producer, Warren Doane. His son, George Jr., is born.

1933: directs his first feature at Universal, *The Cohens and the Kellys in Trouble*. Then moves to RKO Studios, where he works on "The Blondes and the Redhead" films, beginning with *Flirting in the Park*.

1934: directs his first drama, *Laddie*, which is seen by Katharine Hepburn, who chooses him to direct her in *Alice Adams*.

1935: directs *Alice Adams*, which is nominated for an Oscar as Best Picture. He follows it almost immediately with *Annie Oakley*, with Barbara Stanwyck in the title role.

1936: directs *Swing Time*, widely regarded as the best of the Astaire-Rogers musicals.

1937: directs a screen adaptation of J.M. Barrie's *Quality Street*, with Katharine Hepburn. Also *A Damsel in Distress*, with Fred Astaire but without Ginger Rogers.

1938: directs Ginger Rogers without Fred Astaire in *Vivacious Lady*, co-starring James Stewart.

1939: works uncredited on *Having Wonderful Time*, with Ginger Rogers and Douglas Fairbanks, Jr. Produces and directs the smash-hit adventure *Gunga Din*.

1940: directs his last film under contract to RKO, *Vigil in the Night*, starring Carole Lombard, before moving to Columbia Pictures, where he is promised creative freedom by the feared movie tycoon Harry Cohn.

1941: becomes president of the Screen Directors Guild, until 1943. Directs Cary Grant and Irene Dunne in *Penny Serenade*, for which Grant receives his first Oscar nomination.

1942: director of the first film to co-star Spencer Tracy and Katharine Hepburn, *Woman of the Year*; and a comedy drama, *The Talk of the Town*, starring Cary Grant, Jean Arthur and Ronald Colman.

1943: directs *The More the Merrier*, for which he will be voted Best Director of the Year by the New York Film Critics and for which he will also be nominated for an Oscar.

1943–5: appointed head of the Signals Corp Special Motion Picture Unit, which is assigned to photograph Allied military activity in Europe. His films, shot in color in 16mm, will include coverage of the liberation of Paris and the entry of Allied forces into the concentration camp at Dachau.

1945: released from military service with the rank of lieutenant colonel, five battle stars, the Legion of Merit, and a special citation from General Eisenhower. Two of the films on which he worked, *The Nazi Plan* and *The Nazi Concentration Camps*, are to be shown to devastating effect at the Nuremberg war crimes trial. Establishes Liberty Films with directors William Wyler and Frank Capra and producer Samuel Briskin.

1948: Liberty Films is sold to Paramount. Directs a segment of *On Our Merry Way*, with James Stewart and Henry Fonda. Directs his first postwar feature, *I Remember Mama*.

1949: divorce from his wife, Yvonne Sherlin.

1950: Famously routs the forces of Cecil B. De Mille and his cohorts in their attempt to remove Joseph L. Mankiewicz as president of the Directors Guild with his intervention at the legendary Guild meeting of 22 October. Stevens' oration, in which he details and denounces the underhand tactics employed by the De Mille faction in attempting to rig the vote, will later be described by Mankiewicz as "worthy of Clarence Darrow."

1951: release of *A Place in the Sun*, for which he will win an Oscar for best direction.

1952: A delayed release of *Something to Live For*, starring Ray Milland, Joan Fontaine and Teresa Wright.

1953: directs the classic western *Shane*, for which he will receive his third Oscar nomination as best director.

1954: At the Oscar ceremony on 15 February receives the Irving G. Thalberg Memorial Award, awarded to "creative producers whose body of work reflects a consistently high quality of motion picture production."

1956: directs *Giant,* the final film of James Dean. He will win his second Best Director Oscar and also the Screen Directors Guild Award for the film.

1958: President of the Academy of Motion Picture Arts and Sciences for one year. Awarded the D.W. Griffith Award for Lifetime Achievement by the Screen Directors Guild.

1959: directs *The Diary of Anne Frank,* for which will be nominated for an Oscar for best direction.

1965: sues NBC and Paramount Pictures for screening on television a version of *A Place in the Sun* that has been cut to make room for commercials. A judge rules that Paramount cannot cut the film, but that NBC can continue to insert commercials in their showing of films. After five years in the preparation and the making, *The Greatest Story Ever Told* is released but is a critical and commercial failure.

1968: marries long-time partner, Joan McTavish, in Paris.

1969: directs his final film, *The Only Game in Town*, with Elizabeth Taylor and Warren Beatty.

1975: dies unexpectedly of a heart attack in Los Angeles on 8 March.

Introduction: Hollywood Giant

"George was a master psychologist. I thought directing was telling people to do what you wanted them to do. What I learned from George was that directing is really about *allowing* people to do what you want them to do by making them think it was their idea."—Robert Hinkle, *Call Me Lucky: A Texan in Hollywood*

During a visit to Hollywood in 1954, the critic Kenneth Tynan interviewed Mae Marsh, star of D.W. Griffith's silent movie classic *Intolerance* (1916) and asked her if she thought there was anyone of Griffith's stature in present-day Hollywood. "Did you see *Shane?*" she replied. "I wrote this Mr. Stevens who directed it.... He reminded me of Mr. Griffith. He had that pioneer feeling" (qtd in Silvester: 439). Prompted by this exchange, Tynan went to interview Stevens and was not disappointed. "A shambling baby elephant of a man," was his description of him, "who radiates integrity, tolerance and insight ... a trustworthy film-maker of striking compassion" (Silvester 440). In some ways, this book can be seen as a detailed elaboration of that encapsulation of Stevens' character and career.

His cinematic progression is often seen as a slow dissolve (his most characteristic stylistic trait) from being master of comedy to poet of sentiment. The truth is a little more complicated, but it is certainly the case that his career demonstrated the possibility of quality and variety in an industry supposedly given over to commerce and conformity, and the possibility of making personal films that won the praise of critics, the support of audiences, and the admiration of his peers. Few directors could claim a greater knowledge of his craft from such a thorough grounding in the profession, In a period spanning over 50 years from his beginnings in the industry during the silent era to his final film in 1970, his film experience ranged from the popular duo of Wheeler and Wolsey to the legendary partnership of Tracy and Hepburn, from Annie Oakley to Anne Frank, from photographing Laurel and Hardy to filming the Bible. Beginning as an assistant cameraman for Hal Roach, Stevens learned his screen craft when comedy was king in the 1920s but he came to full artistic maturity in a very different era when America emerged from World War into Cold War.

The 1930s features particularly highlight his refined comedy style, which is slow-burning rather than screwball, romantic more than frenetic. They also demonstrate his felicitous handling of stars like Hepburn and Stanwyck, James Stewart and Cary Grant, all of whom blossomed under his direction. The films include the most elegant of the Astaire Rogers musicals, *Swing Time* (1936); one of the decade's most underrated comedies, *Vivacious Lady* (1938); and one of the best-loved of all adventure movies, *Gunga Din* (1939). In the early 1940s, he teams Spencer Tracy and Katharine Hepburn for the first time in a battle-of-the-sexes comedy, *Woman of the Year* (1942), which famously culminates in a classic comedy routine where Hepburn progressively wrecks the kitchen in her anxious endeavor to give her husband his breakfast. This extended sequence is matched for comic precision in another early 1940s comedy, *The More the Merrier* (1943), when the housing shortage in Washington has compelled Jean Arthur's government worker to share her apartment with two men who promptly reduce her rigid morning routine to total chaos. Yet it is Stevens' first major film, *Alice Adams* (1935), in which Katharine Hepburn gives her most touching screen performance, that offers the clearest intimations of things to come. The heroine's social ambitions and determination to better herself have sometimes been taken as an allegory of Stevens' own cinematic intentions. Whether he exchanged early freshness for later pomposity, or whether the earlier frivolity gives way to later profundity, remains the central critical question of his career. Andrew Sarris thought the former, describing Stevens as "a minor director with major virtues before *A Place in the Sun,* and a major director with minor virtues after" (Sarris: 110). My own feeling is that his greatest films are the post-war American Dream trilogy, *A Place in the Sun* (1951). *Shane* (1953) and *Giant* (1956), while fully acknowledging that the earlier comedies, even when being frivolous, are never facile and remain unerringly stylish and enjoyable.

This two-part division of Stevens' career is something of a simplification anyway, since dramas such as *Shane* and *Giant* are spiced with quiet humor, and comedies such as *Woman of the Year* and *The More the Merrier* have serious undercurrents. Nevertheless, there is a pronounced change of sensibility, brought about by Stevens's experience in World War II, when, as head of a Special Film Unit to record the Allied advance in Europe, he is part of the force that liberates the concentration camp at Dachau, an experience he is later to describe, in an interview with William Kirshner in 1963, as "like wandering around in one of Dante's infernal visions" (qtd in Cronin: 19). Thereafter comedy recedes, and his former optimism is now qualified by tragic sacrifice, untimely deaths. *The Diary of Anne Frank* (1959) and *The Greatest Story Ever Told* (1965) will be the culmination of this progression, stories of spiritual uplift but told with a somber reflectiveness. The post-war films seem to be reaching for something beyond a replication of the real world towards an ideal. You get the same feeling in the novels of Henry James and the plays of Anton Chekhov—the tension between realism and romanticism, between the world as it is and the world as it ought to be. Discussing *A Place in the Sun* with Jim Silke in 1964, Stevens reflected that "I think I am *totally* for reality, but I am aware that I adapt this truth to the romance of the way I would like things to be" (qtd in Cronin: 48).

In fact the tragedies occurring in Europe were casting shadows over Stevens' work even before his first-hand observation of the unimaginable horrors he encountered. During the 1930s he had wanted to make films of *The Mortal Storm* (about political prisoners in pre-war Nazi Germany, to be filmed by Frank Borzage in 1940) and *Paths of Glory* (Humphrey Cobb's novel about military catastrophe and cover-up during World War I, later to be filmed by Stanley Kubrick in 1957). His hospital drama *Vigil in the Night* (1940) is appreciably darker than A.J. Cronin's novel, for it concludes at the time of the outbreak

clever chiasmus

of World War II. *Woman of the Year, The Talk of the Town* (1942) and *The More the Merrier* all have troubling subtexts beneath their comedy exteriors, borne out of an anxiety at the Fascist assaults on Europe and the urgency of American involvement to safeguard democracy. Like fellow filmmakers such as Frank Capra, John Ford, John Huston, William Wyler and others, Stevens was quick to enlist and put his career on hold when America entered the war, for he had no illusions about the dangers ahead nor any doubts about the sacrifices required to serve his country in a just cause.

Courage and integrity were two constants in Stevens' career, which is the reason that he was venerated by his cinematic peers. In his pursuit of excellence, he would defy the front office and have his own strategy of seeing off potential interference, which an admiring Fred Zinnemann called his "Indian look" as he was being berated for being behind schedule by desperate producers. "Stevens would just sit there and listen without any expression on his big impassive face, never say a word," Zinnemann recalled, "and when the producer ran out of breath, he would say, 'Thank you very much,' get up, and go back to work. His pictures made millions" (Zinnemann: 53). His intervention at the Screen Directors Guild meeting of 22 October 1950, when the Cecil B. DeMille faction tried to oust Joseph L. Mankiewicz from the presidency, is the stuff of legend, a speech that Robert Parrish was to describe as "an articulate, devastating list of charges" against the anti–Mankiewicz faction and which, apart from the group around DeMille, brought the entire membership to its feet in applause (Parrish: 209). Stevens had been president of the Guild himself and a director's right of self-expression was sacred to him. One aspect of this is that, unusually among Hollywood directors of his generation and someone whose reputation did not benefit greatly from it, Stevens was a fan of the so-called "auteur theory," which ascribed most of the responsibility and achievement of a film to its director. "Those are the kind of films I like to see, as singular as you can make the point of view," he told his interviewer, Mary Anne Fisher in 1963. "Only then does a film take on definition for me. The 'auteur' concept is certainly the most desirable form of filmmaking from my point of view" (qtd in Cronin: 28). The directors he admired wanted to make films, first and foremost, and only secondly to make money. He stood up for the creative independence and artistic integrity of the director, instigating a lawsuit against Paramount Pictures and NBC for a television screening in 1965 of *A Place in the Sun* which had cut the film and interrupted its transmission with commercials. The case was lost (the station retained the right to insert advertisements) but Stevens was widely admired across the directing community for his endeavor to protect other directors and the medium itself from the whole business of selling movies to television and having their work adulterated to suit the commercial imperatives of the newer medium. Warren Beatty was to reflect that it was Stevens' idealism with regard to such professional matters that, when he ran into trouble over the shooting schedule of *The Greatest Story Ever Told,* directors of the stature of David Lean and Jean Negulesco volunteered to help without payment.

Stevens' own working methods were very individual. He would shoot a vast amount of footage and spend months in the editing room afterwards. When his son asked him one afternoon in the projection room why he was still fiddling around with *Giant* after three enthusiastic previews, he replied: "When you think about how many man-hours people will spend watching this picture, don't you think it's worth a little more of our time to make it as good as we can?" (Stevens Jr.: 221). He would not be rushed; and, more often than not, it paid off. When Paramount executives were grumbling about his going over the budget on *Shane* and indeed exceeding the box-office returns of the usual Alan Ladd movie, a junior assistant (later fine director) Alan J. Pakula responded: "He's not making an Alan Ladd movie, he's making a George Stevens movie." In its first year of release, *Shane* had made over twice as much at the box office as any previous Ladd movie. When the head of Warner Bros., Jack Warner, was growing apprehensive over the spiraling costs of *Giant* and was apoplectic over the film's low-key ending, he was soon to be mollified when the film turned out to be the biggest hit in the studio's history up to that time

Stevens' painstaking care over detail was not simply an aspect of his professional perfectionism but also of his reflective personality. "I am aware I deal with outsiders," he said once, " because I have always felt more at home as an observer than a participant in various situations" (qtd in Phillips: 83). His visual style invites an audience not simply to watch but gives them room to reflect on what they are seeing. Expressing his deep appreciation of *The Diary of Anne Frank,* Steven Spielberg told George Stevens, Jr., that "we admire Stevens today because he never rushed his images, casting long spells on us, only asking us to be patient with him—and when we were, he rewarded us with one indelible image after another" (Stevens Jr.: 220). As examples of this, one need only think of the slow dissolve at the end of the mother's phone call in *A Place in the Sun,* or the opening shot of the burial scene in *Shane,* or the revelation of Angel's coffin on the railway cart in *Giant.* They are all sustained shots which invite quiet contemplation of a kind that resonates beyond the immediate narrative situation.

Actors sometimes found Stevens' methods exasperating. He liked a quiet set and would sometimes wander off alone before starting shooting, deep in thought, leaving the actors standing around and waiting. What was he thinking about? The story goes that Carole Lombard once rang him at 3 a.m. to express her firm conviction, in her customary colorful language, that he was not thinking about anything at all. Method actors such as Montgomery Clift and James Dean found him difficult, although as Robert Hinkle's epigraph to this Introduction suggests, Stevens had his own way of drawing the desired performance from an actor; and the performances he drew from Clift and Dean, while not necessarily their most representative, are arguably their finest on screen. In his memoir *Letters from an Actor,* William Redfield included an amusing anecdote about Stevens' method of dealing with Method actors. "During the filming of *The Greatest Story Ever Told,*" wrote Redfield, "George Stevens (a really excellent film director) was queried by an actor as to 'motivation.' 'Young man,' he said, 'while you were resting yesterday, I went up in those hills over there and I shot a lot of sequence with a herd of cattle. Not one of those cattle asked me about motivation, and believe you me, they did just fine'" (Redfield: 111). Admittedly, Stevens was an exceptionally fine director of animals. Still, when one simply looks at the list of actors who gained Oscar nominations for performances in his films—Katharine Hepburn (twice), Cary Grant, Jean Arthur, Charles Coburn (who won), Irene Dunne, Oscar Homolka, Barbara Bel Geddes, Ellen Corby, Montgomery Clift, Shelley Winters (twice, including an Oscar win), Brandon de Wilde, Jack Palance, Rock Hudson, James Dean, Mercedes McCambridge, Ed Wynn—one could hardly claim that his methods did not deliver. Shelley Winters thought him a genius and called him "my favourite director in all the world" (Winters: 111). In his journal, *The Actor's Life,* Charlton Heston described him as "surely one of the best directors who ever lived" (Heston: 159).

Revisiting Stevens' films has been an inspiring and, in certain respects, surprising experience. It was inevitable that *Shane* would loom large, for I have loved that film since childhood and countless subsequent viewings have only enhanced my appreciation of its artistry; so it was an especial delight to see Joseph McBride, the distinguished biographer of John Ford, no less, describing *Shane* as "the greatest of all westerns" and Stevens as "the most underrated American director today" (*Sight and Sound,* October 2017: 93) The revelation for me on reacquaintance has been how far so many of the films transcend their time. George Stevens, Jr., once told me that, when he was driving home with his father after the latter had won a Best Director Oscar for *A Place in the Sun*, he was surprised to find the much coveted statuette had been tossed casually on the back seat of the car. As explanation, his father told him: "We'll see how much it's worth in 25 years' time." Sadly, Stevens died of a sudden heart attack in 1975 just before he could test his prediction; and, in any case, he was, if anything, underestimating the time necessary for a true evaluation of the longevity of his achievement. More than sixty years on, the films look more revelatory and relevant than ever, so that, for example. one can now see that *Penny Serenade* contains one of the most sophisticated uses of flashback in the history of Hollywood cinema; that *The Talk of the Town,* as well as its delights as a romantic comedy-thriller, articulates thoughts about what is cherishable about the American Constitution that were not only vital in 1942 but resonate even more powerfully today; that *Woman of the Year* is as much a war film as a romantic comedy and the exact opposite of the anti-feminist tract it has often been taken to be; and that *Giant,* away from its significance as the last screen performance of James Dean, is a daring demolition of patriarchy; one of the most originally structured of all film epics; has a last shot of a Mexican American infant as symbol of the future which now looks startling in the context of Trump's America; and one of the most thoughtful and wide-ranging depictions of a marriage in American cinema.

Marriage is a key theme in Stevens' films (there are four weddings—and a funeral—in *Giant* alone) reflecting the fact that all his films are love stories of one kind or another, albeit very different. What marks them out as original is that marriage is, more often than not in Stevens, a starting point for a film and not its romantic resolution. If many films ended on a note of "happily ever after," Stevens' films are invariably more interested in the "after" and the strains and complications that can test the ties that bind. Connected with that is the prominent role of women in his films. His heroines are not seen as secondary romantic interest, but are of equal importance to the heroes and often are the main driving force behind the narrative. While some critics at the time and over the years seemed to think his films dated and old-fashioned, which perhaps explains the relative sparsity of commentary on his work compared with that on, say, Ford and Hawks, his films now look progressive, pertinent and prescient. Fellow directors saw him as a trail-blazer and he was to be an inspiration to a succeeding generation of filmmakers. Woody Allen, Mike Nichols, Steven Spielberg, Martin Scorsese, Sam Peckinpah, Robert Mulligan, Alan J. Pakula, David Mamet, John Sturges and Budd Boetticher are only some of the people who have paid tribute to Stevens' example. Perhaps the finest tribute of all is George Stevens, Jr.'s, documentary on his father, *George Stevens: A Filmmaker's Journey* (1984), assuredly one of the best documentaries on a film director ever made.

Stevens thought of the screen simply as a white sheet with shadows on it. The task of the director, he said, was "all about making sure the film bounces off that sheet and comes to life in the minds of the audience" (Stevens Jr.: 234). He succeeded; and in films that revealed his mastery of his craft, his artistry as a poet of human aspiration, and the fundamental decency of the man.

ONE

The RKO Period, 1935–1940

Stevens' route to his first significant feature, *Alice Adams* in 1935, was a somewhat circuitous one. Before that film he had been almost exclusively associated with comedy. He would always acknowledge the influence of Laurel and Hardy on his comedy style, particularly in his approach to realism and deliberation in the construction of comic business and where, although the humor might derive from escalating chaos, it should be rooted in relationships with which an audience could empathize. His first feature, *The Cohens and the Kellys in Trouble* (1933) was made for Universal, and was the last in a series which featured George Sidney as Cohen and Charles Murray as Kelly. The reunion between a millionaire, Cohen, and a tugboat captain, Kelly is complicated by the reappearance of Kelly's ex-wife (Jobyna Holland) demanding alimony; and the narrative is driven mainly by Kelly's attempt to get out of this obligation. The romantic interest is provided by Maureen O'Sullivan as Kelly's daughter and Frank Albertson (who was to play Katharine Hepburn's brother in *Alice Adams*) as a young naval officer. The most inventive piece of comic business occurs in a scene in which a live lobster drops first into Cohen's and then Kelly's oyster stew and proceeds to make mischief under the surface.

After being fired by Hal Roach over a disagreement concerning a script, Stevens was offered a contract by RKO in 1933 and made a series of comedy shorts for producer Lou Brock. His first feature for RKO, *Bachelor Bait* (1934), was a routine assignment starring Stuart Erwin as the head of a matrimonial agency, Romance Inc., who almost pairs off a millionaire to a woman he loves until the millionaire is claimed by a golddigger of 1934. He also made two films with the popular comedy duo Bert Wheeler and Robert Wolsey. In the exhilarating *Kentucky Kernels* (1934), they adopt a small boy as a means to an inheritance and become involved in a murderous feud between two families. Among a number of comic highlights, there is a delightful musical number which begins with Bert Wheeler serenading his sweetheart before the number expands to involve not only all the participants at a party, but also a dog and a donkey; a gunfight in which berries take the place of bullets; a wild chase led by an intoxicated horse whose vision becomes progressively blurred and its progress necessarily more perilous; and Margaret Dumont at her most charmingly imperious. In *The Nitwits* (1935), Wheeler confesses to a murder to save his girlfriend (Betty Grable) from execution; Woolsey confesses to save Wheeler; and none of them happens to be the guilty party, who is a blackmailer terrorizing the city. All is enjoyably resolved in a chase climax. The most significant of his early features was the least typical, *Laddie* (1935), a tale of country folk in Indiana, based on the novel by Gene Stratton Porter, and starring John Beal as Laddie Stanton, a young farmer who is in love with Pamela Pryor (Gloria Stuart), but whose romance is opposed by the young woman's stern and snobbish farmer (Donald Crisp). A seven-year-old Virginia Weidler gives a scene-stealing performance as Laddie's little sister. When the film was critically well received, it came to the attention of Katharine Hepburn as she was discussing with producer Pandro S. Berman who should direct *Alice Adams*. It was to prove a decisive turning point in Stevens' career.

father?

Alice Adams (1935)

> "Is it life to spend your time imagining things that aren't so and never will be? Beautiful things happen to other people, why should I be the only one they never *can* happen to?"—Booth Tarkington, *Alice Adams*, Chapter 9

During a break in the filming of *Alice Adams*, George Stevens was having lunch with his star Katharine Hepburn when they were joined by the agent Leland Hayward, with whom at that time Hepburn was romantically involved. Hayward was in a state of high excitement and spent the next few minutes enthusing about the lucrative deal worth millions of dollars he had concluded on behalf of one of his clients. Stevens listened in silence, but after Hayward had departed, he suddenly leaned across the table, put his arm around Hepburn, and kissed her on the lips. "Money, money, money," he said. "I can't bear that talk. It's what we do that's great, isn't it?" It clinched Hepburn's complete confidence in a director who shared her integrity and ideals.

Musing on the films Stevens had made before *Alice Adams*, notably the popular Wheeler and Wolsey comedies, Andrew Sarris always wondered what it was that Hepburn had seen in his previous work to pick him (Sarris: 356). Apparently, when Hepburn and producer Pandro S. Berman were discussing who should direct, they had narrowed their preference to either Stevens or William Wyler and were preparing to decide on the toss of a coin. One might think that Wyler would be Hepburn's preferred choice, for he certainly had the stronger track record at that stage, with films such as *A House Divided* (1931) and *Counsellor at Law* (1933) already demonstrating his sound instincts for drama. One would have expected Berman to favor Stevens, partly because he had worked compatibly with him before and partly (taking financial considerations into account) because Stevens would be less expensive to hire. However, although the toss went Wyler's way, on an instinct, Hepburn opted for Stevens. She had enjoyed Stevens' previous film, *Laddie* (1934), for its warm-hearted depiction of late nineteenth century rural America and had a hunch that Wyler might be too European for this very American subject.

Their first meeting was inauspicious. Sharing an intimate moment with Charles Boyer in the back of a studio car, Hepburn was annoyed to be interrupted by a knocking on the car window by a bedraggled looking Stevens, who had just hurried from filming a messy slapstick sequence in *The Nitwits* to remind her that they had a script conference appointment in ten minutes' time. At their first conference in the company of Berman, Stevens had been entirely silent, causing Hepburn to wonder whether she had made a big mistake in her choice of director. The explanation for Stevens' silence was twofold: mainly because he had not yet read Booth Tarkington's novel; but also because he wanted to study Hepburn. Later his collaborators would recognize that silence as an aspect of Stevens' taciturn, watchful personality.

Alice Adams was to prove a turning point for both actress and director. After her previous three films had failed at the box office, Hepburn was in need of a hit to revive her career; and *Alice Adams* gave her not only a welcome success but the opportunity to give one of her finest performances, gaining her an Oscar nomination. She was to lose out to Bette Davis for her performance in *Dangerous* (1935), but Davis was gracious enough to concede later that "there was no doubt Hepburn's performance deserved the award" (Davis: 150). For Stevens it was the first film in which, in Sarris's words, he could reveal "a fully mature personal style" which blended "Wyler's meticulousness and McCarey's sentimentality" (Sarris: 357). Even the theme of "bettering oneself" seemed to strike a chord with him, reflecting his desire to do more ambitious work than had hitherto presented itself. Some of his later key themes are adumbrated here: the sympathy with the outsider, the critique of snobbery and cold-hearted materialism; the anguish of social humiliation. With *Alice Adams*, he emerged as a director to be reckoned with, skillfully treading a fine line between romantic comedy and downbeat drama.

Published in 1921, Booth Tarkington's novel *Alice Adams* had won the Pulitzer Prize for that year, in this respect emulating the success of a previous novel of his, *The Magnificent Ambersons* (1918). Alice Adams is a young woman in a small Midwestern town who dreams of social grandeur but whose aspirations are being constantly thwarted by her circumstances. In a society where prestige and success are fundamentally determined by money, Alice has been left behind, for, while the families of her former school friends have flourished financially to the benefit of their children, Alice's sickly father has been content to remain in his lowly job as a clerk in the employment of the wholesale drug manufacturer Lamb & Company. The situation comes to a head when Alice has a humiliating evening at a society dance, but attracts the interest there of a wealthy young man, Arthur Russell. Goaded by Alice's mother, who is sensitive to Alice's situation and exasperated at what she sees as her husband's indolence and lack of ambition on their daughter's behalf, the father is finally prevailed upon to go into business for himself as a glue manufacturer, exploiting a formula that he and Lamb had jointly created many years before. However, the venture is sabotaged when Lamb erects a larger competing glue factory nearby, and then further undermined when it is discovered that Alice's brother, Walter, who works for Lamb, has been embezzling money from the company. "A rain of misfortunes," Tarkington writes, "had selected the Adams family for its scaldings; no question" (Chapter 23). The father has a stroke and is unable anymore to support his family. The mother is compelled to take in boarders. All romantic hopes now dashed, Alice resigns herself to a menial job at Frincke's Business College, whose doorway she had earlier likened to an entrance to Purgatory and had seen as the end of youth and hope. Approaching the doorway at the end, she bravely faces a less exalted, more realistic future. "Halfway up the shadows were heaviest," Tarkington concludes, "but after that the place began to seem brighter. There was an open window overhead somewhere, she found; and the steps at the top were gay with sunshine."

Criticized by some reviewers for not being as humorous in this novel as in some of his earlier stories, Tarkington's response was: "Oh, Gosh. AA was intended to be as humorous as tuberculosis" (qtd in Schwartz: 220). He was similarly unimpressed when some critics complained that they found Alice unsympathetic, for he stated simply that "the girl is drawn without any liking or disliking of her by the writer who is concerned only with making a portrait of her insides and outsides" (qtd in Tibbetts and Welsh: 8). However, he was mindful of the fact that if his novel were to be filmed, the ending might need to be changed, for the Hollywood of the early 1920s, he thought, was not yet ready to accommodate the comparative bleakness of his vision.

A silent film version was actually made in 1923, directed by Rowland V. Lee, produced by King Vidor and starring Vidor's wife, Florence, but the film has since been lost. From available evidence it seems as if it stuck quite closely to the novel. When Stevens came to make it in 1935, the points of controversy were all the ones that Tarkington had identified when his novel first appeared. One can certainly claim that Stevens' film is funnier than tuberculosis (the great writer-director Joseph L. Mankiewicz called it a "great, great comedy" and freely admitted that it influenced his 1949 Oscar-winning drama, *A Letter to Three Wives*), but it is also true that the film's funniest scene (Alice's dinner party for Arthur) is simultaneously its most anguished, a scene that Stevens called, in his production notes, "a crescendo of suffering." Critics at the time and since have had mixed feelings over where their sympathies should lie in relation to the individuals in the Adams family, but Stevens typically is careful to make one aware of the validity of everyone's point of view. If Depression audiences might have little sympathy with Alice's dream of social grandeur when they were preoccupied less with social status than simple survival, Katharine Hepburn felt a strong empathy with Alice. "I particularly liked my character in *Alice Adams*," she told Charlotte Chandler. "It reminded me of the way small-minded people treated my mother, shunning her and us children, not because they thought we weren't good enough, but because they thought *we* thought that we were *too* good" (qtd in Chandler: 90). The film's enforced happy ending, which both Stevens and Hepburn opposed, rankles to this day, but is treated so perfunctorily by director and star that the happiness is made to seem decidedly hollow.

The film's opening concisely evokes the context of the drama. A banner celebrating the town's anniversary proudly proclaims the setting as "South Renford, Indiana, The Town With a Future." The camera tracks from left to right across the main street, passing the News building and the Vogue Smart Shop before stopping at Samuel's Five-Ten-Fifteen Cents Store. In medium shot, a black mother is seen exiting the store with her two children, followed by Alice, who hurriedly moves away to avoid being seen and only pauses to inspect her purchase (a compact) outside the more select Vogue Shop. Instantly Alice's social status is established, and also her discomfiture with it; indeed the black family who have preceded her out of Samuel's seems in some way to anticipate the appearance of Malena, the black maid at Alice's later dinner party for Arthur, who will cast a comical yet also critical and conspicuous shadow over Alice's social pretensions. When Alice now visits a florist and enquires about some orchids and gardenias for her corsage for the Palmer ball that evening, Hepburn's hesitations and slightly tremulous voice marvelously convey an outward display of choosiness that only barely masks the fact that the flowers are completely out of her price range. We next see Alice as she furtively picks violets in Bellevue Park before the camera pulls back to reveal the sign: Do Not Pick the Flowers. The contrast between her social airs and social actuality is nailed in barely five minutes of screen time. The film will be exquisitely polarized between humor and pain, as the hapless aspirations of Alice take place in a romantic haze of her own making, with Stevens, one feels, willing the outsider to succeed while recognizing that he or she rarely does.

When Alice returns home, we have our first encounter with what Pauline Kael provocatively described as "that nightmare of a ghastly family; Fred Stone as the infantile father; Ann Shoemaker as the pushing mother; Frank Albertson as the vulgar brother" (Kael: 283). Audiences and indeed critics at the time did not see things in quite that way. Whereas Kael saw Alice as "one of the few authentic American movie heroines" (282), the *Variety* review at the time of the film's release called her "a silly little ninny in her pretences." Andrew Sarris noticed that Meyer Levin of *Esquire* had more sympathy for the down-to-earth father and brother than for Alice (Sarris: 357); and in her engrossing 1977 chapter on the film, Nancy Schwartz recorded that a 1938 Commission on Human Relations, which encouraged the inclusion of film in school curricula, asked of the title character of *Alice Adams* (in a manner that seemed to signal its disapproval of her): "Was Alice realistic about what was important to her community? Alice was not hungry, she had clothes to wear, food to eat" (Schwartz: 220). In fairness to the film, it is a point that Alice makes herself to her mother; and it is her mother who frets more on her behalf, as she watches Alice's former childhood friends, with only a fraction of Alice's natural ability and attributes, seeming to prosper socially while Alice is reduced to picking flowers and embroidering an old dress to make a presentable front at a party. When she asks Alice what dress Mildred Palmer will be wearing at the party, she must surely notice the slight wistfulness in her daughter's voice when she replies, "The one she brought back from Paris" (and the close-up of Hepburn at this point locates a momentary sense of pathos and sad envy). Whereas Kael was dismayed by what she called "the revolting, nagging, massive-bosomed mother" (Kael: 283), a later critic Gene D. Phillips approvingly quoted an alternative view of Mrs. Adams from Elliott Sirkin in *Film Comment* who thought it "clear that in her indignation over the coldness shown her daughter by the town's newly organised first families, she is the spokeswoman for Stevens and the film" (qtd in Phillips: 84). Up to a point perhaps, but it is also clear that her indignation is directed equally at her husband, whose lethargy has left their daughter floundering while her schoolmates have prospered.

Meanwhile Virgil Adams languishes in his sickbed upstairs, seemingly thankful for small mercies that his boss Mr. Lamb might bestow but giving the impression of a man bypassed by the modern world. He and Alice are obviously devoted to one another, but one can understand the mother's frustration at the way Alice seems to pander to her father's docility and self-pity. "Poor old daddikins," Alice says to him, when Virgil is weakly, even tearfully, bemoaning Mrs. Adams' perception of him as a failure. Rather than face up to his wife, the father will raise the volume of his radio to drown out her criticism. Sympathies across the family members are drawn with some complexity, which is a measure of Stevens' endeavor to give each character his or her due, in terms of strengths and faults, and to replicate Tarkington's own stated objectivity in his presentation of the characters. A review in the *New York Times* of 16 August 1935 caught this sense of ambivalence, when noting that a Depression audience might be unsympathetically disposed towards a social climber like Alice, but adding that "the plight of the Adams family becomes genuinely heartbreaking when we realize how accurately delineated these people are in terms of small-town life before the Depression."

Conversation between mother and daughter about the dance is brusquely interrupted by Alice's brother Walter (Frank Albertson), who seems as brash and selfish as Alice is bright and sensitive. Yet, in being singularly unimpressed by Alice's social aspirations and her circle of acquaintances ("I'm no society snake," he says), Walter does add a shot of realism to dilute Alice's air of romantic reverie and the mother's tone of rueful regret. He also introduces a touch of caustic humor into the proceedings. Reluctantly agreeing to drive Alice to the dance but refusing to indulge her air of social grandeur, he chooses (much to Alice's horror) to borrow a friend's jalopy rather than hire a limousine. The shot from behind the car as it hesitantly splutters into life is the first overtly comic moment in the film, and, as Stevens intended, the image of its wobbly wheels in precarious motion is pure Laurel and Hardy. Yet the social point is being made also. The vehicle is in such grotesque contrast to the sleek limousines beginning to pull up in the Palmer driveway that Alice insists he parks the car some way from the house, even though it is raining. After all, getting soaked will be preferable to social mortification. (In the same vein, despite her mother's insistence that she take her father's coat to protect her against the weather, one senses Alice would rather die than be seen wearing it, and she will hand it quickly to her brother once inside the house to put in the cloakroom.) Alice's sensitivity to appearance is played off against her brother's complete indifference to it, but the observation is beginning to cut deeper than comedy, for Walter's perception of the hollowness of this world does not preclude a sense of protectiveness towards his sister and a desire to shield her from being hurt. When she comes down the staircase clearly looking to make an impression, Walter says, "Relax, nobody's looking at you." It might seem as if he is sneering at her grand manner, but he is actually right; nobody is paying attention. He is also right when he observes that Alice's so-called friends "passed you like you had something catching." Almost as an act of defiance, his dance with Alice is a display that consciously has more energy than elegance and sets them apart from the other dancing couples rather than integrates them into the general experience. Alice's embarrassment seems almost complete when Walter cheerfully hails the black orchestra leader, Skinny Sam, who is taking his band, the Hot Shot Stooges, through the music for the evening and who clearly knows Walter from less luxurious social settings and occasions. If one has some sympathy for Alice's predicament, one can also appreciate Walter's carefree attitude, where his indifference to status and decorum seems preferable to the prevailing snobbery.

When Richard Eyre had dinner with Mike Nichols in 1996 and they began sharing their experiences about directing films, Nichols said that, when he started, to direct, "he looked at Bergman films to see how to work with actors, and at George Stevens for staging" (Eyre: 348). This ball sequence might well have been one of the examples Nichols had in mind of Stevens' mastery of composition and dramatic flow, as the steady accumulation of snobs and snubs begin to undermine Alice's hopes. A social occasion, about which she has at home daydreamed in the mirror, in actuality is turning into a slow nightmare of disappointment. The violets, which she has so assiduously collected for her corsage, begin to wilt, as do her spirits. She is obliged to dance with Frank Dowling (Grady Sutton), whom everyone else is avoiding, partly because he is a terrible dancer (he treads on Alice's foot) and partly because of his overbearing mother. She catches a snatch of conversation from two passing socialites disparaging her two-year-old dress; and the young hostess, Mildred (Evelyn Venable) walks past her without acknowledgment. Even when she secretly drops her dying corsage to the floor in the hope of concealment, Mildred's cousin, Arthur Russell (Fred MacMurray) notices and returns the bouquet to their owner, unaware that his act of courtesy only serves to magnify Alice's discomfort. (She will eventually manage to dispose of the dead flowers by secretly dropping them in a large plant pot in the hallway.) One extraordinary shot shows Alice to the left in the background of the frame; dancing couples flitting around in the foreground;

and with the space in between representing the yawning gulf between Alice's situation and the social status she yearns for.

In the novel, Tarkington writes: "She had now to practice an art that affords but a limited variety of methods, even to the expert; the art of seeming to have an escort, or partner, when there is none" (Chapter 7). Pauline Kael thought that what she called Katharine Hepburn's "pantomiming" here was some of the best American acting she had ever seen (Kael: 282). During this process of deception, Alice commandeers an empty chair; communes with herself; feigns jollity in her voice that is contradicted by the panic in her eyes; in her agitation, seems not to know whether to sit or stand; and finally situates herself on the edge of a sofa and on the fringes of a conversation between several old ladies, not one of whom she knows but a group to whom a casual observer might think she belongs. This in turn adds to her discomfiture when Arthur Russell asks her to dance and she has to excuse herself for withdrawing from a company of people who were unaware of her presence to begin with. The dance itself is pleasurable, but even that pleasure is tainted when, having asked Arthur if he would mind finding her brother, she realizes after he has done so that he will have discovered Walter playing dice in a back-room with the black cloakroom attendants. Her social mortification is complete. "Let's go home," she says to Walter.

The mood of gloom is continued as she enters the house in darkness, with the waltz from the dance now heard over the soundtrack in the form of a slow dirge, wanly reflecting Alice's state of mind. In the novel, when the mother asks her if she has had a nice time, Alice tries momentarily to put a brave face on it, but then throws herself sobbing into her mother's arms. In the film, Stevens extends and enriches the moment. Alice responds cheerily when her mother calls to her from her bedroom, and only when she is alone in her room does she break down. The script originally had Alice throwing herself on her bed at this point, but Stevens suggested that she walk over to the window and then lean against the cold window pane, at which point she would begin to cry, her tears making a visual match with the rain pattering outside on the window. At first Hepburn found this difficult to do, the coldness of the window seeming to obstruct her attempt at tears. An uncomfortable confrontation with the director ensued, Hepburn suggesting that they go back to the original concept, and then sensing that, although Stevens acquiesced, he was silently furious that she had undermined his authority on the set. (He did confess later that, at that point, he was considering walking off the picture.) She turned back to the window and leaned her face on the windowpane; and suddenly the tears came. The shot of her face from outside the window is one of the most poignant of the film; and one of the screen's most elegant examples of pathetic fallacy. Hearing his daughter's sobs, the father stirs in his bed, but the fadeout at this point seems to indicate less a shift in his attitude than a further retreat for the time being into his black hole of self-pity and inaction.

When Alice meets Arthur Russell again, she is halfway up the steps of the doorway to Frincke's Business College and about to ask for a job. This is the situation with which the novel will end; but, in the film, it follows a scene when Alice has told her father that she would like to go on the stage and her father's reaction has been one of condescending laughter, not derisive exactly but not very sensitive either, dashing Alice's hopes as delusions even before they have been fully expressed. At this precise point in the film, it seems momentarily as if Alice has resignedly foregone all thoughts of self-advancement, acceded to her father's advice, and is proceeding towards what Tarkington in the novel, on his heroine's behalf, has called "a doorway to Purgatory." She is stopped in her tracks by a greeting from Arthur, who has noticed her while having his shoes cleaned by a black shoeshine boy. Stevens is always careful to show the marginal role of the black population in the town's growing prosperity; and the shot intriguingly anticipates a similar image, also featuring Fred MacMurray, in a film that might owe something to *Alice Adams*, namely Billy Wilder's 1960 classic, *The Apartment*, which casts a wry and unflattering look at mid–20th century capitalist expansion and social climbing.

Ironically, although she has quickly abandoned her theatrical ambitions, Alice now puts on an act; and her following conversation and walk with Arthur will be pure performance and dramatic imagination. She was only visiting the College, she explains, to enquire about a secretary for her father. Explaining away Arthur's discovery of Walter playing dice with the black cloakroom attendants at the party, she says Walter is a writer and tells wonderful "darky stories." She pretends she has overcome her stage fever and wanting to act, and invents tales about her dancing instructors. It is all designed to impress. There is a delightful touch in the screenplay here which nicely finesses a moment in the original when they arrive at Alice's house. In the novel she gives an affected apologetic little speech about where she lives before bidding adieu ("It's a queer little place, but my father's so attached to it the family has about given up hope of getting him to build a real house further out"). In the film, however, she actually tries to walk past it, only to be stopped by the postman, who can gratefully hand her the family's mail and save his energy without having to make the journey to the front door himself.

It is a funny detail, but also significant in that Arthur seems completely unfazed by Alice's embarrassment. While she is desperately trying to conceal the "real me" behind this façade, Arthur seems fascinated precisely by this concealment and what is actually behind the display. As acted by MacMurray, there is no suggestion that he is being taken in by anything Alice says; what fascinates him is how different Alice is from the other people in his bland social circle. MacMurray's finely judged naturalistic restraint contrasts nicely with Hepburn's equally well-judged tumble of words and the slight edge of hysteria in her tone, which are just enough to convey the character's nervous excitement and her fear of being found disappointing. When Arthur asks if he might call on her, her joy overflows to the extent of even giving her astonished brother a kiss on the cheek. Alice might think her strenuous affectations have worked in engaging Arthur's interest, but Stevens allows us to suspect that it is really the motivation behind the affectations—the real Alice—that intrigues Arthur.

The film is building towards the classic set piece when Arthur will be invited to dinner at the Adams' house. The romance between Alice and Arthur has progressed a little after that walk. "He will call, he won't call," Alice has mused, as she anxiously awaits his appearance while arranging some flowers in the manner of "he loves me, he loves me not." Flowers are used extensively in the film to symbolize the fragility of Alice's romantic hopes. She is actually throwing out some dead flowers and emptying the vase of water when Arthur finally turns up to ask if he might accompany her to Henrietta Lamb's party, on the mistaken assumption that Alice has been invited. For Alice's mother, overhearing this exchange, this is the final straw. Once again she berates her husband as being the cause of Alice's social exclusion; and when Alice breaks down in her father's presence, he can no longer evade the consequences of his modest social position. "Dang, dang," he moans (neatly circumventing a Hollywood Code that did not permit profanity), finally goaded into developing and investing in his glue works as a means (not without risk) of raising his family's status. "The way the world is now," the mother has said, "money *is* family."

Two particularly well observed scenes precede the disastrous dinner. There is a hesitant love scene between Alice and Arthur at a café, which is charmingly counterpointed by the leader of the café's small band of musicians clearly wanting the romance to move at a more rapid pace so they can all go home. When at last the couple get round to a chaste kiss, he obviously feels he has contributed his bit to the romantic ambience, and, quickly bringing the waltz to a close, packs up his violin with a sigh of relief. The second scene occurs at a later stage of the narrative. As Alice and her mother are making preparations for the dinner, we cut to the country household of the Palmers, with a head steward bringing in lunch for Mr. and Mrs. Palmer, their daughter, Mildred, and Arthur, their nephew, who has been thought to be a likely future husband for Mildred but whose recent absence from the family gatherings has been noticed. They are discussing invitations for an imminent garden party and the name of Alice Adams comes up. "A pushing sort of girl," says Mrs. Palmer (Hedda Hopper, in her element exuding hauteur and arrogance) while Mr. Palmer (Jonathan Hale) recalls that the name of Adams is in the news for stealing a glue-making formula from his employer, Mr. Lamb, who is angry at this act of betrayal. As this exchange is taking place, we see Mildred darting a quick look at Arthur, who looks serious and troubled, Stevens here revealing an early gift at filming conversation in a way that can locate complicated crosscurrents of tension that go beyond the ostensible topic under discussion. If Mildred knows of Arthur's interest in Alice and is therefore intent on trying to decipher his reaction to this news, the Palmers think that Arthur's silence is simply an indication of boredom and even tacit understanding, and they suggest that he and Mildred take a walk in the garden and concentrate on "something prettier than thieving clerks." In fact, as eloquently conveyed by MacMurray, Arthur's unease might be prompted not so much by the revelation concerning Alice's father but by the sense of unsympathetic superiority communicated by Mildred's stuffy parents. It is a deceptively important scene because, while it ostensibly casts a shadow over Arthur's forthcoming dinner with the Adams family, it might also be giving him a stark insight into the kind of society into which he is expected to marry. Is this really the kind of future he wants? Is the placidity of Mildred preferable to the pretensions of Alice, irrespective of their backgrounds? It is a scene that might give a different slant—and even a justification—for the film's unexpected ending.

Arthur's arrival at the Adams' house coincides with a loud crash off-screen, which undermines the elegant ambience the mother has labored to create. The cook, Malena (Hattie McDaniel), has fallen down the stairs. (Virgil's cry, "Did she break any of our things?" does not contribute either to the desired atmosphere of sensitivity and refinement.) Later the polite, if awkward, conversation between Arthur and the family preceding the meal is suddenly interrupted by a loud crashing and banging as Malena tries to negotiate the sliding doors before lurching into the room to announce sullenly that "Dinner is served." (Again Virgil's response does not help much towards the formality of the occasion: "That's good—let's see if we can eat it"). Such expressive off-screen slapstick testifies to Stevens' comedy roots, as do the lingering close-ups of Fred Stone as Virgil, whose expression as he puzzles over and struggles with the unfamiliar food has something of the bemused stoicism of an Oliver Hardy.

The humor is there as counterpoint to the humiliation. In his production notes for the dinner scene, which defines what he saw as the scene's central significance, Stevens wrote that a "kind of doom is settling over a young girl's aspirations.... The fates were against her and she's setting a battlefield ... that's going to lead to her own destruction" (qtd in Moss: 37). Hepburn feared that the scene would be "as funny as a baby's open grave" (qtd in Leaming: 303), but she reckoned without Stevens' comedy expertise and the humanity that underlines it, which is compassionate rather than cruel. There has been something endearing about Alice's obsessive moving of chairs and flowers in the room prior to the young man's arrival, reflecting her anxiety that everything should be right. During the dinner itself, when Alice's desire to impress is continually undermined by the developing domestic calamity, her conversation will become little more than cheerful chirpings of embarrassment to conceal her underlying despair. We are seeing (to borrow a Joseph L. Mankiewicz phrase to define all Katharine Hepburn's best comedies) a "hoity-toity girl brought down to earth," but in Stevens' hands, our heart also goes out to her.

As Stevens notes, everything seems to have conspired against Alice: the hot weather, which has withered the flowers and melted the ice cream; the food, which has been either unfamiliar (the Brussels sprouts), unsuitable (the hot soup) or inedible (the caviar sandwich); her father's starched shirt, which has kept popping open at inopportune moments; and perhaps, most of all, the cook, Malena, whose services have been procured to add a touch of class to the evening but whose presence has only served to exaggerate Alice's subterfuge. Hattie McDaniel's performance as Malena is a superb comic cameo, whether retrieving one of Virgil's stray Brussels sprouts by sweeping it off the table with the aid of brush and dustpan, or trying to serve coffee when her little waitress's cap keeps falling in front of her eyes. Yet the characterization is also relevant to the film's themes, for, like Alice, Malena is clearly dissatisfied with her place in this society and also, like Alice, is here pretending to be something she is not. As her cap slips down her nose to show the artificiality of this attempt at etiquette and elegance (Malena is no society waitress), so too might it represent an equivalent to the slipping of Alice's mask of refinement and respectability, exposing the desperate reality behind the façade.

"A penny for your thoughts," Alice says to a pensive Arthur as they adjourn to the porch after the meal. On reflection, she modifies this request. "A poor dead rose for your thoughts, Arthur," she says, the rose seeming a sort of distant relative of the ill-fated corsage at the dance and which similarly symbolized the wilting of her romantic hopes. This withered remnant of what was planned as part of a joyous floral display more or less sums up the mood of the evening; and it also demonstrates how astutely Stevens can switch the mood of a scene, from broad comedy to wistful drama. "George Stevens could do anything," producer Pandro S. Berman told interviewers late in his life when he was recalling the directors he had worked with over a long career. "Break your heart or make you laugh" (qtd in Yeck and Jewell: 19). Hepburn is especially fine in this scene with Arthur on the porch, playing not with melodramatic excess but with a quiet and dignified resignation, even as she recognizes that the next five minutes might be the last time she will ever see him. She even teases Arthur slightly, trying to draw him out of his contemplative shell "What's the matter, little boy? Tell auntie," she says: it's a line direct from the novel, but it also anticipates a famous moment in *A Place in the Sun* when Elizabeth Taylor adopts a motherly tone to Montgomery Clift when the young man seems suddenly tongue-tied and emotionally overwhelmed by the situation in which he finds himself. In attempting to draw Arthur closer, Alice feels she has actually driven him away; and, as she puts it, "when anything's spoiled, people can't do anything but run away from it."

What seems to have been "spoiled" in her eyes is his image of her. As a furious row breaks out in the background between father and son over money that Walter has stolen from Lamb's, which brings the edifice of refined family life crashing down about her ears, she says a quick goodbye to Arthur before giving him a chance to respond and retreats back into the misery of a home which must now seem more like a prison from which she cannot escape.

It is in these final few minutes that the film deviates most markedly from its source. Unlike in the novel, Walter's act of theft has been motivated not by personal greed as by a desire to help a friend in the mistaken hope that the money will be repaid before its loss discovered, which somewhat ameliorates the crime. In the novel, Lamb has set up a rival glue-making business which will effectively ruin Virgil's factory; and, after a bitter denunciation of Lamb for his needless destruction of what the factory has meant to Virgil in terms of self-esteem and the future of his family, Adams has had a serious second stroke. The film retains the speech and Virgil's denunciation of Lamb as "a doggone mean man … it didn't make two cents worth o' difference in your life and it looked like it'd mean all the difference in the world to my family." It is Fred Stone's most powerful moment in the film, when the father finally gives voice to his simmering frustration. In the film, however, Lamb's conscience is to be stirred, particularly after Alice has intervened to say that it is really all her fault and that her father's actions have essentially been prompted by her desires above her social station. "Circumstances can beat the best of you," admits Lamb, and he will propose some form of collaboration in the future between him and Adams ("Together we can show the world about glue") as well as promising a way of dealing with Walter that will not involve his going to jail. Tarkington always recognized that the bleakness of his novel would need to be negotiated differently for the big screen, and the film's adaptation ensures a resolution that is much more attuned to Depression-era sensibilities, the common man being treated with compassion and consideration rather than being crushed by the imperatives of competitive capitalism.

The very ending of the film, however, is something else. Stevens and Hepburn both wanted an ending closer to the realism of the novel, with Alice having given up any romantic notions of Arthur and preparing for the prospect of a secretarial job at business college with, as Stevens' production notes say, "head up and a conquering eye" (qtd in Moss: 39). However, director and star were overruled by producer and studio, who thought a romantic ending would be better box office and would be Alice's just rewards. Accordingly, after a moving scene between Alice and her father, where he has described Alice as "the smartest girl in the world" and told how much he liked Arthur (Alice has just laid her head on his shoulder at this, as if the weight of her sorrow has pulled it down: beautifully acted by Hepburn), she has wandered forlornly onto the porch, only to discover that Arthur is still waiting. He has heard all that has gone on and declares his love for Alice. The film closes, conventionally enough, on a romantic embrace.

"The happy ending is a bad enough falsification; as acted by MacMurray," Pauline Kael wrote, "it's hopeless. Alice's disbelieving "Gee whiz!" is matched by the audience's disbelief" (Kael: 283). Perhaps significantly, the only time previously in the film when Alice has used that exclamation has been her horrified reaction on seeing the dilapidated car in which Walter has taken her to the Palmer dance. Might this have been Stevens' and Hepburn's cunning way of smuggling in their protest at an ending in which neither of them believed? Certainly the treatment of this final love scene is so perfunctory that it puts one in mind of those "ironic happy endings" favored by Douglas Sirk in his 1950s melodramas, where there is a happy ending provided for audiences who like that sort of thing but where space and evidence are provided for another kind of audience who might be tempted and permitted to recognize the hollowness behind the happiness.

Even so, the ending might not be quite as arbitrary and implausible as it seems. When one thinks back to that luncheon scene at the Palmers' home, when the comfortably complacent mother and father are smugly distancing themselves from any association with Alice and her father, and the Palmers' daughter sits in silent complicity, is it entirely unlikely that Arthur might prefer the enigmatic but energetic Alice to the elegant but empty Mildred; or indeed prefer the bumbling but essentially good-natured Adams family to the cultivated but essentially cold-hearted Palmers? After all, he has eavesdropped on Alice's speech to Mr. Lamb, which has given him a new insight into the real Alice; and he has heard Virgil's passionate denunciation of Mr. Lamb, which has given him a new perspective on Virgil's behavior and character and on a person who seems quite different from the "thieving clerk" disdainfully characterized by the Palmers.

Whatever one makes of the ending, it does not alter the fundamental character of the film: its shrewd observation of the changing nature of American society in the early twentieth century; its assessment of the role of women in society and the limits placed on their life opportunities, which will become an important subtext of a number of his films; and its sympathy for the social outsider, which will become one of Stevens' main themes. Also notable is its visual grace and its stylish and seamless blend of comedy and seriousness. All the future fingerprints and masterstrokes are there in *Alice Adams*. With one stride, a major director had emerged on the Hollywood scene.

Annie Oakley (1935)

Celebrating at a party on Sunset Boulevard after a successful preview of *Alice Adams*, Stevens suddenly realized he would have to leave and get a good night's sleep. No time for resting on his laurels, for he was beginning a new film the following morning. When he started shooting *Annie Oakley*, initially all he had to go on was a 15-page treatment and a third of the screenplay, which at that time was all that had been completed. With the aid of screenwriters Joel Sayre and John Twist, he managed to hammer out a script that kept just ahead of the shooting schedule, incorporating a lot of entertaining comic business that he had picked from his experience with the likes of Laurel and Hardy and Wheeler and Wolsey.

Born in 1860, Annie Oakley, whose full name was Phoebe Ann Oakley Moses, had achieved fame in her lifetime (she died in 1926) by becoming the shooting star of Buffalo Bill's Wild West Show. She had appeared alongside her husband, Frank Butler (called Toby Walker in Stevens' film), whom she had met when beating him in a shooting contest and who had teamed up with her to form a successful double act. The film's prologue states, rather hopefully: "No fiction is stranger than the actual life of Annie Oakley who came out of a backwoods village half a century ago to astonish the world." There is nothing particularly strange about the fiction Stevens and his writers construct from Annie's actual life, leading to a romantic, happy ending. Still it is noteworthy that, when Irving Berlin came to immortalize Annie Oakley in his 1946 Broadway musical, *Annie Get Your Gun*, the storyline did not differ that much from Stevens' film. Contrary to the sentiments of Irving Berlin's song, Annie proves that you can get a man with a gun. Whether the man is worth getting is another matter; and *Annie Oakley* is not the only Stevens' film of the 1930s and early '40s to call into question the worthiness of the male for his female partner.

Annie's shooting prowess is well known in her particular community. One of the locals comments that "she can knock out the eye of a bumblebee at fifty yards." When Buffalo Bill's manager, Jeff Hogarth (Melvyn Douglas), organizes a local contest to show off the marksmanship of his new signing for the show, the great Toby Walker (Preston Foster), Annie enters the competition and is matching Walker shot for shot until she senses the dangers of wounding Walker's pride, and deliberately misses a shot so that he can win. The gesture does nothing to diminish Walker's arrogance, but Annie, who has felt an instant attraction when first seeing his picture on the poster, explains later to her disappointed friends that "I couldn't beat that fella, I didn't have the heart to." If Annie is attracted to Walker, she too is an object of admiration to Hogarth, who has recognized Annie's deliberate sacrifice in the shooting contest. Also, although entrusted to place the bets by the townspeople on Annie's victory, Hogarth has fortunately not done so, so the money they have gambled can be returned. (It is a nice touch that we never know whether Hogarth has actually forgotten, or whether it is an explanation he invents on the spur of the moment as an act of generosity and affection towards Annie.) He proposes to Annie that she joins the show; and although Buffalo Bill (Moroni Olsen) is at first skeptical, thinking her inclusion might be seen as a gimmick and that the presence of a woman in the troupe might unsettle the boys, he is persuaded when, during their show in front of a number of dignitaries in Washington, Annie's shooting skills are admired by one of the most important guests, Chief Sitting Bull (Chief Thunderbird). Previously invited to join the show but so far unimpressed by what he has seen, Sitting Bull now agrees, but only on the condition that Annie is part of it. "Little Sure Shot," he calls her, an allusion perhaps to the fact that, in real life, Annie was barely five feet tall.

The story development from here is fairly predictable. Toby and Annie fall in love, with Toby even admitting privately that Annie is the better shot. For the sake of the show, they secretly agree to keep up a pretense of antagonism and rivalry as it seems to be good for business. This further alienates Walker from the rest of the boys, who deride his boasting of being acquainted with the likes of Lily Langtry and Sarah Bernhardt and who are disdainful of rifle skills acquired by him not in the authentic West but in the shooting galleries of New York. Things are complicated still further when, unknown to Annie, Walker suffers powder burns to his eyes when intervening to save Sitting Bull from being shot at by a drunken cowboy. At a shooting display in Annie's hometown, he is goaded by the crowd into competing with Annie in one of their most difficult routines and accidentally shoots her in the hand. Along with the rest of the troupe, Buffalo Bill assumes he has done it deliberately out of jealousy and, to Annie's dismay, he is dismissed from the company. A lovelorn Annie will join the company on their European tour, but confides to Hogarth that the show on their return in New York will be her last. Now convinced that he has no hope with Annie, Hogarth shows her a newspaper report in which the doctor who has treated Toby for his eye injuries has confirmed Toby's insistence that his shooting of Annie was an accident caused by his impaired vision. Annie asks for Hogarth's help to find Toby when they return to America.

In fact, Toby has returned to New York and is running a shooting gallery again, not participating in the shooting practice but still boasting of his former acquaintances, including Annie Oakley, to the disbelief of the few people who attend. Hoping to be inconspicuous when he attends Buffalo Bill's Show, he is spotted by the hawk-eyed Sitting Bull, who disrupts the show by following Toby from the performance tent to the place where Toby works. The Chief then leads Annie to Toby's shooting gallery, where he is setting up his targets. When they are suddenly shot down with bewildering speed and accuracy, Toby does not even need to turn round to identify the marksman—or, more accurately, markswoman. As he embraces Annie, he turns to the young boys at the stall, and says, "Did I know Annie Oakley!" It is a most felicitous ending that amusingly captures both the boys' total surprise but also Toby's renewed self-vindication. This ostensible braggart was telling the truth after all. It is also a rather brilliant visual conceit. When Hogarth has earlier refused to talk to Toby after the shooting accident, he has sent him packing to what he calls "a future that's behind you." Now, when Toby sees those targets going down, he does not need to look back to see who is doing the shooting. The future is indeed behind him—and, at last, happily so.

Although the film might be light on surprises, it is full of delights. Its re-creation of an innocent slice of Americana is done with great affection. The period detail relating to the preparations for the shows, and actual events from Annie's life (for example, the famous occasion when she shot a cigarette from the lips of Crown Prince Wilhelm in Germany) are all nicely observed. The show routines themselves, from the dazzling feats of horsemanship by the Russian Cossacks to the simulated attacks on a wagon train, are splendidly reproduced, with reaction shots of excited spectators and wide shots from a distance, as if one were a spectator in the stand watching the performance, all giving a real sense of what it must have been like to be present at these spectacular entertainments, which, of course, preceded the birth of cinema. At this time people were still coming to terms with the telephone, which the hotel owner, MacIvor (Andy Clyde), sees as an instrument of torture. Stevens creates a moment of quiet charm as the members of Buffalo Bill's Show pose for a group photograph and an extended panning shot from left to right not only demonstrates the time it took in those days to compose a picture but also seems to freeze a moment of precious American folklore.

The performances are all perfectly pitched. Preston Foster communicates a smidgeon of sensitivity lurking behind Walker's swell-headedness which could credibly attract someone of Annie's perceptiveness; Melvyn Douglas's Hogarth is a sympathetic portrait of someone whose unrequited love does not rob him of a fundamental decency; and Moroni Olsen brings a showbiz swagger to his Buffalo Bill, appropriately charismatic in his public appearances, amusingly vain in private, particularly in his attentiveness to his flowing locks of hair. Above all, Barbara Stanwyck makes a splendid heroine, with lingering close-ups (which are becoming a Stevens trademark) drawing out her beauty, and the performance revealing a character of great warmth, courage and independence. In retrospect, it seems a remarkably shrewd piece of casting. No other screen actress of that era went on to command such important roles in Westerns, which was customarily a male-dominated genre. Stanwyck's Annie Oakley is the forerunner of her performances in such films as Cecil B. DeMille's *Union Pacific* (1939), William Wellman's *The Great Man's Lady* (1942), Anthony Mann's *The Furies* (1950), Allan Dwan's *Cattle Queen of Montana* (1954) and Samuel Fuller's *Forty Guns* (1957) to name but a few, which established her as undoubtedly Hollywood's premier actress at portraying women of the West whose femininity was allied to a formidable strength of character.

There are three main themes that run through the film; and, for all the movie's seeming modesty and conventionality, they are all themes that now look ahead of their time.

The most prominent of these is one that also dominated *Alice Adams*: the restricted role of women in society and the social discomfiture caused when a woman is seen not quite to fit the prototype nor the place that society has designated for her. For the most part, the theme is played for comedy, as in the scene when Toby's former partner, Vera (Pert Kelton), scandalizes the small-town community by entering the hotel barroom. When told that ladies are not allowed in the saloon, she replies, nonchalantly, "O, I'm no lady" and proceeds to enter. (A little later we overhear a mumbled conversation between two shocked locals, where one of them says, "Next thing you know, they'll be smoking cigarettes!" and his friend replies testily, "Oh, talk sense," as if this is taking masculine paranoia into the realms of fantasy.) Much of the early comedy of misunderstanding arises from the assumption that Toby's shooting competitor, A. Oakley must be a man: the alternative seems not to cross anyone's mind. There is a variation on this later when Buffalo Bill has to introduce Annie to his all-male company, and the men are so taken aback by this improbable development that in unison they momentarily retreat, as if flinching from a blow. Yet it is not all played for humor. During the early shooting contest, we know that Annie has already taken a fancy to Toby and would be uneasy about showing him up publicly by beating him (when explaining later why she deliberately lost, she says, among other things, "he was just too pretty," a prim way perhaps of expressing female desire). But there is also a wholly unexpected intervention from Annie's mother (Margaret Armstrong), when she whispers to Annie, "I hope you ain't gonna be the cause of that man losing his position." It is a telling comment (and the only full sentence the mother utters in the entire film); and it might not be too fanciful to suggest that, in ten years' time at the end of World War II, a lot of working women in America are going to be confronted with that same dilemma. When women start competing successfully in what is traditionally the masculine domain, social tremors occur.

All of this makes what Stevens called the "foregone conclusion" of the ending more ambiguous than it might appear. Toby has become more sympathetic not when he has fallen in love with the heroine but when he has acknowledged her superiority. Annie is no conscious precursor of feminism, but certain actions of hers indicate an assumption of equality, as for, for example, when in St. Petersburg she inadvertently but instinctively violates protocol by shaking the hand of the Czarina before that of the Czar. So when Annie and Toby are reunited in the finale, it might seem a felicitous conclusion, but, in terms of the film, it could also be seen as being as equivocal as the abruptly happy ending of *Alice Adams*. After all, what does the future hold? Toby cannot return to the Wild West Show: even if they accepted him, his eyesight is no longer good enough. Annie has said she is leaving the show, but, if she changes her mind, would this mean that she were the main wage-earner in the partnership and thus subvert the economic dynamic of a patriarchal society? One could imagine that the man in the saloon, who grumbled "Talk sense!" at the prospect that ladies might one day take to smoking cigarettes, would be apoplectic at the prospect of women taking on the main financial responsibility of a household. The film's ending now looks far less conventional, and more provocative, than Stevens might have realized at the time.

There are two supporting characterizations in the film who, like the leads, are based on real-life personages but whose presence add a significant thematic dimension beyond the one just discussed. The first is Ned Buntline (played in the film by an uncredited Dick Elliott), who was the pre-eminent dime novelist of his era and who is referred to in the film as Buffalo Bill's "press agent." (It is an alarming thought that popular celebrities had press agents even as early as the 1880s.) In one scene we see Bill reading aloud Bunt-line's latest account of his exploits and his entirely fictitious discovery of the "Prairie Primrose" who will later develop into the great sharpshooter, Annie Oakley; Bill reckons the volume will sell at least 50,000 copies and make Annie famous. When Toby grumbles about Annie's publicity, it is Buntline's idea to exploit the rivalry between Toby and Annie to boost the show, an idea that, as we have seen, almost literally backfires. Buntline's presence in the film is important because it shows how *Annie Oakley* is anticipating something that will begin to preoccupy a number of revisionist Westerns of the future: namely, the way the myth of the American West is already overtaking the reality even before the frontier has closed; and also the way the American West is becoming not simply a crucial part of American history but also of American showbiz. For example, the figure of the reporter, who will become aware of the gap between the adventurism he is idealizing and the grubbier actuality, will play an important role in later Western classics such as Arthur Penn's *The Left-Handed Gun* (1958) and Clint Eastwood's *Unforgiven* (1992). Also the West as part of America's burgeoning entertainment industry will be depicted with ironic affection in the opening of Sam Peckinpah's *Ride the High Country* (aka: *Guns in the Afternoon*, 1962), but with satirical bitterness in *Buffalo Bill and the Indians* (1976), Robert Altman's characteristically provocative and iconoclastic gift to the American Bicentennial and in which the role of Buntline will be played by Burt Lancaster. In *Annie Oakley*, the tone is predominantly affectionate, but the sentiment is moving towards that iconic moment in John Ford's *The Man Who Shot Liberty Valance* (1962), when the newspaper editor, having been told the truth about who really shot the notorious outlaw, tears up the story. "This is the West, sir," he says, in that famous refrain: "When the legend becomes fact, print the legend." It is a sentiment all the more ambivalent, given that Hollywood's foremost poet of the West, John Ford, has just printed the fact.

The other supporting real-life characterization, adding a particularly interesting and even problematical dimension to the film, is that of Chief Sitting Bull, who must still have been a divisive figure in 1935 let alone in the period in which the film is set. After all, the battle of the Little Big Horn would seem like comparatively recent history to some of the audience. In their history of RKO studios, Richard B. Jewell and Vernon Hibbin seemed less concerned with the film's sympathetic portrayal of the Chief than with what they saw as its racial condescension. Referring to the "humorous subplot" which shows Sitting Bull attempting to cope with life in New York, they conclude that: "Today the joshing treatment of his frustrations would be considered in very poor taste" (1982: 90). A scene they would have in mind would be one in his hotel room, when the bed folds into the wall behind his back, and when he turns round, he is baffled by its disappearance (though the folding, or collapsing, bed was pretty standard comic equipment in screen comedy of the time: see Chaplin in *One A.M.* and indeed Stevens' variation on the joke in *Vivacious Lady*). In a later scene, when Sitting Bull has rushed from the show, still clutching his tomahawk, to follow Toby's exit from the tent, he will collide with a drunken citizen exiting a saloon with his friend, causing the man's wig to fall off. The Chief will solicitously return the man's hairpiece, while his friend, who has just stumbled across the scene and misinterpreted what he has seen, rushes off in panic. It is a scalping scene in reverse and, in its three-part comic structure (the initial collision, the Chief's return of the wig, the friend's mistaken assumption), could almost be a routine out of Laurel and Hardy.

"In very poor taste"? In this era of political correctness, perhaps, though the comedy seems no different in kind from the humor directed at the hotel owner MacIvor's Scottish meanness or Buffalo Bill's vanity about his flowing locks; the stereotyping is affectionate more than astringent. If Sitting Bull is perplexed by the gadgetry and technology of a society that now has electric lighting, so too is MacIvor with his new-fangled telephone. What is important in the Chief's case is that he is not simply there for comic relief. Like the presentation of the "woman in a man's world" theme, the humor does not tell the whole story. For instance, there is a very striking close-up of Sitting Bull when he is a spectator at the show in Washington and sees a simulated attack by whooping Indian braves on a wagon train. Jumping into the arena to inspect the bodies, he needs to be reassured that "it's all in fun." At first sight this might seem a joke at the Chief's expense and a further dig at his simple-mindedness, but the close-up of his serious expression suggests something deeper: possibly, the reawakening of painful memories, and even a sense of disquiet that the bloody skirmishes of the recent past, in which lives were lost, are now being offered as a public spectacle and a branch of entertainment. It is also at this show that the presence of Annie Oakley will persuade him to join Buffalo Bill's circus. He might admire Annie's shooting, but again one senses that the motive goes deeper: the Chief's sense of a certain kinship between them; that they are both outsiders in the worlds in which they have to move. Whatever it is, it is the turning point of the film. Without Sitting Bull, there would have been no nationwide Annie Oakley to drive the second part of the film; without him, there would have been no one to bring Annie and Toby together in such a felicitous conclusion. Far from being simply the butt of some allegedly tasteless and tactless humor, Sitting Bull is another archetypal Stevens outsider; and the linchpin of both plot and theme. For all its air of pleasant predictability, this rum romantic comedy cum offbeat Western springs a few surprises.

Swing Time (1936)

With Mark Sandrich's *Top Hat* (1935), *Swing Time* is generally the most highly esteemed of the ten film musicals that paired Fred Astaire with Ginger Rogers.

When Stevens asked choreographer Hermes Pan for advice on directing a Fred Astaire musical, Pan's response was simple and succinct: "Just make sure you get his feet in." Resisting the cinematic bravura and choreographic patterns characteristic of a Busby Berkeley musical of that era, Stevens took care to shoot the dancers in full figure to highlight their dancing prowess. In adding unusual dimensions of character and dramatic nuance to the musical numbers, he brings an unexpected realism and depth to the film musical. The emotions expressed in dance are invariably subtler than those expressed in words.

Dancer and gambler Lucky Garnett (Fred Astaire) is in New York with his friend Pop Everett (Victor Moore) to make $25,000 in order to demonstrate to his prospective father-in-law Judge Watson that he is a worthy match for the Judge's daughter, Margaret (Betty Furness). "I always admire any young man who can make money," says the Judge. "It shows character." (The Judge's character is forcefully portrayed by the director's own father, Landers Stevens.) However, Lucky falls in love with a dancing instructor, Penny Carroll (Ginger Rogers), and is torn between honoring his commitment to his fiancée or deliberately sabotaging his financial prospects in New York so he can stay near Penny. She has fallen in love with Lucky also, but is being romantically pursued by an orchestra leader, Ricardo Romero (Georges Metaxa). When she learns that Lucky is engaged and his fiancée turns up in New York, she accepts Ricardo's offer of marriage. However, Margaret has only arrived in New York to tell Lucky she wishes to break off their engagement, thus leaving the way clear for Lucky and Penny.

Although he thought the dance numbers in Swing Time were "much more excitingly handled" than in Mark Sandrich's Top Hat (1935), Bruce Beresford expressed the view that Stevens' direction overall was handicapped by "inventing detailed characterisation which wasn't supported by either the dialogue or the slim plot. Despite his efforts, it was impossible to care about the characters" (Beresford: 13). It would be fair to say that the comedy business the film contrives between the musical numbers is uneven in quality. The labored routine over wrong trousers ("no cuffs"), the strategy by which the groom's appearance at his wedding is delayed by his dancing colleagues, who fear that his wedding will threaten their careers, gets the film off to a slow start. The same strategy is used by Lucky and Pop to delay the wedding of Ricardo and Penny at the end and is no funnier. Apparently, the forced laughter of Lucky and Pop at Ricardo's trousers, designed to humiliate the groom and which sets everyone else off laughing, was a last-minute inspiration, and it looks it (that is, late, rather than inspired). Some of the supporting performances— Eric Blore's exasperated head of the Gordon Dancing Academy, Gerald Homer as the drunken piquet player—suffer in comparison with the more understated comic interplay between Victor Moore's Pop and Helen Broderick as Penny's best friend, Mabel. Stevens' comic touch seems surer on behavioral detail, like the moment when one of Lucky's friends, intercepting a call from an irate Judge Watson, pretends to be talking to his girlfriend and blows a kiss down the phone, causing the Judge to drop the receiver as if he has been stung. There is a neat scene that follows, when Lucky belatedly arrives at the Judge's house to find that the wedding guests have gone. Greeted by a snarling dog and a hissing cat and where the large portrait of the father adorning the wall seems to be scowling at him, Lucky is so successful at placating the wrath of both his prospective bride and her father that, by the time he leaves, the dog is snuggling up affectionately and even the father's portrait now seems to have acquired a smile.

What is most notable, however, is the way the film deploys its musical numbers to advance both its plot and its characterization. In some musicals, one can feel that the numbers serve mainly as interludes between the development of the narrative and relationships in the scenes without songs, but in Swing Time it feels the other way round: the non-musical scenes are the interludes and it is the songs and the dances that carry the film forward. There are four numbers in particular that mark important stages in the relationship between Lucky and Penny.

Their first number together occurs after a disastrous initial encounter in New York, where, through a series of misunderstandings, Penny has accused Lucky of taking a quarter from her purse, but has been put in her place by an unsympathetic policeman. Feeling that Penny is owed an apology, Lucky has followed her to the Gordon Dancing Academy where she works as an instructor and attempts to ingratiate himself by pretending he has come for lessons and contriving to fall in their first steps together. The comic conceit behind what follows—Penny's frustration at Lucky's clumsiness—is elaborated in a number of delightful ways. In demonstrating his hopelessness, Astaire still contrives to slip, slide and fall more gracefully than most people can dance. Penny sings "Pick Yourself Up" almost as a song of consolation to Lucky, who then, to persuade Gordon (Eric Blore) not to fire Penny for her failure, transforms this number into such a resplendent routine with his teacher that, by the end, Mr. Gordon has not only changed his mind, but fixed them up with an engagement at the redoubtable Silver Sandal nightclub. The comedy carries over into the number's conclusion, when Pop and Mabel (who has also been fired by Mr. Gordon when rallying to Penny's defense) attempt to follow in the dancers' footsteps by doing the same routine: a much more prosaic version of the preceding choreographic poetry and which highlights, by contrast, the magic we have just seen. (Mr. Gordon is unmoved: "*You're* still fired!" he tells Mabel.) For something has happened beyond the comedy. As they have danced together in harmony, Penny has seen Lucky in a new light. By the end of the routine, and without saying anything, or needing to say anything, they have become a couple. The beauty of the number is its revelation of the power of dance which, far more than dialogue, has brought them together.

Lucky's dance routine to save Penny's job establishes a pattern for nearly all of the remaining numbers, which are triggered by, or in response to, some form of crisis. Lucky and Penny have fallen out when his gambling (he has been trying unsuccessfully to win enough money to buy a dinner jacket) has caused them to miss their dancing engagement at the Silver Sandal. When he is finally given the opportunity to speak to her again, she is in another room washing her hair, so Lucky sits down at the piano and serenades her with one of Jerome Kern's and Dorothy Fields' most beautiful songs, "The Way You Look Tonight" (which was to win an Academy Award). Again one feels he is opening his heart to her in song in a way that he never could in words; it seems all the more heartfelt because the song is being overheard more than being delivered directly to its recipient. Stevens' direction really comes into its own here, because, typically, he responds fully to the song's romanticism, cutting between Astaire's performance and the wistful close-ups of his co-star, but also goes beyond romance to touch a strain of endearing humor that brings us closer to the characters. Penny now appears entranced as the romantic apparition of the song, quite forgetting that her hair is still lathered with soap. When Lucky turns to notice her behind him, there is a quick smile and then a hilarious double-take at her appearance; and she, a little taken aback by his reaction but then seeing her appearance in the mirror, rushes back into the bathroom. After this moment, Stevens cuts to a new scene which begins with the orchestra leader, Ricardo Romero crooning the same song in Penny's direction at Club Raymond. It is a cut that concisely shifts the setting from bathroom to ballroom; changes the tone from intimate to public; and moves the plot forward, by immediately suggesting that Lucky has a romantic rival for Penny's affections. Not that the outcome of this rivalry will be in any doubt, but the contrasting styles of the song's performance are cleverly revealing. Romero's rendition is a florid, public display; Lucky's is a private revelation.

There is another obstacle between Lucky and Penny, which is Lucky's engagement to Margaret; and this is to be the subtext of the next number. When Lucky and Pop accompany Penny and Mabel on an outing to the New Amsterdam, Pop is quick to warn Lucky about getting too close to Penny, figuratively and literally. When they arrive at the ramshackle hut, Lucky comments, "Well, if this is the New Amsterdam, I'd hate to see the old one," a remark that unwittingly sets the tone for the scene that follows, which is to be one of deception, disappointment and anti-climax. It is snowing, which seems an encouragement for Penny to snuggle up close to Lucky, but he seems nervous of her proximity. He even smokes a pipe, which makes kissing difficult. Her frustration manifests itself in the song "A Fine Romance," where the word "fine" is coated in irony. Stevens weaves a choreographic spell between two characters who wish to come together, but

who seem separated by an invisible wall. Penny's restlessness is conveyed in her alterna-
tion between movement or sitting still; Lucky follows her path but seems hesitant about
closing the gap between them. When the emotional temperature seems to be thawing
and Lucky is about to kiss her, a timely snowball directed by Pop at his hat reminds him
of his other romantic obligation. When Lucky throws his snowball in return, it misses
Pop but hits Mabel, which seems somehow indicative of the mistakes and misunderstandings that are swirling around in the atmosphere. While Lucky is apologizing to
Mabel, Pop lets slip to Penny that Lucky is actually engaged, so that when Lucky returns,
having decided to throw all restraint aside, he finds Penny as mysteriously unresponsive
as he has been. The song now goes into reverse, as he sings a similar refrain of frustration
to her. It is wittily done, but with an undertow of melancholy. Lucky seems amused by
the incongruity of this "fine" romance, but, with Penny, one gets more of a sense of an
ache of despair. When Lucky has returned to her to query Penny's description of him as
"aloof," she now suggests that he misheard her and that what she said was "a laugh." There
is some significance in that exchange, highlighting again a failure of communication and
the way the scene has oscillated between humor and a more melancholic emotional distance. It is one of the most unusual love duets in the Hollywood musical, in that they
sing their verses separately and never actually harmonize (that will be saved until the
end). Vocally the scene will end on the word "romance"; visually it will end with Penny
starting up the car engine and the wipers blowing snow in Lucky's face, cooling his ardor
and smothering his smile.

Yet Lucky and Penny are in love. For the first time in an Astaire-Rogers musical
(and this is their sixth pairing), Stevens manages to smuggle in a kiss between the two.
In deference to Astaire's hatred of screen kisses, Stevens stages the moment with due
visual decorum, the kiss taking place behind Lucky's open dressing-room door. Only
when the door is swung back by an unexpected visitor is there a visual disclosure of what
has happened and Lucky and Penny are revealed, with Lucky's face smeared with tell-
tale lipstick. His joy will feed into his big production number at the Silver Sandal, "Bojan-
gles of Harlem," which, in a nice touch, he starts happily crooning to himself before the
routine has actually begun.

Hermes Pan was deservedly nominated for an Oscar for his spectacular choreography of this sequence, including a remarkable passage where Lucky shares a dance with
three silhouettes dancing behind him, at times mimicking his movements, at times coun-
terpointing them, and at times with the three shadows each doing their own separate
routine. (Pan said he got the idea when seeing shadows on the set one day and achieved
the effect he wanted through the use of rear screen projection.) It is a dazzling visual
concept and thematically appropriate, because there is a shadow over Lucky's happiness
that will be disclosed when he comes onstage to take the applause and notices in the
audience the last person in the world he wishes to see at that moment: his fiancée.

Unaware of the particular reason for Margaret's visit (her desire to break off her
engagement), Penny assumes that her romance with Lucky is now over and agrees to
marry Ricardo. At this stage Lucky also is unaware of Margaret's change of mind, and
the shared melancholy prompts one of the finest routines in the whole Astaire and Rogers
repertoire, "Never Gonna Dance" (which was originally the title of the film). They are
alone together in the dance hall, and Astaire first sings to her at the bottom of a staircase
as she is about to depart up the stairs: there is a clear echo of Romeo and Juliet here. The
song is deeply personal (the first line, "And so, I'm left without a penny" changes later

to "And so, I'm left without *my* Penny") and profoundly sad, since the sentiment behind it suggests that his loss will terminate his urge to dance: the link between emotion and dance here could not be more explicit. Moreover it seems that the song in itself is not sufficient to convey the mood; it needs dance to confirm and complete it. In her interview with George Stevens, Jr. (7 April 1982), for *A Film Maker's Journey*, Ginger Rogers described what the director, she and Astaire had in mind, a quiet dance of love and tender understanding of a kind they had not done before. "He gave us that opportunity to talk to each other without speaking," she said of Stevens' direction, "to love each other without loving, to acknowledge our admiration for each other without a word. It was all done in a pantomime dance. I loved that." Similarly, in his interview with Stevens Jr. for the documentary (15 June 1982), Hermes Pan thought that the dance had an unusual realism and warmth and, although he and Astaire were essentially responsible for the choreography, he recognized the contribution of Stevens' direction, because, he said, "it was quite an innovation to tell a story in a dance routine on the screen." What happens in the dance is a recapping of their relationship, to the accompaniment of a musical medley associated with their swelling love, as it has moved from initial uncertainty, growing longing, ecstasy, then finally to the sadness of goodbye. Towards the end of the number, Ginger Rogers is required to do several pirouettes at the top of the stairs, being caught by Astaire, and then finally spinning away from him out of the frame. It looks straightforward and natural enough on screen, but it was an incredibly difficult routine to film, causing Ginger Rogers' feet to bleed and requiring 46 takes. Everyone involved evidently thought the effort was worth it, and, for a musical comedy, the number's impact is unusually powerful. At the end of the dance, Astaire is left standing alone, with his arms outstretched, looking down the staircase, as if staring into an abyss.

At the end of Woody Allen's Depression–era comedy, *The Purple Rose of Cairo* (1985), much of whose humor derives from Allen's pastiche of RKO studio style (there is even a black maid evocative of Hattie McDaniel in *Alice Adams*), Mia Farrow's downtrodden waitress consoles herself in the local cinema by watching Astaire and Rogers performing "Cheek to Cheek" from *Top Hat*. Astaire croons, momentarily transporting Allen's heroine away from the travails of her life and reminding us of the importance of the cinema at that time to audiences who temporarily could forget their troubles and escape into the glamor world of the screen. Yet the romantic sadness underpinning Allen's film seems closer in spirit to *Swing Time* than to *Top Hat*. *Swing Time* does end on an upbeat note, with Lucky and Penny united and with each now singing the other's theme song (Lucky sings "A Fine Romance," while Penny sings "The Way You Look Tonight") in a harmonious duet. At the same time flickers of Depression anxiety and social instability are never entirely banished from the scene. As his name suggests, Lucky is dependent on good fortune for his future; Penny is often down on her luck during the film and seems a rather passive personality; Mabel is fired from her job. When Lucky is marching up and down outside Penny's hotel room with a placard proclaiming how unfairly in love he is being treated, audiences of the time would no doubt have appreciated the broad humor, but might also have picked up the subtext whereby he is mimicking the strike tactics of unemployed workers of the time, who were protesting against social conditions. It might be recalled that, in the same year, Charlie Chaplin finds himself inadvertently heading a march of placard-carrying protestors in *Modern Times*, and is promptly arrested by the police. The connection is reinforced by Mabel's taking pity on him finally and saying, "Come in, *comrade*" [my italics].It would not do to overemphasize the serious subtext of an eventually upbeat film but nor would it be right to ignore it. The film does cast an occasionally ironical gaze over the uneasy relationship between money and character, wealth and happiness. In this respect, *Swing Time* might not have been as far removed from *Alice Adams* as Stevens supposed when he first accepted the assignment.

Quality Street (1937)

Quality Street was RKO's attempt to persuade a doubting public that Katharine Hepburn had sex appeal. Based on J.M. Barrie's play that was first produced in 1902, and first filmed in 1927, with Marion Davies in the leading role, it is set in England during the Napoleonic Wars and tells the story of an unmarried schoolteacher, Phoebe Throssel, who takes a revenge of sorts against a soldier who has bruised her romantic hopes. The role requires an actress who can transform herself from a tired spinster to a radiant young woman so successfully that the hero, taken in by the disguise, would be swept off his feet. The studio hoped that Hepburn would have the same effect on an audience. They evidently miscalculated, since the film lost $248,000 at the box office, and Hepburn's performance divided the critics. Whereas the *Hollywood Reporter* thought it "her finest vehicle, not even excepting *Little Women*," Frank Nugent in the *Los Angeles Times* wrote that "her Phoebe Throssel needs a neurologist more than a husband. Such flutterings and jitterings and twitchings, such hand-wringing and mouth-quiverings, such running about and eyebrow raisings have not been seen on a screen in many a moon" (qtd in Moss: 50).

The blame for the film's critical and commercial failure should not be laid at Hepburn's door, however. Even at the time, the material must have seemed dated and too reliant on strained comedy contrivance. Stevens handles the farcical maneuverings with some grace; and, from a later vantage point, David Shipman will observe that "despite her [Hepburn's] overplaying and the ceaseless background music, one is always aware of a civilised, even cultured, director at work, though his skills are really more than the film deserves" (Shipman: 395). Stevens would probably have concurred with the latter point, as at this time the films he really wanted to make were either a screen version of Maxwell Anderson's play *Winterset*, or an adaptation of Humphrey Cobb's novel *Paths of Glory*, which Stanley Kubrick was to direct so memorably in 1957. It was to be years before Stevens was allowed to tackle such dramatic material on screen. In the meantime, he did his best with vehicles such as *Quality Street*, teasing out the humanity and poignancy that lay beneath the mechanics of the well-made play.

The year is 1805, and an introductory caption informs us that Quality Street is a location "where a gentleman passerby is an event." The sound of a horn that declares the appearance of a postman is enough to prompt the women of Quality Street to part their curtains and stare out of their windows in curiosity. When a Recruiting Sergeant (Eric Blore) has the audacity to wink at one of them, it can cause a spasm of excitement sufficient to induce a fainting fit. One of the recipients of his attention, Mary Willoughby (Estelle Winwood) describes his attention as follows: "He closed one of his eyes, then quickly opened it again," before adding ominously, "I knew what he meant." At that moment she is part of a reading circle and listening as a romantic novel is being read out loud and where simply the phrase "there emerged ... a man" is enough to startle the female listeners into a flutter of agitation. The hostess Susan Throssel (Fay Bainter) will steal a quick look at the ending of the story and will confess a "partiality for romance," which she says is the mark of "an old maid." When Miss Willoughby visits the Throssels again a little later, she starts sniffing around the drawing room as if she has scented vermin, and says; "I have no wish to alarm you, but I am of the opinion that there is a man in the house." It is actually the smell of the Recruiting Sergeant's pipe emanating from the kitchen. When he enters the drawing room, even the cat, which one must also assume is female, scurries up the chimney in panic.

All of this feminine palpitation is funny up to a point—but only up to a point. When the women are staring out into the street even at the postman, one notices the bars on their windows and one does register the tightly circumscribed opportunities and outlook on life that women in that society had. The most melancholy symbol of this is a wedding gown of Susan's, which she had begun when she had hopes of an alliance with a naval officer named William but which she had gone on to complete long after these hopes had been dashed. What is striking about this is that she has kept it not in the expectation of a new beau but as a souvenir of a time that has passed and a love irretrievably lost; her "plainness," she thinks, makes her unsuitable as a marriage prospect. The gown might now serve its purpose as a wedding gift for her younger sister Phoebe (Katharine Hepburn), who has just bustled into the house in the expectation of a visit and a proposal of marriage from Dr. Valentine Brown (Franchot Tone).

The visit takes place. It is introduced by a portentous shot of a man's cane knocking at the front door. We do not at first see the identity of the caller, and the knock sounds less like a request to enter than a call to attention, almost like the Fate motif of Beethoven's 5th Symphony (which is only three years away). Needless to say, this significant sound is immediately followed by four shots of women's faces at their respective windows, wondering what this call might portend. Such shots will be a recurrent motif at similar moments, both to illustrate the empty lives of these women (as if they have nothing more substantial to get excited about) and to emphasize that nothing happening in the street goes unnoticed (this will in turn form the basis of some of the comedy in the film as Phoebe's dual identity as both herself and her "niece" becomes more difficult to sustain). Brown has indeed come calling on Miss Phoebe with some exciting news, which he will break to her in the garden whose quiet attractiveness, he says, always calls her to mind. However, the news is not a marriage proposal but to tell her he has enlisted in the Army. "In these stirring times," he says, "a man cannot stay at home," the unspoken subtext to that speech being that a woman cannot do anything else. Rising from the garden seat and fiddling awkwardly with a rose in her hand, Phoebe returns with him into the study. She quickly forestalls Susan's anticipation of a happy announcement by telling her sister the actual reason for his visit is "to say good ... bye": Hepburn inserts a poignant caesura before that second syllable, giving it a real droop of disappointment After Brown has left, Susan puts away the wedding gown, and Phoebe reproaches herself for being "unladylike." The soldiers march past; the Recruiting Sergeant winks at Miss Willoughby; Brown waves a cheery farewell; and the two sisters will be left staring out of their window at the departure not only of the soldiers but of their own hopes for the future. They are now framed like the other women of the street at the beginning, as if their fates are to be the same, at which point the screen fades to black.

There is a satisfying but also sad symmetry to this opening, as the uncomprehending males stride off to do battle while the sheltered females are left passively to wait, watch and worry. Donald Richie included *Quality Street* as one of those films of Stevens that are "evocations of a golden past" (Richie: 14). I am not so sure. One can see how this opening could have been played up as a comedy of misunderstandings, but there is something about the intensity of Stevens' direction—the deliberate pacing, his care for the characters' feelings, his withholding of the big close-ups of Hepburn until the romantic letdown—that tends to work against the humor. The more somber mood is reinforced by Fay Bainter's poignant performance (as sensitive a foil to Hepburn's romanticism as she will prove to be to Bette Davis's in the following year in her Oscar-winning performance in *Jezebel*): the worried look she steals at her tearful sister as Phoebe waves farewell at the window speaks volumes. "The windows become so many eyes, with the camera staring out or peeping in," says Richie (49), but it is always the women who are framed like that, confirming them as onlookers rather than participants, with the windows as a barrier to active experience. What does the future hold for them? Stevens does seem to sense this shadow side, and seek to convey the limited role and dismal lot of the single female in that society. Even amid the period frippery and inconsequential narrative events, one still sense the sensitive hand of the man who directed *Alice Adams*.

It is a while before the mood of melancholy lifts and the film can shift into its central comedy conceit. Ten years will pass; and the caption on the screen will not only record this passage of time but give it an emotional coloring. "And for ten *weary* [my italics] years the war went on," it says; and it is clear that this weariness refers not simply to the prolongation of the war itself but to the women at home waiting for their men to return, or indeed just waiting. The caption will be scrolled over a window shot of the Throssel home which a panning shot reveals has been turned into a school, with registrations being taken for their eleventh season. The implication is that the sisters have opened the school almost immediately after Dr. Brown has left for the war and dashed Phoebe's romantic hopes. No sense of dedication or vocation is suggested: Phoebe is giving routine dancing lessons; and some mild humor is generated from Susan's hapless math lessons, where she is slower than her pupils and intimidated by the bigger boys. When the soldiers return and march through the streets, Phoebe is initially disappointed that Brown is not among them; but an even bigger disappointment is to come, for when he does arrive, he is clearly taken aback by how Phoebe has aged and how tired she looks. When the children are leaving the classroom, they are instructed to salute or bow as they go past Captain Brown. While this is happening, Susan supervises the children but Phoebe never takes her eyes off the Captain. In contrast to his dashing life as a soldier, he says, "how much more brave are the ladies who keep a school." He may be right, for in that society men have a role to play, whereas for women past a certain age, life will be a long frustration. In the play Brown has returned having lost his left hand in the war, which might at least suggest a hero somewhat chastened by experience. In the film he has come back unscathed. It is a small detail and perhaps a concession to sentiment, but it does give the impression that Brown has come back not only unchanged physically but also no wiser psychologically, and a man whose superficiality will make him ripe for deception.

Before Phoebe's transformation, the maid Patty (Cora Witherspoon) has been talking to Susan and been making a lugubrious observation about the opportunities for women in their post-war situation. "This will be a great year for females," she has said. "Think how many of the men strutting to the wars have come back limping. Who is to take off their wooden legs of an evening, Miss Susan?" Not an appealing prospect perhaps, but not an insignificant observation either: at least women there will be useful and not simply ornamental or marginal. In the meantime, Phoebe, who has seen a picture of herself taken ten years ago and gone off to find the dress, suddenly appears at the doorway in that outfit and looking ten years younger, as indeed does Hepburn. It is the film's greatest visual moment, because in it is invested not only the credibility of the second half of the film but also the studio's investment in Hepburn as a romantic actress. When Brown now returns and Patty, on the spur of the moment, tells him that this beautiful creature before him is Phoebe's niece, Livvie, the deception proper begins.

Brown seems instantly smitten. Deftly Susan is drawn into the charade. The Willoughbys are deceived, with only Mary remaining suspicious. Stevens now takes the opportunity to open out the play a little, with scenes of a ball, of boating on the lake and croquet on the lawn, all of which are designed to illustrate Miss Livvie's seeming flirtatiousness and Brown's growing jealousy of the attention she arouses. A momentary crisis occurs when in the park she tells him Miss Phoebe is ill and he insists on leaving her and hurrying back to see what is the matter. However, she manages to beat him back to the house, evade the visit of the Willoughbys, rush upstairs and dive under the bed covers, re-emerging as an enfeebled Phoebe just as he enters the room. Hepburn is at her funniest here, and Stevens augments the comedy when Susan notices the hat Livvie has been wearing lying at the foot of the bed and Patty secretes it out of the room without Brown's noticing. After he has gone, Phoebe tells Susan her plan. She will accompany him to the Ball that evening in her disguise as Livvie. Knowing that he is infatuated with her, she will allow him to propose marriage, at which point she will dismiss him with a withering, "La, you're much too old." Her revenge will then be complete. " Phoebe, how can you be so cruel?" asks Susan, at which point, in the film, Phoebe pauses and bursts into tears, and the screen fades to black, leaving both the character and the audience to ponder that question and to take that curiosity into the last part of the drama. In Act III of the play Phoebe has given an explicit answer to that question. "Because he has taken from me the one great glory that is in a woman's life. Not a man's love—she can do without that—but her own dear sweet love for him. He is unworthy of my love; that is why I can be so cruel." One suspects that the decision of Stevens and his writers to cut that speech might have been determined by a feeling that it would undermine the ultimate happy ending; also that it might seem overexplicit and that they would prefer audiences to answer that question for themselves. It is an intriguing anticipation of a key moment in William Wyler's later film, *The Heiress* (1949), when the heroine, who is preparing a calculated and brutal rebuff to a returning suitor who has earlier deserted her, is also accused of cruelty by a relative who has been hoping for a romantic reconciliation. "Yes, I am cruel," Wyler's heroine says. "I have been taught by masters." *Quality Street* does not have that same edge of anger and bitterness, but there is still in Phoebe's strategy, even if only momentarily, a similar protest at patriarchal insolence and injustice.

In the final part of the film all will be resolved. Stevens contrives a ball sequence that is a gem of comic choreography, as he weaves his characters in and out of the frame in what seems like a desperate dance of deceit that is forever teetering on a precipice of disaster, all building to the point where Brown will disclose to Livvie that he now realizes that he was in love with Miss Phoebe all along, which in turn knocks all her plans of vengeance awry. Gradually Brown will see through the deception and contrive a departure for Miss Livvie that will satisfy the snooping of the neighbors. Eric Blore's trademark double-takes have rarely been used to better effect than in the finale here, where the Recruiting Sergeant fights a losing battle in trying to comprehend what is happening as the machinations multiply; and where even his mutton chop will become an important prop to keep the prying Miss Willoughby off the scent and end up being served up as an unlikely breakfast for a supposedly delicate female invalid. Amid the farcical maneuverings, however, the feminine theme never goes away, and Hepburn gives it due gravity. "You went to the great battles," Phoebe will tell Brown. "I was left to fight in a little one. Women have a flag to fly, Mr. Brown, as well as men, and old maids have a flag as well as women. I tried to keep mine flying." It is a forceful assertion of the importance of women in society, even when they seem to have little access to the levers of social and political power; and it is a theme to which Stevens will return, in *Vigil in the Night*, for example, and perhaps even in *The Diary of Anne Frank*, where finally the most resonant declaration of a fundamental unquenchable belief in humanity, even amid the wretchedness of war, will come from the diary of a teenage girl.

A Damsel in Distress (1937)

"A disaster, and Stevens' last attempt at a musical."—Eugene Archer

"Two of the dance sequences, Astaire playing the drums with his feet, and Astaire, Burns and Allen in the hall of mirrors, are amongst the greatest ever filmed."—Bruce Beresford

On a 15 month sabbatical from Ginger Rogers, who evidently wished to step out from under her dancing partner's shadow and into more dramatic roles, Fred Astaire eased his way into this classy Gershwin musical that was part scripted by P.G. Wodehouse. Yet, to the surprise of *Variety*, who thought the film had "plenty for the b.o.–dancing, comedy, marquee values, the usual sumptuous investiture by Pandro Berman, and those Gershwin songs," *A Damsel in Distress* was a flop on release and the first Astaire musical to lose money.

The failure might partially be attributed to the flimsiness of the film's plot, which Marilyn Ann Moss neatly summarized in just two sentences: "Astaire is Jerry, an American musical comedy composer [and performer] who travels to London and there meets the aristocratic Lady Alyce (Joan Fontaine), herself in love with another American whom her family forbids her to see. When she escapes the castle one day with her butler Keggs (Reginald Gardiner) trailing her, she runs into Jerry and eventually falls in love with him" (Moss: 52). Also the musical numbers are not integrated into the narrative with anything like the imagination or innovation of *Swing Time*: indeed, if one removed the numbers entirely, the narrative would hardly be affected. The public might even have been put off by the misleading publicity, for the film's poster, which promised "Mad Adventure! Daring deeds! White hot love with music!" was hardly a reliable guide for what the film had to offer. Yet the principal reason behind the film's failure with both critics and public does seem to have been their disappointment that the damsel in distress was not Ginger Rogers. Ironically, at this stage in their careers, both Astaire and Rogers were looking for a degree of freedom from each other; and Stevens was being nothing if not obliging in this regard, for he was to follow this film of Astaire without Rogers with a film that had Rogers without Astaire.

The casting of Astaire's female co-star was to prove the film's main area of controversy. Jessie Matthews turned down the role of Lady Alyce; Ruby Keeler was very keen to do it, for her career seemed to have temporarily stalled and she could certainly dance;

Stevens' preferred choice was Carole Lombard, with whom he longed to work. Surprisingly, RKO gave the role to one of their new actresses under contract, Joan Fontaine, who had appeared briefly under Stevens' direction in a minor role in *Quality Street*. After around four weeks of shooting, both Astaire and Pandro Berman were agitating to have her removed from the picture, for she had two fundamental weaknesses for a leading role in a musical: she could neither sing nor dance. Stevens was concerned that replacing her would have a demoralizing impact on Fontaine, whom he thought was emotionally fragile; and that, if they removed her, he would have to leave the picture also. In those circumstances, Astaire agreed to continue with what they had. In its review of the film (6 December 1937) *Time* magazine caught the prevailing feeling: "Not so lissom a heroine as light-footed Ginger Rogers ... actress Fontaine goes gamely but somewhat lumberingly through the curvets and caracoles required of her." Harshly but accurately, the review noted that Fontaine's dancing was not only decisively inferior to Astaire's but also to that of Gracie Allen, who is essentially there as supporting comic relief.

How much Fontaine's limited dancing ability affects one's overall enjoyment of the film is, however, a matter of debate and possibly personal taste, particularly if one subscribes to the view that one goes to an Astaire musical mainly to watch Astaire, irrespective of his dancing partner. Admittedly, in the case of *Damsel in Distress,* the romantic balance of the film is affected if the musical weight is carried, vocally and choreographically, almost exclusively by the male. It is significant that the film's main love song, "A Foggy Day in London Town," is a melodic monologue by the hero as he strolls by the creek, while the heroine is reduced to watching him wistfully from her room window. Yet how superbly Astaire delivers the song, possibly his finest vocal performance on film; and how beautifully the sequence is photographed by Joseph August, the light shimmering through the mist to simulate the sense of the sun's shining everywhere in foggy London town and bathing the song in a warm romantic glow. The couple's one number together, "Things Are Looking Up," is done almost as a hide-and-seek sequence in the castle grounds, with Stevens joining in, gallantly attempting to hide his heroine's dancing deficiencies by putting as many obstacles in the way of a spectator's field of vision—trees, hedges, bridges, tree trunks—as he can find. There is a dramatic justification for this. The Ginger Rogers character in *Swing Time* can credibly match Astaire's expertise because she is a dancing instructor, whereas it might look incongruous if Fontaine's sheltered English aristocrat should suddenly reveal footwork on a par with her partner, who, in this film, is actually playing the part of an exceptional musical comedy performer. There is something quite touching as well as amusing about Fontaine's awkward, demure attempt to enter into the spirit of Astaire's graceful expression of love. She might not be Astaire's ideal dancing partner, but one could tell from this performance alone (the shy insecurity, the suggestion of romantic vulnerability, even the character's father-fixation) what might have prompted David Selznick and Alfred Hitchcock later to cast her as the nameless heroine in *Rebecca* (1940).

Ample compensation for Fontaine's shortage of musical comedy skills comes in the form of those seasoned vaudevillians, George Burns and Gracie Allen, a much more formidable supporting duo than Victor Moore and Helen Broderick in *Swing Time*. Burns plays Astaire's overenthusiastic publicity agent, whose exaggerations on his client's behalf (particularly over the latter's supposed amatory conquests) lead to Astaire's being besieged by fans on his arrival in London and later complicate his relationship with Alyce, who thinks she is just the latest in a long line of former sweethearts. Gracie Allen plays the scatterbrained secretary who cannot even sharpen a pencil without ruining it and who is, to the bemusement of those who come into contact with her, constantly mangling and misinterpreting what she hears. (When introduced to Montagu Love's Lord Marshmorton, she immediately starts addressing him as "Lord Marshmallow.") Burns and Allen add to the film's comic and choreographic gaiety so that when Astaire moves into the cottage near the castle and launches into a tap dance routine for the number "Just Begun to Live," Burns and Allen can not only follow but revel in the master's footsteps, matching his every move. The exhilaration is such that even the suit of armor standing against the wall suddenly raises a metallic leg in salutation.

This trio of talents particularly excels in the film's remarkable funhouse sequence. The inspiration for the sequence came from Hermes Pan after a visit to a funhouse at Ocean Park. Thinking this would make a wonderful idea for a number, he asked Stevens if it could be worked into the script in some way. "Well, I have one house in England," replied Stevens, and they took it from there, inserting a country fair into the action and with Pan asking the set designer for everything they had that could be used for the occasion: fairground rides, turntables, moving boardwalks, distorting mirrors, and so forth. The scene builds up amusingly, as Astaire (literally and symbolically) crashes through the barrier that separates him and Fontaine and, misinterpreting her signals, kisses her in "The Tunnel of Love" (the kiss shown in complete darkness, in obeisance to Astaire's known antipathy to kisses on screen, and followed anyway by a slap). Gracie Allen becomes temporarily but gracefully trapped on a large turning disk from which she cannot immediately escape, one of a number of such images in the film to suggest the way in which the characters seem often to be going round in circles in an abortive attempt to communicate with each other. Things come to a head when they enter a hall of mirrors and the dancers are turned upside down, their legs elongated, and the screen at one stage split horizontally to distort their images still further. By this time all the spectators at the fair (including a couple of drunks, who have created their own unwitting choreography in unsteadily following Astaire into the funhouse) are joining in to enlarge the sense of joie de vivre. The "Funhouse" number deservedly won an Oscar for Hermes Pan for Best Dance Direction (the last Oscar of its kind to be awarded); and Carroll Clark was also to be nominated for Best Interior Decoration. The whole sequence is a visual tour de force. It might not advance the narrative, but it undoubtedly lifts the film.

When elaborating on his preference for *Damsel in Distress* over *Swing Time*, Bruce Beresford wrote: "This time Stevens gave up trying to direct the serious bits in the Carl Dreyer manner and played the whole thing for laughs, never mistiming his built-up gags and low-key humour" (Beresford: 13). Although it would be hard to mistake *Swing Time* for a Carl Dreyer film, Beresford was right to praise Stevens' comedy timing in *Damsel in Distress*. There is a particularly felicitous scene early on when, in the manner of traditional romantic comedy, Astaire and Fontaine meet quite by chance when taking refuge in the same taxi (he from marauding fans, she from the family's butler, who has followed her to London). Stevens' orchestration of developments from that meet-cute is masterly, as an attraction is instantly suggested; Fontaine slips out of the car unnoticed when she is about to be discovered; Astaire distracts attention with a brief dancing routine ("I'm dancing and I can't be bothered now") which ends with his hopping onto a London bus and disappearing into the distance; and the hapless butler, Keggs, inadvertently harasses a London bobby and ends up having to spend a night in jail. Reginald Gardiner's performance as Keggs is one of the pleasures of the film, suitably pompous when anticipating a visit of the castle premises by tourists ("we shall be overrun by the proletariat," he moans); mischievously nefarious when he attempts to rig the sweepstake in his favor when betting on Lady Alyce's future husband by concealing his piece of paper inside the hat band; but oddly sympathetic when he secretly discloses a passion for operatic arias which he longs to sing. It gives a sudden dimension of emotional release to a character who elsewhere has taken formality to the point of rigidity. Caught in the act of singing at one stage by Lady Marshmont (the reliably stylish Constance Collier), he is sternly rebuked for such excesses. "A man of character, Keggs, should learn to control his passions," he is told, and his head droops in shame and acquiescence. Later in the film, however, he spies a window of opportunity when he can indulge his obsession before returning to his public role; and, on his own and in a moment of wish fulfilment, he launches a full-throated aria into the night air. This was surely the inspiration for that magical moment in the film-within-a-film sequence in Woody Allen's '30s pastiche, *The Purple Rose of Cairo*, when the head waiter seizes an opportunity to step outside the role to which he has been consigned by the film and goes into a tap-dancing routine that he has wanted to do all his life.

It is customary that the course of true love never does run smooth in the usual romantic/musical comedy, otherwise there would be no film; yet it is noticeable even at this stage in Stevens' career that the obstacles tend to be societal or monetary rather than personal, and that the main protagonist is required to bridge or even leap over a social gulf that separates him/her from his/her beloved. As in *Alice Adams*, *Swing Time* and in the forthcoming *Vivacious Lady*, one of the pair is an outsider in the other's community; and in *Damsel in Distress*, as an American entertainer in pursuit of an English aristocrat, Astaire is an outsider who is often left literally outside, barred from entry into the Marshmont castle. This is exploited for its comic potential, notably when Astaire manages to infiltrate an ensemble of madrigal singers and gives their traditional English airs an injection of American modernity and swing, but it is also an example of the way Stevens is here treating comically themes that in his later films he will treat seriously. In a way one can see how all roads are leading imperceptibly but inevitably to *A Place in the Sun*, where social division and inequality will not be the source of comic incongruity but the stuff of romantic tragedy.

In the stage version of *A Damsel in Distress*, adapted by Wodehouse and Ian Hay from the former's short story and first produced at the New Theatre, London on 12 August 1928, the American with whom Lady Alyce has originally fallen in love does actually make an appearance. In the film he does not, and one of the most endearing scenes is one in which she talks about the American to Jerry (Astaire), who mistakenly assumes that it is actually himself whom she is describing. "In the first place, he's the most charming man in the world," she says, with which Jerry readily concurs; but when she then says, "In the second place, he's *divinely* handsome," Astaire has the appealing modesty to look a little bemused by that: love might be blind, but this is clearly a case of mistaken identity. No one would describe Astaire as "divinely handsome"; his "divinity," as one might call it, is from the ankles down. Still there are few better examples of it than in the film's final number, when his euphoria is expressed through a dazzling drum solo with his feet to the accompaniment of "Nice Work If You Can Get It." It is then topped with a final flourish when, to clear the way on exiting the castle with Lady Alyce, he does a graceful fly-kick left and right that sends both Keggs and young Albert, who are scrambling on the floor to piece together the winning sweepstake ticket, sprawling out of the shot on either side of the film frame. If it is not in any way a classic musical (nothing can quite disguise or compensate for the romantic hollowness at its heart), *Damsel in Distress* still has passages of vintage Astaire, and Stevens knows how to put his directing skills at the service of his star's artistry. He lets his feet do the talking.

Vivacious Lady (1938)

> Helen (the hero's former fiancée): "I'll give you a piece of my mind!" Francy (unbeknown to Helen, the hero's wife): "O, I *couldn't* take the last piece."—
> The Prom sequence in *Vivacious Lady*

Vivacious Lady was originally scheduled to be made before *Quality Street* and *Damsel in Distress* and designed to show off the acting skills of Ginger Rogers away from her partnership with Fred Astaire. However, shooting had to be suspended after a fortnight, because James Stewart (who had been requested as her co-star by Rogers and who was on loan from MGM) fell ill and then was required for another MGM production. In the interim, Stevens completed the other two films, which were both box-office failures, so *Vivacious Lady* suddenly assumed an unexpected importance in being a production that needed to restore Stevens' status in the eyes of the studio. Fortunately the film was a great success. *Variety* described it as "entertainment of the highest and broadest appeal," and the studio's historians, Richard B. Jewell and Vernon Harbin were to claim it as "one of RKO's finest comedies of the decade" (119). It was also to be nominated for two Oscars: best cinematography (Robert De Grasse) and best sound recording (James Wilkinson).

In a New York nightclub to collect his wayward cousin, Keith (James Ellison), and take him back to Old Sharon University where they both work, a young botany professor, Peter Morgan (James Stewart), is instantly smitten with singer, Francy (Ginger Rogers), who is performing there. He likens the impact of her presence to his memory of being run over by his father's car when he was four (a car is to perform a similarly striking function in the film's finale). By the time the evening is over, they are in love; and by the time he catches his train home, the two are married and Peter has a new bride to introduce to his family. However, through a series of circumstances and misunderstandings, he finds himself unable to break the news to his father (Charles Coburn), who is dean of Old Sharon University, anxious for his son to take his place, and who would certainly disapprove of his son's marriage to a showgirl. A further complication is that Peter is unofficially engaged to someone else, Helen (Frances Mercer), who is at the station with Peter's father to greet him on his return home, leaving Francy and Keith to go off together while Peter tries (unsuccessfully) to explain the situation. For a while Francy has to pretend to be an unlikely postgraduate student of biology to justify her continuing presence in town and her evident eagerness to see Peter at every opportunity: in the classroom, in the storeroom, and in the women-only apartment block where she is temporarily accommodated under the beady eye of the apartment manager (Franklin Pangorn at his officious and supercilious best). Eventually things are resolved, but not before the marriage of the young couple has been brought to breaking point, as has the marriage of Peter's parents, for Mrs. Morgan (Beulah Bondi) has finally become as exasperated by her husband's overbearing demeanor as Francy has by Peter's irresolution.

"It's just a matter of chemistry, see," Peter will explain to Francy as part of his lesson on the science of attraction. "Anodes attract cathodes." Aided by Stevens' sympathetic direction, the screen chemistry between Rogers and Stewart (shared off-screen also, apparently) gives conviction to their whirlwind romance; and, as he will demonstrate in *The More the Merrier* (1943), Stevens is particularly astute in directing love scenes where a couple, ostensibly sharing a serious conversation, find they have something else on their mind. When Peter and Francy are saying goodnight to each other after their tour of New York, Peter, while seeming to listen intently, is more intent on Francy's lips than the words coming out of her mouth; and Francy, as if reading his mind, seizes the initiative and quickly kisses him, recognizing that this is one of those kisses from which there is no turning back. As well as making a good romantic team, Rogers and Stewart are a good comedy team also, one acting as a foil to the other. Rogers is not a natural comedienne, but she does know how to deliver an astringent comedy line, and the slightly tart edge to her screen persona offsets Stewart's comic earnestness, just as her cool melancholy can nicely chill Stewart's sentimental intensity. Rogers is a graceful dancer more than a slapstick performer, though she does manage to contain her romantic rival in an impressive headlock during their riotous confrontation at the Prom, where they exchange blows (168 of them before Stevens was satisfied, apparently) and where Francy unfortunately fells her father-in-law by mistake, an error which will also delay a proper introduction. However, the physical comedy business is mainly left to Stewart, whether absent-mindedly gulping down whole a sample of mouthwash in a drugstore while his mind is distracted by amorous euphoria; or noticing the unexpected appearance of Helen below, as he is dangling compromisingly from a stepladder while making a secret exit from Francy's room (his momentarily paralyzed posture causes one fleetingly to think ahead to *Vertigo*). His rebelliously drunken turn in front of his embarrassed father and an amused benefactor, capped by a spectacular falling on his face, has something of the panache that will anticipate his Oscar-winning comedy performance in George Cukor's *The Philadelphia Story* (1940).

While maintaining the utmost visual decorum, Stevens' romantic comedies at this time are quite bold in their sexual suggestiveness. Although Stevens was to describe it as a comedy about the frustration of non-communication, *Vivacious Lady* is equally a comedy about the frustration of non-consummation. It is true that Stewart's principal mannerism—the struggle to get anything said—is deployed very deftly, so that his failure to communicate with his father (who tends not to listen to anyone anyway) is convincing as well as humorous. But even on the train home after their whirlwind marriage, Peter and Francy find that their compartment is already occupied by an elderly married couple whose bickering is not exactly an encouraging augury of the joys of wedded life. Stevens heightens the comedy through a clever use of overlapping dialogue and a contrast between what is happening in the background of the shot (Peter and Francy trying to whisper sweet nothings above the noise) and what is happening in the foreground (the elderly couple locked in an argument, which is drowning out the intimacies of the newlyweds and souring the romantic atmosphere). Even when they escape to the observation car and snuggle up next to each other in the darkness, a guard passes through and switches the light on again. "Can't we ever be alone?" Francy will moan at one stage, and she has a point, for when the couple seem at last to be together on their own, a hand will suddenly materialize from the side of the frame to tap on Peter's shoulder, and a private moment will suddenly be opened out to the public gaze.

The frustrations begin to accumulate. The married couple spend their first night back home in Old Sharon sleeping away from each other and, having as their sleeping partners, a miniature model of bride and groom (from the wedding cake that Keith has bought them) rather than the real thing. When Francy has to continue her pretense to be a postgraduate student in Peter's botany class and he is introducing her to the course she is purporting to follow, she says, feelingly, "There are a lot of things I have to catch up on": one can confidently surmise that she is not only referring to her studies. Given the restrictions of the Hays Code at the time, Stevens takes tasteful visual and verbal innuendo about as far as it can go without straying into impermissible explicitness. One particularly funny moment in this regard occurs when Francy has met her mother-in-law in the ladies room during the Prom, though at this stage neither of them knows the identity of the other. They have got on immediately, sharing a cigarette; and Mrs. Morgan reveals that she has to do this in secret because her husband does not allow her to smoke. After she has left the room, the maid-in-attendance (Hattie McDaniel), who has overheard the conversation, says emphatically to Francy, "If my husband wouldn't let me smoke, I'd find me a way to get a husband that would!" Francy turns and replies, smartly, "It depends on which you enjoy the most!" before exiting. Stevens lingers for a good ten seconds on a shot of the maid as she resumes her cleaning while slowly absorbing what Francy has just said. When the penny drops and she swivels to face the camera, she has the amazed expression of a woman who can hardly believe what she has just heard. The infinitely expressive Hattie McDaniel, who is not actually listed on the film's credits and does not appear again, has surely been cast for that single close-up. In lingering on the moment, Stevens is inviting the audience also to savor the suggestiveness of Francy's remark and join him in enjoying this mischievous circumvention of the Hollywood Code.

The most overt symbol of frustration is the bed in Francy's room in the Martha Gregory Apartments block where she is being accommodated. It is one of those beds that folds into the wall when not in use, but this one has a habit of crashing down when a wind blows through. On noticing this when he comes to visit Francy, Peter keeps finding a pretext to open and close drawers and doors in a surreptitious endeavor to cause a sufficient draught for the bed to descend. It is a motif that will provide a neat finale when Peter and Francy are at last alone and the bunk bed in their cabin obligingly pops down, at which point Peter closes the door.

Unlike the more madcap comedies of directors like Howard Hawks and Preston Sturges of the late 1930s and early 1940s, Stevens tends to root his humor more in everyday situations. He also takes his time, allowing audiences a more leisurely opportunity to relish the performances and identify with recognizable situations and conflicts. This also gives an audience the opportunity to ponder the more serious undercurrents. Although *Vivacious Lady* is primarily a light-hearted romance that makes the most of its relatively slim comic situation, one does have the chance to register Stevens' characteristic observation of the kind of social disparity and snobbery that can destabilize the possibilities of human happiness. There is a particularly interesting exchange between Francy and Peter's father, when the latter more or less accuses her of seducing his son ("You hooked him") for social and financial advancement, and Francy has to point out, very delicately, that she was probably earning more as a nightclub entertainer than Peter as an associate professor. However, when he threatens to ask for Peter's resignation from his post because of this unfortunate association, Francy feels she has no alternative but to abandon the marriage and return to New York.

The theme of marriage will be at the forefront of a number of Stevens' films, and particularly the sacrifices and adjustments that the women in particular have to make, which in turn can fuel dissatisfaction and disappointment if their weak-willed husbands do not live up to their expectations. We saw it in the parents' marriage in *Alice Adams,* and marital strife will also loom large in *Penny Serenade* and *Woman of the Year,* as well as being treated with unusual maturity in later films such as *Giant* and unexpectedly perhaps in *Shane* (one does not expect the marriage theme to feature quite so prominently in a western). Although non-consummation is the thing that takes the marriage of the young couple in *Vivacious Lady* to the point of near-breakdown, it is non-communication that almost blows apart the marriage of Peter's parents. The authoritative performances of such seasoned professionals as Charles Coburn and Beulah Bondi ensure that this comes over with some force. We learn that Mrs. Morgan's fainting fits are feigned not real, a convenient strategy to give her some respite whenever her husband raises his voice in exasperation at some university matter; it is how she has survived living with him for thirty years. Yet it has clearly taken its toll. The scenes between Rogers and Bondi are rather moving, because of the sense they give of the mother's recognition, in Francy's vivacity, of a spark and vitality which she once had and her domineering husband has over the years extinguished. When Francy and Keith begin to demonstrate the new dance routine, the Big Apple, for her and insist that she joins them, the mother's growing involvement and spontaneity convey a joyous sense of release, as if she is shedding invisible chains; so that when her husband enters and can barely believe what he is watching (his monocle seems to jump from his eye of its own volition), the abrupt change of mood takes the film into a different emotional realm. "Have you quite finished?" he says to his wife, who is in some sartorial disarray, for, in losing some of her inhibition, she has lost a glove. She has also finally lost patience. When her husband orders her to come along, she mimics the instruction as if she is a dog being called to obedience and gives vent to her frustration at always being expected to be at his beck and call. Typically, he is paying so little attention to what she is saying that he does not quite pick up her mood. "Coming, my dear?" he says, as they are leaving Francy's room. "Coming?" she repeats, indignantly, before correcting him: "I'm *going!*"

The ending is a bit of a mess. The film was begun without a completed script, and, for all the odd structural and stylistic felicities in the finale, the ending does not quite conceal the air of quiet desperation. Both Francy and Mrs. Morgan have left their husbands, and Stevens pans from Fran's weeping in her train compartment to the next compartment along, which, unbeknown to Francy, is occupied by her mother-in-law who is also in tears: the split screen visually unites them in their sorrow. Francy realizes the identity of the woman when the porter (Willie Best) brings her a half-cigarette from the passenger next door, who has insisted to the porter that she could not take the last cigarette when knowing another has requested one; the gesture is unmistakable. Their shared misery is offset by the antics of the porter, who is shuffling back and forth between them and is alternately bewildered by, and then empathizes with, their tears.

Meanwhile father and son have contrived to derail the women's departure by the alarming strategy of leaving their car across the track and thus causing the train to halt. Even by the standards of romantic comedy, this seems an extraordinarily irresponsible action. Father comes down from his high horse by feigning a heart attack outside his wife's door; he thus gains admission to her compartment and, it seems, a readmission into her affections by a neat but possibly dubious subterfuge. Peter is finally alone with Francy, and, as the door closes and Stevens pans to the sign which reads "Quiet for the

Benefit of Those Who Have Retired," even the train itself seems to be hooting a wolf whistle. But where is all this heading? The train is temporarily stalled; and the relationships are also in a sort of limbo, with a resolution some way off. In feeling, it anticipates the climax of Preston Sturges's *The Palm Beach Story* (1942), where a voice at the end intones, "And they lived happily ever after," before adding: "Or did they?" In *Vivacious Lady*, one might be tempted to think back to the moment where all this started: Francy's song in the nightclub, "You'll be Reminded of Me," and the movement of the camera towards her—one of the most striking camera movements in the film—to suggest Peter's instant attraction and the divergence this represents to his former plans. Not for the only time in the film, however, he becomes so absorbed in her that he does not immediately take in what is being said, for the song seems actually a recollection of a relationship that has failed because of the man's deceptions but that he is the one who will be tormented by its failure. The song is not exactly prophesying the future of their relationship; but it does sound a warning.

Gunga Din (1939)

> "Though I belted you and flayed you,
> By the living God that made you,
> You're a better man than I am, Gunga Din!"
> —Colonel Weed, reciting Rudyard Kipling's
> poem at the end of *Gunga Din*

Based on Rudyard Kipling's famous poem from his *Barrack Room Ballads* of 1892, *Gunga Din* was originally acquired by RKO as a project for Howard Hawks, who was scheduled to direct a screenplay, co-authored by the team of Ben Hecht and Charles McArthur, that leaned heavily for inspiration on their hit play *The Front Page*. When Hawks was removed from the project (reputedly because of the box-office failure of his new comedy, *Bringing Up Baby*, later to be regarded as a classic), the production was reassigned to what the studio probably thought were a safer pair of hands, the dependable George Stevens, who had not tackled anything in the adventure mode before. This decision turned out to be far riskier than the studio had bargained for, though one that was to be triumphantly vindicated.

In taking on the assignment, Stevens first stipulated that the two main characters in the story (one of whom, as in *The Front Page,* is trying to prevent the other from getting married), should be increased to three, to permit more comic and dramatic variety. Stevens' other major stipulation was that the main part of the film should be shot outdoors, which would lengthen the schedule and increase the cost. This was to have repercussions for the rest of his career. Although in generic terms the film is unlike anything Stevens had done before, in logistical terms it anticipates his later working methods. It also initiated his later reputation as a perfectionist who was to become the scourge of studio heads and a hero to his fellow directors.

The film took 104 days to shoot, 75 of which were spent on location in an area flanked by the Sierra Mountains in California, and containing Mount Whitney, which, according to Stevens, was the highest mountain in the United States, and the Alabama hills, whose rock formations suggested the Khyber Pass in India. Studio heads tended to dislike location shooting, partly for financial reasons but also because it made it more difficult to keep an eye on what the director was doing. The length of time taken was partly owing to the difficult working conditions (the temperature on location rarely fell below 100 degrees) and the complicated and elaborate organization required for the spectacular action sequences. It also owed something to the fact that Stevens went into the film without a finished script. This was not an unusual situation for him and he brought in two trusted collaborators, the writers Joel Sayre and Fred Guiol, to work on the screenplay. Nevertheless, there are scenes in the film—the parading of the soldiers, or the dance to celebrate the engagement of Sergeant Ballantine (Douglas Fairbanks, Jr.) to his fiancée, Emaline (Joan Fontaine)—that seem extended beyond their immediate narrative function, presumably (one suspects) to give Stevens and his writers a little more time to work out what happens next. As a consequence, the film went massively over budget, making it by far RKO's most expensive film to date.

Stevens' tactics to frustrate studio representatives, who were sent to chastise him over the escalating budget and bring him back into line, have passed into movie legend. As mentioned in the introduction, Fred Zinnemann described one tactic as Stevens' "Indian look," which would reduce apoplectic producers and financiers to silence. On *Gunga Din,* Stevens' other tactic was to post a lookout on the hills to alert him to the approach of a studio car, so that by the time the representative had reached the location, Stevens had long since gone home. These tactics were usually justified by results. *Gunga Din* proved to be hugely popular, ending the decade for Stevens on a high note (almost literally). Over the next two decades it was to be frequently re-released. An assistant editor at RKO at the time, John Sturges was to direct a Western remake, *Sergeants Three* (1962), with Frank Sinatra, Dean Martin, and Sammy Davis, Jr.; and the George Lucas/Steven Spielberg Indiana Jones films, notably Spielberg's *Indiana Jones and the Temple of Doom* (1984), clearly owed a lot to the Stevens film in terms of their mixture of adventure, spectacle, comedy and heroics. Indeed, in *Adventures in the Screen Trade,* screenwriter William Goldman was to describe *Gunga Din* as not only his "favourite movie of all time," which he had seen sixteen times and which still made him cry, but say that "it is my absolute opinion that in every conceivable way—direction, script, special effects, emotional power—it is infinitely superior to any of the five Lucas Spielberg prizewinners" (Goldman: 154). (He was referring specifically to *Star Wars, The Empire Strikes, Jaws, E.T.* and *Raiders of the Lost Ark.*)

In his American Film Institute interview, Stevens said that "the concept of the film was kind of 'Rover Boys in India' adventure" (Stevens Jr.: 226). It is a comic-book tale of schoolboy heroics in the spirit of romance fiction of the Victorian era which celebrated tales of action by daring and dedicated Englishmen in the defense of Empire. To accept it on these terms, one might also need to accommodate, and even suspend, what a great admirer of the film, Ted Sennett acknowledged as "its blatantly imperialistic viewpoint and its condescending attitude to the natives" (Sennett: 3). Even at the time, the film was condemned in India as "Imperialistic propaganda of the crudest, most vulgar sort" and the sacrifice of Gunga Din as that "of a faithful servant ... loyal unto death, despite the insults that are invariably showered upon him by his White Masters" (qtd in Moss: 61–2). Without wishing to deny the validity of these responses nor deny how the film could jar with modern sensibilities about imperialism and racial stereotyping, one should nevertheless indicate how Stevens brings varieties of nuance and even irony to the broad picture.

The three British sergeants are not offered as typical of the British Army, being often disreputable, rebellious and irresponsible, and whose brawling at the beginning of the film is described by their commanding officer, Colonel Weed (Montagu Love) as "sheer childish, brainless idiocy." "How can we get a nice little war going?" asks Cutter, in thinking of how they can persuade Ballantine to re-join the regiment; in 1939, that must have seemed a particularly irresponsible question. The Thugees are not meant to be typical of other groups and tribes in India; quite the contrary, in fact, since even their own countrymen are afraid of them. At the same time, Stevens does give them a voice and allow them to have their say, which, by comparison, is more than the Apaches are allowed in John Ford's film of the same year, *Stagecoach* (1939). Indeed one might be compelled in this context to reconsider a claim that Nicholas Bartlett once made about Stevens' films. "His people are real, not symbolic," he wrote, "none is wholly good or bad; indeed it is difficult to find a complete villain in all of Stevens' films" (Bartlett: 26). One can imagine his thinking of *Shane* in that context, and Ru Ryker's impassioned and eloquent defense of his behavior towards the homesteaders, but was he also including *Gunga Din*? Eduardo Ciannelli's intense characterization of the leader of the Thugees, Sufi Khan, might seem to contradict this, with his chant of "Kill, lest you be killed ... kill for the love of killing.... Kill! Kill! Kill!" Yet his fanaticism is given some motivation, which is essentially a reaction against the contempt and brutality directed at his own people, whom he describes as "the friendless of the earth ... kicked, spat upon, hanged." At one stage, he likens his dedication to a cause to that of the soldiers he has captured. "I can die for my country and my faith as you do yourself," he says, before throwing himself into the snake-pit which was originally intended for the Englishmen as a horrible death (and the reaction shot of the three sergeants as they watch the death certainly confirms its horror) but a fate which he himself now embraces so that the English can no longer use him as a human shield to thwart his followers. The fanatic who willingly commits suicide in furtherance of a cause in which he fervently believes might resonate even more strongly with audiences today than it did at the time.

Gunga Din's supreme act of courage in giving his life for the British Army is not without its ironies also. RKO executives originally wanted to cast the young Indian actor Sabu in the role after his success in Robert Flaherty's *Elephant Boy* (1937), but he had a prior commitment to *The Thief of Baghdad* (1940) and producer Alexander Korda refused to loan him out to another studio. Stevens anyway preferred an older actor in the role because he thought this would comply more aptly with the way the character is described in Kipling's poem. Sam Jaffe was cast mainly on the strength of his performance as the High Lama in Frank Capra's *Lost Horizon* (1937). The fact that Gunga Din is a man not a boy adds a certain piquancy to the role, since he is mature enough to recognize his lowly station as a water bearer and his exploitation by his masters. His desire to become a soldier in the British Army ("Don't make me laugh," says MacChesney derisively) seems devout and deluded at the same time; and this duality is surely not lost on the director. In his article on the film in *Screen and Radio Weekly 1939*, Stevens posed the question: "Is there a greater story in any language of the heroism of one of a downtrodden class of people?" (qtd in Cronin: 8). The question is rhetorical, but it is also rather ambiguous. Is the act more heroic *because* it is committed by someone of a downtrodden class; or is it more heroic *despite* the fact it is committed by someone of a downtrodden class, and on behalf of a system responsible for its oppression?

These questions particularly impinge on one's interpretation of the ending. Although she generally enjoyed and admired the film, Penelope Houston called the final scene, where Colonel Weed reads the final lines of the Kipling poem over the corpse of Gunga Din, "truly appalling" (Houston: 73). She says he "declaims" the poem to the regiment whereas he is actually reading it only to Cutter, MacChesney and Ballantine, with Kipling (Reginald Sheffield) also in attendance, and she thereby somewhat misrepresents the tone of the scene, which is more private and intimate than public and declamatory. Unfortunately, she did not spell out exactly what it was about this scene that "appalled" her. Certainly the final shot, which superimposes an image of a smiling Din in the corporal's uniform he has been posthumously awarded, can seem dangerously sentimental and patronizing if one takes the film as a straightforward imperialist adventure. Yet the final scene can be felt as profoundly ironic as well as emotionally moving. Behind the praise sounds a note of reproach. When the Colonel says the line, "Though I belted you and flayed you," there is a close-up of MacChesney (Victor McLaglen) in tears, as if he is remembering his own mistreatment of Din and also perhaps his hypocritical condemnation of the Thugees' flaying of Cutter, when he has threatened Din with something as bad if not worse. (He threatens Din with the firing squad at one point, saying "I've a good mind to split you in two and shove you up an elephant trunk.") Cutter's tears are more restrained, but perhaps even more poignant because they are being shed by Cary Grant, who elsewhere has been the film's main source of comedy. His tears are more in the way of private grief for the loss of a friend, whom he has taught how to salute and allowed to keep his bugle, and who answered Cutter's request for "a large tool" to help him escape from jail by bringing him Annie the elephant. There is a suggestion of an unspoken kinship between the two men, in that they are both outsiders and both trying to better themselves. In this regard, and for all their difference in social status, Cutter might have more in common with Din than with his soldier friends. It is striking that it is Din, and not MacChesney and Ballantine, whom Cutter chooses to accompany him on his search for the temple of gold.

Originally Grant had been cast in the role of Ballantine, and it was Grant who expressed a preference for the role of Sergeant Archibald Cutter. Changing his role in the film from romantic to comic (and calling the character Archibald—Grant's actual first name—is surely intended as an in-joke) has the effect of changing the nature of the material, and undoubtedly for the better. His manic comic energy sets the tone of the film and lifts it onto a humorous level that plays effectively against the heroism, which one can enjoy without being asked to take it too seriously. Fittingly Stevens ensures that his entry upstages that of his comrades in terms of comic finesse. Whereas the introduction of MacChesney and Ballantine is done as broad slapstick, with their appearance being preceded by the sight and sound of their adversaries being hurled through a window during a brawl, Cutter appears at his window, still clutching the Scottish soldier who has sold him a worthless map for a buried treasure. "Take your hands off that man!" orders Sergeant Higginbotham (Robert Coote), and Cutter duly obliges, sending his hapless adversary crashing to the ground. He then shrugs slightly and opens his hands in a gesture of mock innocence that seems to imply that he has blamelessly carried out an order and cannot be held responsible for the consequences. Grant's comedy persona invariably tended towards the manic, and Cutter's antics are often laced with a touch of absurdity. When he and Din are crossing the rope bridge that leads to the temple, Cutter suddenly realizes that its unsteadiness is being hugely exaggerated by the attempt to follow them of Annie the elephant. "Annie, take your trunk off!" cries Cutter desperately, as if that might lighten the load. When he first sees the temple of gold, Grant does one of his priceless reaction shots, whinnying like a horse to suggestion a combination of excitement, anticipation and frustration.

A peak of absurdity is reached when, in order to distract attention from Din's escape from the temple of Kali to warn the approaching company of the danger, Cutter noisily interrupts the Thugees in their ceremony of worship by singing a rousing song about the roast beef of England before blithely informing them that they are all under arrest. "Her Majesty's very touchy about having her subjects strangled," he explains. "Wrap up your gear. You're coming with me." It is hard to think of another actor who could have played that moment with quite such brazen audacity and insane conviction. We have seen that Cutter is a fantasist, and Grant gives the impression of a man who genuinely believes he has them all surrounded. As well as being funny, it gives a certain credibility as to why he is not killed there and then. The followers are just too startled and bemused; and foolhardiness on that scale, particularly when allied with great courage, is momentarily fascinating. Sufi Khan seems as much struck by admiration as by anger at this unseemly interruption, while quickly appreciating that the man's capture can be more useful for tactical advantage than his death.

In view of his preceding pictures, one would expect Stevens to handle the comedy well. Although the engagement dance sequence goes on too long for its function in the narrative, the comedy surrounding the punch bowl is well sustained: from MacChesney's anxious "Leave some for the elephant," as Cutter enthusiastically laces the punch with Annie's medicine; to Robert Coote's amusingly abrupt swivel and fall as the punch has its devastating effect; it even causes a flower to wilt in an instant. Joan Fontaine is beautifully photographed in the film, but her character makes no impression, even though MacChesney's description of her impact on Ballantine is stark: "She's charmed him like a snake." When one considers the role of snakes later in the film, the remark could hardly be more misogynistic. The absence of a strong female role in a Stevens film is uncharacteristic and invariably unfortunate (his choice of *Vigil in the Night* for his next film might have been a subconscious response to that).

What is undoubtedly new is Stevens' confident handling of the spectacle. An early scene when the troop of soldiers enters what appears to be a deserted village but is actually surrounded by Thugees, in hiding and ready to strike, is superbly shot. A close-up of a soldier's anxious look around the area is ingeniously merged with a long shot, as we subliminally spot sinister events going on behind him in the far distance and of which he is unaware. At the film's finale, when Din blows the bugle which alerts the British of the danger of ambush, the action that follows seems to spill out into every corner of the screen, with soldiers and natives engaged in life and death struggles that are choreographed into a visual frenzy of ferocity and fear. Bruce Beresford thought it rivalled the samurai films of Kurosawa in terms of excitement and beauty, and there can be no higher praise than that (Beresford: 13).

Stevens was never again to make a film quite like *Gunga Din*, and, in some ways, one is grateful. Even he recognized that, if made a year later, its simple celebration of what he called "the rumble of the drums and the waving of the flags" would have looked incongruous and anachronistic. In Hollywood's golden year of 1939, it seemed to speak to a more innocent time, naively insensitive to issues of race and Imperialism, but also still idealistic enough to believe in selfless and reckless heroism. In taking on the project, Stevens' task was to make the material work on its own terms, and this he undoubtedly succeeded in doing. "The comic-book movie doesn't have a great deal to do with life as it exists, as we know it to be," wrote William Goldman. "Rather it deals with life as we would prefer it to be" (Goldman: 153). Interesting, though, that, in this particular adventure story, victory is so closely associated with tragic sacrifice. That theme is to be at the heart of Stevens' war experience and his greatest films to come.

Vigil in the Night (1940)

> "There is nothing in the world so bad as a bad nurse. Nor so good as a good one. Remember that, Nurse Lee. Remember it all your days."—A.J. Cronin, *Vigil in the Night,* Chapter 6

> "Perhaps *Vigil in the Night* is about the war. In the film the great irritation of the war overcomes the lesser irritation of their mundane activities, which was something I was really aiming for."—George Stevens

Vigil in the Night is one of Stevens' oddest and most neglected films. Like the later *Something to Live For,* it is regularly dismissed in a single-sentence summary in critical surveys of his feature-film career or sometimes ignored entirely. Even the compendious anthologies of reviews in *Variety* make no reference to the film. Two conspicuous exceptions to this general critical neglect are Leonard Maltin and David Shipman. In his *Movie Guide* of 2009, Maltin summarized the film as a "compelling drama of provincial hospital life in England, with outstanding work by [Carole] Lombard as dedicated nurse, [Anne] Shirley as her flighty sister, and [Brian] Aherne as doctor" (Maltin: 1493). And although he felt the main characters never came to life, David Shipman thought the film good elsewhere, and that "rare among American directors of the time, Stevens allows no caricatures of the British, and he shows an understanding of the national character; and since the life of the hospital is as convincingly portrayed as in any movie then or since, the whole is preferable to the film of *The Citadel*" (Shipman: 397). Such praise, however, was far from typical of the reception as a whole. A problem for commentators on Stevens' work has always been where to put it in the director's development and how to assess its significance. Does it mark the end of something; or is it a new beginning, or what Eugene Archer called "an ill-advised change of pace" (Archer: 29); or is it a logical continuation of what has gone before? The simple answer to these questions is that it is, in some ways, all of these things.

It did mark the end of Stevens' contract with RKO; and he was soon to be followed out of the studio by his regular executive producer, Pandro S. Berman. It was Berman who had asked him to consider as his next project a film version of this A.J. Cronin story, which had just been published in *Good Housekeeping.* King Vidor's film of Cronin's novel, *The Citadel* (1938), had been very successful, and Berman no doubt thought a similar kind of medical drama was a box-office winner. Stevens was initially reluctant, and it is tempting to see the film as a project the director simply took on to fulfil the terms of his contract before departure. He was feeling tired after the rigors of *Gunga Din* and being called in to rescue *Having Wonderful Time* (1939); he was frustrated in his thwarted endeavor to interest the studio in two war subjects that particularly excited him, *The Mortal Storm* and *Paths of Glory*; and for the last five or six years, he had been regularly putting in a seven-day working week, which had not only placed increasing strains on his marriage but was also, he thought, compromising the quality of work he felt he was capable of achieving. One suspects the exhaustion he was feeling seeped into the final film.

Although it might at first sight seem uncharacteristic, one can sense a continuity from his previous films. Like *Alice Adams, Annie Oakley, Quality Street* and *Vivacious Lady*, it is essentially a female-driven narrative, and one that, even more than the other films, is concerned with the theme of female sacrifice, which is here seen in personal and professional (and, by implication, even global) terms. When Nurse Anne Lee (Carole Lombard) is upbraided by the Manchester tycoon Matthew Bowley (Julien Mitchell) for diverting funds to facilitate effective treatment for a smallpox epidemic and reminded that such funds might be needed in the event of war, she replies: "It's war and sacrifice *all* the time for us … our war never ends. You can't sign a peace treaty with disease." It is the only time she ever raises her voice; and her outcry recalls a similar sentiment uttered by Katharine Hepburn's heroine in *Quality Street* about the battles women still have to fight when men go to war. The war in Europe was very much on Stevens's mind when he was making this film. (He had begun filming in September 1939.) He wished to include a moment in the final part of the film when Nurse Lee and Dr. Prescott (Brian Aherne) listen to the British Prime Minister, Neville Chamberlain, over the radio as he announces that his country is now at war with Germany. However, the head of RKO was so perturbed that he travelled from New York to the studio specifically to insist on its deletion.

Rather than suggesting that the subject had intimations of war, RKO chose to advertise the film as a romantic melodrama. "The world's most famous doctor," the posters proclaimed, "rips the veil from the hidden lives of bitter women who knew men too well—yet must somehow find love in the midst of terror, toil and disillusionment." It would be hard to recognize the film from that description, particularly as the doctor is anything but world-famous (he is struggling to find sufficient funds to do what his job requires) and Nurse Lee quite explicitly prioritizes her nursing above any ideas of romance. No wonder audiences might have been bemused; and the casting of Carole Lombard would only have added to the bewilderment. The most scintillating screwball comedienne of her day, Lombard in this film is required to play a poker-faced angel of mercy who not only fails to sparkle but is scarcely allowed even to smile. Audiences were not impressed and the film made a loss of $327,000. It was a sad end to Stevens' tenure at RKO, but the film remains intriguing for the way it anticipates the seriousness of Stevens' post-war work.

A somber mood is established at the outset. After the credits have taken place over a shot of a lamp flickering in the darkness (suggestive of both "vigil" and "night"), Stevens cuts to a dawn scene where a storm is raging. The camera pans past a sign, "Shereham County Hospital" and then a building that is labelled "Isolation Ward" before moving towards a window where we glimpse a solitary nurse keeping vigil over a child who is suffering from diphtheria. In her biography of Stevens, Marilyn Ann Moss slightly misremembers this opening, as she identifies the nurse as Lucy. In fact, when Stevens dissolves to a shot of the nurse, he reveals that it is actually Anne, who is coming to the end of her shift, is visibly tired, but still alert enough to clear the tube which is helping the child to breathe. The five-year-old boy smiles trustingly at Anne before going back to sleep. Anne looks at the clock which is now showing nearly ten minutes past the hour; her relief is late.

Stevens' camera placement is typically precise when Lucy does finally arrive, for, as she comes to the top of the stairs, she is framed from the inside of the kitchen with a kettle in the forefront of the shot, as if already suggesting her priorities before tending to the child. It takes only a brief dialogue exchange to underline the difference in attitude to nursing between the two. When Lucy repeats the Ward Sister's mantra, "There's nothing as good as a good nurse and nothing so bad as a bad one," she does so in a derisory tone, whereas for Anne, it is clearly a sentiment very close to her own heart. Nevertheless, when signing off, Anne, in a typically protective gesture, falsifies the register and signs in her sister as having arrived on time. It is an action that will have serious consequences.

Having cursorily checked her charge, Lucy leaves the room for a moment in order to make herself a cup of tea in the kitchen. Stevens crosscuts agonizingly between the two rooms, as, while Lucy nonchalantly prepares her tea, in the sick room the tube which is helping the child to breathe has become blocked. During her absence, the child dies. When Lucy returns to the room and realizes what has happened, the camera closes in on her to convey her heightening panic, but she does not scream; Alfred Newman's music (insistently and incessantly piling on the melodramatic agony) does it for her. Instead her immediate reaction is to call and run for her sister. Later an angry doctor, after examining the dead boy, insists on getting to the bottom of how this can have happened. Anne and Lucy seem initially uncertain about what to say, but Nurse Gregg (Helena Grant) has discovered that tea was being made in the kitchen which suggests that the nurse on duty was out of the room when the tragedy occurred. At this point Anne not only takes the blame upon herself but also lies, saying that she had left the room at five minutes to six to make tea and had left the boy unattended. She is dismissed from the hospital. Only her exemplary record prior to this, she is told, saves her from more serious punishment.

It is a shocking development, for it is evident even at this early stage that Lucy scarcely seems worthy of her sister's sacrifice. (The casting of Anne Shirley as Lucy would have been quite resonant for audiences at the time; she had been Oscar-nominated for her role as the daughter for whom her mother sacrifices everything in King Vidor's classic 1937 melodrama, *Stella Dallas*.) One senses that this might be something of a recurrent pattern in their relationship, with Anne being in the habit of putting Lucy's interests ahead of her own. We never hear anything of their parents or their upbringing: has Anne needed to look after her younger sister from an early age, so that her protective attitude has become almost second nature? She will indicate that her primary motive in this instance is that Lucy would have more to lose from dismissal as she has not completed her training whereas Anne has her certificate and will be able to find work elsewhere. Yet one wonders whether this is the whole explanation. Does she derive a secret satisfaction from self-abnegation? Has she something of a martyr complex?

Her action has implications for her emotional life also. Because of the disgrace of her dismissal, she feels it necessary to leave the area, which in turns means leaving the man who wishes to marry her (Joe, played by Peter Cushing), but who will later (on the rebound?) marry Lucy instead. This might seem another example of Anne's sacrifice, yet it is noticeable that there is no strong indication that she reciprocates Joe's love. When Lucy calls after her, she very quickly turns from him to respond to the more urgent call of her sister, and the farewell between them is much more emotional than the one she has shared with Joe. Her final words to Joe are to ask that he takes care of Lucy.

"O Anne, how could you ever forgive me?" Lucy has asked, but there is no element of reproach in Anne's response and no sense that she has any doubt that she did the right thing in the circumstances. There is more pride than pain in Lombard's performance at this point, implying a character who might even enjoy subjugating her own feelings to what she feels is a superior cause. Later in the film, when Anne is promoted in her job at Hepperton Hospital and gets a new uniform, she is filmed by Stevens in such a way that, as Marilyn Ann Moss has rightly noted, "she looks like a nun, like a Madonna, in fact" (Moss: 66). She checks her reflection in a mirror and one feels that this vision is not so much Stevens' perception of her as the character's perception of herself and of her role as a nurse as being like that of a nun: selfless dedication to a higher cause which takes precedence over the personal life. It is a significantly different emphasis from that of the novel.

Although the film follows the novel quite closely, Stevens and his screenwriters (Fred Guiol, P.J. Wolfson and Rowland Leigh) have been quite adept at telescoping events and injecting a bit of variety into the overall mood. Anne's roommates at Hepperton Hospital, Nora (Brenda Forbes) and Glennie (Rita Page), are both equipped with a quality entirely absent from A.J. Cronin's story: namely, a sense of humor. Glennie's wit suggests she might be a fan of Groucho Marx. "The bed might look hard and feel hard," she says to Anne on their first acquaintance, before adding, "but don't let that fool you: it *is* hard." Nora has something of the manic whimsy of Harpo. When Matron unexpectedly enters their room for a quick inspection, Nora quickly conceals her forbidden and still lighted cigarette by hiding it inside her mouth, then smiling innocently even as smoke is coming out of her ears. Matron is not entirely deceived. Revealing a touch of humor and humanity behind the severe exterior, she remarks as she departs, "Nurse Dunn, your sinuses are on fire." This is entirely consistent with the way the character of Matron has been established, for she is in the habit of greeting prospective nurses with a fearsome litany of rules, regulations and privations at the inadequately resourced hospital, before concluding, "I hope you will be happy here," and following this incongruous sentiment with a quick smile that seems more automated than spontaneous and has vanished almost as quickly it appeared. The role is played by that grand actress, Ethel Griffies, probably best known to moviegoers as the expert ornithologist in the café scene in Hitchcock's *The Birds* (1963). The irony is that, for all the hardships and harsh conditions, Anne *is* happy at Hepperton. In an elaborate montage to suggest the passage of time and which uses dissolves and superimpositions in a manner that will anticipate his future style, Stevens shows Anne as she bustles enthusiastically through her duties. Her intervention during the operation on the wealthy Manchester businessman Mathew Bowley in the operating theater only enhances her prestige. Although at first it seems a serious breach of medical ethics (nurses who watch operations from the balcony are required to keep silent), Anne notices that one of the swabs has been left in the patient, and she has the courage to speak out when she sees something amiss. Once again she is shown to be willing to risk her own career in the service of something she deems as more important than any personal concerns. Her observation brings her to the attention of Dr. Prescott (Brian Aherne), who has been performing the operation. The significance of her intervention and what it might have cost her is clearly not lost on him.

At this point there is another interesting deviation from the novel, with the appearance at Hepperton of Nurse Gregg, who was present during the incident of the child fatality at Shereham. In the novel her re-appearance occurs much later and in a different context, though her behavior will have a similar undertow of malice, using her knowledge of Anne's past in what the novel will call a form of "spiritual blackmail" to exact special favors. This will be nipped in the bud when Anne tells her whole story to Dr. Prescott, and the rebuke issued to Nurse Gregg will be so severe that, somewhat improbably, she will apologize abjectly to Anne for her behavior and become a model nurse under her command. By contrast, the film treats the character's malice then transformation more melodramatically perhaps but also more convincingly. The gossipy Nurse Gregg is about to tell Matron the secret about Anne's nursing past and the reason for her dismissal when the bus on which all three of them are travelling is caught up suddenly in a storm and overturns. A similar accident occurs in the novel but is not linked in any way to Nurse Gregg or disclosures about Anne's past. In the film it is as if Fate has intervened on Anne's behalf to make amends for the earlier miscarriage of justice that took place on a similarly stormy day. No one dies in the accident, fortunately. Nurse Gregg will be severely concussed, but Anne's prompt and expert action in treating her has helped to save her life. When Anne visits her later in her hospital bed, Nurse Gregg is mute but it is clear from her expression that a change of heart has taken place. Her contrition is now given a powerful motive.

Anne's future at Hepperton Hospital will be threatened a second time, but this time the outcome will be an unhappy one. Since his operation, Mathew Bowley has taken an interest in Anne's progress and promotion. It becomes apparent that his interest is more personal than professional when he invites Anne to meet him in his office after a Hospital Board Meeting. Stevens opens the scene with one of the most elaborate shots in the film, pulling the camera back in a single movement from the meeting itself to behind the curved window in Bowley's office to the door as Anne enters his room prior to the meeting. From where she is, she is able to hear what is going on and hear Dr. Prescott's unsuccessful plea for funds for his new hospital. At the conclusion of the meeting, Bowley joins Anne in his office, while, unbeknown to him, we can see through that curved window the arrival of Mrs. Bowley (Doris Lloyd) in the now empty boardroom. It is a neat visual strategy because her proximity adds suspense to the moment when Bowley starts pressing his unwelcome attentions on Anne (he will help fund her private practice, he says, in return for what he calls her "companionship"), for if she arrives in the middle of Bowley's advances, it might look as if Anne were encouraging him and place her unwittingly in a compromising situation. This is what happens. Seeing her husband start guiltily at her unexpected entry, Mrs. Bowley not only castigates him for his foolishness, but shouts insults at Anne, accusing her of attempting to seduce Bowley in order to extract financial backing for Dr. Prescott's hospital. She threatens a scandal if Anne is not immediately dismissed. Although the truth of the situation is apparent to all, Bowley is too cowardly to admit what he has done, and, for the sake of the hospital, Anne agrees to resign.

Again the adaptation makes small but significant changes to the novel. In Cronin's novel, Anne's roommates never know the real cause of her resignation (it is said to be for family reasons), whereas in the film, in an affecting farewell scene between the three, it is clear that Glennie and Nora are under no illusions about what took place between her and Bowley. Indeed Nora reinforces the point by going into a long tale about a similar experience of hers as a young nurse, when a patient she refers to as "an old baboon," who supposedly "had one foot in the grave and four toes in the other," was so rejuvenated by monkey glands that had been put into him in Vienna that she was finally reduced to hiding from him up a tree. The fanciful anecdote lightens the mood, but not by much. The film also interestingly deviates from A.J. Cronin when Anne says goodbye to Dr. Prescott.

In the novel he gives her a letter of recommendation but also criticizes her for indiscretion, for, when he had told her of his future plans, he says, he had assumed he was speaking in confidence. (Mrs. Bowley's insinuations have obviously been brought to his attention.) In the novel Anne is "hurt beyond endurance" by this rebuke, "could merely hang her head" at his reaction, and afterwards, "broke down and sobbed as if her heart would break" (Cronin: 90). The film's Anne is made of sterner stuff. When he quietly rebukes her for breaking a confidence, the close-up of her suggests anger as well as hurt, and she walks out without taking his letter of recommendation, as if principle will not allow her to accept a favor from someone who has so grievously misjudged her. She says nothing (she is a character prone to internalizing her deepest feelings); also there are no tears. In the film, Anne will break down only once, and that is after the death of her sister.

The London scenes are the dullest in the film. Stevens' direction is at its most per-functory here, seeming to derive no inspiration from the change of setting (the evocation of London is reduced to two stock establishing shots) or from the drama of the situation (Lucy's interrogation at the coroner's court, following the suicide of a prestigious patient in her care at the notorious Rolgrave Rest Home). Anne has arrived in London to seek work and see Lucy, only to find that she has left Joe and is embroiled in another case of medical neglect. Dr. Prescott is also (very) coincidentally in London, seeking alternative funding for his hospital project after his falling-out with Bowley, and providentially hap-pens to see the newspaper story about Lucy's troubles. He comes to Lucy's defense at the coroner's court, rather improbably being allowed to cross-examine the Home's owner and reveal that she has a history of medical malpractice. Equally implausibly, the twelve-man jury concludes, without needing to confer, that Lucy has no case to answer for she was only following an incompetent doctor's instructions. All of this is dispatched with the minimum of visual and dramatic interest, and indifferently acted by Anne Shirley at her most simpering, Brian Aherne at his most pompous, and with Carole Lombard reduced to reaction shots of glacial gratitude.

From this point, however, the adaptation re-shapes the novel's events in quite an ingenious manner. In the novel, Lucy wishes to atone for her miserable nursing record (after all, she now has two patients who were trusted to her care and came to an untimely end when she was out of the room). Informed by Dr. Prescott of the desperate need for nurses following a fever epidemic in Wales, she volunteers to offer her services as a nurse; to Prescott's dismay, Anne resolves to go with her. In the film, the writers shift the crisis closer to home, for it is a smallpox epidemic at Hepperton Hospital, which will necessitate Anne's return to a place where she has previously been dismissed. This is to have signifi-cant repercussions; and Prescott is still dismayed, and not only by Anne's possibly placing herself in danger. "Is nursing your whole life?" he asks. "Yes, I thought you knew," she replies, and he only barely manages to conceal his disappointment.

Despite the matron's pleading, the nurses at Hepperton have refused to volunteer to serve in the Isolation Ward. An impassioned outburst from Nora at a meeting of the nurses makes clear the reason: why should they put their lives at risk when their condi-tions of work are already so appalling and so poorly rewarded? It is a theme that the novel will take up forcefully, and Anne will become secretary of a strong Trade Union to fight for nurses' interests. One would not expect a Hollywood studio film of this time (or any time, for that matter) to take such a strong pro-union stance, and it is Anne's return and example rather than any collective solidarity that will break the deadlock. On hearing that she has volunteered to serve in the Isolation Ward, Nora and Glennie and later Nurse Gregg will join her as an act of personal friendship and loyalty that overrides their institutional misgivings. Anne warns them that, once they go through the door to the Isolation Ward, there is no turning back. The remark prompts a fleeting recollection of Stevens' deceptively un-emphatic medium shot when Anne and Lucy have gone to the Ward for the first time and there is just the slightest hesitation on Lucy's part (perhaps a momentary shiver of premonition?) before closing the door behind her.

With no concern for budgetary constraints, Anne will gradually effect a complete transformation of the children's conditions, bringing in builders and carpenters to con-struct better facilities and surroundings for staff and patients that will aid recovery and bring the epidemic under control. "It's the first time I've seen men work as hard as nurses," comments the Matron, pointedly. Dr. Prescott has returned, having had no success in raising funds in London, and his solicitude towards Anne is such that even Matron turns her head in curiosity; she recognizes that Prescott is in love with her even if Anne herself does not. Prescott's bitter denunciation of Bowley's penny-pinching is tempered when he sees that Bowley's son is one of the latest smallpox victims; and Bowley's anger at what he has construed as Anne's profligacy turns to fear and apprehension when he and his wife watch helplessly behind a window as Matthew Jr. is wheeled, unconscious, into the ward. The film has cleverly telescoped two separate events in the novel into this one central focus, and intensifies the drama still further by making the child in peril not Bowley's niece (as in the novel) but Bowley's son. In their roles as the boy's parents, both Julien Mitchell and Doris Lloyd are very moving at this point. The profit motive disin-tegrates under the pressure of personal crisis, and one can see in Mitchell's face alone the sudden change in Bowley's priorities, as the human being displaces the businessman.

The film's main suspense sequence concerns Lucy's all-night vigil at the bedside of Bowley's son. Stevens and his editor Henry Berman (Pandro's brother) build a compelling montage, cutting between shots of Lucy's anxious face, her application of cold compresses to the boy's forehead, the thermometer readings that keep track of his progress, and faces of other children in the ward who become curious onlookers at this life-and-death strug-gle. At one moment Stevens dissolves from a shot of young Bowley asleep on his pillow to that of the child who had died in Lucy's care at Shereham, to suggest that that earlier event is at the forefront of Lucy's (and the audience's) consciousness as she tends to her patient. When she turns momentarily away from the bed and young Matt stops breathing, Stevens' camera moves in to catch Lucy's reaction in precisely the same way as he had when filming the earlier tragedy, as if a nightmare is about to repeat itself. Initially Lucy again panics and runs for help. However, seeing that she is the only nurse on duty, she rushes back to give the child the kiss of life that will also be, for her, the kiss of death, a chance, as she will say, "to give back a life for the one I lost." In the morning she carries the boy to the window and shows his recovery to his parents, who have been waiting all night for news. It is the first daylight shot in the entire film.

Some time has passed. Bowley has now agreed to finance Dr. Prescott's venture. When Anne tells him that her work is done at Hepperton and she is planning to return to London, an emboldened Dr. Prescott takes her hand in the most emotional gesture shared between them so far and declares, "I'm not going to let you go." It is a moment that resembles Anne's scene with Joe when she is about to leave Shereham, and once again it is Lucy who will interrupt a potentially romantic moment. This time it is Nora and Glennie who are calling on Lucy's behalf to tell Anne that her sister has collapsed. Without even responding to what is essentially a declaration of love from Dr. Prescott, she turns and rushes to be with her sister, with Prescott following. They will be too late.

Stevens pans from Nora and Glennie, then to Anne seated by Lucy's bedside and holding her hand, and then to Nurse Gregg, who turns to look at Anne when Lucy says she has written to the Matron at Shereham Hospital to tell her what actually happened that tragic morning. It is a sudden reminder that Nurse Gregg has until then always thought Anne to be culpable. The theme of atonement not only implicates Lucy and Bowley, it seems, but Nurse Gregg also, who has unwittingly atoned for her earlier misjudgment by becoming a strong ally. When Lucy dies, Anne squeezes her hand for a moment, then gets up, and walks out of the room without saying a word. I am always reminded at this point by that line in Shakespeare's *King Lear* to describe Cordelia's reaction to news of her father's suffering: "Then away she started/ To deal with grief alone" (Act IV, Scene 3, II.31–2). Only when she is on her own in the now deserted children's ward does she give way to emotion, leaning against a window, sobbing painfully, and murmuring almost inaudibly, "My baby." It is a very powerful moment, for Anne has spent the entire film withholding her emotions until, at this point, the pressure of restraint becomes no longer supportable. It is a great piece of acting from Carole Lombard whose performance grows in stature the more I watch it: disciplined, rigorously unsentimental, and with a stoical nobility on a par with Garbo (whom she startlingly resembles at certain moments).

How long she stays in the ward in such extreme distress is unclear. When we see her next, she has resumed her customary composure, able to deal with a distraught Joe, who blames her for luring Lucy into the nursing profession against her natural instincts, and also with Dr. Prescott, who is devastated by self-reproach. "When the time comes to help someone I love, I fail," he says, but Anne ignores the confession of love to state her conviction that what they do is worthwhile and fulfilling, even if they cannot always be the final arbiter of who lives and who dies. "It's not for us to doubt His judgment," she says. Their role is to do the best they can for the good of mankind to the limit of their expertise and courage, and leave the rest to God. In a war context, the speech anticipates by two years the sentiment of the sermon that famously closes William Wyler's hugely popular propagandist tear-jerker, *Mrs. Miniver* (1942).

At the end of *Vigil in the Night*, there has been a mining accident and Dr. Prescott's services are urgently required. "Come, my Dr. Prescott," says Anne, joining him as he prepares to leave, "there's work for us to do." Lombard places a slight emphasis on the word "my," but it seems to me that the word "work" is more significant. Even at the end she never addresses him by his first name; and (unlike in the novel) she never says she loves him. It is striking how emphatically Stevens sidesteps the possibility of a romantic love story in order to highlight instead the urgency of service and the beauty of sacrifice. Equally notable is the prominence he gives to the specific date when his story ends: 3 September 1939. The war in Europe has begun. It is a war in which Stevens himself will become deeply involved, and which will change his sensibility forever.

· Two ·

Men in Chaos,
1941–1943

Penny Serenade (1941)

> "I have often humbled actors, creating stories that will bring a kind of humility out of them, rather than letting them come forth on the screen in their established aura. *Penny Serenade*, with Cary Grant and Irene Dunne, is a good example."—George Stevens, 1967

When Columbia's star director, Frank Capra, came to the end of his contract and left for pastures new, the studio's head of production, Harry Cohn, turned to George Stevens as a replacement and offered him a three-picture contract. He thought Stevens would prove an ideal substitute, sharing Capra's ability to blend comedy and drama and having a good track record of critical prestige and commercial success. Stevens made one condition: that, for the duration of the contract, Cohn would not speak to him (that is, interfere with his shooting of the films on the studio floor). In return, Cohn asked Stevens to refrain from smoking on set, thereby conforming to the studio's fire regulations and also setting a good example to the studio employees. Both men seem to have kept to their side of the bargain, though with some difficulty. When he was working as an assistant director on *The More the Merrier,* Budd Boetticher (later to become a fine director in his own right, of course, particularly renowned for his series of westerns with Randolph Scott) recalled that one of his main jobs was to keep Cohn at bay when he visited the set by tossing Stevens a tennis ball to play handball by himself while Boetticher dealt with Cohn. When Cohn angrily demanded that "that son-of-a-bitch Stevens" come over to speak to him, Boetticher lost his temper and shouted back, "That son-of-bitch you're referring to is probably the best son-of-a-bitching director in all of Hollywood." Boetticher, who described Stevens as "my favourite director in all the world," thought he would lose his job as well as his temper, but, as Fred Zinnemann was also to discover, Cohn liked nothing better than someone to stand up to him, and helped further Boetticher's career.

Stevens' first project for Columbia was *Penny Serenade*, based on a semi-autobiographical short story by Martha Cheavers titled "The Story of a Happy Marriage," which was due to be published in the August 1940 edition of *McCall's* magazine. It was perhaps a more downbeat project than Cohn had anticipated, for it seemed to continue the solemn mood of *Vigil in the Night* and similarly has the death of a child as its dramatic core. Just as Carole Lombard had been cast against type in that film, so Stevens deliberately cast Cary Grant and Irene Dunne, whom audiences will have remembered as a scintillating comedy duo in Leo McCarey's *The Awful Truth* (1937), in roles that are significantly different from those with which they had been mostly associated. The opening sets a melancholy tone, with Julie Adams (Irene Dunne) preparing to leave her home. One of the few items left is an old record player, and while playing through a collection of records, beginning with "You Were Meant For Me," Julie will revive memories of her marriage to Roger Adams (Cary Grant), which is drifting towards separation after the death of their adopted daughter.

"Here's the story," wrote *Variety* in its review (16 April 1941). "Irene Dunne and Cary Grant adopt a six-week old baby and raise her until she is six, when she dies after a brief illness. Then they adopt a boy of two." In his review of the film, the English critic James Agate provided an even blunter plot summary than that. "A tear compeller," he wrote, "showing how Cary Grant and Irene Dunne lose first their own baby and then the one they adopt. Which, as Lady Bracknell would certainly have observed, looks like carelessness" (qtd in Halliwell: 640). As the Agate review indicated, *Variety* (although it went on to commend the film for the way in which "the yarn approaches the saccharine, only to be turned back into sound comedy drama") had neglected to mention a key point in the story: namely, that, prior to the death of their adopted child, Dunne has earlier in her marriage suffered a miscarriage during an earthquake, as a result of which she can no longer have children. Donald Richie was uncharacteristically cynical about the film's supposed narrative manipulation to bring about this eventuality: "Hundreds are destroyed in an earthquake so that Irene Dunne's miscarriage may be successfully accomplished" (Richie: 28). It is somewhat surprising, given his expertise on Japanese cinema and history, that Richie seemingly failed to acknowledge the fact that Stevens was actually recreating the devastating Tokyo earthquake of 1923, when many thousands, not hundreds, were killed, and where it is entirely plausible that a young couple living in that environment at that time would have experienced tragedy. Modern filmgoers might recall that the event is memorably recreated in Hayao Miyazaki's final film, *The Wind Rises* (2014). The earthquake was so effectively done in Stevens's movie that Frank Capra was to smuggle a shot from it into one of his most controversial war documentaries, *Know Your Enemy— Japan* (1945).

If it seems a bit unkind, then, to accuse the film of narrative manipulation at that point, commentators on the film have had other reservations. Its oscillation of mood has proved a problem for some critics. Leslie Halliwell thought it "a well-played but uneasy film which veers suddenly and disconcertingly from light comedy into tragedy" (Halliwell: 640). The structure of the film does not support this description. By beginning his story in the present before moving into flashback, Stevens ensures that a pall of melancholy and foreboding hangs over the film from the outset. Whether one surrenders to the film's sentiment is perhaps a matter of personal taste. As Richard Schickel has demonstrated, it is easy to make the plot sound sentimentally contrived, if you are impervious to the nuances of Stevens's direction and yearn for precisely the kind of melodramatic excess that Stevens is at some pains to avoid (Schickel: 104–7). By contrast, Eugene Archer thought the film "emerges as a triumph of form over content" and praised, among other things, "its unconventional handling of romance" and Stevens's "skilled application of the moving camera (circling round rooms and corridors, gliding up flight of stairs) as a lead into precise but unconventional frames" (Archer 29–30). Although necessarily concise, Archer's critique of the film seems to me pertinent and suggestive, and his repetition of the word "unconventional" in the same paragraph is particularly telling, for it is precisely Stevens' oblique and unusual dramatic and stylistic approach to the material that makes it so exceptional.

The film's cyclical structure (beginning and ending with a shot of a framed photograph of the married couple) might seem conventional, but this is deceptive. The film's narrative actually begins at the end before moving into flashback; and the ending suggests the possibilities of a new beginning. In the first scene the open door of what was once a child's bedroom is a confirmation of the wife's sadness and determination to leave, and she closes it; but at the end we see the husband and wife re-entering this room, leaving the door half-open in a gesture that quietly suggests an endeavor to bring both their marriage and their longing for a child back to life. The film's flashbacks are all prompted by records that have some special meaning for the heroine, and the movement from present to past begins with a close-up of the center of the record before irising out to reveal the scene. It is a clever device because it means that, rather being tied to a standard chronological development of the relationship over time, the film can leap to key moments without having to fill in the gaps.

What might also have been in the mind of Stevens and his excellent screenwriter, Morrie Ryskind, is Noel Coward's phrase in his play *Private Lives* about "the extraordinary potency of cheap music." The popular songs not only evoke time and place but have an emotional connection with the characters. In this respect, one curious detail is the use of the classic Arthur Freed and Nacio Herb Brown song, "You Were Meant for Me." This was composed in 1929, which is the year when the plot of *Penny Serenade* ends, yet Julie remembers it as the song which was playing when she and Roger first met. A chronological error? A memory lapse? Or another example of the way beginnings and endings are oddly conjoined in the film? Eugene Archer noted how Stevens sometimes ends emotional scenes at a point before completion as an instance of the director's restraint and avoidance of sentimentality. The scene where Roger pleads before the judge to retain custody of their adopted daughter, which ends before we know the outcome, is a memorable example of that. Conversely, some scenes seem paradoxically to begin at a point of closure, an example being the scene when the doctor at the San Francisco Hospital says, "Well, that's all," and we have gradually to piece together the fact that he has just told Julie that she cannot have children. Even one of the running jokes of the film (every time the door to one of the rooms in their apartment is pulled open, the open window slams shut) seems to be a reversal of the norm. The saying is that, when one door closes, another opens; in this film, when a door opens, something immediately slams shut. In some ways, that will be a metaphor for the development of the relationship. Even the recording that first draws Roger to Julie has a crack in it that causes the needle to stick in the groove, prophetically suggesting perhaps that their romance will not proceed as smoothly as they might wish.

The growth of the romance is handled with that offbeat charm one recognizes from Stevens' early comedies. Seeing Julie through the window of the Brooklyn music store where she works, Roger has come into the record shop in the expectation that she will serve him, only to be disconcerted by the appearance of another young lady behind the counter, Dotty (Ann Doran), and it takes some improvised ingenuity on his part to maneuver her out of the frame. His attraction to Julie is suggested by a typical piece of Stevens indirection: not through anything as obvious as words or a kiss, but the fact that he buys 27 records from her before admitting that he has does not actually possess a phonograph. The romance blossoms to the point when Roger combines the news of his promotion to be his newspaper's Tokyo correspondent with a proposal that they be married before he departs. His proposal occurs at a party on New Year's Eve at the stroke of midnight, and the personal elation merges with the public celebration, swelling the sense of joy. Yet the marriage service itself seems to introduce a momentary chill. The wedding in the registry office is introduced with a shot from outside the window and with snow falling; and we only hear Julie's vows in the final part of the service, ending with the words, "Till death us do part." That phrase will be reiterated on three separate occasions during this section of the film, as if its promise of a life-long devotion might come back to haunt them or take on a meaning that at that time they did not foresee. Death will indeed bring them perilously close to parting, but the death will be that of their adopted daughter. This might be seen as another aspect of the complexity of the flashback structure, in the way it adds a retrospective irony to Julie's memory, for she is now recalling warning signs of troubles ahead that she did not pick up at the time.

Retrospective irony also underlies an early scene on the beach, which is ostensibly straightforwardly romantic. Played with impeccable timing by Grant and Dunne, the scene suggests that their romance is becoming serious but also hints at some underlying problems or differences that could in the future imperil their happiness. One or two throwaway comments by Roger become more ominous in retrospect. He has been teaching Julie how to swim, reassuring her that "when you're with me, you're safe"; it is an assurance that he will not be able to fulfil. "I wish every day could be a holiday," he tells Julie, "and I need never go back home or go back to work." At the time the comment seems a perfectly understandable declaration of his happiness of the moment in Julie's company, and it is only with hindsight that one picks up a sense there of Roger's tendency to lethargy and irresponsibility that will have consequences for them later. One might connect that with a later moment in their relationship when he excitedly tells her of the job in Tokyo but is worried by how she will react and wondering how it will affect their relationship. "Listen, little boy, of course I want you to go," says Julie, recognizing it as a great opportunity, not wanting to stand in his way, and stirred and moved by his obvious excitement. Yet the phrase "little boy" is intriguing there. It is as if, almost subconsciously, she has recognized an immaturity in Roger that will take years and hard experience to eradicate. In their first marital row after she has arrived in Tokyo and told him she is expecting a baby, Julie will tell him that "You're acting like a child," when he seems ready to squander most of their inheritance on a round-the-world trip. Roger's reaction to this (and Cary Grant does this superbly) is to sulk, unwittingly confirming Julie's judgment.

One of the items which links the early romantic scene on the beach and the later Tokyo earthquake tragedy is a fortune cookie. Julie and Roger open their fortune cookies, but the messages they contain turn out to be (depending on which angle you take) either wrong, ambiguous, or right, but not in the way intended. It is noticeable that both are reluctant for the other to see what the message contains, as if it touches on an unconscious or undisclosed desire that each wants to conceal from the other. Julie's message reads: "You will get your wish. A BABY." From her expression it seems clear that this is her wish, but the moment is followed by the interruption of a little boy who, to Roger's annoyance, has scattered sand on him before departing. "Go on, beat it," Roger says roughly to the boy, and Julie's wish is therefore somewhat dashed by the thought that Roger does not like children. Roger's message has read, "A wedding soon," but this is so opposed to his inclination that he secretly crumples it before Julie can see it and opens another one that reads: "You'll always be a bachelor." "Oh, those things are silly," says Roger irritably, "they never come true," and in a way he is right: Julie will not have a baby, and he will not always be a bachelor. Yet the way the two are so secretive and uncomfortable about them gives the scene a slight edginess. Why does the prospect of an early wedding alarm Roger so? Is he afraid it will inhibit his freedom or demand a sense of responsibility from him of which he is not sure he is capable? Admittedly the two are to be married in haste, but Roger can almost immediately escape to his new job overseas, though not before making his wife pregnant. Like most of Roger's actions, it is unplanned, and the consequences are not fully thought through.

When she joins him in Tokyo, Julie will at first be reluctant to tell Roger the news of her pregnancy, and indeed breaks the news indirectly by showing him her original fortune cookie prediction, which she has kept and treasured in a small jewelry box. Again it is a charming detail which becomes disquieting on reflection: she has not told him before because she has been afraid of his reaction. This anticipates a time when their communication, which is often indirect about things that are important to their relationship, will break down completely. When the devastating earthquake hits, Julie's miscarriage will be conveyed by a brutal piece of visual symbolism: her cherished fortune cookie on the floor after having fallen out of its box, and momentarily glimpsed before being covered and crushed by falling debris.

In her pioneering feminist text on the treatment of women in the movies, *From Reverence to Rape*, Molly Haskell wrote of *Penny Serenade* that "the Irene Dunne character is defined by her obsession to have a child that quite clearly precedes, and culminates, in her marriage to Grant, and that finally wrecks his career and emotional stability" (Haskell: 128). Her suggestion that Dunne's character marries Grant primarily to have a child (she calls this the film's "sick premise") seems unduly perverse, since. Julie's prime motivation for marrying him is because she loves him, which takes precedence over her fear that he dislikes children. It is also hard to accept Haskell's argument that the woman's "obsession to have a child" is the cause of Grant's career failure and the man's "emotional instability." Roger's failure to deliver as a husband and father might certainly owe something to his inability to recognize his wife's deepest needs. The scene when he visits her at the San Francisco Hospital portrays that very well, as he tells her of the country newspaper he has bought in Rosalia that will enable him to buy clothes and furniture ("it's what *we* [my emphasis] always wanted." he says, mistakenly), while Julie attends less to his words than to the sounds of the pram wheels and baby cries that she can hear outside her hospital room. Yet his failure is equally the result of financial irresponsibility and an ambition that is matched neither by ability nor by achievement, something which even he acknowledges at the end of the film. There is a particularly telling detail when they are applying to adopt and being interviewed by Miss Oliver (Beulah Bondi). Roger grossly exaggerates his earnings; and when Julie upbraids him outside for this, he says that it was a strategy to ensure that they would still be in consideration for having a child by the adoption agency. Yet Julie's comment to him, "Why do you have to be a big shot?" seems closer to the mark. The lie is less the result of his wanting a child (after all, in a sharp detail by Grant, he secretly smiles to himself when they are told the process could take a year) and more the product of pride, the scarcely acknowledged defensive posture of a man who is failing to live up to what he promised and is not yet ready to face up to the fact. Stevens reveals this rather cunningly in a montage of the circulation figures of

Roger's local newspaper. Conventionally, this would show the figures rapidly rising; here the circulation moves from 901 to 908. Again it is worth recalling that this is Julie's flashback (we are never given Roger's perspective) and that the memories are not only a recollection of happier times but also an explanation of why she is leaving him.

Significantly the idea of adoption comes not from Roger but from his best friend Applejack (Edgar Buchanan), who has joined him as press manager when Roger has taken over the ownership of the *Rosalia Courier*. The fact that a baby is still preying on Julie's mind is shown by their initial entrance into the newspaper premises. The first thing she spots is a prominent baby poster in the window, whereas, in his excitement on entrance, Roger not only fails to notice the poster but fails to pick up Julie's difference of mood from his own. Applejack, who is himself adopted, will raise the issue with Julie one evening when they are sharing a meal together while Roger is away on business. It is as if he senses this as a good opportunity, as it is still too sensitive an issue to raise with them both, even though we learn later that it is now two years since her miscarriage. Julie reveals that she has not discussed the matter with Roger, saying he was so disappointed about the miscarriage that "I just didn't have the courage." It is another example of their failure to communicate or understand the needs of the other which now seems to be looming larger in her memory. Indeed one wonders whether she is right or entirely honest about Roger's disappointment over the miscarriage, and that the real reason she has not raised the subject of adoption with her husband is that she is afraid of a negative response. This would explain her excitement when Applejack tells her that he and Roger have been talking about adoption and that "he's all for the idea." She almost willfully fails to notice Applejack's discomfort when Roger returns. When Julie gently reproves her husband for discussing such a personal matter with Applejack without discussing it with her first, Roger clearly has no idea of what either of them is talking about. It is a cleverly written, directed and acted scene, in which all three characters are caught a little off balance and have to adjust their bearings and the actors are required to hint at a subtext to what they are saying. Applejack's description of his conversation with Roger and Roger's enthusiasm for the adoption is most probably a fabrication, designed to bring about what he believes is a desired conclusion for his closest friends; Julie affects to believe him not because he is especially convincing but because she desperately *wants* to believe him, whether what he says is true or not; and when it belatedly dawns on Roger what has been fixed behind his back (and Applejack is a very good fixer of things), he realizes he has been presented with a *fait accompli* that he can neither deny nor back out of. As Applejack has effectively brought the child into being before the adopted parents have agreed to it, it is a lovely and appropriate touch when, in one of the film's most celebrated scenes, he will play mother to the new arrival and give a demonstration to Julie and Roger—in what looks like a single take—on how to bathe and change a five-week-old child. Edgar Buchanan provides characteristically solid and sympathetic support to the two leads throughout the film, but particularly so in this scene, where he adds what looks like a stroke of inspired improvisation when, after completing the bathing and clothing of baby Trina, he sprays a little talcum powder on himself as a token of congratulation.

In the interview at the adoption agency, Julie and Roger have stated a preference for a curly haired two-year-old boy. "When they're two years old, they're more or less housebroken, aren't they?" says Roger, as if they are rescuing a pet more than adopting a child. When Miss Oliver later drops round unexpectedly at the newspaper office to inspect their living quarters, Julie is gaily dancing the Charleston while doing her housework and the apartment is in something of a mess. She invites Miss Oliver to sit down, before realizing belatedly that there is actually nowhere to sit. "Moving from room to room," Bruce Beresford wrote, "she [Miss Oliver] obviously thinks (as does the audience) that the couple are unfit to adopt anything; then she moves into a sparkling, spotless nursery. Sentimental, but handled with conviction," he concluded, shrewdly noting that this is just one example of a particular feature of Stevens's direction in this film, where he will use the element of surprise to deflect the danger of sentimentality (Brewster: 13).

Over the next twenty minutes or so, Stevens and Ryskind will take us humorously and humanely through the process whereby Roger and Julie will adopt, over Roger's initial objections, a five-week-old girl, Trina and bring the child back to her new home. There is a host of endearing detail: the contrast between Roger's shock and Julie's delight when they are informed that a new-born girl is awaiting adoption; the way Beulah Bondi as Miss Oliver smoothly accommodates Roger's unease and, almost imperceptibly, switches her appeal to the more receptive Julie; the moment when Roger, still desirous of a boy, gestures towards a two-year-old, saying "What about him?" and Miss Oliver has to point out that this is a nursery and the youngster already has parents (the boy, anyway, seems to wave Roger disdainfully away); and the return home and first night with their baby, when every noise, be it a squeaky stair or a dropped parcel or an alarm that refuses to be switched off, seems to be magnified, and where the stirrings of love are never far away from feelings of panic and inadequacy. No parents of a newly born child could fail to empathize with these feelings and Stevens is not afraid to take his time here, delightfully combining sympathy with slapstick as the new parents struggle with their new situation. He even slyly circumvents the Hays Code by sneaking in a shot of the married couple sleeping in the same bed, albeit with their newly adopted child between them. Yet, again if one recollects this as Julie's flashback, there is one moment that strikes a powerfully discordant note. When Julie sits down in the nursery and holds Trina for the first time, Roger sits next to her and allows the child to grip his finger. But has he grasped what has happened? "Well, you've had your look, dear," he says, "how about going back home?" Julie swivels round as if she has been struck to stare at him in genuine shock, and Irene Dunne (who is alert to every nuance of the character) makes the most of the moment. Although Roger will quickly become devoted to the girl, one could surmise that that moment of total misunderstanding might have lingered in Julie's mind and is now being recalled as something that portends their future misalliance. She might also have been remembering that, even when they first arrived home with the baby, Roger mistakenly referred to the child as "him" and then later as "it."

An element of surprise has been one of Stevens' weapons to ward off the dangers of sentimentality; he now deploys suspense. Roger's lie about his income has come back to haunt him. Arriving for an inspection when the baby is two years old, Miss Oliver is surprised to find the newspaper office inactive and deserted, and dismayed to discover that Roger is out of a job, a situation which could lead to Trina's being taken from them and returned to an orphanage. Significantly it is Julie who has to admit to Miss Oliver that they have "no income." After she has left, Roger, as is his wont, seeks to deflect the blame from himself. "Old battle axe! She doesn't want us to have Trina!" he cries, an outburst of petulance and rage that only thinly disguises a displacement of his own sense of guilt. Julie's appraisal is more temperate and accurate, as she reassures Roger of Miss Oliver's support, but her anxiety is every bit as great, for she cannot be certain whether that support will be enough.

The following scene is perhaps the film's most striking example of what Eugene Archer meant when he referred to Stevens's "precise but unconventional frames." With Julie's help, Roger is preparing to leave the apartment with Trina to plead the case for adoption before a judge. The action is organized visually around a close shot of Trina's doll propped up against the bars at the top of the stairs, in readiness for collection when Roger and Trina are on their way out. At this juncture one might recall subliminally that shots of stairs and steps have portended significant events in the film: Julie has been climbing the stairs when the earthquake in Tokyo has struck; Miss Oliver's first sight of Julie in their apartment when coming with the news of a child awaiting adoption has been through the bars of the stairs. The toy dominates the frame, while we see just the legs of Roger and Julie moving back and forth in the background. No dialogue or close-ups; the movement itself suggests the urgency of the situation; and the visual focus on the doll is a concise way of emphasizing the main subject of the scene and what is upper-most in the adults' mind. Stevens withholds a shot of their faces until the end of the scene when Roger, carrying Trina and halfway down the stairs, reaches back for the doll, and Julie hands it to him before moving to the window and watching them depart. It is a masterly, unexaggerated organization of all the dramatic elements of the situation in a concise visual form. Stevens is careful not to overplay his hand at this stage, for the film's biggest emotional scene is still to come.

The scene in which Roger pleads his case before an initially unsympathetic judge (Wallis Clark) is one of the most highly charged and dramatically challenging of Cary Grant's screen career. Mark Harris has noted that, during the making of the film, Grant had learned that five members of his family (his aunt and uncle, and their daughter, son-in-law and grandchild) had been killed in a Nazi bombing raid on his hometown of Bris-tol, so it is possible that the actor is drawing upon a raw and recent sense of personal loss (Harris: 81). Some critics have a tendency to sneer when stars like Grant step outside the parameters of their usual screen persona, suggesting that such an extension of their range is a mistaken craving for critical respectability and a denial of the uniqueness of their talent: see, for example, Andrew Sarris's disparaging comments about Humphrey Bogart's great character performances in John Huston's *The Treasure of the Sierra Madre* (1948) and *The African Queen* (1951). If they are nominated for an Oscar in the process (as Grant was to be for his performance), then their critical disdain is only heightened. Richard Schickel dismissed Grant's performance in this scene as a miscalculated "bid for prestige" and wrote that he pleads for the baby in "a defeated monotone" (Schickel: pp. 104–5). To say the least, this does less than justice to the range of Grant's vocal perform-ance in the scene. By contrast, David Mamet, who knows something about directing actors and how difficult they find the kind of self-abasement that a scene like this requires, described his performance in this scene as "a magnificent piece of acting. Cary Grant … actually pleads. He bares his soul before the judge who holds the fate of his daughter in his hands" (Mamet: 169). He makes no big dramatic gestures; his hand movements are economical; his physical movements are mostly confined to either sitting on a chair or suddenly standing, as if unable to decide whether deference or assertiveness will best further his cause; and, although he once almost loses control and shouts, his voice mostly just throbs with sincerity and sorrow. There are a couple of places where he stumbles over his words, unusually for an actor so dexterous with dialogue. Whether this was intentional or not, it effectively reinforces the character's sense of desperation and fear of failure.

Grant's performance is expertly supported and enhanced by two other features of the scene; the presence of Bondi as Miss Oliver; and Stevens's visual framing. Simply in the way she sits and listens, Bondi gives the scene an additional emotional weight, as a compassionate presence situated between sympathy for the plight of the father and recognition of the legitimate requirements of the law. When Roger makes his most personal direct appeal, acknowledging faults in himself that have led to this crisis ("I've always been kind of careless and irresponsible") but pleading in the best interests of the child, Stevens resists the temptation of close-ups and instead composes a medium shot of Roger and the judge on either side of the frame, with Miss Oliver in the center in the background, as if inviting the audience objectively to weigh the merits of the case. There is a silence and then the camera retreats just slightly; it is like a short intake of breath. Stevens ends the scene at the precise moment before the judge delivers the verdict, delaying the revelation in his framing until Roger returns home, opens the front door and climbs the stairs. It is only then, at the top, that we—and Julie—see that he is carrying Trina.

There is one other feature of this sequence that seems to me of particular significance, and relates again to the sophistication of the flashback structure. The scene at the court is the only one in the film in which Roger appears without Julie. Yet, if this is Julie's flashback, how should we interpret what has been shown? Is it Julie's imagination of what must have happened, given the successful outcome? Possibly; but there is an additional psychological twist, that reveals something about Roger and will validate the film's ending. Roger can abase himself before the judge in a way that, one feels, he would have found impossible in Julie's presence: it would have involved too much loss of face and self-esteem. "I'm not a big shot now," he tells the judge. It is one of the deepest ironies of the film and of the flashback structure that, at this juncture, it is their separation that enables them to keep their child and their family together. Yet it also prepares one for the ending. When Roger acknowledges his failure and broken promises to Julie, it is a major step forward in honesty and self-realization.

On returning home from the court with Trina, Roger has handed over their little girl to an overjoyed Julie with the words: "She's yours, dear, now and forever. Nothing can ever take her from us." Nothing is forever, of course; and, recalling the sadness of the opening prior to the first flashback, audiences at the time must have sensed the unwitting irony behind Roger's words and have been steeling themselves for the tragedy to come. A full-blown melodramatist might have opted for a childhood accident, as in *Gone with the Wind* (1939) or a death-bed scene that Michael Curtiz was to contrive in *Mildred Pierce* (1945), but this is not Stevens's way. Nevertheless, there is something almost subversive in the way his more temperate sensibility undercuts expectations of Hollywood mawkishness and morbidity. There are certainly opportunities aplenty for a tragic accident in the six-year-old Trina's participation in her school's Christmas play, where she has to ascend a ramp unseen, carrying a cloud and a star behind the Nativity scene, and then sing as an echo the words of "Silent Night." She does indeed fall on the way down, but Stevens defies audience expectations of calamity by first playing up the sentiment (the reaction of Roger and Julie as they hear Trina's voice as an echo behind the stage) but then turning Trina's disaster into an unexpected moment of slapstick, as her fall causes the cloud and star she is carrying to hurtle across the background in unseemly haste. So how then will be the tragedy be handled? Screen convention would seem to demand a heart-on-sleeve dramatic culmination. Stevens delivers instead a stunning anti-climax, all the more devastating for being unseen and unforeseen.

Miss Oliver opens a Christmas letter from Julie and, as she starts to read, we see her expression change. It is striking that Stevens does not use a voice-over for this scene. We are compelled to read the letter along with Miss Oliver and hence share her shock on learning that Trina has died after a short illness. As she slowly absorbs the terrible news, Stevens punctuates her reading with the imposition of separate close-ups of Roger and Julie at home, physically separated by only a few feet but mentally miles apart. The rain lashing down outside their window is a potent piece of pathetic fallacy, suggestive of the tears of grief being shed inwardly by them both but which they seem unable to share. Roger is so cocooned in his personal pain that he appears almost literally deaf to everything around him. When Julie asks him to attend to a door in a separate room that is banging or answer a knock at the front door, he makes no move to do either. The knocking at the door will only add to the distress, for it turns out be a mother seeking help because her car has broken down on the way to the Christmas play with her son. Roger will give them a lift, but this act of charity is simultaneously a dagger to the heart that will make his anguish unendurable, for it is a reminder of Trina; and after dropping off mother and son at the play, he will tell Julie he is leaving, because he can no longer bear the thought of going home. The record Julie is playing as these memories crowd in is the popular song "Together," which can hardly be less appropriate, with lines such as "we'll always be together" seeming to mock their situation. Even the line in the song "laughed at the rain together" has a bitter ring. It is raining hard when Roger says goodbye; there is no laughter then.

In the final scene, after Roger's self-recrimination that surely stems not from self-pity but a deep and genuine anguish that he has lost and let down the two people in the world he most loves, there is a phone call from Miss Oliver. A child is awaiting adoption, she tells them, and she thought of them because it fits the description of the child they had requested in their first letter to her: a two-year-old boy with curly hair. An excessively contrived and convenient turn of events? Yet it is hard not to feel that Roger's brave, belated self-recognition and Miss Oliver's redemptive phone call are in some way connected. "A reconciliation is effected, both plausibly and movingly, *in extremis*," wrote Gilbert Adair, and dismissed the idea that this was just another sentimental happy ending in the Hollywood mode. "For if sentimentality is nothing more than the flaky crust of an *unearned* emotion," he argued, "then Stevens' best movies really can't be judged sentimental" (Adair: 8). The couple are being offered a chance to start again not simply to facilitate a happy ending but because, on the basis of what we have seen, they deserve it. And the tone is one of subdued optimism more than euphoria: the period is, after all, the Depression and jobs will be hard to come by. The ending is all the more satisfying because of its restraint and recognition of the difficulties ahead. In some way it reminds me of the marvelous ending of Billy Wilder's *The Apartment* (1960), where the happiness of the couple is modified by their jobless situation and the visual gloom of their bare surroundings. Wilder's way of defusing sentiment is through Shirley MacLaine's brisk, unforgettable rejoinder to Jack Lemmon's declaration of love over a game of gin rummy: "Shut up and deal." Stevens will cap his narrative not on a close-up and embrace of the reconciled couple, but with a shot of the two of them tentatively, almost instinctively, turning back from the top of the stairs, and, with their backs to the camera, shuffling in tender but tentative proximity into the child's room and starting to assess what needs to be done. No big romantic fadeout, then; just a gentle, poignant suggestion of the possibility of new beginnings.

Woman of the Year (1942)

> "*Woman of the Year* sees Tess as a disruptive element that needs to be brought into line…. George Stevens … tacked on a final sequence that called into question everything the Hepburn image seemed to stand for."—Barbara Leaming

> "*Woman of the Year* shows a lapse in Stevens's generally fond regard for the female character. Instead his camera takes a persistent pot-shot at her, insisting that she ultimately acquiesces to the demands of her partner."—Marilyn Ann Moss

> "Over and over again these days, we hear the phrase 'The world is in chaos.' The world is *not* in chaos…. Men are in chaos."—Dorothy Thompson

Woman of the Year is famous for being the first film to pair Katharine Hepburn with Spencer Tracy, introducing an on-screen romance that was to lead to eight more films together, and an off-screen romance that was to endure until Tracy's death in 1967. As the above epigraphs indicate, the film is also notorious among female (and some male) critics for its undermining of the career woman and for an extended comic finale in which the heroine is progressively humiliated for her failure as a dutiful housewife to cook breakfast for her husband. Eugene Archer thought this "disastrous episode ruins the conclusion and diminishes the film" (Archer: 30); and Andrew Sarris found it "ponderously unfunny" and added on "presumably to give more punch to the *Taming of the Shrew* motif" (Sarris: 453). Joanne Stang's *Films and Filming* article on Stevens (July 1959) has a still from the film with a caption that reads "Katharine Hepburn was Stevens' *Woman of the Year* in 1942. Spencer Tracy played her husband who finally tamed her into being the perfect wife" (Stang: 10). Although conceding that the heroine is relentlessly undermined during the film, Marilyn Ann Moss goes on to offer an explanation and defense of Stevens's strategy in arguing that the story has a "very overt political agenda" (Moss: 81). The film can indeed be seen as a political allegory entwined with a romantic comedy, but I will offer an alternative interpretation of what the allegory means, and a reading of the film which challenges the above critical consensus.

The inspiration for the film originated with screenwriter and director Garson Kanin, who, after noting the success of George Cukor's *The Philadelphia Story* (1940), "believed at that time that I had discovered the formula for a Hepburn success. A high-class or stuck-up or hoity-toity girl is brought down to earth by an earthy type, or a low-brow, or a diamond in the rough" (Kanin: 80). Kanin had spent an evening in the company of the celebrated political journalist Dorothy Thompson, who at that time was married to the Nobel Prize–winning novelist Sinclair Lewis (and whose 1935 novel about the danger of rising fascism in America, *It Can't Happen Here,* has recently been seen by a number of critics as remarkably prescient). The following day, Kanin had received a letter from the renowned boxing journalist Jimmy Cannon. Suddenly he had the idea for a movie. Female political pundit and male sports journalist work on the same paper; they clash in print; and then, as Kanin put it, they "meet and clash in person; both wrong, both right—not bad!" (80). Hepburn would be ideal casting for the heroine, and Spencer Tracy seemed perfect for the male role.

Because he was shortly to be drafted and spend the war making documentaries for the Office of Emergency Management and eventually collaborating with Carol Reed on the Oscar-winning documentary about Operation Overlord, *The True Glory* (1945), Kanin was not able to develop the project personally. He bequeathed the idea to his brother Michael and the upcoming screenwriter Ring Lardner, Jr., later to acquire notoriety as one of the Hollywood Ten. The two submitted a screenplay that was two-thirds complete to Katharine Hepburn, who was enthusiastic and proposed it as her next project to the head of MGM, Louis B. Mayer, requesting a salary of $100,000 for the writers, the same for herself, plus $11,000 to cover the costs of her agent and other expenses. When Mayer passed the project on to producer Joseph L. Mankiewicz for consideration, Mankiewicz assumed that, because the fee being asked for the script was so high, it must be the work of an experienced team such as Ben Hecht and Charles McArthur, who had been reassigned to another project. When the deal was agreed, he was surprised to find that the screenplay was the work of two relative unknowns. One might have expected the writers to be grateful to him for agreeing to a financial deal beyond their wildest dreams. However, Mankiewicz was to be instrumental in changing the ending of the film after an unsuccessful preview and coming up with a different conclusion that played well with audiences but has been a bone of critical contention ever since. When they won the Oscar for the best original screenplay of the year, the writers pointedly refused to shake Mankiewicz's hand as they passed his table on their way to the podium to receive their award.

Normally Hepburn would have sent the script for a new romantic comedy to her great friend, George Cukor, as a possible future collaboration, but, in this instance, because of the story's sporting background, she thought Cukor would be wrong for the film (as she said, "he didn't know a baseball game from a swimming match"). Instead she turned instead to Stevens, who, as well as being fond of Hepburn personally, had always felt a sense of gratitude to her for giving him his first big break with *Alice Adams*. The material seemed congenial, for aspects of the heroine's predicament echoed that of the heroines he had treated sympathetically in *Alice Adams, Annie Oakley, Vivacious Lady* and *Vigil in the Night*. It was also the kind of comedy he did best, where the humor arises not from gags or slapstick but essentially from the reality of the characters and their situation. The sticking-point for Stevens was the studio. Hepburn was under contract to MGM and insisted on making the film for them. Stevens was still under contract to do two more films for Columbia and was not sure Harry Cohn would be best pleased if he seemed to be transferring his allegiance to a rival studio. Cohn seems to have raised no objection and, as it happened, Stevens was to prefer working at Columbia where he was much more his own boss. MGM was not known as a directors' studio ("too many damned story conferences," Stevens grumbled), and although he made it there as a favor to Hepburn, it was to be his only MGM film. *Woman of the Year* was to prove immensely popular, but its blend of comic and serious material now looks arguably more abrupt and problematic than in *Penny Serenade*, partly because it does not have the structural sophistication of the earlier film. What it does have is the onscreen chemistry of Tracy and Hepburn, which *Variety* felt, in an otherwise rather hostile review that lamented the film's length and predictability, went "a long way toward pulling the chestnut out of the fire" (1 April 1942).

The film begins somewhat deceptively in the same vein of romantic comedy as *Vivacious Lady*. Once again Stevens is telling the story of two people who had no business getting together, but did, and then having them experience the pleasant frustration of non-consummation, though, in both cases, the frustration is to lead to near-separation.

Before we see Tess Harding (Katharine Hepburn), we are shown a series of newspaper headlines either by or about her, revealing a personality who bestrides the world of international politics; has meetings with world leaders such as Churchill and Roosevelt; and tells her readers what she thinks and, by inference, what they should think also. A newsstand has a placard for the *New York Chronicle* that reads: "Hitler Will Lose, says Tess Harding." Stevens pans left to reveal another *Chronicle* headline: "The Yankees Won't Lose, says Sam Craig" (Spencer Tracy). Which should claim precedence? The lines of combat have been instantly drawn. In Pinkie's bar with his journalistic cronies, Sam is outraged when Tess over the radio advocates the abolition of baseball for the duration of the war in Europe so that Americans might focus their minds on more important matters than sport. "We're concerned with what we like to call the threat to our way of life," cries Sam at the radio. "What's the sense in abolishing the thing you're trying to protect?" He is sufficiently needled to write an article for the *Chronicle* attacking Tess's point of view, to which she then responds. The editor, who obviously does not want two of his star reporters to be seen quarrelling with each other in the same paper, summons them both to his office to negotiate a truce.

When Sam enters the office, his attention is caught first by the sight of Tess's shapely leg as she straightens the seam on her nylons. His instinctive response is to back out again in embarrassment, but the editor calls him in. Nevertheless, what Gilbert Adair was to describe as the "startling eroticism generated by Tracy and Hepburn in *Woman of the Year*" (Adair: 7) is established immediately before a word has been exchanged, and will continue in their romantic scenes together. In a scene in her apartment, for example, Stevens frames their embrace in silhouette, which seems to add an additional cloak of privacy and makes us feel we are eavesdropping on a secret love affair (which, in a way, we are).

When the two of them leave the editor's office, Tess becomes aware that Sam seems to be following her, entranced. She turns a corner and then stops on the stairs, catching Sam by surprise and pointing out to him that, if he is supposed to be on his way to the sports office, he is heading in the wrong direction. In the ensuing conversation, they circle warily about each other in a sort of romantic roundelay, with Tess careful to maintain her advantageous position above him. It is one of a number of occasions in the early part of the film where Stevens plays witty visual games within the frame to suggest the shifting balance of power in their relationship. For example, there is a shot of the bartender Pinkie (William Bendix) engaged in a strangely awkward conversation with Sam, not quite making eye contact. The reason for the awkwardness is only revealed when Pinkie steps away to disclose the presence of Tess alongside Sam in a reverse mirror shot, as if displacing Pinkie's image by magic and certainly supplanting him in importance. Their subsequent drinks evening at Pinkie's will end with Tess literally under the table, whilst still trying to explain to Sam the intricacies of Spengler and fascism. In the cab back to Tess's apartment, Sam tells her that there is something he must get off his chest; and Tess, who has a habit of taking what he says literally, dutifully moves her head. What he wants to say is that he is in love with her. "Even when I'm sober?" she asks. "Even when you're brilliant," he replies. The word "even" is telling in that context, and it is a sentiment that is to be tested over the course of the film.

It has already been noted how often in a Stevens film the main driving force behind the narrative is female, but it is particularly marked in *Woman of the Year*. It is Tess who suggests that she should accompany Sam to a baseball game; who invites him to her apartment after she has finished her broadcast; and who insists that Sam, rather than her secretary Gerald (Dan Tobin), drives her to the airport after her talk on women's rights. When he asks why, she says, coyly, "I thought you might wish to kiss me goodbye," making the first move in their courtship. When they arrive back at her apartment after their drunken night at Pinkie's, the cab driver asks Sam whether he should wait, but it is Tess who answers on his behalf, and who unmistakably intends that they should spend the night together. (A rather bold and daring thing to suggest in a Hollywood movie of that era.) In fact, Sam, as in his first meeting with her, will make a strategic withdrawal when Tess goes to fetch him a glass of milk; he will later say that it is an indication of his seriousness about their relationship. Yet, although he proposes marriage, it is Tess who decides the date and place of their wedding, scarcely having time even to tell her maid, Alma (the ever dependable Edith Evanson), who, when she sees Sam carrying his new bride over the threshold into Tess's apartment, assumes that she must have been injured. Tess is invariably the initiator, though when she oversteps the mark, she does apologize, which is more than can be said for Sam. Nevertheless, it is striking how, in a film traditionally read as anti-feminist, and indeed in an industry traditionally seen as duplicating a predominant patriarchal ideology, the heroine is so much more active than the hero, whose movements seem mostly confined to his office, the appropriate sports stadium, and to his favorite bar. The full implications of this are to be revealed in the kitchen scene at the end when Sam's immobility becomes as eloquent and suggestive as Tess's chaotic activity.

The character contrasts are particularly affirmed in two early scenes where each enters the world of the other, though how one is intended to interpret the scenes is somewhat ambiguous. Laughter is undoubtedly part of the intention, but at what, and at the expense of whom? When Tess accompanies Sam to the baseball game, she causes a flutter in the press box which has previously been an all-male preserve. (As one of the reporters has said earlier: "Women should be kept illiterate and clean, like canaries.") Stevens extracts a lot of comedy from Tess's large white hat, which is inappropriate for the occasion, for it is not raining and partially obscures the view of the spectator behind her (a nice little cameo, which Hepburn greatly admired, by an uncredited Jack Carr). There are also chuckles from the press corps when Sam has to explain to Tess the intricacies of the national sport, though one feels he is more embarrassed by how he might look to his colleagues than by Tess's ignorance. Marilyn Ann Moss wrote that "Sam smirks condescendingly each time he has to explain a play to her" (Moss: 85), but that underestimates the subtlety and restraint of Tracy's performance here; in fact, condescension would be quite misplaced and out of character. Because of his feelings for her, he wants her to understand and enjoy what he does, not wallow in his superiority. "You're wonderful!" he exclaims proudly, when, by the end of the game, she is getting as excited as the men around her. By that time she has even made a friend of the spectator whose view she had earlier obscured. When they have to leave the game at a point when the game is tied, the reporters are not laughing patronizingly at Tess but sizing up the romantic score on the basis of what they've seen. "Looks like the ball game isn't the only thing tied up here," says one of them, as he watches Sam's departure with his female guest.

As she gets into a cab to take her to her broadcast at NBC, she hands Sam her card and invites him to visit her at her apartment that evening at 8:30. She has not time to explain that she is hosting a reception there for foreign dignitaries following her broadcast, and Sam turns up, mistakenly expecting a quiet intimate evening. Touchingly, he seems quite nervous and is scrupulously on time, and carrying a box of flowers. He is quite surprised to be greeted by the maid, Alma, and even more startled by the sound of foreign voices from within. There is a typical piece of endearing comedy business from Stevens here, as Alma takes the flowers from a flustered Sam; hands them to Tess who has rushed to greet Sam and who then hands the flowers back to Alma so she can take his hand. What began as an intended romantic gesture turns inadvertently into a gently embarrassing game of pass-the-parcel. Just as Tess has entered Sam's masculine terrain in the afternoon, Sam now finds himself in Tess's world, and at sea. Tess reveals her fluency in French, Russian, and Slovenian as she weaves in and out of the guests as a good hostess should. Knowing no language but his own, Sam feels a complete outsider until he hears English being spoken between two men who are having a private conversation. "Dr. Livingstone, I presume?" he says brightly as he joins them (which would have been seen at the time as a cinematic in-joke, in that Tracy had played Stanley to Cedric Hardwicke's Livingstone in the 1939 film), but their response to his intrusion is to resume their conversation in a foreign language and move away. Yet this extended sequence of the comedy of non-communication is to close in a rather strange, disquieting way. Sam will find himself seated next to an Asian gentleman, who seems as lost as he is and whose only English is the word "Yes." On realizing this, and in full knowledge that the man will not understand a word, Sam says to him: "You're a silly-looking jerk with that towel around your head, you know that, don't you?"

It is difficult to know how one is intended to react to that line. Nowadays one would imagine that many audiences would find the line objectionable, offensive, or even casually racist. One wonders whether, even at the time, audiences were taken aback by Sam's gratuitous rudeness and the way it seemed indicative of American insularity (one could call it xenophobia) at its least appealing. In context, of course, it could simply reflect Sam's sense of frustration, and he will leave shortly afterwards. Yet these two scenes taken together—at the baseball game, and at Tess's apartment—are very revealing about the two of them. When Tess enters Sam's world (at the game, at the bar), she does so voluntarily; endeavors to accommodate herself to the environment; and enters into the spirit of things. When Sam strays into Tess's world (at her apartment, at the Women's Meeting), he does so accidentally or reluctantly and is a disruptive rather than supportive presence. This is worth bearing in mind when Sam is complaining that Tess is preoccupied with her career and not paying him enough attention. It is also worth remembering when critics argue that the sympathies of the film are slanted far too much in Sam's direction and that, because of the screenplay's hostility towards the stereotype of the career woman, Tess becomes, in Molly Haskell's words, "a Lady Macbeth of overweening ambition" (Haskell: 8). As Haskell goes on to note, Stevens is too canny and sensitive a director to allow that impression to predominate; and I will argue that Stevens has an alternative agenda that will effectively subvert allegations of male bias.

As in *Penny Serenade,* a crisis in their marriage will occur through their adoption of a child. Prior to that, the film has more resembled *Vivacious Lady* in its comedy of non-consummation, when Sam and Tess's wedding night is disrupted by the sudden arrival at Tess's door of a prominent Yugoslavian refugee, Dr. Lubbeck (Ludwig Stossel), whose plight Tess has been highlighting in her column and who is in flight from the turmoil in Europe. He is accompanied by two bodyguards and later by members of the Yugoslavian Embassy who crowd into Tess's bedroom to express their gratitude. A blissfully unaware Sam, who has been changing in another room, now emerges, and in a droll medium shot, we see that Alma, who is at that point just leaving, hesitates for a moment, as if to warn him, but then thinks better of it. As he strolls over towards the bedroom, Sam is to be set upon by Lubbeck's bodyguards. As the celebrations develop, Sam organizes a kind of counteroffensive by inviting Pinkie and his friends to join the party; and the newlyweds are left surveying the jollity until it dawns on the entourage of both Lubbeck and Pinkie the rather special occasion that they have inadvertently interrupted. It is a typically well-organized Stevens comedy sequence that builds cumulatively towards ultimate chaos (the classic Laurel and Hardy structure), but it is also an augury of difficulties to come, where privacy is hard to come by, where two separate professional lives seem rarely to coincide, and where small niggles, such as Tess's failure to notice that Sam is wearing a new hat, can be blown out of proportion and develop into full-blown argument. Almost imperceptibly the comedy is receding to reveal a marriage that is running into trouble.

Nevertheless the whole episode involving the adopted child does sound a rather jarring note in that it both changes the mood and strains credulity. Sam suspects that something is up when Tess waits up for him one night and then serves him breakfast in bed (courtesy of Alma) the next morning. "What would you think about having a child?" she asks him. Mistakenly (and understandably) thinking it is her way of telling him she is pregnant, Sam is overjoyed, so the shock is all the greater when she explains that, without consulting him, she has adopted a young Greek refugee (George Kezas) and introduces him to Sam. The boy quickly picks up Sam's hostility, and Tess could hardly have handled the delicate situation less tactfully, particularly as the adoption seems to stem from a humanitarian reflex more than a considered maternal desire. Ironically, on that very morning, she learns that she has been voted "America's Outstanding Woman of the Year." ("Would you have voted for me, Sam?" she asks; he doesn't answer.) Things come to a head on the evening of the ceremony, when it seems that, to Sam's astonishment, Tess is intending to leave the boy to play on his own in the apartment while they all go to celebrate her award; they will only be gone four hours or so. "He can do a lot of crying in four hours," says Sam and refuses to accompany her, his harsh parting shot as she leaves being that "the outstanding woman of the year isn't a woman at all." "I'm sorry," says Tess and then departs, leaving us perhaps wondering exactly what she is sorry for: the argument? ignoring the best interests of the child? failing to live up to Sam's concept of womanhood? or that he does not understand the importance of this occasion to her?

Unsurprisingly, a number of feminist (and other) critics have objected to what they feel is the extreme slanting of the material against the career woman at this point in the narrative. It does seem extraordinary that Tess seems not to have considered the simple expedient of hiring a baby-sitter. (While accompanying Tess at the ceremony, Sam has assumed that Alma would have been looking after the child in their absence, but it turns out that Alma is going as well.) Molly Haskell accused the writers of "doing everything possible to sabotage the career woman played by Katharine Hepburn ... with so little of 'the milk of human kindness' that she is guilty of criminal negligence toward the child she and her husband Spencer Tracy have adopted." This is a fair point, but she goes on: " Tracy by contrast is a doting father—though never to the neglect of his newspaper work, which seems to say that love and ambition can co-exist in a man but not a woman" (Haskell: 8). The contrast is not that straightforward. If what Tess has done is shocking, what Sam proceeds to do seems to me more shocking still and completely demolishes any idea of his being "a doting father." His response to her departure is not to stay in and look after the child, which he has intimated would be the responsible thing to do. He reacts by returning the child to the Greek Children's Home, without any consultation with Tess, and in such a way as to cause the maximum embarrassment to his wife (for they know with whom the boy has been placed). When Tess returns to her apartment with some press photographers in tow, she will find that both her husband and her adopted son have gone and without any explanation. Only by noticing the address ringed in the phone book does she realize that the little boy has been taken back to the Home. When she goes to claim him back, she quickly realizes, and sadly accepts, that he would rather stay where he is.

It is an oddly harsh interlude in a predominantly romantic film. It is a critical commonplace either to condemn the heroine for her behavior or to condemn the film for making her behave like that, but I find it remarkable that few critics seem to have been similarly struck by the callousness of the hero's behavior. Tess might have been guilty of crass insensitivity in adopting the child without her husband's blessing and then in neglecting the child; but then how much more admirable is the husband's action of dumping the child back where he was without any discussion with his wife? Is the balance of sympathies (or, in this case, lack of sympathy) quite as one-sided as has often been made out?

By this time the two have separated and Sam has gone back to his own apartment. They still work in the same newspaper building, but when Tess rings him to tell him about an urgent telegram from her aunt (Fay Bainter) that involves them both, it is noticeable that he refuses to come up to Tess's office and that she has to go down to meet him. Once again he has shown his reluctance to enter Tess's feminine territory; once again she demonstrates her willingness to enter his. When she shows him the telegraph which requests the presence of both at her aunt's on a matter of great urgency, Sam refuses to accompany her, saying he has a championship bout to cover. The impression given is that his absence is less a matter of professional priority than of simple petulance: one feels he would not have accompanied her whatever the circumstances. (He more or less confirms this in their final breakfast scene.) The urgent matter referred to is the aunt's marriage in a civil ceremony to Tess's father (Minor Watson); and their disappointment at Sam's absence—they know nothing of the marital break-up—momentarily threatens the proceedings from taking place. (Sam never shows any sorrow at causing this distress or offers any congratulation.) In a marriage ceremony that will anticipate a later scene in *Giant*, Tess is moved by the words of the wedding vows and their applicability to her own marital situation; and we are given a close-up of Hepburn in tears as the words are heard over the soundtrack. David Shipman felt that "the writers should have found something stronger than the words of the wedding service to trigger Hepburn's inevitable act of repentance," but added that her "maladroit attempt to prepare breakfast under Tracy's baleful gaze, is one of the classic sequences of screen comedy" (Shipman: 470). In a similar vein, another perceptive critic of Stevens' work, Penelope Houston, who had been concerned by the film's gathering solemnity, thought it recovered for what she called "an unerringly timed final sequence of inspired comedy, in which the career-woman, intent on proving her domestic ability, battled increasingly desperately with the implements of a mechanised kitchen" (Houston: 74). However, the issue that has concerned critics since is not so much its success as a finely contrived piece of screen comedy but its assault on a career woman for her domestic incompetence, which seems designed to make her appear an inferior female.

This was not the original ending to the film, which had formerly concluded with a reconciliation between Sam and Tess at a world championship fight and with Tess affirming her determination to be a good wife and her wish to be known as Tess Harding-Craig. However, this had not gone down well with preview audiences. According to Joseph L. Mankiewicz, the audience had reacted in the way they had because the film dramatized "the incredible superiority that Hepburn exuded over other women" but without "giving her the come-uppance always essential to making her palatable to the average American audience" (qtd in Geist: 106). Accordingly, and with the aid of screenwriter John Lee Mahin, he suggested an ending along the lines of a favorite sequence of his in Stevens' *Alice Adams*, where Alice's attempt to impress a man she loves culminated in a dinner which went comically and catastrophically wrong. The changed ending would satisfy both male and female members of the audience, as the average American housewife, abashed by Tess's intelligence, wit, beauty and linguistic fluency, could still claim superiority in the kitchen and might even find her more sympathetic now that she has been cut down to size. According to Marilyn Ann Moss, market research revealed that women in the audience "enjoyed Tess's defeat no less than men" (Moss: 82). One does wonder, however, how many of them, while laughing at the heroine's humiliation, might also have secretly empathized with her plight as a newly married woman, expected to be a domestic goddess to her husband, and feeling overwhelmed by the task.

Undoubtedly one can sense behind the sequence the hand of someone who is a master of comedy timing and detail. Even if one did not know of Stevens' background in photographing Laurel and Hardy comedies, one might have been reminded of them in this sequence simply in the way one of the characters is looking on askance and in disbelief as the other unwittingly creates chaos before his eyes. Stevens knows how to utilize tiny bits of credible detail for cumulative comic effect: the way the straps on Tess's dress keep falling down to inhibit her movement; the draught from the closing of the refrigerator door, which blows over a page of the recipe she is following without her noticing, with disastrous consequences; the egg yolk which drops on her shoe. All of this will build to calamitous proportions as the coffee starts boiling over, bread starts flying out of the toaster behind her, at first unnoticed and then compelling her to catch a slice in mid-air. What started out as a surprise breakfast becomes a kind of comedy of nervous breakdown.

There is one rather startling statistic about this final sequence: it lasts all of 15 minutes. Stevens's comedy has always tended to be slow-burning rather than frantic, but this takes slowness almost to the point of slow-motion. Whatever the intent behind the deliberation, it allows viewers time not only to watch but to weigh up a variety of possible responses to what they are watching. For example, it is not implausible that Tess should find herself so utterly bemused in Sam's kitchen; nor is it inexcusable. She has, after all, been brought up as a diplomat's daughter and would, one supposes, have had little experience in preparing her own breakfast, let alone someone else's. Moreover, as Penelope Houston noted, it is a mechanized (i.e., masculine) kitchen that even an experienced housewife might have found initial difficulty in negotiating, so it is not surprising that Tess has trouble in working out where everything is. Indeed at one stage she shows some ingenuity when, experiencing problems in lighting the gas, she manages to strike a match on her shoe that does the trick. As all of this is going on, are we only being invited to reflect on and enjoy Tess's progressive domestic difficulty? Might we not also be tempted to admire the effort, however wayward, she is making on Sam's behalf, particularly as it is something which we never see reciprocated?

Sam is unimpressed. He interrupts her preparations and thinks it is just another of her feminine wiles to win him over. Even when she offers to give up her job, he does not believe she is sincere. Only when she has to confess her helplessness at the end in the face of total domestic disorder does he relent a little. He does not want her to be "Mrs. Sam Craig," he says, a meek housewife constantly in his shadow. "Why can't you just be Tess Harding Craig?" he asks, a rapprochement she happily accepts. What this will mean in practice is left open, but, as in *Penny Serenade*, we are left with the sense not so much of an ending as of a new beginning. Because the Tracy/Hepburn chemistry works (and continued to work) so well, the edge is taken off any potential disquiet; and, in retrospect, one might be tempted to see *Woman of the Year* not in isolation but as just the first install-ment in a series of nine films this magical screen partnership made together. The har-monious resolution is ostensibly of the kind one would expect of a romantic comedy of the era, even if its sexual politics might appear dated.

Yet there is an important political dimension which seems to me to give a wholly different perspective to the way in which the central relationship of the film has been commonly perceived. It is a coincidence that the film was previewed during the weekend of Pearl Harbor. More pertinent is the fact that, around this time, Stevens had had a private viewing of Leni Riefenstahl's documentary of the Nuremberg rallies, *Triumph of the Will* (1934), her hymn to the spirit of Hitler youth and the invincibility of the German army. He had been both awed and appalled. He was to say that its immediate impact on him was two-fold: a feeling that he must enlist at the earliest opportunity to join with the Allied forces against Hitler; and a sudden recognition that "all film," including his own, "was propaganda," even a comedy like *Woman of the Year*. In her chapter on the film, Marilyn Ann Moss has argued that the film "collapses the figures of Leni Riefenstahl and Tess Harding" and that Tess is to be understood as a Riefenstahl surrogate, a dan-gerously seductive political animal who represents "the threat to America by anything European, anything related to foreign governments or citizens, anything that happened to do with 'otherness' at a time when war seemed imminent and traditional American values needed to be shored up, protected and secured" (Moss: 81). In this regard, Sam's ultimate victory over Tess could be seen as a political rather than sexual victory; and that the film's so-called anti-feminism should be viewed and understood in the context of a larger political agenda that promotes the American way of life.

I also believe that *Triumph of the Will* cast a long and significant shadow over *Woman of the Year,* but I interpret this differently. It seems to me that the prototype for the Tess Harding character is not Leni Riefenstahl but the American political journalist Dorothy Thompson, who had been described by *Time* magazine in June 1939 as second only to America's First Lady Eleanor Roosevelt as the most influential woman in the U.S. (Pinkie explicitly quotes this comment in his bar while listening to Tess on the radio along with the sports journalists, thus making the link between Tess and Dorothy Thompson quite unmistakable.) Thompson was the absolute antithesis of Leni Riefenstahl; and indeed in the year that Riefenstahl was composing her paean of praise to Hitler's regime, Thompson was becoming the first American journalist to be expelled from Nazi Germany on account of her hostility to Hitler. In 1932 she had published a highly unflattering portrait of the dictator, *I Saw Hitler!,* which included a description of him as "formless, almost faceless, a man whose countenance is a caricature…. He is inconsequential and voluble, ill-poised, insecure. He is the very prototype of the 'Little Man'" (qtd in Hertog: 191). If she can be criticized for underestimating the danger that Hitler represented (and she was hardly alone in that), it is nevertheless apparent that her opinion of him is as far removed from Riefenstahl's adulation as could possibly be imagined.

My view is that Stevens sees Tess as the genuine heroine of the film and substantially endorses what she stands for; and that it is Sam whose isolationist values have to be challenged in the broader context of the world situation. Stevens' sympathy for his heroine would certainly be more consistent with the treatment of the heroines in his films thus far. More than that, though, Tess's world outlook at that time was much closer to that of Stevens than Sam's. When Tess is literally bringing the seriousness of the European situation home and indeed into their bedroom, not as an abstraction but in the physical form of political exiles and child refugees, Sam's instinct (implicitly, America's) is to eject them as soon as possible as having nothing to do with him. This was the opposite of Stevens's attitude. We have already seen that his first impulse on seeing *Triumph of the Will* was not to barricade his home against outsiders but to enlist in support of the Allies. He could have made a strong case for staying at home, justifying it by making uplifting films to bolster morale. After all, he was nearly 40; he had a wife and young son to support; he was president of the Screen Directors Guild, which was a position of some responsibility; he was still under contract to Columbia Pictures, at a time when his career was beginning to soar, but with no guarantee that he would be able to resume it on the same footing after the war, even if he survived. He also had an asthmatic condition which could certainly have got him excused from any form of military service on medical grounds. (Indeed, in January 1943, while he was finishing the editing of *The More the Merrier,* he was rushed to hospital to undergo an emergency appendectomy.) Nevertheless, at some considerable sacrifice to his own domestic comforts, he chose to become involved, believing that the situation was too serious to stand idly by in the hope that the crisis would not be brought closer to home. This makes him Tess's ally in the film, not her antagonist.

As additional confirmation of this interpretation, one can cite *Vigil in the Night,* which Stevens saw as a war film; began shooting on the day war was declared in Europe; and was prevented by RKO executives from including a radio broadcast announcing the outbreak of war for fear it might be construed as going against America's policy of isolationism. Nevertheless, he did go on to defy Hollywood convention by rejecting the novel's romantic ending in favor of a more practical one, when Carole Lombard's heroine, brushing aside the hero's romantic overtures, says, "Come, my doctor, we have *work* to do." It is a sentiment that anticipates something which Tess Harding will say when she is addressing her Women's Convention: "Our place is no longer only in the home; it is also in the first line of battle."

So where does this leave the final breakfast scene? Although conceding that *Woman of the Year* was a good movie, the *New Yorker* (7 February 1942), suggested that it might have been a better idea to have made it about a woman who persuades her man to "give up writing stories about games played by other people and take a grown-up interest in the collapse of the planet" whereas "the film has it just the other way around." My view is that Stevens not only recognized that, but agreed with it, and that this breakfast scene is overelaborated to the point where audiences are invited to come to the same conclusion. In this regard, it reminds me of the epic fistfight between Gregory Peck's pacific Easterner and Charlton Heston's belligerent Westerner in William Wyler's *The Big Country* (1958), which Wyler films for the most part in detached, even disdainful long-shot, as if emphasizing the absurdity of this contest of masculinity that Peck goes through precisely to expose its pointlessness. At the end of this exhaustingly inconclusive encounter, he turns to Heston and says: "Tell me, what did we prove?" It seems to me that Stevens' ultrapatient contemplation of his heroine's domestic inadequacy has a similar implication. So she cannot brew coffee or make waffles. So what? What does that prove? Doesn't America, and the world, have rather larger things to be worried about at that moment?

In fact, Stevens insinuates a telling brief coda to enforce the point. In the middle of their reconciliation, Tess and Sam are interrupted by the arrival of Tess's officious secretary, Gerald, who rushes in with a bottle of champagne to remind her that she is due to launch a ship that morning. Sam ushers him out onto the balcony; we hear a crash; and Sam returns to tell Tess that he has launched Gerald. A light comedy ending perhaps, but Sam has earlier referred to Gerald as "the little corporal," which was Churchill's phrase for Hitler (denoting his size and lowly status). In now opposing Gerald for the first time, might one suggest that, symbolically at least, Sam has finally come off his fence of isolationism and taken his tentative first step in the fight against fascism?

One flashes back to the placards at the opening of the film. "Hitler Will Lose, says Tess Harding." In the dark days towards the end of 1941, that was anything but a foregone conclusion; but she was right. "The Yankees Won't Lose" says Sam Craig in the *New York Chronicle*. Sam was right also; but, in the grand scheme of things, that prediction now looks far less important.

The Talk of the Town (1942)

> "This was one of the more successful screen attempts in the forties to combine man-woman screwballish entertainment with serious-minded moral enlightenment."—Andrew Sarris

> "Some people write novels. Some people write music. I make speeches on street corners."—Cary Grant as Leopold Dilg in *The Talk of the Town*

Was Steven Spielberg watching *The Talk of the Town* shortly before making his fine Cold War drama *Bridge of Spies* (2015)? When one views them in close proximity, one is struck by their similarities. Both deal with the growing friendship between a condemned man and a senior member of the law profession who will overcome his initial reluctance to get involved and become a staunch defender of the accused man's rights under the Constitution. In both films the lawyers make impassioned speeches that invoke the basic principles of the American Constitution in guaranteeing the right to justice and protection under the law of every citizen brought to trial, irrespective of ethnicity or ideology; this guarantee is at the root of what America stands for. Both films are critical of media manipulation and wary of the volatility of public opinion at a time of political and social unrest. In Stevens's film, the talk of the town is articulated not by the townspeople themselves but by a series of exclamatory newspaper headlines and by those in power and for their own ends. In Spielberg's film also, Tom Hanks's hero finds his family physically threatened by a populace whose rage has been calculatedly stirred by the owners of the press and by television.

The condemned man, Cary Grant in *The Talk of the Town* has something of the fatalism of Mark Rylance's character ("Would it help?") in *Bridge of Spies*, being a lone voice in a wilderness of entrenched opinion and hostile, even death-demanding opposition.

Rylance's phony Soviet family, produced by the authorities in the Embassy in Berlin for Hanks's benefit, has its equivalent in *The Talk of the Town,* with the phony girlfriend, Regina (Glenda Farrell), supposedly grieving for her boyfriend, Clyde Bracken (Tom Tyler), who has allegedly perished in the fire, but actually being in the pay of the corrupt mill owner (Charles Dingle). Ronald Colman's law professor in the Stevens film, like the Hanks character in the Spielberg, has to go through an experience that takes him outside of his previously cocooned existence and brings him into contact with the real world, a move that jeopardizes his career and places him in physical danger, but an experience that will modify his perspective on life. Hanks will move from his enclosed boardroom and comfortable home environment to Berlin at the height of international tension; Colman will move from his ivory tower of academia to an awareness of judicial and corporate corruption in small-town America that will culminate in a confrontation with a lynch mob. The humor involving food—the fried eggs in *Talk of the Town,* the marmalade in *Bridge of Spies*—is offset by the scenes in the Supreme Court of both films, which are suitably solemn and dignified. Both films show how conversation more than confrontation can dissolve divisions; where even ideological opposites (as embodied by the two main characters in each film) can find common ground and a shared humanity; and, in so doing, give some hope even in the darkest of times about the future.

Although nominated for seven Hollywood Academy Awards, including Best Picture, *The Talk of the Town* tends to be surprisingly neglected or even disparaged in discussion of Stevens's work. Stevens himself never seems to have talked about it in any of his published interviews, probably because he was never asked. Most articles about Stevens only mention it in passing, if at all; and even some of Stevens's most eloquent advocates regard it as a misfire. For example, Douglas McVay thought its "eccentric humour mixed with a serious attack on judicial corruption" was " an uneasy amalgam, which only Capra at his pre-war best could, one feels, have satisfyingly blended" (McVay: 10). Eugene Archer felt much the same, describing the film as "a motley conglomeration of farce and social significance [that] mixes melodrama and satire in uneven and unsuccessful proportions." He concluded: "This curious film, largely derivative in both script and direction, suffers from contrast with the originality of Preston Sturges' comedies of the same period, and conclusively proves that the Capra mantle, to which Stevens may have aspired, was well beyond his range" (Archer: 30).

However, it is possible to see the film not as an attempt to blend the characteristics of Sturges and Capra but to steer a middle course between them, tempering the raucousness of the former and the sentimentality of the latter and emerging with a warm and wry (but not blinkered) view of humanity that is distinctively Stevens's own. Certainly it has an unusual concoction of ingredients that requires the deftest of touches from director and stars, but Stevens's gift for civilized comedy and thoughtful drama was demonstrably the equal of any Hollywood filmmaker of the time, so it is no surprise that he could combine the two. Also, in Cary Grant, Jean Arthur and Ronald Colman, he had performers with all the requisite poise, polish and precision that one could possibly wish for in realizing his intentions.

Wittily scripted by Irwin Shaw and Sidney Buchman, *The Talk of the Town* is a comedy drama-cum-thriller about a labor organizer, Leopold Dilg (Cary Grant), a thorn in the side of management because of his allegations of cost-cutting and corruption at the factory where he works, who is framed for arson and murder. He is then tried and sentenced to death by Judge Grunstadt (George Watts), who is in the pocket of corporate and governmental interests. Escaping from his prison cell, Dilg hides in the rented cottage of a teacher and former school friend, Nora Shelley (Jean Arthur), on the very night when an eminent law professor, Michael Lightcap (Ronald Colman) turns up early to take up occupancy. The first part of the film deals with the growing friendship between Lightcap and Dilg, who at first pretends to be the gardener, Joseph. He engages Lightcap in stimulating games of chess and in discussions of the law, where his first-hand knowledge of its manipulation by powerful civic forces clashes with Lightcap's trust in its cold logic and objective precision. When Lightcap discovers Dilg's true identity, his instinct is to turn him in to the police, at which point Dilg knocks him out and goes on the run again. The second part deals with the Professor's modification of his legalistic rigidity when he becomes aware that it is not always synonymous with justice. There are two complicating factors. Lightcap is in the process of being appointed to the Supreme Court and is made aware that he must steer clear of any publicity or involvement with a case that might impair his reputation for impartiality. Also he is falling in love with Nora, who is often the arbiter of commonsense between two intelligent men who, in extreme circumstances, are apt to behave like naughty boys.

Stevens wastes no time in launching his narrative. Barely has his name vanished from the credits than the screen is engulfed in flames, with a series of headlines in the *Lochester Sentinel* proclaiming the arson attack on Holmes's Mills and the death of a man inside; the arrest and trial of the man accused of the crime, Leopold Dilg; and his conviction and death sentence. The sweep of the narrative parallels the rush to judgment that permits little time for contemplation, investigation or shades of doubt. It is reminiscent of the mood and even style (with its use of dark shadow to accentuate the shady processes of the media and the law) of Fritz Lang's first American film, *Fury* (1936), an enduring indictment of mob hysteria. The ominous atmosphere continues as Dilg overpowers a guard and makes a desperate escape bid in a violent rainstorm. It is evident from this section alone that Stevens would have been stylistically capable of film noir if his temperament had run that way; but, almost without breaking stride, he swerves nonchalantly into comedy as Dilg begs Nora Shelley for protection before passing out with pain, only to be revived again when Nora pours water on his face but has the courtesy to apologize before doing so.

The comic business escalates as Dilg's intrusion into Nora's abode coincides with the arrival of its paying guest, the distinguished (and unsuspecting) dean of the Commonwealth Law School, Michael Lightcap. The suspense of concealment is adroitly combined with the mechanics of farce, replete with unexpected openings of doors; surprised occupancy of rooms; one of the protagonists being completely unaware of the motives and actions of the other; and a madcap heroine running from room to room and at various times required to juggle with an umbrella, a candle, and a telephone cord in her desperate attempts to keep up a pretense of near-normality. In the process she is required to invent ever more outlandish excuses to account for her continued presence in the house. "She must have adenoids," Lightcap muses, as he hears loud snoring emanating from another room (it is actually Leopold) and she quickly confirms his diagnosis to alleviate suspicion. When she has first returned unexpectedly and is discovered by Lightcap, she has to fabricate a story about an argument with her mother (Emma Dunn), which has led to her storming out of their home and having to come back to the cottage to spend the night. To add credence to the story, she asks if she may borrow a pair of Professor's Lightcap's pajamas, which will in turn lead to a delirious series of misunderstandings in the morning, as the house is besieged by a local reporter (Lloyd Bridges), who thinks they are the latest in ill-fitting fashion; her mother, who jumps to completely the wrong conclusion; a posse of delivery men; the police; and Dilg's lawyer, Sam Yates (Edgar Buchanan). All of this mayhem is supremely timed and has been prefaced by two great comedy moments: a wonderful shot where, at the end of a singularly eventful evening, the camera has done a deadpan reconnaissance of the premises as if to check where the occupants have finally ended up; and a moment in the morning, when Nora, in Lightcap's unflatteringly floppy pajamas, pauses before a mirror and murmurs "Lovely, lovely" at her reflection. Jean Arthur delivers the line with a mischievous vocal impression of Katharine Hepburn. The peak of Nora's (and Jean Arthur's) comic invention will occur later when, noticing that Professor Lightcap is about to read his morning newspaper, she screams and slides a pair of fried eggs (sunny side up) over a front-page picture of Dilg that would give away gardener Joseph's identity. She even has the presence of mind to furnish an explanation for such behavior to the astonished Professor: "It's not your egg morning!" Stevens thought Jean Arthur was one of the greatest comedians the screen had ever seen; and if anyone wanted confirmation of this, her performance in *The Talk of the Town* provides ample evidence.

On one level, the film might seem to fit the formula of a conventional Hollywood romantic comedy, with Jean Arthur torn between two men, both of whom she loves and who both love her, but in completely different ways. Who to choose? One incident encapsulates her confusion to perfection, when Nora kisses Lightcap in gratitude for knocking Dilg unconscious and then, to the Professor's bemusement, turns to kiss Dilg in the hope of his quick recovery. The balance of attractions is so delicately poised that Stevens shot two endings and allowed preview audiences to vote on whether she should end up with Grant or with Colman. According to Marilyn Moss, "audience opinions ranged from the logical to the outlandish" (Moss: 96). One pollster thought she should marry Grant because he needed her more than Colman did, while others shared that preference but for different reasons (e.g., Colman's beard made him look suspicious and, anyway, he was such a gracious loser in films). Stevens delays the resolution until the very last shot, when after a romantic kiss with Lightcap in his chambers at the Supreme Court, Nora confronts Dilg and kisses him. Dilg walks away and exits left out of the frame, then suddenly reappears, and takes Nora with him, leaving an audience staring at the closed door of the Supreme Court, which is now in session. With Dilg's gesture seeming almost like an afterthought, this finale is absolutely in keeping with the nature and tone of a film that has kept an audience continually off-balance or on its toes. Visually the romantic coupling that one expects at the end of a traditional Hollywood movie could hardly be more decentered.

The choice has been made for the heroine, but is it the correct one? While respecting the wishes of his audience in the matter, Stevens slyly allows for an element of doubt. The fact that he gives more visual weight to the kiss she shares with Lightcap than the one she will then share with Dilg might be a tease to add to the ending's frisson of surprise, but it might also signal where his own preference lay. "I wonder if I can say this just as I want to," says Lightcap in his chambers to Nora; it sounds almost as if Stevens is wondering whether he can make this convincing. Lightcap argues that he has attained his dream and has more happiness than anyone has a right to expect; and therefore hopes that his great friend Leopold deserves equal happiness with a fine woman who can love him for the rest of his life (and perhaps save him from himself?). Nora cannot fail to pick up his drift, yet is there the faintest hint of self-sacrifice on the part of both of them? As Nora leaves the Supreme Court Office to follow Dilg, she turns and looks back in the direction of Lightcap before exiting. In his final close-up, Lightcap looks down and seems momentarily pensive and thoughtful. Even Dilg, as he hurries away from the session, seems surprised when she calls out to him. "Our country's in good hands," he says of Lightcap, and, significantly, gives a lot of the credit for this to Nora. "The woman's touch," he says. "Indispensable." (A Stevens' sentiment if ever there was one.) When she kisses him, it takes him a moment to appreciate its significance as a declaration of romantic preference. The last shot suggests that he still cannot quite believe it, but had better quickly take advantage before she changes her mind. Yet, on consideration, Nora is passing up a career in Washington to return to a small town she despises and whose inhabitants she has described at one stage as "bloodthirsty idiots" (and there is nothing in the film that would contradict this assessment). Dilg, who has been described as the town's "only honest man," is returning to a place whose populace not long before had formed a mob which had stormed the court with placards that read, among other things, "Quick Justice for Dilg," i.e., a lynching. One cannot think that the removal of an ignorant judge and a corrupt factory owner is going to make that much difference to the town's complexion. Stevens might be paying lip service to the conventions of romantic comedy with his ending and satisfying his audience's wishes, but he seems also to be signaling that his priorities and preferences lie elsewhere.

The romantic triangle is an odd anticipation of *Shane*, in which Jean Arthur will once again be torn between two men she loves and who at one stage will be shrieking in horror as the two men are driven to fight each other. "They're both nuts!" she exclaims in *The Talk of the Town*, when they are acting according to a code of honor that seems to her absurd; and in *Shane* she will be similarly exasperated by foolish, possibly fatal displays of masculine pride, though in the later film the tone will be much more anguished (as if reflecting how much more serious Stevens had become in the meantime). Even the basic situation is structurally similar to *Shane*: a stranger arrives in a household and— at first reluctantly and then decisively—becomes drawn into the dilemma of its beleaguered hero and has finally to act as his savior. An important thing it has in common is its ambivalence towards violence. There is a moment early on in the film when Lightcap has just arrived at the cottage and is complaining about the mess, at which Nora turns on him ferociously and claims that everything would have been okay if he had not arrived a day early, so he has no one to blame but himself. Taken aback by her vehemence, he responds: "There's a certain justice in what you say, but the violence." That could be the most important line in the film. He is objecting to the violence behind the expression of the sentiments rather than the substance of the sentiments themselves, but it prefigures a key theme in the film, which will be the relationship between justice and violence and whether, in a situation of extreme crisis, the logic and letter of the law will be sufficient to prevent injustice or whether more extreme measures will be called for.

Lightcap has come to his summer retreat at Sweetbrook to write a book on the relationship between literature and legislation in the 18th century. As the so-called "Age of Reason," the 18th century is Lightcap's ideal of civilization, the "highpoint of man's intellectual development," as he puts it. However in his disguise as Joseph the gardener, Dilg will argue with Lightcap that this is impossibly idealistic; and that, in his trust in the impersonal application and cold logic of the law as a guard against intemperate imagination and emotion, the Professor is investing too much faith in rationality and ignoring the way the law can be twisted to serve the needs of the powerful. Dilg, Nora and Sam Yates conspire to try and "thaw" Lightcap a little and bring him down from his pedestal by taking him to a baseball game in town. Donald Ritchie wrote of this development that Lightcap "is softened up by that great spiritual tonic, a real American baseball game" (Richie: 18), but this is not actually what happens. Although it might appear similar to the sports scene in *Woman of the Year,* where Katharine Hepburn is taught the rudiments of American football in order to understand better the national character and then gets carried away with enthusiasm, Colman's Professor shows not the slightest interest in the game. What changes his attitude is his encounter in the stadium with Judge Grunstadt, who is gloating over the way the Dilg case has brought him to national prominence and reveals that he has made up his mind about Dilg's guilt and is writing up his opinion before he has seen all the evidence. This is contrary to everything that Lightcap believes about the law's impartiality, objectivity and scrupulous weighing and presentation of fact. It is not American baseball that turns his head; it is his awareness of flagrant judicial bias.

Later that night another incident occurs that will act on Lightcap's sensibility. Police dogs have picked up Dilg's scent and are nearing the cottage. In hiding from them, Dilg leaves his slippers outside his bedroom door; and in absent-mindedly slipping them on his own feet when going downstairs, Lightcap finds himself suddenly being pursued by rampaging hounds. It is a good example of the film's deft combination of comedy and seriousness, for, while the chase makes for good farcical fun, one is also aware that, in literally stepping into Dilg's shoes, Lightcap has suddenly been made directly aware of what it feels like to be a fugitive from the law and in fear of one's life.

When Lightcap storms into Judge Grunstadt's courtroom towards the end of the film with the real guilty party in tow, he has to fire a gun to make himself heard and to stop in its tracks a crowd that is baying for the accused man's blood. It is the culmination of an escalation of violence in which he has been involved and which has turned him from a disinterested outsider into a moral crusader on behalf of American justice. As we have seen, it has begun with his doubts about Judge Grunstadt, and also his doubts about the credibility of the supposedly dead man's girlfriend, Regina. He has taken to heart Nora's denunciation of him, when she accuses him of hiding behind the procedures of the law (and also behind his beard, supposedly signifying the maturity of middle age) and, in so doing, allowing the persecution and possible execution of an innocent man. To the strains of Wagner over the soundtrack and in defiance of his assistant, Tilney (Rex Ingram), he will shave off his beard as a way of acknowledging his new openness to the world. (The big close-up of Tilney in tears might be gilding the lily somewhat, but it is perhaps designed to emphasize in a funny and sentimental way the grandeur of Lightcap's sacrifice.) Deferring to Tilney's superior advice and experience in such matters, he will inexpertly take Regina on a date, ostensibly for romantic reasons, actually to extract information. Earlier he has lied to the police when he has claimed that the borscht he had purchased in town was for himself and not for Dilg. Later he is compelled to knock Dilg unconscious to stop him from turning himself in to the police, which the Professor now recognizes will mean almost certain death. When they trace and capture Clyde Bracken, whom Holmes, for his own ends, has insisted was killed in a fire started by Dilg, both the Professor and Dilg are compelled to use force in overpowering Bracken. Indeed Stevens endorses the use of violence by inserting a shot of Nora's taking a wrench out of her pocket, clearly in readiness to join the fray herself and use it as a weapon if

Bracken cannot be subdued. In the car-drive back to Lochester, Bracken is threatened with further violence if he refuses to confess his role in the framing of Dilg. All of this is a very long way from Lightcap's earlier belief in the power of reason and the application of legalistic logic to bring about justice.

While noting that the film was "not primarily frivolous," Penelope Houston suggested that "a fair amount of lecturing on corruption and civic duty was adroitly camouflaged by the smooth and civilized surface of the comedy" (Houston: 74). Yet it is not finally the comedy that the film is foregrounding, but the need for involvement. In this sense it is a continuation of the argument of *Woman of the Year*: that is, it is not enough to sit on the sidelines complacently extolling American values and the American way of life; the time has come for action against dangerous demagoguery. The real theme of the film is not who will win Nora's heart (which is the reason that Stevens can be so visually non-chalant about it) but the political education of a clever and decent man (immaculately played by Colman) who will come to acknowledge the inadequacy of his bookish and theoretical approach to life when it comes into contact with the harshness of modern times. Early on Professor Lightcap has told Nora that "there is a nervous impulsive quality in you that I find in my students—a disease of the age." In fact, Nora (and Lightcap's students) have a good deal to be nervous about; and the disease of the age is not nervousness or impulsiveness but moral complacency. The Age of Reason might have been Lightcap's ideal, but that is not the age we live in; and it certainly was not the case in 1942. Hence the disturbing evocation of mob mania, which bursts the bounds of romantic comedy; hence the Professor's speech in the courtroom, reminding the townspeople of the values enshrined in the Constitution which cherish judicial fairness and individual freedom. "Think of a world crying for this very law," he says, and declares that it is something worth battling for, "for our neighbors as well as ourselves." The application of these words to the global situation could hardly be clearer, for these values are now imperiled across the world. Madness and fanaticism are on the march; reason on its own will not be enough to stop it. Once again one senses that what was uppermost in Stevens's mind when he made this film was not who should end up with Jean Arthur but the war in Europe. It is a sparkling and entertaining movie, but behind the film's camouflage of comedy and romance is a call to arms.

The More the Merrier (1943)

> "I quit the film business to go into the army. I wanted to be in the war—I really didn't want to make films at that time. I had the opportunity to go overseas right away if I went into the army at a certain time, as soon as I'd finished *The More the Merrier*. I previewed that picture two nights in a row, then I left for North Africa and never heard about the picture until I was in England three months later."—George Stevens, 1967

> "One of the most sophisticated and charming home-front romantic comedies of the era…. Stevens created a romantic fairy-tale with one foot in contemporary reality."—Mark Harris

In his 1974 interview with Patrick McGilligan and Joseph McBride, Stevens said about *The More the Merrier* that "we had fun on that picture…. I knew it was my last picture, and I had a limited time to do it, and I wanted to enjoy it" (qtd in Cronin: 112). His reference to it as "my last picture" thirty years after the event is quite striking. He might simply have meant that it was his last film in fulfilment of his Columbia contract. As he was shortly going off to war, he knew it might also be his last film in the sense that he could not be certain of his own survival. Also, as his agent at the time Charles Feldman kept reminding him, it was not inevitable that, given the possible duration of the war, there would be a job waiting for him when he returned. As it happened, on the completion of *The More the Merrier,* Harry Cohn had circulated an internal office memo (1 February 1943) to inform staff that Stevens was leaving at the end of the week to serve his country and that "anyone to whom you assign this office must take it with the understanding that he will vacate it when Mr. Stevens returns." To Cohn's undying chagrin, Stevens was to sign up with Liberty Pictures on his return, causing a rift between the two of them that was never repaired and which Stevens always regretted.

There could have been other implications behind Stevens's feeling at that time that *The More the Merrier* might be his last film. Would he want to renew his directing career? And if not overtly a farewell to the cinema, *The More the Merrier* does look like a summation of his career thus far, with frequent allusions to his earlier work. It is the concluding part of what could be regarded as his unofficial War Trilogy with comedy overtones, but whereas the two preceding films (*Woman of the Year, The Talk of the Town*) carry a serious message beneath the comedy camouflage, *The More the Merrier* is the other way round: the war context is more overt, but the comedy is more insistent. It is undoubtedly the merriest of the three films. The situation of a woman torn between two lovers or suitors refers back to similar situations in *Annie Oakley, Swing Time* and *The Talk of the Town.* Jean Arthur's first romantic encounter with Joel McCrae, with her face covered with cream, recalls the moment in *Swing Time,* when, having lovingly crooned "The Way You Look Tonight," Fred Astaire turns to find Ginger Rogers with her hair covered in shampoo. When we watch Jean Arthur crying in her room after the discovery of her diary, with the rain on the window seeming to match her tears, we are reminded of a similar image in *Alice Adams* that carries the same poignant charge. There is an elaborate comedy set piece (the heroine's morning schedule) that is as extended and inventive as the disastrous dinner party in *Alice Adams,* the baby-changing routine in *Penny Serenade,* and the breakfast scene in *Woman of the Year.* And there are two visual tropes that mark out the film as unmistakably Stevens's work. The first is the plethora of window shots. "No one but Stevens uses windows in so peculiar and personal a fashion," observed Donald Richie (49), and one has already noted this in *Alice Adams, Quality Street, Vigil in the Night,* and *The Talk of the Town,* where there is also sometimes a storm raging outside that is either a correlative to, or portent of, the torments within. Richie thought these recurrent window shots were an aspect of Stevens's interest in the outsider, but, in *The More the Merrier,* the window shots are used for a variety of purposes: comedy, visual variety, narrative compression, and sometimes for a suggestion of togetherness even though visually separated, which will culminate in a finale where the movement of McCrae into Jean Arthur's window space will signal an unexpected and satisfying comic denouement. All of this is related to the second unmistakable Stevens' touch, which is his expressive use of cinematic space. If one recalls that Mike Nichols thought that was one aspect of screen direction in which Stevens was unrivalled, then the material of *The More the Merrier* could hardly have been more congenial, because the use of space (in coping with Washington's wartime housing shortage) is actually the film's main theme.

As a farewell film, Stevens might also have thought he could indulge his sense of mischief. Frank Capra once observed that "committee-hating directors were attracted to Columbia," naming Stevens alongside himself, John Ford and Leo McCarey as the main agitators (Capra: 202); and Stevens must have chuckled at the headaches he was leaving in his wake for the studio heads and the censorship bodies. After all, his new film was a comedy that nevertheless touched on sensitivities about the war, something he had been challenging since *Vigil in the Night*; and also studio sensitivities about making films that could be seen to be poking fun at people in the services (which Stevens would not have dreamt of doing). It was a film that could be seen as mocking FBI paranoia during the period. (Stevens might have pleaded guilty to that.) When one remembers that only four years previously, David Selznick had been forced to pay $5000 to the Motion Picture Producers and Distributors of America for the right to use the word "damn" in *Gone with the Wind* (1939), it was certainly provocative for Charles Coburn's tycoon in *The More the Merrier* to have "Damn the torpedoes! Full speed ahead" as his personal mantra. (Admittedly, he is quoting the words of the nineteenth century American Admiral David Glasgow Farragut at the battle of Mobile, so the profanity has a respectable heritage, but the frequency with which he utters it—at least a dozen times in the film—does give the impression that Stevens is pushing the Code as far as he can.) The Hollywood Production Code scarcely allowed for a subject that necessarily showed men and women sharing accommodation space, a situation that tended to vex the censors even if the people in question happened to be married (remember how cleverly Stevens gets round this in *Penny Serenade*). It might also have been wary of a film that highlighted the situation in Washington at that time, where, because of the number of men away at war, the female population outnumbered the male by a ratio of 8 to 1. Its apprehension would only have been intensified when Stevens makes no attempt to disguise the licentious possibilities, particularly in a shot where a male employee has to run the gauntlet of a queue of female office workers who, as they are signing off after their day's work, start wolf-whistling after the departing figure and seem almost to be salivating with lust.

Stevens was to receive his first Oscar nomination for his direction of the film. It was one of six nominations it secured, the others being for Best Picture; Best Actress (Jean Arthur, in what was astonishingly her only Oscar nomination); Best Supporting Actor (Charles Coburn, who won); Best Original Story (Frank Ross and Robert Russell) and Best Screenplay (Richard Flournoy, Lewis R. Foster, Frank Ross and Robert Russell). The screenplay credit literally reads: "Screenplay by Robert Russell & Frank Ross; Richard Flournoy & Lewis R. Foster," which is the only screenplay credit I can recall where the collaborators are separated by a semicolon. This strangely punctilious punctuation could be interpreted as suggesting that it is the product of two joint collaborations: the first between Robert Russell and Frank Ross (who at that time was Jean Arthur's husband); and then between Richard Flournoy (best known as the screenwriter for the popular *Blondie* series of films for Columbia in the late 1930s and 1940s) and Lewis R. Foster (an Oscar winner for his screen story for Capra's 1939 classic, *Mr. Smith Goes to Washington*). However, according to the biographers of both Harry Cohn and Jean Arthur, these credits give little indication of the story and inspiration behind the actual writing of the film.

The screenplay was, it seems, mainly the work of Garson Kanin, who at that time had been drafted and was serving in the Signals Corp at Fort Monmouth. Transferred to the New York headquarters of the film division of the Office for Emergency Management, he had learned of the difficulties of his friend Jean Arthur, who was on suspension from Columbia for having turned down nine scripts in succession. Kanin offered to write one for her in exchange for $25,000, which was far in excess of what he was being paid by the army. This he accomplished in the space of two weeks in collaboration with his fellow draftee, Robert Russell, with the script at that time being called *Two's Company*. Kanin could not be credited on the screenplay, because he was at that time under contract to RKO. He and Russell sold it to Jean Arthur and her husband producer, Frank Ross, who then offered it (with Kanin as intermediary) to Harry Cohn for free, who was naturally suspicious of such seeming generosity from a star with whom he was in almost perpetual conflict. Possibly to eliminate any pre-judgment or bias, Kanin suggested that he read the script aloud to Cohn in his New York office, but, in fact, he did not need to get much further than reading the opening sequence to obtain Cohn's approval.

Stevens had originally wanted Cary Grant for the leading male role, but he was unavailable. (Coincidentally, Grant was to play the Charles Coburn role in the uninspired 1966 remake, *Walk Don't Run*, which was to prove his final film before retiring from the screen.) At an initial production meeting and read-through, Grant's replacement, Joel McCrae seemed uncomfortable and unenthusiastic and let it be known through his agent that he wanted out of the picture. However, Jean Arthur was insistent that he stuck with it; and he was to give a perfectly accomplished performance, his interplay with Arthur being a particular pleasure. There is a delightful scene between them when McCrae has bought her a travelling bag as a peace offering-cum-wedding present and is explaining to her how it works. The scene is mostly done in a single take and seems semi-improvised, until Stevens cuts to a close-up of them together which becomes an almost tangible leap in emotional proximity, the moment when two people are falling in love with each other before they are even aware of it themselves.

The film begins as a Washington travelogue. As the narrator solemnly introduces us to the delights of the capital, among which he includes its pleasant and leisurely lifestyle, its epicurean and gourmet delights and its welcoming atmosphere, his words are being comically undercut by what we actually see: a bustling populace scrambling for transport and for food in overcrowded diners, and particularly for accommodation where every boarding house has a sign that proclaims "No Vacancies." When the businessman Benjamin Dingle (Charles Coburn) finds he cannot move into his hotel room because he is two days early, he must quickly find alternative accommodation. On the way to an advertised room for rent, he passes the statue of the Admiral David Glasgow Farragut, whose declaration, "Damn the Torpedoes. Full Speed Ahead" will provide the impetus behind the behavior of Dingle for the remainder of the film, anticipating the way he will barge into hotels, apartments, conversations, personal diaries, and other people's love affairs. Whatever obstacles are put in his path, he will simply either bypass or walk straight through them. For example, when faced with the queue of people who have assembled outside Constance Milligan's apartment in response to her advertisement of a room for rent, he will simply walk past them up the steps; take down the "Room For Rent" sign; and then calmly inform the people, who have been too engrossed in their newspapers to notice his arrival, that the room has been taken. One quickly surmises that this is a man who is used to getting what he wants and is not too scrupulous about how he gets it. When Miss Milligan (Jean Arthur) says she cannot possibly share her apartment with a man, he has a ready answer for that also, saying how much more convenient it will be for her if she is sharing with someone who will not always be borrowing her clothes and the pretty dress she is wearing. "How would you like it for her to spill a cocktail all over it at the party you couldn't go with her to," he argues, "because she borrowed your dress to wear to it—in?" As is revealed in that example, Dingle's go-getting attitude is even reflected in a sentence structure that sometimes outpaces his thought and which he then finds difficult to conclude in an orderly manner. ("Of all times, Miss Milligan, this is no time to be indecisive—in.") When Connie Milligan has exhausted all the reasons he cannot possibly stay, Dingle simply suggests that they try it for a week and, if it does not work out, "we'll flip a coin to see who moves out." The character could have come over as overbearing and even unpleasant, but Charles Coburn plays it with such a light touch, that one can discern a kind of charm and even courtesy behind the browbeating and an authoritative manner that does not conceal a basic good nature.

However, the arrangement will be sorely tested the following morning. Connie has designed an intricate schedule which will enable them both, without getting in each other's way, to arise at 7 a.m., bring in the milk and morning paper, wash, dress, make their beds, make the coffee, and breakfast, in order for her to be out of the apartment by 7:30 a.m. in readiness for the day's work. Given Stevens's silent comedy experience and his work with Laurel and Hardy, where nothing was more hopeless than a plan of action, it is the kind of sequence he could probably have directed in his sleep, which does not make it any the less clever in construction and hilarious in execution. Connie's schedule, which demands clockwork precision in its execution, will descend into choreographed chaos. During the routine both of them will at different times find themselves locked out of the apartment. In trying to get back in, Dingle will have to climb through another window and appear alarmingly at Connie's bathroom window, gesticulating madly as she is brushing her teeth unaware of his presence outside until the sight of him scares her out of her wits. In trying to fill the coffee pot with water, he inadvertently soaks himself with spray from the shower. He is startled by a collapsing bed, and then he himself collapses equally sharply when Connie unknowingly flattens him by pushing hard at a door behind which he is standing. In hurriedly making his bed, Dingle throws a sheet over his trousers and then cannot find them, a joke which Stevens will ingeniously extend with some elaborate comic business, including a wonderful moment when the suspenders on the trousers get accidentally hooked on a door handle, and, unseen by Dingle, hurtle like an arrow back through the room to land on the ledge outside of his open window. He never does discover how somehow they wind up back on his bed. No sequence illustrates more clearly Stevens's desire to have fun with the material, but without allowing the comedy to stray too far away from recognizable human folly and into contrived slapstick. In narrative terms, it is important because it convinces Dingle that, if he is to continue in that apartment, he will need to recruit another male tenant as ally. In thematic terms, it will anticipate Connie's realization that life has a way of disrupting even the most meticulous of timetables. After all, what could be worse timing than falling in love with a man who is due to go off to the War in less than two weeks' time and whom she might therefore never see again?

The subsequent romantic rapport between hero and heroine will be imaginatively foretold by Stevens before the two even meet. When Connie arrives home that evening, unaware that Dingle has invited a fine upstanding young man, Joe Carter (McCrae), to share his room, she switches on the radio and starts almost involuntarily doing a dance to the music she is listening to, a rumba version of "What Is This Thing Called Love?" Hearing it as he leaves the shower and passes Connie's room, Joe also starts to move instinctively to the rhythm of the music. In a later scene at Dingle's hotel, Joe will dance with Connie to this tune, by which time their attraction to each other has become very evident. Earlier that evening, in order to be with Joe, she has tried and failed to foil an evening date with her fiancé, Charles J. Pendergast (that ever reliable supporting actor, Richard Gaines), surreptitiously slipping the phone off the hook so that his anticipated call cannot get through, only for the receiver to be zealously replaced by a young man, Morton Rodakiewicz (Stanley Clements), who has inconveniently called on Connie for her advice about whether to join the Boy Scouts and sees this as an opportunity to do a good deed. Her date with Pendergast happens to be at the hotel where Dingle is staying and where he has invited Joe for a drink, hence the opportunity for them all to meet and for Dingle to maneuver things so that Joe and Connie can be together. The music helps. Whereas Joe and Connie are in perfect step when dancing to "What Is This Thing Called Love?," Pendergast finds that the music "disturbs me" (it should) and that he cannot concentrate, at which point Dingle whisks him away to his hotel room so that they can discuss business quietly in private. The coast is still not entirely clear. The ratio of men to women in Washington at that time is made manifest when Joe literally finds himself surrounded by eight of Connie's office friends and is led apprehensively to a table that seems to cut off any prospect of retreat as Connie is called to the hotel phone. Fortunately it is Pendergast who is ringing from Dingle's room, suggesting that, as he and Dingle have important business to discuss, perhaps Joe might see her home; he has been reassured by Dingle that it will not be very far out of Joe's way.

On returning home, Connie and Joe sit on the steps leading up to her apartment building and she starts talking about her marriage plans. The scene is similarly structured to the earlier one between them when Joe has been introducing her to the intricacies of the travel bag, but now it is imbued with heightened emotional intensity. It seems semi-improvised and mostly done in a single take; and, as in the earlier scene, what is being said is less important than what is being felt, at which point Stevens cuts to a close-up of the two to signal a rise in romantic temperature. She keeps talking about her future plans with Mr. Pendergast while simultaneously removing Joe's hands from her neck, her arms and her waist, and Joe murmurs a response but is so irresistibly drawn to Connie that at one moment he distractedly kisses her engagement ring. Her awkwardness and restraint derive obviously from the fact that she is already engaged, but also from the fact that their amorous sparring is being played out in public, with other couples in the block adding to the sense of self-consciousness, and where even a cop walks past at one point. Part of the humor comes from the contradiction between the dialogue (at one point Connie starts talking about her cousin's stamp collection) and the visuals (her resistance of Joe's amorous advances); and also from our recognition that, in trying to fend off Joe's advances both verbally and physically, she is also trying—and in vain—to fend off her own attraction to him, with the words merely a cover for the underlying emotion. Unable any longer to resist the deaf acceleration of desire, the two kiss passionately. But what then?

As in *Swing Time, Vivacious Lady* and *Woman of the Year*, erotic feeling seems closely bound up with sexual frustration. In a Stevens film, the course of true love is invariably circuitous and especially in the comedies. Connie is due to be married; Joe is due to be sent to Africa; the timing for the characters (in contrast to the exquisite comedy timing of the two leads) could not be worse. As usual, Stevens comes up with a tender but then hilarious coda. The two are in such a romantic daze, that, in saying goodnight, Connie almost trips on the steps and Joe, tipping his hat and turning away, momentarily forgets that this is where he actually lives. When they move dreamily inside and turn on the light, there is a sudden roar of collective outrage, and they discover that the parlor has been turned into a dormitory for businessmen, who are trying to get some sleep and have little patience with the bittersweet longings of the lovelorn. The more the merrier? Not really. Later that night, lying awake in their separate rooms, the two will converse quietly about the hopelessness of their situations, and both will be close to tears. Stevens will frame them in a shot from outside their windows, with the wall between them splitting the screen in two and giving the sense that they are lying side by side.

The reverie is rudely interrupted by the crashing entry of two FBI agents, who have come to detain Joe on suspicion of being a Japanese spy. They are acting on a tip-off from that keen Boy Scout, who has seen Joe pointing a pair of binoculars in the direction of a government printing office. (He has actually been pointing it at Connie as she is being escorted into a cab by Pendergast, who at that stage Joe has never seen.) For verification that Joe is a sergeant on Special Duty and that Connie is indeed his landlady, Pringle has been sent for, and he arrives at the police station with Pendergast, who is surprised to see Connie there and then appalled to learn that she and Joe share the same address. The engagement is called off; and a hasty marriage is arranged by Pringle between Joe and Connie to avoid a scandal. There are some funny moments in this final section (Pendergast's slippery slide across the rain-soaked street, as he desperately tries to stop a reporter from writing a scandalous story about his break-up with Connie, is a spectacular piece of slapstick), but I tend to agree with Andrew Sarris when he writes that "the resolution of the romance is saddled with very contrived farcical devices" and that " the movie runs out of steam before the final black-out fade-out" (Sarris: 360). Yet the very ending of the film does have its felicities, managing to be sexy, nostalgic and moving all at the same time. When Joe has returned to the apartment with Connie to pack his things, they are talking together for quite a while before they notice that they are actually in the same room. At which point Dingle (for it is he who has organized the demolition of the division) completes one of the film's running jokes when he changes the name plate on the apartment door to read "Sergeant and Mrs. Joe Carter." He then joins his cronies on the stairs to sing his theme tune one last time to the newlyweds. The saucy sexual innuendo in the lyrics is unmistakable and must have seemed rather bold at the time. At the same time the situation of a newly married couple having to make the most of their short time together before parting is a suddenly sad reminder of *Penny Serenade*. In having Dingle tear down the physical barrier that has previously separated two people in love, Stevens is perhaps paying an affectionate homage to the famous "Walls of Jericho" motif in one of Columbia's greatest successes, Frank Capra's *It Happened One Night* (1934), a parting joke and gift to Harry Cohn and the studio Stevens was leaving. Yet, even amid the happiness and the humor, one cannot quite forget that Joe (like Stevens, in fact) will very shortly be leaving for Africa and might never return. The film fades momentarily to black before the final fade-out. It offers a subliminal moment of reflection, and perhaps even a shiver of apprehension, as we recognize that a war that has brought this couple together is also forcing them to part.

• THREE •

From World War to Cold War, 1943–1948

"I want to say something not only about George but about some of the other men who were his colleagues, like Capra, Huston and Litvak. These were men who were highly successful, who were way past military age, who were all rather pacifistic.... And one and all they gave up very lucrative and very prestigious careers and went right in, as soon as they could, into the army.... You mustn't forget that aspect of Hollywood. Hollywood has been so attacked, including by me, but we must not forget some of the marvellous men who came out of it. People who sacrificed themselves and their careers to serve their government."—Irwin Shaw, 1982

"After seeing the camps, I was an entirely different person. I knew there is brutality in war and the SS were lousy bastards, but the destruction of people like this was beyond comprehension.... You're disturbed by being of the human race."—George Stevens, 1967

Near the end of Irwin Shaw's classic World War II novel, *The Young Lions* (1949), when the Allies are liberating the concentration camp at Dachau, there is a scene where one of the survivors, a rabbi, asks the American officer in charge, Captain Green, if he can hold a religious service for the dead. An Albanian diplomat, who has been advising Captain Green, counsels against it, as he says a Hebrew religious service will create a lot of bad feeling and that the other prisoners will not stand for it. Green promptly orders the service to go ahead and tells the Albanian that anyone who attempts to interfere with the service will be summarily dealt with; and that, if the Albanian ever sets foot in his office again, he will be arrested. Afterwards the novel's main character, Noah Ackerman, who has been listening intently to this exchange, says loudly to his friend Michael Whitacre that "I have a lot of hope for Captain Green.... When the war is over, Green is going to run the world, not that damned Albanian" (Shaw: 804). Shaw acknowledged that the character of Captain Green was modeled on that of his own commanding officer, George Stevens.

Stevens had left Los Angeles for military service in February 1943, having recently recovered from a bout of pneumonia. Despite his recurrent ill health and being way past military age, which could easily have excused him from military service, he never wavered in his determination to do his duty, as he saw it, in the fight for democracy. He was made a major in the U.S. Army Signals Corp whose overall assignment was to compile a photographic record of Allied activity during the war. He saw his role as a link between covering what was happening in the war and reporting it as honestly as he could to the people back home while recognizing the importance of boosting morale. To begin with, he had been sent to Africa to cover combat clear-up in the North African campaign, and he also had spells in Persia and in London. His major assignment occurred when he received orders from General Eisenhower to organize and co-ordinate a 45-man Special Coverage Unit, attached to Supreme Headquarters Allied Expeditionary Force, to film the invasion of Europe, from D-Day 6 June 1944 to the day of Germany's surrender on 7 May 1945. The Unit was to become known as "Stevens' Irregulars," with Stevens leading from the front in a jeep that had "Toluca" printed on it, to remind him of Toluca Lake back home. The Unit included Ernest Hemingway's brother, Leicester; the writers William Saroyan, Irwin Shaw and Ivan Moffat; and the cameramen William Mellor and Joseph Biroc. After the war, Moffat and Mellor were to become key collaborators on Stevens' films, and Joseph Biroc was to go on to photograph Capra's *It's a Wonderful Life* and many films for Robert Aldrich.

As this book is a critical study of Stevens' films and not a full biography, his war experience can be seen as a sort of intermission in his filmmaking career, though a profoundly significant one. The finest written account of Stevens' war experience is contained in Mark Harris's magnificent book, *Five Came Back*. The most evocative and moving visual account is contained in the documentary, *George Stevens: D-Day to Berlin* (1998), directed and introduced by George Stevens, Jr. Historically the documentary covers roughly the same ground as Carol Reed's and Garson Kanin's Oscar–winning *The True Glory* (1945). However, whereas the Reed/Kanin film is an official visual record of the campaign in Europe, edited from over six million feet of film compiled by over 700 front-line cameramen and endorsed by General Eisenhower, George Stevens, Jr.'s film is an edited compilation of the footage that his father filmed as a personal diary during his coverage of the Allied advance, with the unique characteristic that his footage was shot in color. Among numerous striking moments are: the captain on board the HMS Belfast reading aloud to his men the "band of brothers" passage from Shakespeare's *Henry V* as they prepare to be the first warship to land on the Normandy beach (hard not to suspect that Steven Spielberg was heavily influenced by this section when he came to make *Saving Private Ryan*); the stunned reaction of the camera team at the destruction they encounter as they move through towns and villages; and Stevens's filming of the liberation of Paris, achieved by his obtaining the written permission of the French General Philippe Leclerc for his unit to join the French 2nd Army Division to secure this exclusive footage ahead of the Allied forces. We see Stevens and his team taking the salute from General de Gaulle in Paris before rejoining the American Army offensive. Stevens was to tell his son that this day (25 August 1944) was to be "the greatest day of his life," a state of euphoria also felt by his comrade Irwin Shaw, who bet him that the war would be over by October. Alas, as the film notes, the Germans were to launch a counteroffensive (the Battle of the Bulge), which would prolong the conflict for another year; result in a further 68,000 American casualties; and leave the Belgian countryside devastated. Crossing the Rhine, the Stevens unit is shown filming the discovery of the huge underground factory at Nord-hausen, where the V.I. flying bomb was constructed; and on 25 April 1945, covering the first link-up between Allied and Russian troops at Torgau. As well as covering the military events, Stevens's home movie also finds time to capture more intimate moments: haircuts for the men; listening to Glenn Miller on the radio; Stevens himself delightedly displaying a Christmas present from his son.

Although they had seen terrible casualties on their journey and filmed the haunted demoralized faces of thousands of German prisoners of war traumatized by the prospect of imminent defeat, nothing could prepare Stevens's film unit for the horror that confronted them when they join the Allied forces in the liberation of Dachau concentration camp. The documentary shows but does not dwell on the terrible footage; it does not need to. The commentary reports that 122 SS guards were shot as reprisal and a typhus epidemic that was sweeping the camp had to be contained. Stevens' final act of the war was to visit Hitler's mountain hideaway and then head to Berlin to see the Olympic stadium that had been the setting of Leni Riefenstahl's infamous documentary which had done as much as anything else to confirm Stevens's determination to fight the evils of fascism. He would later collaborate with Budd Schulberg on a film about Germany's war crimes, *The Nazi Plan,* which would be presented with devastating impact as evidence at the Nuremberg War Crimes trial of Herman Goering and twenty other German officers in December 1945. Stevens was eventually demobilized in March 1946 with the rank of lieutenant colonel.

When William Wyler returned to Hollywood after distinguished military service and then made his masterpiece about the problems of readjustment of returning war veterans, *The Best Years of Our Lives* (1946), he wrote an article for the journal *The Screen Writer* (February 1947) in which he mentioned how his fellow directors had gained a more realistic view of the world through their experience. "Frank Capra has told me that he feels this strongly," he wrote, "and I know George Stevens is not the same man for having seen the corpses at Dachau." Wyler's phrasing there is very telling. Stevens had not simply been shocked and horrified by what he had seen at Dachau: in Wyler's view it had fundamentally changed him as a person. It follows that it would fundamentally change him as a film maker as well.

"After the war, I don't think I was ever too hilarious again," Stevens was to tell his friends. Listed by Ingrid Bergman as one of the five directors she particularly wanted to work with (the other four being Wyler, Billy Wilder, John Huston and Roberto Rossellini) and approached by her to do a comedy together entitled *One Big Happy Family,* Stevens eventually felt compelled to withdraw because he was just not in the mood for comedy. What he had seen had alerted him to the potential Nazi in every human being and caused him to turn away from any religious faith. He became silent and withdrawn, and his marriage began to fall apart. (He and Yvonne were to be divorced in 1949.) Capra told George Stevens, Jr., that he felt his father was bitter about the people who had stayed home and made all the movies. This might have been part of the reason behind the animus he felt towards Cecil B. DeMille. When I interviewed Joseph L. Mankiewicz in 1984, he could still recall the occasion when De Mille at a board meeting had challenged Stevens to say what he was doing when De Mille's job at Lux Theatre Radio was being threatened by union activity, and Stevens had witheringly replied: "I was snowed in at Bastogne while you were piling up your bloody capital gains." (Elia Kazan also recalled that moment in his autobiography.) This was a forerunner of the famous Screen Directors Guild meeting in October 1951, when De Mille's attempt to unseat Joseph L. Mankiewicz as the president of the Screen Directors Guild was fatally undermined by Stevens's intervention, which outlined and denounced the underhand tactics of the De Mille faction and whose presentation, Mankiewicz told me, would have done credit to Clarence Darrow. While he was engaged in the war, Stevens had lost all interest in Hollywood; and unlike most of his colleagues, was slow to restart his career on his return. When he did, a different sensibility emerged, no less sensitive and humane but now much more contemplative and serious.

Four

Interlude,
1948–1951

On Our Merry Way (1948)

As part of his tentative reassimilation into the Hollywood filmmaking scene after his traumatic experience in the war, Stevens accepted a generous monetary offer to direct a comedy sequence starring James Stewart and Henry Fonda for the episode film *On Our Merry Way*. The film was produced by actor Burgess Meredith and former real-estate dealer now eccentric independent producer Benedict Bogeaus, who had previously produced one of Jean Renoir's American movies, *Diary of a Chambermaid* (1946). This time they had the idea of combining three short films with the connecting theme of the influence a child has had on a person's life. The stories are collected by Burgess Meredith, who has told his young bride (Paulette Goddard) that he is a star reporter for the local newspaper when actually he simply answers the phone for classified ads, but who has managed to become a roving reporter for just one day. He interviews random members of the public for stories that relate to this theme.

King Vidor directed two of the episodes and Stevens one. Vidor thought so little of it that he makes no mention of it in his autobiography. Stevens insisted that he remained uncredited for his contribution. A similarly uncredited John Huston directed the lead-in to the Stevens episode. To complicate matters still further, there was originally to be a fourth episode, starring Charles Laughton, in which a minister regains his faith through a miracle involving a child, but it was dropped because it was deemed to be too serious for the film's overall comic tone. David Selznick offered to buy this episode with a view to making it part of a feature-length film, but the offer was refused. Nevertheless, the discarded Laughton episode is the only one which would have had any relevance to the film's original title, *A Miracle Can Happen,* which was the title it went under when it was sneak-previewed in New York.

"The fact that this attempt at whimsy doesn't always come off is incidental," wrote *Variety* at the time, "just look at the names! The pic opens with a pair of surefire names like Goddard and Meredith, and in bed too." That last comment is a reminder that showing a married couple in the same bed in a 1948 Hollywood movie was sufficiently unusual to prompt the industry's main trade paper to comment on the fact. (The fact that Meredith and Goddard were actually married at the time might have encouraged the producers to take the risk.) The other names in the cast that impressed *Variety* so much were James Stewart, Henry Fonda, star trumpeter and bandleader Harry James, Dorothy Lamour,

Fred MacMurray and William Demarest. Raymond Durgnat characterized the film as American populist comedy at its last gasp, describing Meredith's assignment as something that the reporter "hopes will be inspirational," but who, by way of reply, "gets a clutch of disabused episodes" (Durgnat: 178), which is essentially the film's main joke. Like most critics, Durgnat thought the Stevens episode was the best of the three.

James Stewart and Henry Fonda play a couple of jazz musicians who are the leaders of a band named Lank's Rhythm Rascals. When the caravan which is transporting them and their band breaks down in the small town of Sycamore, they become involved in organizing and judging a local music contest. They think they can work the situation to their financial advantage by ensuring the victory of the Lord Mayor's son, but their plan begins to unravel when they hear the superior trumpet-playing skills of a glamorous young female contestant called Lola. The plan is further undermined when Harry James is brought along to judge the contest.

Stewart and Fonda make the most of their comic opportunities, with Fonda displaying an unexpected adeptness in slapstick and Stewart going through a range of facial contortions that humorously reflects the steady erosion of his scheme. The main comedy occurs in the contest itself, which begins with an old lady getting her hand stuck in her horn and a young contestant with more enthusiasm than talent, and is then followed by a montage of different soloists of varying degrees of ineptitude. The Lord Mayor's son has been secretly instructed by Stewart to pretend to play his instrument while Fonda ghosts his performance in a rowboat beneath the bandstand. Unfortunately the boat keeps setting off and unsteadying the performance. As a last desperate measure, Stewart tries to distract Lola from her trumpet playing by making her laugh, but he only succeeds in getting a lemon stuck in his mouth. Fonda emerges, bedraggled and waterlogged, but is unable to offer much help as he keeps having to retreat from the stage in order to be sick. In short, the ruse fails. Indeed Lola will become the new leader of the band, which is renamed Lola's Rhythm Rascals. Because they exaggerate and misrepresent the story to the roving reporter, describing the contest but saying they awarded the prize to a six-year-old child prodigy despite being under strong political pressure not to do so and resisting the temptation of huge bribes from interested parties, one might be tempted to take this as an ingenious example of a lying flashback that anticipates Hitchcock. Stevens commented that the humor was all structural, but it is doubtful whether this was what was uppermost in his mind. It was more likely that he was taking the rare opportunity to have a bit of fun, contriving Laurel and Hardy–type situations for two fine actors and friends, while marking time until the emergence of a subject that fully engaged his interest.

I Remember Mama (1948)

"It was a story of the confirmed period of the past and dissociated from the unresolved present," said Stevens of I Remember Mama, in his interview in 1964 with James Silke (qtd in Cronin: 41). The comment is both a description of the material and an explanation of its appeal to him at that particular point in his life. A young writer, Katrin Hanson (Barbara Bel Geddes) remembers her childhood with her Norwegian family in early twentieth century San Francisco. "I knew old San Francisco," said Stevens. "I had been raised there, I knew what the city looked like, and I knew who these people were"

(41). Consequently he could readily empathize with the young narrator who comes to realize that she can only become a successful writer when she writes about things close to her heart. Stevens could also readily sympathize with the immigrant family, who are still coming to terms with the New World. He similarly felt an outsider in the strange new world of post-war America, to which he had not entirely adjusted.

Produced on Broadway by Richard Rodgers and Oscar Hammerstein, *I Remember Mama* was based on Kathryn Forbes's novel *Mama's Bank Account* (1943), which had been adapted and directed for the stage by John Van Druten. Opening on 19 October 1944 (and featuring the Broadway debut of the young Marlon Bando in the role of the son, Nels), it had proved immensely popular and had run for 713 performances, with the author attributing a large part of its appeal to what he called "the basic humanity in Miss Kathryn Forbes's characters whom it was my pleasure and privilege to present on the stage" (Van Druten: 7). The part of the mother, Marta Hanson, had been played on Broadway by Mady Christians, but when RKO had acquired the screen rights, there were rumors that Greta Garbo might be tempted out of retirement to play the role until she made it clear that she had no intention of returning to the screen. The role was then offered to Irene Dunne, who suggested Stevens as one of her preferred directors. Accordingly RKO secured the services of Stevens on a year's loan from Liberty Films between March 1947 and March 1948. Jessica Tandy was originally slated to play the part of Aunt Trina, but begged to be excused when she was offered a co-starring role opposite Charles Boyer in *A Woman's Vengeance* (1948), and the part was reassigned to Ellen Corby, who was to be nominated for an Oscar for her performance. She was one of the film's four acting Oscar nominees. The other three were Irene Dunne, who was unlucky to lose out that year to Jane Wyman in *Johnny Belinda* (1948); Oscar Homolka as Uncle Chris, repeating the role he had played so successfully (and, according to some reports, indulgently) on stage; and Barbara Bel Geddes in only her second screen appearance and having been preferred in the role of Katrin to Joan Tetzel, who had played the part on Broadway but then had to settle in real life for being Homolka's fourth wife.

Although it has certain similarities with a number of popular '40s Hollywood films that dealt with family life in turn-of-the-century America—for example, Vincente Minnelli's *Meet Me in St. Louis* (1944), Elia Kazan's *A Tree Grows in Brooklyn* (1945) and Michael Curtiz's *Life with Father* (1947)—it has even more in common with previous Stevens' movies. In revisiting the past through the Hanson family, Stevens seemed also to be revisiting and remembering his own cinematic past. The maturation of a sensitive young woman in constricted domestic circumstances is thematically similar to *Alice Adams*; the hospital scenes are clearly from the same man who gave us *Vigil in the Night,* particularly the close-ups of curious children in their hospital beds as they watch the special attention being given by an adult to the child in her care; and the cyclical flashback structure, where a heroine reflects on where she is in the present through selective reminiscences from her past, recalls *Penny Serenade,* as does a running visual joke about a window that will not close properly. Like *Woman of the Year* also, the film is centered on a strong-willed and active woman who will carry its narrative and emotional momentum.

DeWitt Bodeen's skillful screenplay is a largely faithful adaptation of the play, with some minor deletions of dialogue and detail. For example, Mama's disclosure in the play that she had a son in Norway who died when he was two years old is omitted from the film, presumably on the grounds that it serves no dramatic purpose. In deference to the

Production Code, Uncle Chris's language is toned down for the film, particularly in the scene in the hospital with Aunt Sigrid's son, Arne (Tommy Ivo), when he is teaching the boy some swear words to use if the pain in his fractured kneecap becomes unbearable. In the play, both are allowed to say "Dammittohell!"; in the film, the boy is taught to exclaim in Norwegian, much to the horror of a listening nurse, who is then told by Uncle Chris that all it means is "Stupid old goat!" Also in deference to the Code but unlike in the play, it is made clear that Uncle Chris's relationship with his housekeeper, Jessie Brown (Barbara O'Neil), which for years has been regarded as improper by his nieces (except Marta) and which has caused the three to snub "the woman" at every opportunity, is perfectly respectable, for they were married years ago. (That might be seen as a compromise but seems to me a nice touch, for, in not telling the three nieces of this situation, Uncle Chris can mischievously relish their discomfort and keep them at arm's length.) The opening out of the play is relatively modest. Stevens shot some of the film on actual locations with extras dressed in period clothing, but mostly the recreation of San Francisco circa 1910 was accomplished in the studio. A conversation between Marta and Aunt Trina, when the latter tells Marta about her wish to marry a funeral director, Mr. Thorkelson (Edgar Bergen), is moved from the living room to the porch, for the purposes of visual variety; and a conversation between Uncle Chris and Mr. Thorkelson about Trina's dowry has been moved from the hospital's reception area to the gentlemen's toilet, for the purposes of visual comedy (and because the nurse in charge has seen fit to remind the two men that "this is a hospital, not a marriage bureau"). Uncle Chris's outsized personality has been prepared for before we actually see him, for Aunt Jenny and Aunt Sigrid have chuckled at the prospect of the timid Mr. Thorkelson's first meeting with him. ("Uncle Chris will eat him!" declares Jenny.) Accordingly, Stevens contrives an appropriately grandiose entrance, with a sweeping panning shot to the quayside to announce his arrival by ferry. Because he is lame in one leg, he drives an automobile to Marta's house, causing horses to rear and whinny as they stray into his path, and honking the horn at every opportunity as if to warn the community of his approach.

At the beginning of the film, we hear Katrin's voice as it emerges out of a San Francisco fog; it is as if the veils of memory are being lifted. As the camera retreats slowly from inside her attic window, she types the final sentences of her novel; writes "The End"; and then stretches in satisfaction. "A Novel, by Kathryn Hanson," she says to herself. Whereas inside her home she is always addressed as "Katrin," she has Americanized her name for her readership; the process of assimilation has moved forward. It is also interesting that she describes her manuscript as "a novel." At the end of the play, she is celebrating simply the publication of her first story. However, the film carries this idea further and is essentially a re-enactment of the novel that Katrin has just written. As she collects all the pages and starts reading through from the beginning, the film moves into flashback as the older Katrin looks at a younger version of herself in the mirror, scribbling away in her private diary. The shot widens out to embrace the past as young Katrin breaks from her writing to join the family downstairs as they gather round the table for the Saturday night ritual, where Mama counts and allocates the money from the father's weekly wage. It will always conclude with her satisfied declaration: "Is good. We do not have to go to the bank." It is Mama's coded way of saying that they are living within their means. Only at the end will she reveal that she does not actually have a bank account; and that she had concealed this knowledge from her children because she did not wish to worry them.

Although Katrin has referred to her book as "a novel," it is clearly more a memoir, and the film reflects that by being unapologetically episodic. As James Agee remarked in his review in *Time* (5 April 1948), "He [Stevens] felt no timidity about tackling a script that lacked action and a strong plot." These are not all it lacks. There is no conventional love story at its heart (Katrin is far more interested in books than in boys); there is remarkably little dramatic conflict (even when the father is on strike at one stage, this causes barely a ripple on the narrative surface); and although childhood illness plays a part in the narrative, the film, in Bruce Beresford's words, "avoids the trap of over-cute children," which he thought marred *Penny Serenade*. (The performances of the children in *I Remember Mama* are indeed all very good.) In fact, Beresford thought that the film ranked with Capra's *It's a Wonderful Life* as "the best of all the weepies" (Beresford: 14). Yet its sentiment is quite different from that in Capra's fable, where darkness, anger and social rage bubble restlessly under its sentimental surface and contribute to the film's Dickensian richness and complexity. In Stevens' film, there is not an iota of wickedness: foolishness, weakness and thoughtlessness perhaps, but nothing that corresponds with the disturbing undertones of the Capra film. In fact, Stevens seems to have been drawn to this material precisely because the humanity on show is simple and unaffected, with none of the extremes of viciousness, cruelty and evil of the recent past which he had witnessed first-hand.

There is something remarkable and uncompromising about the way the director goes about this. Stevens was famously impossible to harass or hurry on a set; and something of that stubborn calm can be felt in this film's tempo, which is resolutely leisurely and unforced. For a film in which nothing much happens, its running time of 134 minutes is unusually long. It does require from an audience an element of patience perhaps, and Agee thought the film was an hour too long, but Penelope Houston was surely right in suggesting that what she called the film's "slow, reflective pace" was deliberate, and effective in conveying the sense that "it seemed less like something actual and present than like something affectionately remembered" (Houston: 74). When one thinks about the title, it promises not only a portrait of a remarkable character (the "Mama" of the title) but a characterization seen from a particular perspective (the "I" of the title) and filtered through selected memories that have imprinted themselves on her consciousness (the "remember" of the title).

Like the play, the film falls basically into two parts, with each part having three dominant incidents. In Part One, the first such incident is the unexpected arrival at Marta's house of Aunt Trina. She has preceded her sisters, the bossy Jenny (Hope Landin) and the whiny Sigrid (Edith Evanson), in order to enlist Marta's support in her desire to marry an undertaker, Mr. Thorkelson (Edgar Bergen) but also to ask for Marta's help in ensuring that Jenny and Sigrid will not laugh at her. In the play, Aunt Trina says: "If they laugh at me, I'll—I'll kill myself." The exaggeration is presumably meant to be funny, but Stevens thought that Ellen Corby was not injecting the line with sufficient humor, so, for the film, the line becomes "If they laugh at me, I—I yump in the bay!" which drew the required chuckle from the audience. Nevertheless, actual humiliation is no laughing matter in a Stevens movie; and when the sisters intimate that their reactions are tending that way, Martha makes clear that the laugh will be on them if they try anything.

Trina stays behind after Jenny and Sigrid have departed, and therefore becomes involved in a family ritual where they sit around and listen to a performance from their boarder, an out-of-work actor, Mr. Hyde, who is three months in arrears with his rent but who compensates by reading to the family passages from great literature. As Mama puts it: "He reads to us aloud. Wonderful books—Longfellow, and Charles Dickens, and Fenimore Kipling." Mr. Hyde is a relatively small role, but Cedric Hardwicke's perform-ance is so heartfelt and invested with such an undertow of sadness that it becomes one of the film's highlights. That night he reads the last part of *A Tale of Two Cities*; and whereas in the play, the actor is directed to read the final lines and then close the book, Hardwicke delivers the lines "It is a far, far better thing I do than I have ever done" without recourse to the text. It is as if he is personally addressing the family about how he sees his role in their household. Later he will confirm Aunt Jenny's worst fears and steal out of the house without paying his rent, in the film saying farewell by letter rather than in person as in the play, and leaving behind a worthless check—but also his library of books. When Aunt Jenny is crowing that she was right about Mr. Hyde all along, Marta tears up the check and, in a brilliant touch that is not in the play text, says that "he pay with far, far better things than money," as if subconsciously remembering his reading of that night and absorbing its inner meaning. For what he has done has stimulated in Katrin a love of literature which will lay the foundations of her future. At the end of the film, when Katrin sits down and prepares to read her story to the family, Mama insists that she sits in Mr. Hyde's chair, recognizing the connection and the continuity.

The second major incident of this first part is Uncle Chris's annual visit to San Fran-cisco, which this time happens to coincide with the illness of Marta's youngest daughter, Dagmar (June Hedin), who has a mastoid and will need an operation. Uncle Chris will take an active (indeed, overactive) interest in this matter, even insisting that he attends the operation himself. Dr. Johnson (Rudy Vallee) will permit no such thing. "I allow no one to attend my operations," he says firmly, to which Uncle Chris replies, slyly: "Are so bad?" In the play Dr. Johnson is allowed to respond indignantly to this slur on his rep-utation, but in the film (and with greater comic effect), Marta hustles the Doctor out of the house before Uncle Chris can do any more damage; she will deal with him herself. The interplay between the Uncle and Doctor is very well acted and directed and typical of the way the film can find gentle humor even amid the more serious moments. We will learn later that the Uncle's obsession with medical matters is not a fad but derives from his own lameness which he sustained in childhood; and that most of his life savings have been spent on medical treatment for children who have had a similar affliction. When he has first arrived at the house, he has immediately checked on the other children to see if they are in good health and growing properly. What at first might seem overbearing interference is eventually revealed as genuine concern for their welfare.

The operation will prove a success, but it is against hospital regulations for the chil-dren to have visitors for the first twenty-four hours and Mama and Nels (Steve Brown) must return home without seeing Dagmar, as she has promised. Mama is so distraught that, as Nels tells his sisters, "she started talking Norwegian in the streetcar." When she starts distractedly mopping the floor, which she had done the day before, and says, "Comes a time when you've got to get down on your knees," even Katrin's unsentimental younger sister Christine (Peggy McIntire) can see that Mama's heart is breaking, and she rushes in tears from the room. Yet Mama's gesture almost miraculously triggers an inspi-ration. She seems to hear Dagmar's pleading voice and, in so doing and as if in answer to a prayer, she has an idea. Later she and Katrin return to the hospital. There is a different nurse on duty. Giving Katrin her hat and coat and still wearing her apron, Mama slips into the cupboard, which she had noticed earlier in the day while waiting for news of

Dagmar, and reappears with mop and pail and starts cleaning the floor, all the while edging nearer to Dagmar's ward. Stevens maintains the tension by cutting between close-ups of Katrin's anxious face and the kindly face of the nurse at the reception desk, unaware of the deception taking place under her nose. Mama slips into the ward and says goodnight to Dagmar as promised, before singing her and the other children to sleep with a quiet lullaby. Sentimentality is kept at bay by the understated emotional realism of Irene Dunne's performance and a continual throb of danger at the possibility of discovery, particularly when she collides with the side of a bed in the darkness and almost knocks over her mop and pail. This scene is only reported in the play, but is crucial in the film for it visualizes as powerfully as any other event her love for her children and her absolute determination to do everything in her power for their welfare. At this point the film dissolves back to Katrin in the present. There is a slight pause before she resumes her narrative, as if allowing us a moment to relish Mama's dedication but also as if Katrin herself is momentarily and lovingly reflecting on the significance of the incident, for later Mama will similarly put herself out in an endeavor to further Katrin's ambitions. Katrin might also be reflecting that what we have just witnessed will be the subject of her first successful publication.

The three main events in the second half of the film are Katrin's graduation; the death of Uncle Chris; and Katrin's first literary success. The circumstances surrounding Katrin's graduation are among the most dramatic of the film, since the events bring about the nearest we get to a family disruption, with sister against sister, mother against younger sister, older sister in inadvertent opposition to Mama, and with father (the excellent Philip Dorn) and son playing the role of mediators. As graduation night approaches and she prepares for her role as Portia in the school production of *The Merchant of Venice,* Katrin has set her heart on a dresser set from Schiller's drugstore as an appropriate present. One is reminded a little of *Alice Adams,* as the heroine struggles to keep pace with the aspirations of her social peers. Unfortunately, like *Alice Adams* again, family finances might not permit it, for their father is currently on strike and Mama anyway is planning to give Katrin her grandmother's brooch as an heirloom. "But you'll devil Mama into giving you the dresser set somehow," observes Christine sharply, alert to Katrin's tendency to get her own way by overdramatizing things, and she is proved right. Katrin does indeed get her dresser set and drools over it so much that, on the way to the play, Christine feels compelled to tell her that, in order to pay for it, Mama has had to give Schiller the grandmother's brooch in exchange. Returning to the house to have confirmation of this from her father, who says Christine should not have told her, Katrin is distraught and is all ready to pull out of the play in her distress. Papa says she cannot do this, reminding her that "tonight, you are not Katrin, you are an actress. There is a saying—what is it?" at which point Aunt Trina leaps helpfully in with her unidiomatic twist on "The show must go on" ("The mail must go through!"). Katrin acquiesces, but leaves the house in tears.

There is a neat deviation from the original at this point. In the play Katrin has a brief conversation with her school friend, Dorothy Schiller, asking if she may speak with her father after the performance. In the film Stevens dissolves from a shot of Papa as he anxiously watches Katrin's departure from the window to a shot of Mama at the same window later that night, anxiously looking out for Katrin's return. As in *Penny Serenade,* the daughter's appearance in the school production has been something of a disaster, and Mama wants to know what has gone wrong. When she learns that Christine has told Katrin about the brooch, she is angry, because she has made Katrin unhappy and it was none of her business. For her part, Christine is sorry that Mama is angry, but because of the smug way Katrin has acted over the dresser set, she is not sorry she told.

Enter a contrite Katrin with her brother, and with Mama's brooch which she has exchanged back for the dresser set from a reluctant Mr. Schiller. Mama puts the brooch on Katrin. "Christine should not have told you," she says, to which Katrin replies, "I'm glad she did. Now." And Papa agrees. Unlike in the play, at this point Christine returns to the living room and as she moves round the room to bid goodnight to everyone, there is a moving and almost rhythmic sense of family unity being restored and enriched with a new understanding. When Papa now offers Katrin a cup of coffee in symbolic recognition of her newfound maturity, she is too overcome with emotion to drink it and rushes out of the room. But when we return to her as narrator to move the story forward to the next main event, which is the visit to a dying Uncle Chris, we notice a significant detail: as she promised, she is now wearing her mother's brooch.

The death of Uncle Chris is filmed with great artistry. It was bold for mainstream cinema at that time (or any time, for that matter) to include a death-bed scene that lasts for ten minutes, but Stevens accomplishes it with sensitivity and a wise humor. Homolka is at his finest in this scene, the character's failing strength putting a plausible restraint on any tendency of his to overact. Nevertheless the performance here retains a tetchiness that is true to the character, and is physically very convincing in the man's restricted and painful movement. James Agee mentioned one moment—"a sudden shifting of his bulk on the death-bed"—that he described as "almost magical" (Agee: 386); and one suspects that it might be the moment when Uncle Chris twists a little too sharply on the bed when talking to Katrin and quickly bids her to leave the room, as if the pain has made him suddenly aware that the end is near. There is a lovely moment also when, having badgered Marta for a drink, he takes one gulp and grimaces before swallowing, looking first at the glass and then accusingly at her, knowing the drink has been diluted; both characters (and actors) almost laugh out loud at his pained expression at that point. He bids farewell to the children in Norwegian, insisting they do the same to him; he reiterates his dying wish that Nels will become what Uncle Chris always wanted to be, a doctor, in order to help those who suffer ("It is to have a little of God in you"); and he formally introduces Marta to the person whom the other nieces refer to as "the woman" but is his wife Jessie, who has brought him much happiness. The three share a last (undiluted) drink together before he quietly expires. In the play, shortly before he dies, Uncle Chris has asked Marta to draw the curtain a little to protect his eyes from the sun, but in the film, he tells Marta not to do this, clearly resisting the dying of the light until the last moment. Only after he has died does Marta go to the window, gently lower the blinds, and pay a last farewell in the manner he requested: "Farvell, Onkel Chris."

The camera pans left to the nieces who are seated on the porch outside, waiting for news. When Marta appears to tell them their uncle has died, Jenny immediately asks, "Did he say anything about a will?" and sinks back despondently, when they are told there is no will and no money, only an account book on how his money was spent. "Bills from a liquor store," snorts Jenny, but Martha disabuses her of this notion and starts reading from the notebook. In his Preface to the acting edition of the play, John Van Druten has suggested as a guide to any subsequent producer that "Mama, standing higher than the aunts when she reads Uncle Chris' notebook, is much more effective than she would be, standing on the flat" (Van Druten: 6). Stevens respects that suggestion by having Mama remain standing as she reads to her sisters, as if almost instinctively occupying a moral high ground on her uncle's behalf that undercuts their cynicism and disappointment. The notebook is an account of the money he has spent for operations on lame children that have enabled them eventually to walk, and even in the case of Aunt Sigrid's boy, Arne, to "run." Stevens films this in medium shot and almost in a single take, the distance imparting a dignity to the revelation that is somehow more emotionally powerful than if the scene had been played in close-up. The aunts' misconceptions are to be further exposed when Mama introduces "the woman" Jessie to them as Uncle Chris's wife, prompting them to behave towards her with the respect that was always her due. The scene closes with a medium shot of Jessie as she waters the garden, while the sisters file in to the house to pay their last respects to Uncle Chris. We never learn whether we she takes up Marta's offer to stay with the family, although her gratitude is obvious, but for the moment Stevens allows us to contemplate quietly a good woman as she deals with her grief alone, his heart (and camera) instinctively drawn to the outsider.

A brief montage follows to cover the passage of two more years, during which the main event is the marriage of Aunt Trina to Mr. Thorkelson and the birth of their first child. "The old and thrifty ways persisted," says Katrin in her narration, as Stevens shows the family bustling round the house, with Papa none too successfully fixing a window, Dagmar tending to her new puppies, and Katrin opening her tenth letter of rejection that seems to signal the death of her literary ambitions. When Papa reads out an item in the local newspaper about the visit to San Francisco of the celebrated writer Florence Dana Moorhead (Florence Bates), who says that "sincerity" is the recipe for success as a writer, Katrin is scornful and dismissive, but Mama, picking up the idea of recipe and learning that gastronomy is actually Miss Moorhead's main interest in life aside from writing, looks at her picture in the paper and seems to like what she sees. "Is kind face," she says, but when we see the picture later, we are perhaps more struck by the fact (as the author is herself) that she clearly likes her food. As with her idea for visiting Dagmar in hospital, Mama has had an inspiration for how to reach Miss Moorhead. Meeting her in the lobby of the Fairmont hotel, Mama offers to give Miss Moorhead her mother's special recipe for the Norwegian dish, kjodboller (meat-balls with cream sauce) if she will read one of Katrin's stories which she has brought with her. If she could read more than one, she could write out the recipe for lutefisk as well. It is a charmingly played scene in which Irene Dunne and Florence Bates suggest a more or less instant rapport between two innately kind ladies. When Mama visits Katrin later in her attic to tell her where she has been, Katrin is busy destroying her literary efforts and is astonished by what her mother has done. Miss Moorhead's verdict that the stories are not good seems only to confirm Katrin's convictions, but Miss Moorhead has also told Mama that Katrin has a gift for writing and, on her recommendation, to send her agent a story written from her own experience. As James Agee put it, when reviewing the film: "Mama, by swapping recipes, wheedles a successful authoress into reading Katrin's stories and passing on the secret of literary success (write about what you know)" (Agee: 385). In fact, it was advice that Agee himself took to heart for his own masterpiece, the posthumously published novel *A Death in the Family* (1955), which was awarded a Pulitzer Prize, as it is a semi-autobiographical account of his own family and childhood. The advice is a moment of epiphany for Katrin. When she wonders about a specific subject and particularly a central character, Mama says, "Could you maybe write about papa? Is fine man, wonderful man." As she descends the stairs to fix supper, she turns back and firmly declares, "I like you should write about papa"; but almost instantaneously, Katrin has had an even better idea and an even better subject.

The arrival of the letter confirming the acceptance of her story is one of those episodes in Stevens's work informed with what Gilbert Adair called "an impassioned sweetness," which he thought characterized the director at his best (Adair: 8). A horse and carriage has emerged eerily out of the San Francisco fog carrying the U.S. mail and Stevens pans to a window shot of the family seated around the kitchen table, suddenly startled by a ring at the door and a delivery man presenting Katrin with a large envelope. She walks slowly to the open door of her room and in medium shot we see the family watching in curiosity (it is clearly the kind of event that has happened to them only rarely) as Katrin in the background of the frame nervously rips open the envelope. A piece of paper flutters out and drifts to the floor, prompting Katrin to drop almost to her knees in an endeavor to read what it says. It is a check for $500, as payment for one of her stories, "Mama and the Hospital." Can this moment have been rehearsed? Surely not; and yet it seems so right, for does it not echo that moment midway through the film when Mama has said "Comes a time when you've got to get down on your knees," a sort of involuntary prayer that is answered when she suddenly thinks of a way she can visit Dagmar in hospital. I have no idea whether Stevens calculated that connection or even had it in mind when filming; it is perhaps one of those touches of film magic that just happens. When Mama instructs Katrin to sit in Mr. Hyde's chair and calls the family round the table to listen to their new story-teller, she is taken aback to learn that the story is not about Papa but about her and is momentarily too agitated to sit down with the rest. She moves to the window, in what seems like a mixture of self-consciousness, embarrassment and pride. As Katrin begins her reading, which will essentially be the story we have just watched and bring the narrative full circle, Stevens will track away from Mama's face at the window, the curtains veiling her tears, and then pan to a San Francisco and an America in which the Hanson family now truly belong.

"I have a real affection for that film in certain ways, in some of the most simple ways," Stevens told his interviewer James Silke, when Silke had told him that the film moved him so much that he found it impossible to look at critically. "I think some of the movement in the film, of the people is absolutely beautiful" (qtd in Cronin: 39). Some details catch the dramatic essence of a moment while feeling completely natural, as when Katrin, in her anxiety, collides with a chair ("Pick up your feet, Katrin," instructs Mama) as she leaves the living room after the news of Mr. Hyde's hurried departure; or when Jessie stumbles slightly as she goes to water the plants in her garden, distracted by Marta's kind offer of somewhere to stay and still numb with grief at Uncle Chris's death; or when Mama, coming to tell Katrin of her meeting with the writer, knocks her head against the light in Katrin's attic, a gesture that suggests she has entered unfamiliar territory, which in turn suggests that she has something very important to impart. Such incidents in their context seem spontaneous, yet Stevens went way over budget and schedule in order to catch such moments (Irene Dunne said she earned more from the overtime she worked on that film than from her actual salary) and shot so much film that, apparently, it could have been edited in six different ways and still made sense. In fact, the film is brilliantly edited by Robert Swink; subtly photographed by Nicholas Musuraca; sensitively scored by Roy Webb in a style of restrained romanticism that never overpowers the film; and has a design that is rich in detail without suffocating an audience in period decoration. Even Dagmar's pet cat Uncle Elizabeth, fully living up to Aunt Jenny's description of its appearance as "horrible-looking," manages to establish an indelible persona of aggressive self-assertion with just two close-ups. The music critic Donald Tovey once wrote: "One of the first essentials of creative art is the habit of imagining the most familiar things as vividly as the most surprising." This is what Stevens achieves in *I Remember Mama*. More than a comeback film for him after the trauma of war, it was a restoration of faith in the basic goodness of people and his homage to the consolatory beauties of close family life. He will have been thrilled by the congratulatory telegram he received from fellow director Michael Curtiz (read out by George Stevens, Jr., in the film's 2004 DVD release) who called *I Remember Mama* "without exception, the most perfect picture I have seen in years."

Something to Live For (1951)

> "I know that [Jacques] Rivette likes *Something to Live For*."—Francois Truffaut, in a letter to Luc Moullet, 1956

Originally entitled *Mr. and Mrs. Anonymous, Something to Live For* is something of an anomaly. It is the shortest and least discussed of Stevens's post-war features. The film came between *A Place in the Sun* and *Shane* and has been eclipsed by both. Rather like another film of this era for Paramount by one of Hollywood's greatest directors, William Wyler's *Carrie* (1952), *Something to Live For* seems almost to have been disowned by the studio, who shelved it for a while and then released it with minimum publicity. It had begun shooting in May 1950, but was not previewed until August 1951 and then not released until March 1952, when it was poorly received by both press and public. While not among Stevens's major works, it is deserving of re-appraisal. Its depiction of professional alienation, midlife crisis and domestic discontent in a materialistic American society anticipates the '50s melodramas of Douglas Sirk, particularly a film like *There's Always Tomorrow* (1956). Its satire on the Madison Avenue advertising world looks forward to the ambience of Gene Kelly and Stanley Donen's notably astringent musical, *It's Always Fair Weather* (1955), not to mention a television phenomenon of our own time, the hugely successful series *Mad Men*.

The screenplay is an original by experienced dramatist and screenwriter Dwight Taylor. He had based it partly on the life of his mother, Laurette Taylor, a great theatrical star of the 1910s and 1920s whose career had been blighted by alcoholism, but who, before her death in 1946, had made a stunning comeback on Broadway in the role of Amanda Wingfield in Tennessee Williams's first great theatrical triumph, *The Glass Menagerie* (1943). Her equivalent in the film is the actress, Jenny Carey, soulfully portrayed by Joan Fontaine, whom we first encounter in a drunken stupor alone in her room at the Olympia Hotel in New York. The elevator operator, Billy (Harry Belaver), has rung for the services of Alcoholics Anonymous, inadvertently giving the impression that it was he who needed attention, which is the reason that the AA representative who turns up is a man, Alan Miller (Ray Milland), rather than, as is the policy of AA, someone of Jenny's own gender. In the course of their first meeting, we learn that Alan is a former alcoholic who now offers help to sufferers on their road to recovery, and that Jenny is a budding actress who is up for a part on Broadway but who has already missed two rehearsals on account of her drinking. As they confide the reasons behind the anxieties that led to their drinking, the two will grow increasingly dependent on each other and fall in love, despite the fact that Alan is a married man with two children and a third on the way. As David Shipman, who uniquely among critics preferred the film not only to *A Place in the Sun* but also to anything that Stevens did afterwards, observed: "The lovers teeter on the edge of a precipice, not because of infidelity but because of their shared alcoholism, which Stevens conveys with understanding…. Few films better illustrate the changes that can be wrought on sub-standard material by sensitive and polished direction" (Shipman: 855).

Whereas David Shipman thought the film's style elevated the content, other critics felt it overwhelmed it. Nicholas Bartlett called it an "odd film," where "Stevens brought all the technical flair of *A Place in the Sun* to bear on an anecdote about alcoholics and the theme could scarcely stand up to the treatment" (Bartlett: 28). He thought it was still worth seeing for the technical flair and the performances of the three stars. By contrast Eugene Archer thought the acting superficial but the film "admirable and even brilliant in its technique: seldom has a romance been treated with such ornate visual symbolism, the ingenious interplay of lights and shades affording marvellous contrast between the wholesome normality of the hero's glittering home life and the dingy gaudiness of his sensual liaison." Archer's acute identification of a key aspect of Stevens' visual conception nevertheless did not prevent him from dismissing the film as "a pretentious soap opera" (Archer: 31). That was also the view of Bosley Crowther, when he reviewed the film for the *New York Times* (8 March 1952) on its first release. Describing Stevens's direction as being "as sleek and professionally efficient as any you are going to see around," Crowther still thought Dwight Taylor's script "a fearsomely rigged and foolish thing" and indeed bad enough to drive anyone to drink. "Bartender, toss us a beer," he concluded.

Crowther's conclusion puts one in mind of (and might even be a deliberate homage to) James Agee, who had famously signed off his review in *The Nation* of Billy Wilder's classic drama about alcoholism, *The Lost Weekend* (1945), with a pseudo drunken flourish. "I undershtand that liquor interesh: innerish: intershtsh are rather worried about this film," wrote Agee. "Thash tough" (Agee: 184). Just as the hero's concern for the dipsomaniac actress begins to cast a lengthening shadow across his marriage, there is no doubt that *The Lost Weekend* cast a long shadow over Stevens's film, not only because of the similarity of theme but because of the casting of Ray Milland in the main role in both. It tempted some critics to regard the film almost as a sequel, with Milland's recovering alcoholic, now with a wife and family, coming perilously close to slipping back into alcoholism again. The film signals that previous lapses have happened during the marriage, for Miller's wife, Edna (Teresa Wright), seems always on high alert. She stirs sleepily when Alan comes into the bedroom late at night after his first meeting with Jenny, but she then flinches abruptly when he trips over an electric cord, as if fearful of what that signifies: it might be an accident but it might be a drunken stumble. We will learn later that he has not had a drink for fourteen months, which is commendable enough in itself, but his two young boys are substantially older than that, so the problem has clearly not gone away with his marriage. The craving is still there; and temptation is all around. Stevens often dissolves to shop windows that either display or advertise drink (Jenny's hotel is actually next door to a liquor store, with a neon sign that flashes the word "Liquors"); and he frequently foregrounds, and occasionally magnifies, drinks or bottles in the frame, bringing an audience as close as he can to the alcoholic's craving and the difficulty of resistance.

In the morning after Alan first met Jenny, Stevens does not depict the conventional hangover, for Alan's visit has temporarily distracted Jenny from the urge to drink. However, in dissolving between the two of them as they encounter the pressures of a new day, he seems to draw them closer together in their shared weakness and vulnerability. The morning becomes a tale of two rejections, of a failure that is partially self-inflicted in both cases, but which could have lasting repercussions, personally and professionally.

Alan has been summoned to see his boss, Mr. Crawley (Herbert Heyes) of Crawley Inc. Advertising to be told that his proposed advertising campaign for Bahama Cruises is terrible. "Romance ... that's your keynote," he is told. "Romance with a capital R." If romance is lacking in his work, perhaps it is lacking in his life too. Sobriety has left him in an emotional limbo. Apparently this is the second time Crawley has called him to his office with a similar complaint: is he losing his touch? Not too subtly, Crawley tries to get at the reason, asking Alan whether he is feeling his age; whether there is trouble at home; and whether he's "been drinking again?" In fact, it has already been intimated that all three of those queries are touching on sensitive areas of Alan's life. He might well be going through a midlife crisis, exacerbated at work by the success of a younger colleague, David Baker (Douglas Dick), who is quickly shown to have the drive and self-belief that Crawley likes and which Alan now lacks. The domestic disquiet is more obliquely suggested. Conversation between husband and wife over the breakfast table that morning has been interrupted by the loud appearance of their two boys in cowboy outfits; and, preoccupied with his own concerns, Alan does not pick up on the fact that something is on Edna's mind that she is finding difficult to disclose. It is a common feature in Stevens's films for a wife to be more attuned to her husband's anxieties than the other way round. It is only later that we will learn that she is pregnant and apprehensive about her husband's response. Alan is telling her about his meeting with Jenny, and Edna says, "I wish I could be more help sometimes," but his reply, "Only a drunk can help a drunk," not only excludes her but seems almost a premonition of his desire for taking the relationship with Jenny further. What is striking about the scene at work is how different Alan seems from the confident man we saw dealing with Jenny, how swiftly his self-esteem can evaporate when faced with a reversal. When he returns disconsolately to his office to break the news to his artist, Joey (Douglas Spencer), about the boss's dissatisfaction, his eyes drift over to a bottle of alcohol on Joey's desk, which he uses to wash out his brushes. It seems an involuntary but inevitable reflex on Alan's part consequent upon his feelings of inadequacy. His immediate reaction is not to call home for moral support, but to call Jenny, who will understand his mood, but there is no reply. After Joey has left the room, Alan tightens the top on the bottle as if he needs to stiffen his resolve, and quickly leaves for lunch, avoiding temptation, but still in turmoil.

In leaving the office at that point, he misses a call from Jenny, who, unbeknown to him, has also had a bad morning and returned to her hotel room in a similar state of distress. Arriving late for her rehearsal, she has seen another actress on stage who has taken her place. The line her replacement (Kasey Rogers) delivers—"I might find out you're the most awful louse"—is enough to drive Jenny out of the theatre, no doubt because she recognizes it as a line from the role she was due to play but also because the sentiment itself might be one that resonates. Having failed to persuade the elevator operator Billy to fetch her some drink, she finds a half-full bottle of whisky in her suitcase and is about to drink it when she notices Alan's card that he has left for her the night before. At this point she begins unknowingly to mimic Alan's actions, phoning him at his office for help, with a bottle within tantalizing reach; and then, after failing to get through, leaving the room in a flight from temptation. When they meet accidentally at the restaurant, Stevens has engineered their parallel fates so deftly that, when they eventually encounter each other, it seems more like fate than coincidence.

This lunchtime scene is full of precise and significant detail. The restaurant is not one of Alan's regular haunts, apparently, for he is deliberately trying to escape from his usual workday routine and feels a change of environment might stimulate his creativity. In fact, far from finding a refreshment of outlook there, he is subjected to a succession of small but sharply observed rebuffs and reproaches, tiny in themselves but demeaning enough to unsettle his already fragile self-composure. On arrival he finds there is no vacant table immediately available. "Would you wait at the bar, please?" says the head waiter, whose surface civility mingles with just the faintest hint of intimidating pomposity. The waiter's suggestion could hardly be more unhelpful given Alan's state of mind. When he asks for a glass of water at the bar, the bartender seems barely able to conceal his disdain, as does an adjoining customer whose face we never see. "Never make any money that way," the man remarks, an aside that in a different context might seem harmlessly ironical but here feels gratuitously intrusive and rude. "They seem to be doing alright," replies Alan, matching the customer's sarcasm with a brisk retort in a similar vein, but it is an exchange that would only intensify his feeling of edginess. No sooner has the glass of water arrived than he is jostled by a woman customer who causes him to spill some of it. Testily accepting her apology and downing the remaining contents, he leaves the bar, at which point the woman turns to her friend and exclaims, "That was straight gin!" Obviously still agitated, he tries to phone Jenny, but the booths are all occupied, and indeed one caller (Jody Gilbert) loudly expresses her suspicion that he is eavesdropping on her conversation. The pressure on him is building towards a feeling of panic and almost paranoia. When he finally reaches a phone, his call is unanswered. On his return to the restaurant foyer, he is told there is still no free table and he is once again directed by the waiter to the bar, where a bartender swoops speedily and obligingly towards him to take his order. Emphatic close-ups of drinks and glasses loom large; everything around him seems to be conspiring to break down his resolve. In a spirit of surrender, he orders "an old-fashioned." And it is at that point that Jenny arrives at the restaurant and spots him. When she sees he has ordered a drink, she is shocked, because it surely cancels out everything he has told her the previous evening, and she hurries out of the restaurant, after wishing him all the luck in the world. What she has not grasped is that her fortuitous arrival is actually the saving of him, the spur he needed to decline the drink. He pushes it away from him as it were unpleasant medicine. It is a moment that will define the potential future pattern of their relationship. An affair might save them from alcoholism, but will it also endanger other aspects of their lives?

After fleeing from the restaurant, Jenny has taken shelter from the rain in the now deserted theatre which was the scene of her earlier humiliation. Alan has followed her, and against this setting, the two open up more about their feelings, with the darkened theatre becoming a kind of confessional, particularly appropriate in the case of Jenny, for whom the stage, she will say, has become a religion. However, it is Alan who opens up first to explain what has happened to him that morning and how the reprimand from his boss had shaken him to the point when, as he says, "I suddenly got the feeling that I'd got to the edge of a slide again." When Jenny asks him about his work and whether he likes it, he says, "I can take it, or leave it alone," and then adds, "I've a wife and kids, it's a job, that's what counts." Even Jenny is struck by his lack of enthusiasm for what he does. Equally striking is the casual, almost unconscious, way, he links dissatisfaction with his job to his domestic situation at home. Is there an implication of resentment about the life he feels compelled to lead in order to support his family? Although there is no indication elsewhere of any alternative lifestyle that Alan covets or indeed is fit for, there is a suggestion of the post-war grey-flannel-suited American male frustrated in a job for which he has limited talent and no respect (even his arch-rival Baker calls it a "racket"), but subconsciously blaming the family. This in turn is leading to an increasing alienation from them. You can sense it spatially in the way Stevens moves the characters around in the home. There seems an emotional as well as physical distance between him and his wife, for they never kiss or embrace in the film. This sense of detachment is equally true of his relationship with his children. When later in the film, Edna tells him that the boys "love you very much," Alan's response is to say, offhandedly, "Well, I am their father," as if the one thing automatically follows from the other and quite failing to see what Edna is trying to communicate to him. It is a response that reveals a lot about a certain insensitivity and lack of reciprocity in his feelings towards a family who are devoted to him. We never discover when he first became an alcoholic, and he himself says he does not know the reason why he did, but one can infer that alcohol seems to be his almost subconscious means of filling a void of personal and professional disaffection.

The source of Alan's discontent might be nebulous, but the roots of Jenny's malady are very specific. Enamored of the theatre since childhood, she had come to New York in search of work and been spotted by renowned Broadway producer Tony Colton (Richard Derr), whose eminence is such that even Alan knows him by reputation. Colton had become her mentor—and perhaps something more. However, when she had accepted a part in an out-of-town play for another producer, Colton had taken offense and seen it as an act of professional betrayal. The result was that, when the play had transferred to New York, Jenny had developed a stage fright so severe that she had been unable to perform for fear that Colton would be sitting in the wings and waiting for her to fail. Stevens films much of Jenny's story unusually in long shot as she walks towards the stage, as if careful not to give it too much weight, for it seems to omit as much as it contains. If Colton was her mentor, was he also her lover? "Outside of himself," Jenny says, "he loves the theatre more than anything else in the world." So why his extreme reaction and her terror? Something about her story does not quite add up somehow, as if her hints about Colton's jealousy are disguising what is at the root of her fear: namely, that Colton's disapproval (personal or professional) strikes at the heart of her low self-esteem. "Do you love him?" Alan asks, pointedly. There is a pause before she answers "No" and moves away. When he later asks, "You did stop seeing him?" he has to repeat the question before again she turns away from him and says, "I broke off completely. When I went away, I never saw him again." Both the body language and the hesitancy before she answers suggest that she might not be telling the whole truth.

Alan's insistence also implies something stronger than mere curiosity. When Jenny says she has broken off completely with Colton, Alan turns back abruptly to buy Jenny a plant from a flower stall, in the process almost being run over by a bus. Incidentally, that moment is very powerfully filmed, seeming to take even Joan Fontaine by surprise: it gives an additional frisson to Alan's impulsive gesture. Flowers will become symbolically important in the film, for she will also receive a gift of flowers from a future co-star that will send Alan into a spasm of jealousy; and later a lavish bouquet for her opening night on Broadway by Tony Colton, whose message, "I'll be watching you" will start Jenny on another panic attack. On returning to her hotel room, Jenny is told by Billy that a Tony Colton has called several times, but he has told him that she is not taking any calls. Emboldened by this, Alan accompanies her to her room, asks if he can see her again, and tries to kiss her, all the while insisting that they need each other to avoid lapsing back into alcoholism. There is a sharp knock at the door; Billy has appeared with a jug of ice-cold water. Has he sensed what is going on and wants to pour cold water on it before the adulterous, non-alcoholic affair gets out of hand? It will anticipate a key dramatic moment later in the film when cold water will come to the aid of Jenny to avoid another personal catastrophe.

When we next encounter Alan at work, he has a pair of shoes in his hand and a spring in his step. Stevens deftly suggests the change of mood simply by repeating a shot from earlier in the film, but with a different inflection. Earlier, when he passed Baker on the corridor, Alan has seemed bemused and Baker chirpy; now it is the other way round. When Alan tells Joey they have been given the account for Kennedy Shoes, the artist seems unexcited, but Alan tries to talk up the project and even sees the possibilities for romance. "Anything's romantic if you go about it right," he says, at which point Joey turns and says, "Have you been drinking again?" Mr. Crawley will wonder the same when Alan tells him he will be visiting the Egyptian Room at the Museum. (The film will suggest that this is one of the perpetual dilemmas of the reformed alcoholic which no doubt fuels his frustration: when he is down, friends and acquaintances will assume it's because of drink; but when he seems happy, they will assume the same thing.) In fact, Alan's high spirits are attributable to the fact that he is meeting Jenny, for she has been offered a key role in a Baltimore production of a new play, *The Egyptians*, and she is in the museum doing some research. When he joins her, she tells him the play is about a queen who falls in love with her slave, and they begin to rehearse the play together. "Your looks spoke love.... Love is like the Nile ... our eternity is now." When the queen and slave then kiss and Jenny and Alan do the same, it is apparent to them both that they are not entirely play-acting.

"Hi, dad." Their intimacy is suddenly interrupted by the unexpected appearance of Alan's elder son, John (Patric Mitchell) who is on a school trip to the museum with his class teacher, Miss Purdy (Helen Brown). As a discomfited Alan and Miss Purdy exchange pleasantries, Jenny moves to the foreground left of the frame and stands in darkness, as if a shadow of shame has fallen across her that will not lift until the children leave. When his son reminds him that he must not miss dinner tonight as they are having roast beef, Alan's hopes for an evening with Jenny are dashed and Jenny's feeling of shame intensified.

As they leave the museum, Stevens dissolves strikingly from the inscrutable face of an Egyptian mummy to the serious face of Edna at home, which implicitly brings Alan crashing down to earth and to his family obligations. It is also a droll visual pun on the word "mummy," for Edna has just told Alan that she is pregnant again and assumes that Alan's somber mood is that he is not too enchanted by the news. When he complains that she should have told him earlier, she replies that she was afraid to, because she thought it might make him fall off the wagon again. As he perfunctorily says goodnight to his sons and buries his head in his hands, it is apparent that there might be something more behind his moodiness than the anxieties of parenthood. "Darling, what is it? What's the matter?" Edna asks, adding, cajolingly, "Tell mama" (an unmistakable Stevens touch) Alan blames his mood on his anxieties at work, but it is notable that, when John has mentioned earlier that there was a woman (or "that dumb girl," as he puts it) in the Egyptian Room as well as his father, Edna has looked up quickly, as if taking note. Teresa Wright is marvelous throughout the film at suggesting that, behind this façade of the loving and trusting wife, Edna is intelligent, sensitive, sharply observant of things around her, and knows her husband a lot better than he thinks she does. Later, when she is hanging up his clothes, a play script slips from his pocket and Edna starts reading it aloud: "Love is like the River Nile." By way of explanation Alan says that it is all part of his research for a possible new Egyptian account and he has been doing some sketches of Egyptian architecture. We know that is a lie, but does his wife believe him? An answer to that will be delayed until the film's exquisitely played final scene.

Alan and Edna have been invited to a party at the home of David Baker, who is celebrating his securing of the steamship account. When Alan has hesitated before accepting, Baker has said: "The boss is coming. I know he'd like to see you there." The invitation has thus been made to sound more like a warning. ("I'd give that sharp-shooter a wide berth," comments Joey, darkly.) When they do arrive—and the crowded rooms suggest that they have arrived quite late—Alan is surprised to find that Jenny is one of the guests. She will be equally surprised to learn that Tony Colton will also be coming. It is never satisfactorily explained how Baker knows either of these people, let alone both; and it might be one of the things that Bosley Crowther had in mind in his hostile *New Yorker* review when he complained, referring to Dwight Taylor's script, about "how that long arm of coincidence keeps batting you in the face!"

Yet the party scene itself is so well directed that one can almost forgive its narrative contrivance. Stevens maintains the seeming spontaneity of a social occasion, even spicing it with humor through shrewdly observed incidental detail, yet he never loses the scene's essential dramatic focus or momentum. It is clear that the occasion is designed more to show off than to entertain, and that part of the outward tension arises from Baker's desire to impress his boss and associates, in so doing undermining Alan's status in Crawley's eyes. The inner tension comes from Alan's awareness of Jenny's proximity and more particularly his endeavor to keep a watchful and protective eye on her drinking. All the time he himself is being harassed by a drunken guest who seems determined that Alan should join him in a drink, while another morose guest, mordantly surveying the proceedings, is pressing his attentions on Jenny, noticing her reluctance to drink and making a dull joke about "minding your Ps and Qs," meaning your pints and quarts. The tension goes up a further notch when Edna joins what is now being referred to as the "abstemious quarter" and gets into conversation about her pregnancy with Jenny, while Alan, momentarily cornered by the insistent drunk, looks on helplessly. However, when Jenny's resolve is finally broken and she accepts a Manhattan cocktail, Alan is compelled to move and quickly intervenes before she can take a sip with the offer of some food and a suggestion that they sit together so that he can ask her about the theater. All of this interplay is plotted with great visual finesse by Stevens, who gives the surface pleasantries a constant undercurrent of suspense, not least through his insertions of brief shots of Edna as she follows the path of her husband. This is another layer beneath the surface and an important one. The impression given is that she is quietly observing all that is going on and absorbing what she sees into an unspoken narrative, particularly when Alan rather loudly and rashly is asking Jenny why she has not returned his calls. Jenny looks back in the direction of Edna by way of explanation. Rather like Spencer Tracy's hero in *Woman of the Year* at that gathering of diplomats in the heroine's apartment, Alan's tactlessness seems intensified by his evident unease at a social event in which he feels an outsider.

Enter Tony Colton, to strain the atmosphere still further. It is quite a theatrical entrance; we hear the excitement at his arrival before we see him. It will be the character's only speaking appearance in the film, and Richard Derr does an exceptional job in so concisely conveying the sense of a narcissist who oozes self-importance; whose ostentatiously fluent French and even the elaborately fussy way he orders a cocktail betoken a character who demands center stage whatever the occasion; and who believes he only has to enter a room or conversation in order to dominate it. When he addresses Alan, he pauses slightly before saying his name, as if consciously giving the impression that he cannot quite remember who this inferior is and thereby immediately putting Alan slightly on the defensive (it is probably an ingrained strategy on Colton's part to keep his opposite number slightly off-balance). When he learns that Alan is in advertising, he seems more disdainfully amused than interested, which can only serve as another blow to Alan's diminishing self-regard, but the real focus of his attention is Jenny, permitting us once again to speculate on the precise nature of their relationship. Priding himself on being Jenny's "discoverer," he proceeds to embarrass her by praising the performance of the actress who replaced her in the Broadway production. He makes an obscure reference to American women as being "unsatisfactory lovers" and goes on to muse that, in the theater, talent alone is not enough; what one needs is "emotional stability." The motivation behind these calculated barbs remains obscure. It could reflect the twisted satisfaction of an egotist relishing the failure of someone who mistakenly believed she could succeed away from his guidance. Or, beneath the show of suave civility, is it the calculated spitefulness of a former lover who has been spurned by his protégé and who is now taking his revenge? Whatever the intention, the effect is immediate, for Jenny rises and rushes out of the room before Alan can stop her. During the exchanges, we notice that Edna has occasionally been taking quick looks over to their table; and in the taxi home with Alan, she muses on Jenny's abrupt exit. "I think I know the kind of girl she is," she says, thoughtfully. "She can be easily hurt." As if in response to Edna's observation, Stevens sympathetically dissolves to Jenny's sobbing in her hotel bedroom, traumatized by her encounter with Colton, tormented by her growing feelings for a married man, and with the phone ringing unanswered for (at a rough count) the eighth time in the film. Worried when she has failed to answer, Billy has entered her room and answers the phone on her behalf, telling Alan that she is fine and not to worry before replacing the receiver and telling Jenny that Alan is reassured that all is well. As he leaves the room, he turns to say: "If you believe that, you'll believe anything."

Billy is right. The scene dissolves to an aerial shot of Madison Avenue, with Alan looking forlornly out of his office window at the scene below and wondering whether to call Jenny. By now it is obvious he needs her support and reassurance quite as much as she needs his. Indeed he actually has the phone in the hand when he is interrupted by a secretary, who tells him he is needed at once in Crawley's office as the owners of Kennedy Shoes have arrived to assess and give their verdict on the company's proposed advertising campaign. The subsequent scene is the one occasion where Stevens permits himself to inject some humor into this predominantly somber film, partly at the expense of the strait-laced executives and partly at the unabashed hyperbole of advertising copy. We are surely meant to enjoy the deflation of the brashly confident Baker, whose romantic pitch for the product goes down like a lead balloon. "Who was the first person to drink champagne from a lady's slipper?" he ventures helpfully by way of explanation of his design, but the elderly executives look more perplexed than ever. On the other hand, everything about Alan's pitch for the product seems to strike the right note: the slogan, "Its Strength Is in the Arches"; the illustration of an Egyptian temple, whose archway reinforces the theme and has been plainly inspired by Alan's time at the museum with Jenny; and the emphasis on durability more than romance. "It tells the truth," says one of the Kennedys, appreciatively; and another says, "You've hit the ball squarely, young fella." (That last phrase is particularly satisfying, since Baker's youth has been used on previous occasions as a way of undermining Alan, by Crawley and, obliquely, by Tony Colton.) When the third of them says, solemnly, "It should get them … here," and touches his heart, Alan gives him a quick quizzical look: it is all he can do to restrain himself from laughing out loud. Yet their preference for Alan's approach over Baker's (durability being victorious over shallow romance) has some relevance to Alan's current emotional confusion and indeed to the state of his marriage, the significance of which he will not fully comprehend and accept until the final scene. For the moment he is still suffering from a hangover of melancholia that even his delighted boss notices. "You act like this beautiful baby of yours isn't yours," says Crawley. Momentarily the expression causes a slight jolt, as if Alan's future paternity is being alluded to rather than the campaign. "Well, it isn't entirely," Alan replies, adding to the discomfort of the moment, for he is thinking of how his meeting with Jenny in the museum has given birth to the idea. Trying and failing yet again to get through to Jenny to tell her the good news, he rings Billy at the hotel, who tells him that Jenny and the company are testing the new play in Baltimore and she will be departing from Pennsylvania station on the midnight train.

The spirit of David Lean's classic film of doomed romance, *Brief Encounter* (1945), hangs heavily over the scene of Alan and Jenny's farewell: the setting of the railway station; a tormented heroine in flight from an emotional entanglement that is spiraling out of control; the lovelorn hero unable to express the depth of his feelings and returning to his old life, with the long shot of his departure from the near deserted station powerfully suggesting the immensity of his self-pity. Consciously or not, in terms of ambience, mood and narrative, *Brief Encounter* seems much closer to *Something to Live For* than does *The Lost Weekend*, with which it is more often compared. Victor Young's lush piano main theme is so like Rachmaninov (one of Young's favorite composers) that one wonders if he had the use of Rachmaninov in *Brief Encounter* in his mind as a musical touchstone. In both films, the very word "romance" carries great significance, as has already been shown in analyzing the Stevens film; in Lean, it fits in with "delirium" in the crossword that Laura helps her husband with. Billy Wilder always said that his classic, *The Apartment* (1960), had been inspired by *Brief Encounter* and his speculation about the doctor's friend, whose flat the lovers are about to use for their guilt tryst. I wonder if Stevens was similarly inspired by Lean, but this time choosing to tell its story of doomed love not from the point of the wife (Celia Johnson) but from that of the married man, Alec Harvey (Trevor Howard) with whom she has fallen in love.

The connections between the two films are very striking. Like Trevor Howard's Alec, Ray Milland's Alan has two sons. As in *Brief Encounter*, hero first meets heroine when he goes to her assistance. Similarly, in both films, they will meet again accidentally over lunch, and continue their acquaintance afterwards: in Lean's film, at the cinema; in Stevens's film, in the theater. In both films it will be the hero who will be insistent about meeting again, in the face of the heroine's initial reluctance. In both, an intimate embrace will be interrupted by an embarrassing intrusion: in Lean's film, by Alec's friend; in Stevens's film, by Alan's son. In both films, it will be the heroine who breaks off these encounters because she feels "ashamed" of what is happening. Although we never see Alec's home life in *Brief Encounter* during the period of his unconsummated affair, one could imagine that it is something like that portrayed in *Something to Live For*: the boys running round the house, unconcerned and unaware; the husband seeming preoccupied, his mind elsewhere; his wife sensing that something is wrong but not sure how far to enquire. Given these connections, it is curious that David Lean's film has been acclaimed and loved over the years whereas a similar film by a director of comparable stature has been all but forgotten. One reason for this might be the different point of focus in both films. In Lean's film we see things almost entirely from the point of view of the wife and share her anguish through Celia Johnson's heartrending performance. In Stevens's film we see the film mainly from the point of view of the married man, whom audiences probably found significantly less sympathetic, not simply because of his pursuance of the affair itself (however much he defends it as essential to his survival from sinking again into alcoholism) but also because his wife is pregnant with his child, which adds an extra dimension of cruelty and irresponsibility to the proposed infidelity. *Brief Encounter* will be invoked again in the final scene, and with a few deft variations.

Some weeks have passed; Christmas is coming; and Alan and Jenny are destined to cross paths one last time. Jenny is back in New York for the Broadway premiere of *The Egyptians*, nervous and superstitious; she is very quick to prevent her co-star Albert (Paul Valentine) from walking under a ladder outside the theater. Meanwhile Alan is sitting glumly alone in his office, still wearing his hat and coat even though the office party is in full swing down the corridor. He will duly be joined by the revelers and will ruefully brush off some drink that one of them has spilt on his coat collar; it would not do for him to go home smelling of alcohol. He has been staring at the newspaper headline advertising the opening of Jenny's play that evening, and indeed he must have known about it for he has already sent her a plant for luck on the opening night. What he does not know is that Jenny has spotted Colton's elaborate bouquet among the messages, with a note to say that he will be there and scrutinizing her performance, which has prompted a recurrence of the flood of self-doubt that has driven her to the bottle to begin with. She hurries away from Albert, ostensibly to get some rest before their big night, actually to get some drink.

When Alan returns home, Edna and the boys are putting the finishing touches to the Christmas tree. He is still evidently out of sorts and a tiny gesture is very telling; he tosses his coat over the back of a chair rather than hangs it up, as if he does not feel quite at home. While the children are out of the room and bringing the stepladder so that their father can put the angel at the top of the tree, Edna again tries to find out what's wrong. "You're a very nice man, Mr. Miller," she says, "even if you don't think so yourself." It is one of those lines that, in an endeavor to cover over a weakness in the script, arguably only highlights it, for the film has not been as effective in projecting Alan's virtues, particularly in the home context, as his self-doubts. Again one might compare the film with a similar scene in *Brief Encounter*, when the husband is trying to discover from his wife what is troubling her and where there is a sense of a deep bond between them that seems missing in the Stevens' film, largely as a result of the hero's coldness. In Lean's film, the husband will suggest that they go out together to the cinema. In Stevens's film, Edna will suggest that they have a night out together and perhaps take in a new play. At that point the telephone rings; it is for Alan. "Somebody's in trouble and it might be serious," he says, picking up his coat and heading for the door. While on the ladder and decorating the tree, Edna says she will try to get tickets for a show and suggests trying for the opening night of a new play which is featuring the actress whom they met at David Baker's party. She has her back to the camera at this point, but there is something about Teresa Wright's delivery of the line that suggests that she *knows*; that she has sensed all along the root cause of Alan's melancholy and, in all likelihood, knows where he is going. At this point Stevens includes what is arguably the finest visual moment of the film: a medium shot of the home, with Edna on the far left side of the frame and half way up the stepladder, Alan on the far right of the frame hesitating at the door, and with the partition that separates the hallway from the living room almost dividing the screen in two. The evocation of distance, separation, precariousness and hesitancy in a single shot eloquently conveys the sense that, at that precise moment, a marriage is in the balance.

The film follows what is arguably its finest moment with what is probably its weakest scene. The call has been from Billy, who has heard the telephone ringing unanswered in Jenny's room and has been disturbed to find her door locked, at which point he has summoned Alan's help. When they burst into the room, they find that Jenny has been drinking again and is barely conscious. Sending Billy out to fetch coffee and some food, Alan takes charge. His arousal of her from despair does not convince and has a slightly unsettling tone. The dingy room seems to emphasize the predominant furtiveness of their romance. When Alan kisses her passionately and browbeats her into confessing her love for him (he reiterates "You love me, don't you?" three times), one could be forgiven for being less interested in her response than appalled by Alan's bullying behavior, particularly when one recalls that, in the previous scene, his wife's sincere statement, "I love you, Alan" has elicited no reaction from him whatever. When Jenny admits that she loves him but says, "Nothing can come of it," he replies: "There's a strength in it, don't you see?" He has pulled through these last few weeks without a drink because of his love for her; she can do the same because of her love for him. It sounds a rather fragile solution, as does his solution for her survival of the threat of Colton's scrutiny, which is simply to plunge her into a cold shower. Even if she can wash away the Colton curse that easily, there will still be the Broadway critics to face.

It is hard to know how seriously we are intended to take the play. From what one has heard from their reading in the museum and the snatches one sees on the stage, it looks frankly terrible. Considering its stilted archaic language and blatantly artificial sets, one wonders whether Stevens is deliberately satirizing Cecil B. De Mille, particularly *Samson and Delilah* (1949). Was Dwight Taylor paying affectionate homage to the now hopelessly outdated blood-and-thunder melodramas that his father, the theatrical producer and writer Charles Taylor, had brought regularly to Broadway in the early years of the century? Either way, at a time when the New York theatre was playing host to exciting new masterpieces from the likes of Tennessee Williams (*A Streetcar Named Desire*) and Arthur Miller (*Death of a Salesman*), one does have doubts about the longevity of the play and some qualms about the impact of that on Jenny's paper-thin confidence. Nevertheless, in terms of the film's development, what will be happening on stage between the Egyptian queen and her slave will be less important that what happens in the auditorium between Alan and Edna. If the film has faltered towards the end, it regains its balance in the final moments.

Alan has arrived at the theater just in time before the curtain rises. "There were two of them," he says quickly to Edna as he takes his seat beside her. "They got into a kind of tail-spin, but they're alright now." Because of her perceptiveness and her suspicions, Edna will doubtless have noticed the phrase "there were two of them" and suspected who the two were. Watching the play as it comes to the love scene between queen and slave ("Love is like the Nile…. Our eternity is now"), she recognizes the lines from the play script that has dropped out of Alan's pocket. Teresa Wright subtly conveys this with a very slight droop of the head and a barely perceptible glance towards her husband, who is close to tears. When filming *A Place in the Sun*, Stevens told Shelley Winters that "movie acting is talking soft and thinking loud" (Winters: 43). Here, in a supreme piece of movie acting, Teresa Wright does not need to talk at all to convey the loudness of her thoughts. At the end, she will be like the husband in *Brief Encounter*, recognizing the unspoken private agony endured by one's married partner, but, with infinite tact and compassion, offering a restoration of stability. *Brief Encounter* will call it "self-respect" and "decency"; in *Something to Live For*, it will suggest itself as "durability." Indeed Edna will surprise Alan by telling him of her own acting talent and ambitions when she was younger, laying them aside when she committed herself to marriage and children. "You can't have everything in this world," she tells him, "something had to give." Behind this is a wise and tender message: when you can't have what you love, you should love what you have. And she will cap this with a particularly shrewd payoff line. "By the way," she says, "did Crawley give up on that Egyptian account?" It is an obliquely subtle way of discovering whether Alan's infatuation is over. "Yes," he replies, "yes, I guess he did."

Alan's answer seems like that of a man coming out of a dream. *Brief Encounter* has sometimes been seen as the dream of an ordinary housewife with a romantic disposition who, seated in her armchair and listening to the music of Rachmaninov, fantasizes a doomed love affair that brings perilously close to the surface the dissatisfactions of her bourgeois life before she returns to the safe moorings of her marriage. Something of that feeling also pervades Stevens's film, particularly when one recalls that it begins with the curtain rising for the play, so the rest of the film could be a flashback, or a reverie perhaps, of a middle-aged Madison Avenue male with a drink problem, a dull job, and a stultifying family life who fantasizes a preferred narrative from his attraction to the leading actress on stage but who, by the end, has exorcized his forbidden longings and come to terms with the life he has.

It is a curious film certainly, full of bottled up emotions. Penelope Houston described it as "lugubrious" and "an unqualified failure" (Houston: 72); and although this now seems a little harsh, one would hesitate to argue that it was a success. Ray Milland's character seems ultimately unworthy of the two women who love him; maybe a voice-over would have helped in giving him a deeper, more sympathetic, interior personality. The relationship between Jenny and Colton is never fully explained, though Stevens might even have been drawing on his own experience when directing a young Joan Fontaine in *Damsel in Distress* and fearing her precarious self-confidence could have collapsed completely if she had known of the objections of Fred Astaire and Pandro Berman to her performance. Stevens was to direct Fontaine in four movies and, outside of Max Ophuls, no director has ever photographed her more beautifully. Teresa Wright somehow manages to turn the underwritten part of the wife into a fount of wisdom and understanding. For all its weaknesses, the film is still worthy of attention, for it upholds three central characteristics of Stevens's cinema: that you can freeze any frame in it and the camera always seems to be in the correct position; that however many times you watch it, you can always find something that you never spotted before; and that few Hollywood directors can match him for insight and subtlety when it comes to the portrayal of a marriage. You would expect this from the director of *Penny Serenade* and *Woman of the Year*; but it might surprise you when it turns out to be equally true of *Shane* and *Giant*.

• Five •

The American Dream,
1951–1956

The following three films constitute the summit of Stevens' achievement as a director and, in my opinion, are among the supreme masterpieces of American cinema. They marked a turning point in his career and a change of direction in his style. One can certainly see the same kind of sensitivity, compassion and comedy that marked his earlier films, but the trilogy is altogether more ambitious in scope than anything else he had attempted and the product of a more contemplative personality whose war experience had changed his sensibility. The films are all deeply American stories, infused with a unique sense of landscape and character that make up the personality of the country. Set partly in the past but bringing the story up to the present post-war era, the films reflect on the character and destiny of America. At the core of each is an outsider striving for assimilation and the promise that the country offers and whose aspirations become tantalizingly close to fulfilment, but whose ultimate dream of success and happiness will elude his grasp. Is it a failure of character or is the Dream itself a delusion? The endings of each of the three films defy convention and indeed classification—tragic? elegiac? hopeful?—but are each in their own way a magnificent summation, for they leave the conclusion to the audience.

A Place in the Sun (1951)

> "No themes are so human as those that reflect for us, out of the confusion of life, the close connexion of bliss and bale, of the things that help with the things that hurt, so dangling before us for ever that bright hard medal, of so strange an alloy; one face of which is somebody's right and ease and the other somebody's pain and wrong."—Henry James, Preface to *What Maisie Knew*

> "It will be a very good film, I think, but sad."—Ivan Moffat, associate producer on *A Place in the Sun*

After attending a preview screening of *A Place in the Sun*, Charlie Chaplin was heard to say that "it was the greatest movie ever made about America" (McCann: 49; Bosworth: 213). Considering the remark was made during the days of the HUAC investigations and prior to the imminent era of McCarthyism and the blacklist, such a tribute from a political hot potato like Chaplin might seem a dubious accolade and an impossible claim to live up to anyway. Still, no filmmaker worth his salt could accept such a compliment from a cinematic genius like Chaplin as anything but a tribute to cherish; and over the years the film has continued to receive equivalent acclamation from Stevens's colleagues and cinematic peers. In an interview in *Sight and Sound* (August 1956), Nicholas Ray was to put the film alongside *The Grapes of Wrath* and *Citizen Kane* as a Hollywood movie that demonstrated the possibility of appeasing the Front Office while being made without compromise. In an interview at the American Film Institute, Billy Wilder cited *A Place in the Sun* alongside *Battleship Potemkin* as a film he wished he had made (Stevens Jr.: 332). Woody Allen's *Match Point* (2005) is an homage to *A Place in the Sun,* not only in terms of its thematic similarity (social ambition leading to thoughts of murder) but even in terms of how hero and heroine first meet (in the games room). Mike Nichols claimed to have seen the film around 150 times, "because it's not only my favourite movie, it was my Bible" (when he was preparing to make his screen directing debut with *Who's Afraid of Virginia Woolf?*). He went on: "There's nothing you can't learn from George Stevens the way he shot *A Place in the Sun* and what it is" (*Becoming Mike Nichols,* HBO documentary, 22 February 2016).

Winning Stevens his first directing Oscar, *A Place in the Sun* was a turning point in his career. Gilbert Adair suggested that the subject of the film—the hero's pursuit of social status and a romantic ideal as an alternative to the mundane reality of his life thus far—was analogous to Stevens's own artistic ambitions at that time: his pursuit of what Adair called "self-conscious artistry" in preference to "the homelier virtues of his genre-related work" (Adair: 6). The film undoubtedly represented a more serious sensibility than in any previous Stevens film and one that would be sustained until the end of his career. The reason for it, however, had as much to do with autobiography as with artistic ambition. After what he had seen at Dachau, Stevens felt temperamentally unable to return to the realm of comedy on which he had built his reputation.

The film is an adaptation of Theodore Dreiser's mammoth sociological novel, *An American Tragedy,* which had been published in 1925. Dreiser had been inspired by an actual murder case in 1906, in which a young worker Chester Gillette (called Clyde Griffiths in the novel), anxious to climb the social ladder, had been tried and executed for the murder of his pregnant girlfriend Grace Brown, who worked with him in a New York skirt factory. Taking her out on a rowboat on Moose Lake, he had struck her over the head with an oar, so the prosecution had argued, before overturning the boat in an attempt to make the crime appear to be a boating accident.

Stevens was being bold in proposing this subject to Paramount, as the studio's previous attempts to bring the novel to the screen had not been successful. In 1930, during his ill-fated sojourn in Hollywood, Sergei Eisenstein had submitted a screen treatment that was acceptable to Dreiser but unacceptable to the studio; and the following year Josef von Sternberg had made a film version of *An American Tragedy* (1931), which Paramount had approved but which Dreiser thought was such a travesty that he filed an injunction against the studio in protest. In a memo to the head of Paramount, B.P. Schulberg (8 April 1930), a young David Selznick had described Eisenstein's scenario as "the most moving script I have read," but added that "when I had finished it I was so depressed I wanted to reach for the bourbon bottle. As entertainment I don't think it has one chance in a hundred" (qtd in Behlmer: 26). When Josef von Sternberg had come to make his film, he said: "I eliminated the sociological elements, which in my opinion were far from being responsible for the dramatic accident with which Dreiser had concerned himself" (Sternberg: 46). As the "sociological elements" were, in Dreiser's eyes, precisely the cause of the tragedy and the reason that he had written the novel in the first place, this approach, from the author's point of view, could not have been more ill-conceived.

Dreiser had died in 1945, so Stevens did not have to contend with the author's view-point, but the film has since been attacked for diluting the novel's social critique and reducing it to a tragic love story. Raymond Chandler was particularly venomous about what he called the picture's "bogus self-importance" (Chandler: 139). More temperately, and in the context of expressing overall great admiration for the film's cinematic skill, Penelope Houston suggested that "by bringing events forwards from the twenties to the 1950s, by softening and romanticising two of the leading characters, George Eastman (Montgomery Clift) and Angela Vickers (Elizabeth Taylor), by playing up the love story at the expense of the social criticism which was the mainspring of Dreiser's novel, the film seriously weakens its own dramatic impact" (Houston: 74). These are important considerations, but it can be argued in Stevens's defense that the changes Houston cites are essential to his conception. He wanted to tell a modern story that he felt was both more personal and more universal. It would not be fair to attack him for not being faithful to the novel, for he could hardly have signaled more clearly his intention to do something different. He changed the title (the new title was suggested by Ivan Moffat). He updated the drama to the present day, so the film's hero could be seen as a returning vet searching for a place in a much changed, money-oriented society. He significantly and symbolically changed the names of the three main characters. The rich heroine is now called Angela, to suggest how angelic she appears in the hero's eyes. The office girl he seduces (Shelley Winters) is given the cumbersome but potent name of Alice Tripp, which suggests how she will become an obstacle to the hero's search for happiness. (In the trial he will even trip on a rope from the replica boat that the prosecutor has produced as an important item of evidence into the courtroom as part of his cross-examination.) The hero's name, George Eastman comes from the real name of the photographic pioneer, Stevens saying that the inspiration came from Eastman-Kodak who had supplied his 16mm color film during the war. Also, in giving the main character his own first name, he might have been suggesting and indeed acknowledging some identification with him. It is a detail that Stevens seems intent on emphasizing: the character is referred to or called by his first name around 40 times in the film. Although Stevens's romanticism is evident throughout, which sometimes gives *A Place in the Sun* more the ambience of Scott Fitzgerald than Theodore Dreiser (*The Great Gatsby* appeared in the same year as *An American Tragedy*), underneath there is always a lurking sadness. For the first time, in Mark Harris's words, Stevens "peered into the ugliest recesses of human nature and personal ambition" (Harris: 440). Yet I would agree with Penelope Houston (and Mike Nichols' response would confirm this) that ultimately "the power of the film rests less in the story than in the skill and virtuosity in the telling of it" (Houston: 76). *A Place in the Sun* is the film of a real auteur.

Everything to come is foretold in the opening three minutes. A young man is standing at the side of an open highway, trying to hitch a lift. We are soon to learn his destination, but our knowledge of what has brought him to this point is delayed until much later. He is initially filmed from behind as he backs towards the camera, before turning and being given what Eric Hynes called "one of the greatest and most gasp-worthy of movie entrances" (Hynes: 48) when he moves into close-up. Montgomery Clift's screen presence has never been more strikingly captured. It is Stevens's way of announcing a new kind of movie hero whose sensitive, turbulent and troubled masculinity will come to typify a decade of rebellious or alienated males. The young man glances up at a huge billboard at the side of the road, featuring a reclining young woman in a swimsuit on a beach under the heading "It's an Eastman." We will learn that the billboard, with its promise of a place in the sun and which features his own name, encapsulates in an instant the ideal he is seeking. He is distracted by the sound of a car horn and he catches a fleeting glimpse of a young woman in a Cadillac speeding past, his first glimpse (although he does not know it as yet) of Angela Vickers and which subliminally seems to strike him like a bolt of lightning. ("I guess maybe I even loved you before I saw you," he will tell her at the later party scene, and this might be the moment when that happens.) When he hears the horn, there is a momentary sense that the dream-girl has stopped to give him a ride, but it is actually a friendly driver in a run-down truck, and George hesitates for a fraction before accepting, as if unwilling to relinquish his fantasy. Already the clash between romance and reality is apparent, prefiguring the way he will be trapped between the two worlds and by what Stevens will call "the extraordinary misfortune of having a mundane ideal presented to him in the most glamorous form" (Quoted in Cronin: 71).

Unwittingly helping George on his way to his tragic fate is his Uncle Charles (Herbert Heyes), president of Eastman swimsuit manufacturers, whose billboard has so entranced George. After a chance encounter in a Chicago hotel where George had been working as a bellboy, he had invited his nephew to call at the factory if he ever passed through that area and needed a job. When George rings his uncle at home from Eastman's office at work, it is clear from the uncle's reaction that he has forgotten this invitation and is somewhat taken aback by the speed with which the young man has taken him up on his offer. Nevertheless he invites him to the house that evening to talk further. A number of important details have been quickly assembled here. On his way to his uncle's office, George has unknowingly stepped into an elevator with his smartly dressed cousin, the aristocratically named Earl (Keefe Brasselle), who has taken no notice of him. It is one of those small events that already hints at the social disparities lurking at the heart of the film. When we first see the uncle, he is discussing business in the games room in his house, which will be the setting of George's fateful first face-to-face encounter with Angela. When Eastman's secretary ushers George into her employer's office so he can make his phone call in private, one senses his awe at the surroundings through the way he sinks into the chair and stares at a cheque for $100,000 to the Internal Revenue Service laid out on the desk, a sum he has most certainly never seen before in his life. Having made the phone call, he wastes no time in buying for the evening some tweeds that he sees in a store window (cost $35). Dissolve to a contrasting shot of Earl, in immaculate evening dress and straightening his bow-tie in the mirror, as Eastman tells everyone of George's imminent visit. The family seems somewhat taken aback and even alarmed. "What are we going to do about him socially?" asks Mrs. Eastman anxiously (a performance of poised snobbery by Kathryn Givney). Her husband assures her that there is no cause for alarm, for he is planning merely to offer him a job in the factory, not integrate him into the family circle.

Few directors can match Stevens for scenes of social embarrassment (think only of the party scene in *Alice Adams*); and the scene of George's visit to the Eastman home is an excellent demonstration. The low-angle shot from the family point of view as George enters the house seems to cut him down to size before he has spoken a word; and the very distance he has to cover in his approach conveys the social as well as physical gulf between them. His ill-fitting tweed jacket and trousers are in conspicuous contrast to the smartly attired Eastmans, who are about to depart for an evening engagement. Stevens's camera placement at every point suggests how out of place George is. Montgomery Clift's richly detailed performance compounds the impression, conveying George's nervousness not only through the hesitancy of his speech but through a series of physical gestures: twisting his hands in a way that reflects his inner tension; seeming slightly off-balance as he sits awkwardly at the edge of his chair, in contrast to the other members of the family who are lounging languidly in familiar surroundings; appearing to shrink slightly into the furniture during the awkward pauses; and rather self-consciously trying to relax by resting his elbow on the chair-arm as he deals with the family's insinuating questions. When his uncle asks if he has anywhere to stay, Mrs. Eastman leaps in fractionally too quickly to suggest that, if not, she would be able to recommend " a quiet little rooming house," barely suppressing her alarm that her husband might be tempted to invite him to stay with them. When George can reassure her that he has already found a room, she says, "That was fortunate," a response where, behind the civility, one can almost hear a suppressed sigh of relief. As George leaves, she whispers to her husband, "Charles Eastman," in gentle admonition of this kind-hearted but socially awkward occasion and no doubt thinking that this will thankfully be the last she will see or hear of this nephew. In fact, a similar gesture of her husband later, brought about by a similar forgetfulness, will nudge the narrative even more decisively along its tragic path.

As George is haltingly explaining the nature of his mother's religious and charity work in response to a slightly patronizing inquiry from Eastman's daughter, Marsha (Lois Chartrand), we hear a car horn outside, which takes us suddenly back to the film's opening and for the same reason: it announces the presence of Angela Vickers. It is something that will occur again in the film and is an example of the way Stevens conceived the soundtrack of the film almost as a dramatic score in its own right, where certain sounds (like Angela's imperious car horn, or the sharp cry of a loon in Loon Lake, or the barking of a dog, or the roar of a speedboat) accumulate significance through the context in which they are heard or recalled. When Angela breezes into the house, one cannot but contrast the ease and confidence she immediately exudes in that milieu to George's earlier entrance, where diffidence has dogged his every step. It is striking that no one thinks of introducing Angela to George; and, in her excited chatter about her new vacation house at the lake ("a dream palace," she says, "I'm going to end my days there") to Mrs. Eastman, she literally does not see him. But once again, her appearance is enough to jerk George's head instantly in her direction as if magnetized. In Book Two, Chapter X of the novel, Dreiser describes the effect on the hero of his first sight of the heroine as "electric— thrilling—arousing in him a curiously stinging sense of what it was to want and not to have—to wish to win and yet to feel almost agonizingly that he was destined to win not even a glance from her" (Dreiser: 225). Later we will see George in his rooming house, drafting a production report to send to his uncle, but with the neon sign "Vickers" lit up outside his window, a reminder of the young woman who has so jolted his senses. There is a newspaper photograph of her in anticipation of her appearance at a soirée at the Eastman home, and we see George waiting outside the gates, just hoping to catch a glimpse. After she has passed through, Stevens gives us a shot of George behind the bars, as if this is a world from which he will always be excluded. Ironically, the shot is a pre-monition of the future as well as a reflection of the present, for, when the seemingly unattainable is actually within his grasp, the ultimate destination of his dream will be a prison cell on executioners' row. The shot is one of many examples in the film of Stevens's extraordinary visual compression, where so many dimensions of the drama coalesce in a single image.

At the request of his father, Earl has assigned George to a menial job at the factory, becoming, in a sense "one of the girls." Feeling that Angela Vickers is completely out of his league, George is drawn to a more down-to-earth object of desire, Alice Tripp, who works with him on the assembly line at the Eastman factory. They have worked together for months, exchanging looks but without exchanging a word, for it is a company rule that male workers at the plant must not fraternize with the female employees who make up most of the workforce. However, after his forlorn sojourn outside the Eastman place, one evening he has gone on his own to the cinema and has found himself sitting alongside Alice, who is also unaccompanied. The movie they are watching is an invention for the film and credited on the poster inside the movie theater as Ivan Moffat's *Now and Forever,* which Stevens's friend and associate producer Moffat was to call a "little affectionate tease." Yet perhaps there is more to this detail than an in-joke. "Now and Forever" is how Alice will come to see her relationship with George, whereas, for George, his relationship with Alice will be "Now" but with Angela "Forever." Some of the dialogue we hear coming from the screen (e.g., "Do you really think we could be happy, never seeing anyone again?") will anticipate some of the things Alice will say to George in their final boat journey, as if almost subconsciously, and poignantly, she is remembering the occasion which first brought them together.

Casting the role of Alice proved quite a challenge. Donna Reed and Ruth Roman were considered, as was Cathy O'Donnell, who was thought to be "too soft" for a part which demands a certain toughness and resentment as the character's prospects and situation deteriorate. Barbara Bel Geddes had been ideal in *I Remember Mama,* but, for *A Place in the Sun,* Stevens told her: "You play that girl, and when the boat goes over and you go to the bottom of the lake, the film goes with it" (qtd in Moss: 160). He knew that if the character was too sympathetic, the circumstances of her death would destroy any sympathy an audience might have for the hero. Indeed this was widely thought to be the reason that von Sternberg's version of the tale had failed, for, when Sylvia Sidney's victim had died, the film had seemed to die along with her. At the same time the audience has to feel some pity for her and her plight, or the hero's dilemma and moral crisis become correspondingly weakened. At that time more associated with the roles of blonde bombshell, Shelley Winters was cast against type and apparently landed the part when she turned up for an audition dressed in the clothes of a typical factory girl and Stevens did not at first recognize her. Later to admire Stevens above all other directors she worked with, Winters initially clashed with him over the role, thinking he was making the characterization too drab; Montgomery Clift also thought Stevens was coaxing a performance that made the character from the start "too downbeat, blubbery, irritating" (qtd in Bosworth: 184). Yet misery is visually unattractive; it would be sentimental to represent it otherwise. And the character is more forceful and sympathetic than Clift's description might suggest. In his assessment of the film, Eugene Archer interestingly contended that women tended "to identify absolutely" with this character, "a circumstance which governs their response to the film" (Archer: 25); and one can certainly see how the majority of a post-war female audience would have much more in common with Alice than with a wealthy socialite such as Angela. Whether or not one agrees with Stevens's concept of the role, it would be hard to deny the potency of Shelley Winters' Oscar–nominated performance of an ill-used young woman grimly, and understandably, determined not to be left in the lurch. Two of the greatest sequences in the film (the scene at the doctor's and the scene on the lake) owe much of their power to the intensity that she brings to the character's despair and desperation.

In his 1967 interview with Robert Hughes, Stevens said: " I wanted her to be the kind of girl a man could be all mixed up with in the dark but come the morning wonder how the hell he got into this. If he was married to her, the sound of her voice would be pleasant, he would be comfortable with her, but because he had other ideas, it's impossible" (qtd in Cronin: 70). This harsh characterization of the hero's behavior would certainly validate Alice's later truculence and her insistence that he must face up to his responsibilities towards her and their unborn child. The presentation of the relationship leaves us in no doubt as to who is the main predator, for in their walk together after the cinema showing, it is Alice who keeps reminding him of the company rule about no fraternization between employees and that he is an Eastman and in a different social strata from the others. "I'm in the same boat as the rest of you," he says, an unconsciously ominous comment in view of later events; and, disregarding her caution, he takes the romantic lead, putting his arm around her, kissing her, and not wanting her to go. As Mandy Merck has noted: "she goes into her room and stands in its window as George looks at her from below—in roughly the same position in which he first beheld the Eastman billboard" (Merck: 127). It might seem as if the billboard image has been transformed in George's mind into that of Alice Tripp, but the ambience is decidedly less romantic and the image literally much darker. He seems genuinely touched by Alice's loneliness, but this makes her all the more vulnerable to his advances.

There are two other details in this scene worth mentioning. As they are walking down the street, they pass a small group of Salvation Army worshippers who are singing hymns and collecting for their cause. George's response—and the close-up of a boy among the group, whom he views almost as a memory of his own past—is typical of the way the film often manages to compress large chunks of the novel into a few images. As Penelope Houston observed, this "momentary street scene … gives us a glimpse of George's whole, harsh, puritanical street mission childhood" (Houston: 76). Indeed it goes further than that, because George's reaction—initially startled, and then physically recoiling from the sight—indicates his hypersensitivity to his background and his consequent resolve to put his past behind him. (It is worth noting that Michael Wilson and Harry Brown's adaptation is also a masterpiece of compression: later in the film, when George gives an account of his background to Angela's father, they manage to summarize in a few lines practically the whole of Book One of the novel.) The other significant moment is Alice's revelation to him that she cannot swim. "I was even scared of the duck pond when I was a kid," she tells him. George is amused by the irony of that for someone who is working in a factory that makes swimsuits; but it is knowledge that he will put to a deadly purpose when Alice is threatening to blight his chances of future happiness with Angela.

The relationship between George and Alice will be an essentially nocturnal affair, because the penalties of discovery would be severe (they could both lose their jobs). Their growing intimacy will also be accelerated by social circumstances, for they have difficulty in finding places where they can be alone. A drunk interrupts their conversation in a café; a policeman moves them on when they are kissing in the car; and a rainstorm forces them to shelter on Alice's porch prior to saying goodnight. When Alice accidentally knocks the volume control on the radio by her open window, George swiftly darts indoors to switch it down so as not to alert the landlady; and when Alice follows, George starts dancing with her in the dark to the music on the radio and closes the door behind her with his foot. We hear Alice sighing, "O George" as the camera moves slowly towards the radio by the window. Almost imperceptibly, the light changes; the rain outside has stopped; it is dawn. We catch a glimpse of someone quickly leaving the room and passing the window, an indirect way of indicating—1950s Hollywood style—that the two have spent the night together.

Cut to a shot of the factory horn as it sounds the start of a new working day. Charles Eastman is visiting the plant and notices with dismay that Earl had assigned George to a routine job on the assembly line rather than somewhere more befitting an Eastman. Attempting to retrieve the situation, he goes over to George and says, "I suppose you thought I'd forgotten all about you" (he has); but is then further discomfited when George asks him whether he has seen the production report he had submitted (clearly he knows nothing about it). In the same way as he had invited George to the house some months ago to cover his surprise when George has phoned him out of the blue, he now attempts to deflect his embarrassment by inviting him to attend an upcoming party at his house. It happens to fall on the same day as George's birthday, which Alice has been hoping to celebrate secretly with him. This invitation, which is virtually an after-thought, will have profound repercussions, for it is at this party that George will meet Angela, and his whole world will be turned on its head.

When George arrives at the party, he is in a cluster of other people and enters unannounced and unnoticed, his outsider status further underlined by the fact that he is wearing a business suit for what is a black tie affair. As he moves into the house, he could be all but invisible, as people seem to be dispersing in different directions and holding animated conversations in which he takes no part. There is an embarrassing moment when his cousin Marcia comes towards him as if remembering the time when they had met before. George is all set to acknowledge her greeting, but she is actually smiling in welcome at the people alongside him and moves past without seeming to see him. As the reception area clears and George is left standing alone, he wanders into the games room and starts occupying himself with a game of billiards. A successful trick shot suddenly draws a quiet response of "Wow" from the direction of the slightly open door; and George turns and comes face to face with Angela Vickers. The alternating large close-ups that follow, as each looms large in the other's eyes, also seem to proclaim "Wow"; the attraction between them is immediate and electric.

In his article on Stevens, Douglas McVay referred to "Angela's unlikely reciprocation of George's passion" (12). This seems to me a criticism that is more applicable to the novel than the film. In Dreiser's novel, the equivalent to Angela, Sondra is a shallow character whose harsh portrayal represents the author's view of the heartlessness of the moneyed classes. In the film, she is much more sympathetic and credible. Even from the point of view of casting, Angela's passion for George seems entirely plausible, for it is well documented that the young Elizabeth Taylor was infatuated with Clift. Yet Elizabeth Taylor is also extremely good in this scene, particularly when one remembers that she was only 17 at the time of filming; had never had any acting training; and, as she was fond of pointing out, prior to *A Place in the Sun,* her leading men had been either dogs or horses. She quickly suggests that Angela is drawn to a certain mystery and sensitivity to George that seems quite different from the self-confident and superficial social set she is used to and might be more in accord with her own complicated, highly strung personality. "Being exclusive? Being dramatic? Being blue?" she asks. She becomes even more intrigued on discovering that he is an Eastman and that he has been following her progress through reading about her in the newspapers. During their conversation Angela has been walking slowly round the billiard table and then has positioned herself behind him to watch. However, billiards is now the last thing on George's mind; and when he turns to face her, the nervous tension and excitement in the air is palpable.

At this moment George's uncle enters, suggesting that George might like to ring his mother to tell her of his promotion. Considering his sensitivity about his background and with Angela in the room, it is actually the last thing that George wants to do, but he is unable to resist his uncle's kindly insistence, particularly as there is a telephone to hand in the room. It is an important dramatic moment, because it is the first time we have seen George's mother (Anne Revere) and in her actual environment (the Bethel Independence mission in Kansas City); and it takes Stevens less than a minute to suggest the background of George's youth from which he is trying to escape. When she hears the pop of a champagne bottle being opened, his mother immediately asks George where he is, and with whom. "It's me, Mama!" Angela shouts jokingly down the phone. When his mother asks who that was, George has to respond, "Just a girl, Mama" (Elizabeth Taylor's reaction shot at that is a picture of amused effrontery), which is the opposite of what he feels and the impression he wishes to make. George's embarrassment throughout the phone call is excruciating, partly because he is afraid it will clinch his character in Angela's eyes as a "mother's boy." (It does anticipate how George's fate will be exclusively determined by the women in his life.) "Did you promise to be a good boy? Not to waste your time on girls?" she asks as he puts down the phone. "I don't *waste* my time," George says in response, retrieving the initiative with what is the most assertive thing he has said thus far in the film. When Angela leads him away to dance, we have the film's most expressive slow dissolve, with the shot of the mother's pensive expression as she replaces the receiver superimposed over that of George and Angela as they move towards the dance floor in the expensive and expansive surroundings of the Eastman home. It is a shot that links George's past, present, and, with the mother's sense of foreboding, his future also. Hours later he and Angela are still dancing. From a close-up of the couple, Stevens dissolves to a shot of Alice's front door and then pans to a shot of Alice's bedroom, where we can see the cake she has prepared for his birthday and, in medium shot, a forlorn Alice half-asleep on her bed as she waits for George to appear.

"I wanted to edit the film together in a way that meant more than the addition of one scene to another," Stevens told an American Film Institute audience on 23 May 1973. "I wanted a kind of energy to flow through…. Shelley Winters bursting at the seams with sloppy melted ice-cream in a brass bed, as against Elizabeth Taylor in a white gown with blue balloons floating from the sky. Automatically that's an imbalance, and by imbalance you create drama" (Stevens Jr.: 233). This imbalance is reinforced by the contrast in mood and camera placement, as the film moves from romance to rancor; and from a close-up of George and Angela together to a medium shot of George and Alice, who is filmed with her back to the camera, so that we are made aware of the dismal room and Alice's equally dismal mood. "We're in trouble, real trouble," she tells George, and even audiences at that time would have needed little prompting to deduce what she means. It is a pivotal point, because from this moment on, there is no scene in the film involving Angela that is not shadowed, complicated or complemented by our knowledge of the situation of

Alice nor is there any subsequent scene where George is not being tormented by his divided emotions and by twin forces pulling in opposite directions of duty and desire.

Dissolve to a shot of Alice and George, where he is now in an office that looks out onto the assembly line. The distance between them has grown physically as well as emotionally, something which Alice has predicted during their first walk together. ("Pretty soon they'll move you up to a better job … and that's the last we'll see of George Eastman.") The following scene takes place in George's rooming house and is framed around two contrasting phone calls, one from George to Alice, saying he has so far had no luck in finding a doctor, and another immediately after, when George is unexpectedly called by Angela, who is inviting him to a party that week. Montgomery Clift conveys George's change of mood simply through a difference in posture: he is slightly crouched when talking to Alice, as if weighed down by the pressure they are under, but straightens noticeably when he realizes the second call is from Angela. Stevens shoots from inside the room and through a half open door as George uses the phone in the hallway; and he holds the shot as George comes back and slumps in his chair, initially elated by Angela's call but returning to his problems on re-entering his room. Stevens then cuts to a shot of George in Angela's car in much the same kind of posture: it's a few days later, but the posture suggests a continuity of mood and a preoccupation that Angela cannot help but notice. "You seem troubled … as though you were holding something back," she says to him, as they dance. (His greeting at the Eastmans', incidentally, is notably warmer than the last occasion, and even Marcia says hello, as if Angela's company confers on him a seal of social approval.) The word "trouble" sounds a warning knell, and he is indeed holding something back, but "the trouble is…" he says, "I'm too happy tonight" and it is that point that he declares that "I've loved you since the first moment I saw you…. I guess maybe I even loved you before I saw you." "And you're the fellow who wondered why I invited you here," she replies, and starts to say, "I love—" before suddenly fearing that people might be watching and rushing out onto the balcony, with George following. She can then say openly, "I love you too! It scares me!…"

In the feature documentary that accompanies the DVD release of the film, Alan J. Pakula has described their scene together on the balcony as "the best kissing scene in movies." It is visually and emotionally overwhelming, particularly as accompanied by Franz Waxman's glorious love theme, one of the most beautiful in film music. Stevens said that he "wanted to get the feeling of them being totally lost in each other," and he does so through the use of huge close-ups, where their faces seem to merge into each other, and through a dialogue delivery that comes out in whispered gasps as if they can hardly breathe through the pressure of emotion. "Oh Angela," George says, "if only I could tell you how much I love you. If I could only tell you all." "Tell mama," she replies, "Tell mama all." Elizabeth Taylor had problems with that line as she did not really understand it, but it links back to that earlier phone conversation Angela was overhearing between George and his mother, her sense of George as a "mother's boy," and the feeling at this moment of an all-consuming protectiveness towards him. Alan Pakula even called this scene Wagnerian, whose ecstasy is, as he put it, "comparable in film ways what Wagner was doing in *Tristan and Isolde*." The comparison might seem exaggerated, but it is apt, because, as well as being infused with a sense of ecstasy, the scene has also an unmistakable sense of impending doom. George is overcome by the one thing that he could never have anticipated in his wildest dreams: that his feelings for Angela might be reciprocated, which can only add to the anguish of his situation and the terrible secret he cannot disclose. When the shot of their kissing is repeated at the end of the film, it is in a context laden with death as he is being marched to the execution chamber. And the shot is not simply a romantic memory but a confirmation that it was Angela's image in his mind at the point of Alice's death and it is that which has led to his conviction.

There follows an abrupt shift of mood: from the ecstasy of Angela to the agony of Alice, as she visits a doctor to inquire about an abortion. Because of the Production Code, the word "abortion" could not be used. (William Wyler was to encounter a similar hurdle when he needed to introduce a key reference to abortion in his film of the same year, *Detective Story*.) Nevertheless, it could be argued that the scene is all the more powerful because of that. Alice is too frightened and ashamed to use the word and she is asking a doctor whom she is visiting for the first time to break the law. For all the indirection and fencing, which is turning a consultation scene into a suspense sequence, it is unlikely that many people in the audience would have been unaware of what really is being discussed between the two of them. In an American Film Institute seminar in May 1975, Ivan Moffat recalled that, when the scene was shown, audiences at the time became, as he put it, "deathly still—they couldn't believe what they were seeing," and he reminded the seminar that "in 1951, there was no question of anyone getting an abortion without extreme difficulty, danger and at great cost."

The impact is undoubtedly strengthened by the way the scene is directed and acted. Stevens begins with a shot of Dr. Wyeland (Ian Wolfe) in the foreground of the frame, filling in a form and then swiveling round in his chair to talk to his patient, so that, like him, an audience is watching Alice as she begins to stammer out a seemingly rehearsed version of the reason for her visit. She gives a false name and says she has been married for three months. Stevens holds the shot for longer than what might be expected, withholding a cut back to the doctor for his reaction, so that Alice's explanation seems to drop into a dangerous void as her awkwardness and hesitancy become more apparent. Shelley Winters is superb here, not playing for overt sympathy, but so tense that even the quiet chiming of a clock in the room makes her start slightly. She is astutely supported by one of Hollywood's most reliable character actors, Wolfe, who precisely catches Dr. Wyeland's change of mood and approach: at first comfortably seated and kindly; then shifting slightly in his chair, as he begins to sense that the patient is holding something back; and then beginning to move around the room when it becomes clear what is being asked of him, albeit indirectly. "Tell me, how did you happen to come to me anyhow?" he asks, pointedly. When Alice tells him she is not married and begins to sob quietly, he says to her, quite sharply, "All right, that won't do any good," before resuming his position behind his desk and assuming again his demeanor as a paternalistic doctor who will do everything he can to ensure the health of her and her child. However, if she is asking for services beyond that, he says, "I cannot help you." It is left ambiguous whether the doctor is also a secret abortionist or whether George (who has set up the appointment) has been misinformed, in which case the doctor's severity towards Alice is understandable. If the latter, then her sense of humiliation would be even more complete. This scene is included in *The Ivan Moffat File*, as an example of Moffat's contribution to the screenplay (see Lambert: 261–5); and it is interesting to note that, in the finished film, there are some minor changes, noticeably to do with Alice's behavior. In Moffat's extract, Alice is more hysterical and grabs the doctor by his lapel at one point whereas in the scene as filmed, she is more passive, Shelley Winters conveying the sense of someone so deadened by shame that she can barely rise from her chair. It is the performance of someone who has just been put through the worst experience of her life. Small wonder that David Mamet, in his personal roll call of great screen acting, included "Shelley Winters' dejection in *A Place in the Sun*" (Mamet: 168).

When Alice comes out of the doctor's office, George is standing across the street in shadow and with his back to the camera. As Alice walks to the car, Stevens pans right as George walks parallel to her on the opposite side of the street, obviously wanting to give the impression for any onlooker that the two are not together. Only at the last moment does he cross the road and get into the car beside her, when Alice tells him what has happened and says that they must get married, and soon. The visual presentation of this scene, with George completely in shadow, has the effect of shrouding his behavior in furtiveness and ignominy, particularly when contrasted to Alice's agonized self-exposure in the previous scene. His face remains in shadow until he returns to his rooming house and switches on the light, when his confusion and self-torment are plain to see. His sought-for place in the sun is turning into a nightmare of the soul. His distraught mood is further accentuated by the neon "Vickers" sign flashing outside his window, as if in mockery of his aspirations; but also by a radio report about the dangers of taking a swim on unpatrolled beaches in this warm weather, which has accounted for at least five deaths in the area. A close-up of George gives the sense of the report's setting off a train of thought deep in his subconscious that he would rather not face, whereupon he throws himself on his bed in a paroxysm of torment and self-disgust. At which point we hear the unmistakable sound of Angela's car horn outside his window, a siren call of desire that is simultaneously a delirious distraction from his mood of despair but also an intensification of it.

There is something painful in the extreme contrast between his delight at seeing Angela when compared with the gloom of his scene with Alice; and between Angela's unbridled joy and Alice's limitless pain, neither of them knowing anything of the other nor that George is the common factor in their contrasting moods. Angela has come to invite him to stay at her lakeside retreat where he can meet her parents, and when he says he is expected at the Eastmans' over that period, she says that the Eastmans are coming too, so there is no problem. A later phone call to Alice, where George asks her agreement to postpone their marriage for a week so he can accept an invitation to stay with the Eastmans, which could be financially advantageous to them both, confirms his deceit and duplicity. There is a moment during his conversation in the car with Angela, when he says almost sheepishly, "And you love me?" as if he still cannot quite believe that this is happening and that the unattainable romantic dream is coming true. Yet there is also something sinister behind the question, which, in the full context of the narrative, makes one's blood run cold. Is he, as it were, testing the water to see where this love might lead? For he must recognize that the attainability of the dream brings the barely contemplated imperative of murder much closer to the surface of his consciousness.

"George, what are you thinking about?" asks Angela, after she has been for a swim in Loon Lake, which she describes as "my lake," a private retreat which few know about other than herself. The question is similar to the one she has posed at the party, when she has sensed he is troubled. From the start, she has seemed unusually sensitive to the depths and complexities of George's moods. ("And I used to think *I* was complicated," she says). As in the party scene, George can give a plausible surface answer to Angela's query—he is worried about how Angela's parents will react to their relationship—but what he is really thinking about is something darker. He has been startled by the cry of a loon and he is also pondering the story Angela has told him about the accidental death by drowning in the lake the previous year and how it had taken five days to find the body. The music pounds ominously over the soundtrack like an anxious heartbeat as he stares out at the lake; and Stevens dissolves very slowly at this point to a shot of a disconsolate Alice as she walks towards her mailbox hoping to find a card or letter from George but finding only the morning paper. As she stands at the center of the frame, Stevens overlaps the shot of the lake, as if to represent George's imagination and what he is *really* thinking about, and also as if in foreboding for Alice's fate, for this is indeed where she will end up. Alice's misery is compounded when she sees George in a picture at the front of the newspaper among Angela's social set and realizes that he has lied to her about his where-abouts, which in turn will prompt her to take action. That newspaper picture will be important in another scene, because when it is discovered by the police in Alice's room and the landlady mentions that she thought Alice had been seeing "an Eastman," it is very straightforward for them to deduce who was meant. At this point, Stevens dissolves from the newspaper to a shot of flames at the Hawaii-style party being enjoyed at the lakeside retreat and being hosted by the Vickers. In context, it looks like simply a means of moving from one scene to the next, though highlighting the contrast between the two social spheres. Yet it is more than that, for it prefigures a matching shot later in the film, when the maid is instructed by Mrs. Vickers to burn any newspapers that contain a report of George's murder trial and we are given what David Mamet in his select category of Good Ideas the example of Stevens's shot of Elizabeth Taylor as "she sits alone, and the fire in the fireplace is superimposed on her, reflected in the window" (Mamet: 106). Those twin images encapsulate the entire tragedy of the film.

When Alice calls George at the Vickers' house from a nearby bus station, one is momentarily reminded of the way George had been unsettled by the phone conversation with his mother at the Eastmans'. The moment he seems to be making a favorable impression and moving into a society he covets, a phone call from what he sees as the less desirable side of his life and personality plunges him back to where he was in the social hierarchy. The phone call this time places the danger nearer at hand, for Alice is threatening to come over or to telephone the newspapers with her story before killing herself if he does not agree to meet her now and to get married immediately. Excusing himself from the table with a story about his mother's illness (not the first time in the film when he has shown himself to be an accomplished liar, something which will undermine his defense at his trial) George hurries to the bus station before Alice can do any more damage and drag their affair into the open. They agree to marry the next day.

Arriving at the office of the Warsaw County Court House, George and Alice walk down to the far end of the hall to the marriage license office. They are faced by a glass door on which is written, "Registry, Births, Marriages, Deaths," which catches the entirety of their dilemma in a single phrase. Almost simultaneously they are confronted with a sign: the office is closed because of Labor Day. Did George know that when he agreed to the marriage the previous evening? The film leaves this ambiguous, inviting an audience to consider this as an intervention of fate which will determine the future course of the action. Would George have gone ahead with his murder plan if he and Alice had married at this point? Somehow one doubts it, and Montgomery Clift skillfully suggests genuine confusion at this unexpected turn of events, mingling momentary relief with a surge of elation, as if this twist of fate is a sign, or opportunity, for what he must do. Why don't they come back tomorrow, he suggests, and just enjoy today by having a picnic in the lake? "When he is making this proposal," said Stevens, "he is committing himself to his destiny." To convey this, Stevens's camera is looking over George's shoulder; and, behind him, and visible through the open door, is the courtroom, the bar of justice, and the judge's empty chair. Like the slow dissolve between the empty lake and Alice's forlorn walk to her mailbox, the shot is both an indicator of what is going on in George's mind (his criminal intent) and an omen of where it will lead (his trial).

Reviewing the film in *Sight and Sound,* a young Karel Reisz was particularly impressed by the scene on the lake that follows. "[It] develops in a series of slow, isolated impressions taken in different settings at different times of day and evening," he wrote, "in which the changing quality of the images rather than any continuous dramatic development creates the powerful effect of hysteria: it is a most daringly conceived piece of cinema" (Reisz: 121). Giving a false name to the boat keeper (Douglas Spencer), George sets off with what seems a clear intention of murder in mind, the suspense heightened by the fact that Alice is unsuspecting and at last able to feel cheerful about the two of them together. As the day lengthens, the atmosphere becomes more oppressive. Stevens alternates between close shots of George and Alice and long shots of the distant boat, looking fragile and vulnerable on the dark lake. Alice chatters cheerfully, her words echoing, perhaps even unconsciously, the dialogue that was playing on the screen when she met George in the cinema ("It's like we were the only two people left in the whole world"). By contrast, George is mainly silent, preoccupied, concentrating on the rowing, though the beads of sweat on his forehead seem less expressive of physical exertion than of inner tension, with apprehension beginning to ooze from every pore. The music is quiet but not peaceful, with an insistent rhythm like a throbbing headache. George is startled by the cry of a loon, a sound that is natural but also subjective, in that it cannot fail to bring back the memory of the earlier scene at the lake with Angela when this plan was first forming in his head. There is a sudden *fortissimo* outburst in Waxman's score when Alice says, "There'll be more than two of us," as if George is suddenly and shockingly reminded that the killing of Alice would also mean the killing of their unborn child. The boat now begins to drift, correlating to George's shift from initial determination to gathering indecision. Eisenstein's treatment for this scene proposed the use of an inner voice alternating between cries of "Kill!" and "Don't Kill!" to convey the hero's torn emotions, but Montgomery Clift needs no words to convey what is going through George's mind: the nervous eye movements that perfectly encapsulate Dreiser's description of them as "terrified pools of misery," the crouched posture, the hands half covering the face, the perspiration on his forehead, all combine to convey the impression of someone struggling with an almost insupportable pressure of conflicting emotion. Everything that has happened to George in his life thus far is converging towards this single moment of an ex-mission boy now on a mission of murder: the impoverished Puritan background; his ambition in conflict with his conscience, his overpowering love for Angela, so tantalizingly within reach, set against his pity for Alice, that is dragging him back from his dream, his reluctance to go against his own moral nature contending with his frustration at the one thing that stands in the way of his fulfillment.

The breaking point must come; and it comes when Alice sees a star. She makes a wish; that George would love her again. "Did you make a wish?" she asks, and again later: "What did you think of when you saw the star?" When George says "I'll make it up to you," he seems to have acknowledged that he cannot go through with his plan, but Alice's continuing description of what their future together will be like only underlines for George the agony of what he has lost. As the music swerves into a distorted version of the love theme to suggest the disintegration of his future with Angela, even Alice can read the meaning behind his tormented features. "Maybe you wished that I was dead," she says. "Is that it?" "No, I didn't!" he shouts, standing up in the boat. "Now just ... leave me alone," he continues, sitting down again. But the movement has caused a sudden instability, and Alice, wanting to apologize ("Oh, poor George! I know it isn't easy for you, I shouldn't have said that, I..."), starts towards him. "Stay where you are!" he shouts, but the boat rocks and before he can catch her, the boat has turned over, throwing them both into the lake.

"All of us involved," wrote Ivan Moffat, "wanted the act itself to appear ambiguous. In taking Alice out on the lake, his motive was murder, but when he came to the point he had second thoughts. The scene was therefore shot and edited with that in mind¬— morally guilty, but, in a narrow technical sense, innocent" (Moffat: 221). It is the perfect metaphor for a character whose every emotion seems divided and whose every motion seems to entrap him further in an insoluble dilemma. Stevens cuts to a medium shot before showing George as he clambers out of the water, so we never know whether he searched for Alice before saving himself, but his escape is only a prolongation of torment. Even when he returns to the Vickers' summer retreat, he seems a doomed, hunted man, unable to shake off even for a moment the memory of what he has done. Perhaps inspired by a passage in the novel when the hero has a nightmare about a savage black dog that tries to bite him, George becomes hyper-aware of the sound of a barking dog, which reminds him of the one he has passed at the Boy Scouts' camp when he is trying to find the road. He starts when a young woman squeals in delight as she is tossed playfully in the water, her scream reminding him of Alice. He winces involuntarily when Angela says to him sympathetically, "Poor George," for Alice has used the same phrase during their final moments on the boat. A police siren sets his nerves jangling, when Angela is pulled up for speeding, but how easily she deals with this infringement of the law; the policeman's recognition of her (and implicitly the family she belongs to) immediately predisposes him to leniency. Ironically, at the same time as the Vickers' family is beginning to warm to Angela's young man for his quiet courtesy and his candor about his background, the police net is closing around him. Weighed down by guilt, George seems now perpetually tired and barely able to lift his head. At one moment Stevens will include a striking deep-focus shot, where the jollity of the Vickers' social set heard on a speedboat in the back-ground is offset by a shot of a portable radio left behind on the quayside as it reports the discovery of Alice's body and the search for the young man who accompanied her. Stevens told Robert Hughes that he took out the sound of the motorboat engine and replaced it with the sound "of a Nazi Spitzinbomber, the ones that used to dive on the people on the road when they were trying to get out of France," so that when the motorboat pulls away, the audience "are hearing a vicious sound that they might associate with other things" (qtd in Cronin: 71). Against this ostensibly exuberant but actually harsh background, the foregrounding of the radio is also inviting us to recall that earlier shot of the radio in Alice's room, playing music as George and Alice danced, prior to the seduction from which the whole tragedy will follow.

Returning with Angela from their drive and noticing the police cars outside the family gates, George tells Angela to go inside: he will join her in a moment. Ever sensitive to his moods, Angela says, "Every time you leave me for a moment, it seems like goodbye." She is right; this will be their last goodbye before their farewell in his death cell. Now openly on the run from the police, he walks, stumbles, falls, then runs through the woods, the drama heightened by Stevens's fast panning shots and accompanied by a remarkable *fugato* passage in Waxman's score to convey the sense, in Dreiser's words, of "a harried animal pursued by hunter and hound" (Dreiser: 433). (Its similarity to a passage in the second movement of Shostakovich's Symphony No. 11 has been much remarked on, all the more extraordinary, because it preceded the Shostakovich by five years and because Shostakovich could not have seen the film in the Soviet Union; another curious coincidence is that Waxman was to conduct the West Coast premiere of the Symphony in 1957.) The hunt is swiftly concluded. George is apprehended by a single trooper and meekly surrenders to his arrest, though denying he has committed murder. His only request to District Attorney Marlowe (Raymond Burr) is that they do not take him back to the Vickers house for questioning, and he is led away to the jail in Warsaw County. In the following scene at the Vickers house, we can see that the family is reeling from the revelation while also taking care to limit the damage to the family name. "Say he's a relative. Came to the house once," Marlowe quietly instructs his assistant, while Charles Eastman offers to pay for George's defense on the understanding that nothing about George's relationship with Angela will come out at the trial. Dressed in white, Angela is led away in what Mandy Merck likened to "a forlorn bridal procession, flanked by Mrs. Vickers and the maid" (Merck: 139), before, alone in her room upstairs and with her image reflected in a huge rectangular mirror that almost fills the screen, she faints.

"The trial scene became a succession of heavy blows and a foregone conclusion," wrote Ivan Moffat about the construction of the sequence, explaining that "it was no longer a question of suspense, but of heavy stones being cast in that courtroom in the name of justice, and of Monty Clift reeling back against their impact" (Moffat: 257). A parade of witnesses is dealt with in a series of quick wipes, the testimony adding up to compelling but not conclusive circumstantial evidence pointing towards George's guilt. The brisk way in which this evidence is presented is economical from a narrative standpoint, but it also gives the sense of the words almost washing over George prior to his own appearance on the stand. As he takes his place and we are given a close-up of his tense expression, the cry of a loon is heard over the soundtrack, sufficient in itself to jolt him back to the scene of the crime, and to the complex of emotions that overwhelmed him that night. The handling of his questioning by both defense and prosecution is quite odd in some ways. There is no mention of the fact that Alice was pregnant; one wonders if Angela ever knew that. Although he appeared to agree earlier to keep Angela's name out of the trial, the DA forces George to admit that he "had left his heart behind" when he was called away from the Hawaiian party at the Vickers by Alice's phone call and that, when Alice was drowning, George at that moment "was thinking of someone else." The inference of who that someone else might be seems dangerously close to the surface. Eugene Archer found the trial scene unconvincing, because of its contest between "a hopelessly negligible defence, which incredibly admits the plan to murder, and the flamboyantly theatrical exaggeration of the case for the prosecution" (Archer: 26). Certainly the defense strategy in having George admit that he had planned to murder Alice but changed his mind seems risky, to say the least; but equally risky are the melodramatic antics of Raymond Burr's prosecutor, bringing a small boat into the courtroom for George to demonstrate what had happened and then angrily smashing it with an oar to suggest how George committed the murder. However, it seems to me that the defense and prosecutor can be taken as two sides of George's divided personality and double life, where the defense is giving him the opportunity to offer a sincere and honest justification of his conduct to himself while the prosecution forcefully represents his self-condemnation and the sordid truth behind his behavior which he himself might not yet fully recognize.

"I don't believe I'm guilty of all of this," he will tell his mother and the Reverend Morrison (Paul Frees) when they visit him for the last time in his cell as he awaits execution for the crime of premeditated murder. It is true that a lot of things have led to this moment. George Eastman is Stevens's definitive portrait of the outsider, for whom the American Dream of social and romantic fulfillment has become an almost tangible reality, but who has found himself constantly pulled back by an impoverished and oppressive material and moral background from which he can never escape. Social disparity and demarcation can still be an insurmountable barrier, and Stevens anatomizes the circumstances by which an ordinary and sensitive individual might be tempted to contemplate murder. After Dachau, he was under no illusions about the darkness that lay at the human heart. Nevertheless, he said, "I wanted the audience to relate to a character whose behavior it might not subscribe to" (Stevens Jr.: 232). George is not an evil man, but is brought to a new realization when he is visited by Angela in his death cell. Eugene Archer thought the scene "of dubious probability," although, noting the presence of Angela's father (Shepperd Strudwick) in the background and remembering the family's influence in the community, I think it may be assumed that some monetary deal has been effected to make this meeting possible. And Archer goes on to acknowledge the scene's "undeniable cinematic effectiveness" (Archer: 26), partly because of Elizabeth Taylor's tenderness in the way she conveys Angela's feelings, and because it seems to resolve a crisis in George's mind and bring him some sort of peace: the judgment on him validated by his love for Angela and by his recognition that it was she, and not Alice, who was uppermost in his mind when the boat turned over.

As George is being escorted to the execution chamber, Stevens pans behind and across the other inmates of Death Row as they call out to him: "So long, kid," "You're going to a better world," "I'll be seeing you." Sometimes dismissed as sentimental, the scene is being faithful to something that occurs in the novel. It also prompts one to reflect that George seemed friendless in the outside world; and also that these condemned men would each have a story to tell. It is well known that Stevens and Clift disagreed over the final close-up, with Stevens wanting him to convey some kind of horror, but Clift feeling that a condemned man would simply look numb and dazed. Franz Waxman's original end title music seemed to favor Stevens's interpretation, with a discordant strident saxophone suggesting a mood of nervous fear, but it was displaced in the final cut by a more neutral-sounding rendering of the love theme as orchestrated by Victor Young and Daniele Amfitheatrof. Nonetheless, the close-up at this stage is in striking contrast to the close-up of him that concluded the opening credits, as he hitched a ride to his destiny, full of expectation, not knowing that it would lead inexorably to his execution. Over Clift's final benumbed expression is superimposed the image of Angela's kiss at the party, the romantic dream to which he clings even as he is escorted to his death.

In a letter to Stevens dated 26 March 1951, his co-screenwriter Michael Wilson congratulated him on the film. "You have given it the compassion of true tragedy," he wrote. "It is a deeply pro-human picture—an inadequate word to describe a crucial quality in a time when our culture is being de-humanized and brutalized" (qtd in Merck: 144). Wilson was referring to an era of McCarthyism in which he would soon become a victim of the Hollywood blacklist, as would Anne Revere for her refusal to cooperate with the

HUAC investigations. She felt her role as George Eastman's mother had been cut for political reasons (she recognized that Stevens fought for her, but, because of contractual obligations, he was limited over what he could actually do), though it seems that the part had been reduced prior to her appearance before HUAC, because it was felt that the final part of the film was too long. Like Michael Wilson, Revere did not care for the ending. "The sloppy love scene at the end of the film was a real tip-off of the times," she said. "It was a cover-up of the real story" (qtd in Taylor: 20). Yet the last shot seems to me the ultimate consummation of consolation and catastrophe that has marked George's progress throughout the film. No film of his better exemplifies the tension between the realist and the romantic in Stevens than *A Place in the Sun*. When staring at that billboard poster at the beginning of the film, George Eastman was envisaging his place in the sun—the girl, the money, the success—with no realistic expectation of achievement, hence his relationship with Alice. By the end, he has briefly *lived* it, and then been destroyed by it. The final close-up is not only a reminder of what he has loved but what he has lost; and also the memory that has led to his execution, for it is surely his thought of Angela over Alice as she scrambled for her life in the water that has convicted him of murder in the eyes of the jury. He has discovered that the pursuit of happiness for someone of his kind must involve social and sexual transgression. For him, the American Dream will slide inexorably into an American tragedy.

Shane (1953)

> Behold, we know not anything;
> I can trust that good shall fall
> At last—far off—at last, to all,
> And every winter change to spring.
>
> So runs my dream: but what am I?
> An infant crying in the night:
> An infant crying for the light:
> And with no language but a cry!
> —Alfred Lord Tennyson,
> *In Memoriam*, Canto 54.

"You don't give a man much choice, do you, Starrett?"—Rufus Ryker in *Shane*

Shane (Alan Ladd) is an archetypal Stevens protagonist, an outsider who must save a society that ultimately rejects him. His violent intervention on the side of homesteaders against cattlemen is glowingly watched by Joe Starrett's young son (Brandon De Wilde), who comes to idolize him, and feverishly followed by the boy's mother, Marian (Jean Arthur), in whom Shane seems to awaken a repressed romantic longing. A film of elemental power and hidden depths, *Shane* is quintessential Stevens, and, for many, the apotheosis of the Western.

Ever since its first release in 1953, when the film was nominated for six Oscars and Stevens was awarded the prestigious Irving G. Thalberg Memorial Award, *Shane* has cast a long shadow over American cinema in general and the Western in particular. Like *Shane,* John Ford's masterpiece *The Searchers* (1956) will similarly end with its hero returning to the wilderness from which he came, unable and perhaps unwilling to claim a place in the civilization he has helped to establish; and in Ford's alternately bitter and elegiac *The Man Who Shot Liberty Valance* (1962), a Westerner will similarly have to come to the aid of a decent man who would have proved no match for the practiced gunslinger, an act which, however, will render him an anachronism. Clint Eastwood's *High Plains Drifter* (1973) will offer a Gothic variation on *Shane,* and *Pale Rider* (1985) a pale imitation; but in *Unforgiven* (1992), Eastwood will accomplish his harshest and most complex homage, in which a former gunfighter will be drawn reluctantly but ineluctably into a situation where he will have to relive and arguably expiate his violent past. Sam Peckinpah was often quoted as citing *Shane* as his favorite Western, possibly because the situation of the ageing gunfighter performing one last deed of fulfilment was to recur in his own films, but mainly because he thought it was the genre's first truthful representation of violence.

The critical literature on *Shane* is far more extensive than on any other of Stevens' films, and much of it is complimentary. In her review of the film when it first appeared, Dilys Powell wrote that "what makes *Shane* so good a film is its combination of simplicity and warmth of feeling with grandeur of composition. The human figures with their humble show of courage and loyalty are set against a magnificent panorama of plain and mountain; or sometimes they are composed in groups finely poised for drama" (qtd in Tookey: 759). More recently Drew Casper has praised Stevens' ability in the film "to make elemental characters, situations and conflicts complexly real, their complexity never short-circuiting the directness of their impact" (Casper: 340). This is well put, but it would be fair to say that, after the initial critical euphoria, the film's reputation has diminished somewhat over the years. Pauline Kael represented a prevailing opinion when she wrote that she thought the film overwrought and over-planned and that "the Western was better before it became so self-important and self-conscious" (Kael: 436). Perhaps the heroic and romantic dimensions that Stevens brought to his re-creation of the American past are now viewed with skepticism in a more cynical modern age and have been progressively demythologized in the light of recent political history. I would also argue that the film's reputation is not as high as it once was because its particular strengths have been overlooked and its intentions consistently oversimplified or misrepresented.

Two influential essays on the Western, published shortly after the release of *Shane* and which were both dubious about its intention and achievement, seem to have had a disproportionate and negative influence on critical opinion. In his 1954 essay "The Westerner," Robert Warshow attacked *Shane* for what he called its "aestheticizing tendency" and Stevens' attempt "to freeze the Western myth once and for all" (Warshow: 150). Although Stevens respected the legend of the West and saw *Shane* in part as an old-fashioned morality play in which a single horseman rides to do battle against tremendous odds, he also saw it as an unusual domestic drama and, as he put it to his interviewer Joe Hyams in 1953, "actually a passive story of a family and its benefactor" (qtd in Cronin: 12). There is no evidence to suggest that any part of his agenda was to "freeze the Western myth"; and, if by "aestheticizing tendency," Warshow meant that Stevens was attempting to render the scenes with as much artistry of which he was capable, that surely should be the goal of any serious director. In his equally famous essay, "The Evolution of the Western," published in the same year as the Warshow article, André Bazin derided the film in a similar vein, referring to *Shane* as "the ultimate in superwesternization" and claiming that, in *Shane,* George Stevens "set out to justify the Western" (Bazin: 152). This seems to me wholly mistaken. Generic considerations were uppermost in Stevens' mind only insofar as he was very insistent on getting the period details right—but that was equally true of all of his films. (He was helped in his quest for frontier authenticity by the contribution of historical expert, Joe De Yong, who advised on details of clothing, hardware, dialogue, etc.) The setting might also have held a particular attraction, for it was close to the location of one of the earliest assignments of his film career, as cameraman on the Hal Roach picture *The Devil Horse* (1926), which starred the later legendary stunt-man Yakima Canutt. Otherwise it is likely that what audiences (and indeed fellow film-makers) have appreciated in the film over the years has been its universal humor and humanity as much as its traditional Western heroism. What Stevens was responding to in the material were elements that, in fact, one can perceive in a number of his films, most notably his fascination and sympathy with the outsider; and his sympathetic obser-vation of the role of women in a male-dominated society. It is also the film whose material, more than in any other of his works, permits him to bring together three vital facets of his artistic personality; the realist, the romantic, and the idealist.

In a 1974 interview with Patrick McGilligan and Joseph McBride, Stevens insisted that *Shane*, rather than being his self-conscious attempt to make the ultimate Western, "was really my war picture" (qtd in Cronin: 116). Contemporaries, such as John Ford, William Wyler, and John Huston, had made films about their war experiences, he reflected; in an oblique and original way, *Shane* was his. The narrative trajectory con-formed to a war-like scenario, in which a struggle over territory leads to intimidation; then to failed attempts at compromise and conciliation; escalating finally to a point of no return where a stand must be taken against brute force by an equally determined force for good. More particularly, Stevens' war experience had altered his whole perspec-tive on violence. "You know, the one thing I wanted to do with *Shane*," he told Robert Hughes in 1967, "was to show that if you point a .45 at a man and pull the trigger, you destroy the upright figure" (qtd in Cronin: 73). A gunshot in *Shane* is not a gesture of bravado, he insisted; it is a portent of death.

The first gunshot we hear does not occur until about an hour into the film; and Stevens famously took a great deal of care over the sound because he wanted to make us jump out of our skin. It is the moment when Shane is demonstrating his prowess to young Joey by shooting at a small white rock in the distance. Not only does the rock jump a good two feet on impact, Joey has to clasp his hands to his ears and is momentarily dazed by the deafening sound. (Stevens achieved that effect by taking out the sound of the pistol and substituting the sound of a small cannon alongside a rifle shot, an effect that Warren Beatty was to imitate when he came to make *Bonnie and Clyde*.) Until then Joey has had to simulate the sound of gunfire himself, using his father's unloaded rifle and his own toy gun; this is the real thing. Alan Ladd is very good at points like these in the film (a similar moment occurs just before this when Joey has confessed to inspect-ing his gun and taking it out of the holster), for his tight-lipped expression conveys the sense of someone momentarily lost in his thoughts and reflecting on something in his past that he would rather not recall.

Unbeknown to both Shane and Joey, this lesson has been watched by Joey's mother, Marian, and the scene suddenly takes on an extra dimension. In the novel, Marian does not appear at this point and the lesson is essentially presented as a teaching experience for the boy, with Shane earnestly insisting to him that "a gun is just a tool. No better and no worse than any other tool, a shovel or an axe…. A gun is as good—and as bad—as the man who carries it. Remember that" (Schaefer: 55). This speech is repeated almost verbatim in the film but this time to Marian, who has insisted that "guns aren't going to be my boy's life" after sending her disgruntled son away to get ready for the Independence Day celebrations. She is clearly unconvinced by Shane's justification of the weapon and is given the last word. "We'd all be better off if there wasn't a single gun in the valley," she tells Shane, "*including yours*" [my italics]. The irony of this is that eventually the life of her husband and the future of her family will depend on Shane's prowess with a gun. And yet, as if to disclose how her words have hit home, one of the last things Shane will tell Joey is "to run on home to your mother and tell her there aren't any more guns in the valley." For behind these words is something unspoken: the growing love between Shane and Marian, which can never be expressed, much less consummated. One of the main reasons that *Shane* was Woody Allen's favorite American film was because of what he called its "tangle of relationships" that, he said, is developed "with the same subtlety as in the most sophisticated kind of urban movie" (qtd in Lyman: 4). "That's where a film gets most interesting to me," Stevens was to tell his interviewer, Mary Ann Fisher, in 1963, "with those aspects of it that are somewhat hidden, the secondary and third levels of interest" (qtd in Cronin: 28).

Published in 1949, *Shane* was the first novel of Jack Schaefer, who had pursued a career in journalism after completing a doctorate in American literature at Columbia University and who at that time, and for some time afterwards, had never been west of Toledo, Ohio. The story had been brought to Stevens' attention by his son, George, both agreeing that it had great cinematic possibilities. Stevens' choice of screenwriter to adapt the novel was A.B. Guthrie, Jr., who had never written a screenplay before, but whose Pulitzer Prize–winning novel, *The Big Sky* (which, coincidentally, Howard Hawks was filming at the time Stevens was preparing *Shane*), had greatly impressed Stevens. Working from Stevens' annotations on the novel, Guthrie produced a substantial part of the screenplay quite quickly, the final part being completed by Jack Sher under Stevens' supervision. It is a remarkably astute adaptation whose subtleties will be explored in greater detail as this analysis unfolds. Some of the changes are slight, but still significant. Even the names seem more convincing in the film: for example, the boy's name has been changed from "Bob" to the diminutive "Joey" to reinforce the connection with his father, Joe ("Goodbye, little Joe," are Shane's last words to him); the name of the rancher has been changed from the relatively bland Fletcher to the more abrasive Ryker (perhaps with overtones of "Reich" playing on Stevens' mind); Morgan is now Ryker's brother rather than just the foreman in the novel; and the names of the characters of Torrey and Ernie Wright have been transposed. Also the settings of some of the most dramatic events have been moved. The gunfight between Torrey and Wilson, for example, which took place in the saloon in the novel, is enacted more atmospherically in the film on a muddy street during a gathering thunderstorm.

Even tiny details of difference matter. In the novel, when Shane is able to identify Wilson as a gunfighter out of Cheyenne from a description given of him, one of the homesteaders, Ed Howells, says maliciously, "You seem to know a lot about that kind of dirty business," and Shane replies emphatically, "I do" (Schaefer: 110). In the film, when Howells (Martin Mason) makes that comment, Shane does not respond, his silence being more in keeping with the mystery of his past. At an earlier point in the novel, Joe Starrett had advised his son not to get to liking Shane too much, because he will be moving on someday and the boy will be upset (Schaefer: 47–8). In the film this comment is made by the mother: a small but profoundly significant change, because it deepens the complexity of the sentiment. When Marian says it, she is being more than simply protective of her son's feelings; she is implicitly protecting the image of her husband, who might seem to be diminishing in their son's eyes in comparison with Shane. Beyond that, it is also a warning to herself, a suggestion delicately disclosed in Jean Arthur's performance at this point through the slight self-consciousness of her tone of voice and the quick way she blows out her son's bedroom lamp before he can see she is blushing slightly.

Stevens and his son went scouting appropriate locations together before settling on an area outside Jackson Hole near a small town called Kelly, with the Teton mountains towering in the background. The setting particularly comes into its own in the opening shot of the magnificent funeral scene, when Torrey's coffin is about to be lowered into the ground and, behind it, one can see both the town in the distance and the mountains behind that. The film's whole conflict—between life and death, graveyard and town, homesteaders versus cattlemen—is encapsulated in that shot. As Stevens put it beautifully in an interview with James Silke in 1964, it was "all arranged in one camera view that had to do with a man being put away in the grave, with the synthesis of the whole story wrapped around it" (qtd in Cronin: 46). A similarly expressive use of location occurs when Shane is riding into town for the final showdown. At the point when the road reaches a rise, we see him framed between the trees that Stevens has taken such care to find as a signal that the characters are approaching the town; and the music swirls in dizzying expectation as Shane rides between them and descends towards his destiny. As much of the shooting was done on location and therefore subject to the vagaries of the weather (as well as Stevens' characteristically painstaking attention to detail), the film took 27 days longer than its allotted 48 day schedule to complete, and, by the finish, the budget had grown to nearly $3 million. The studio perception was that Alan Ladd pictures at that time on average grossed $2.6 million, so Paramount was worried that the movie was destined to make a loss and almost sold the film to Howard Hughes. Fortunately for Paramount, the deal fell through; and *Shane* went on to make over twice as much as it had cost at the box office in its first year of release in the United States, not to mention the additional money the film was to make on the several occasions when it was re-released.

Stevens' original thought for the title role had been Montgomery Clift, no doubt influenced by their collaboration on *A Place in the Sun*. He did have some misgivings about whether Clift was muscular enough to be credible in the uprooting of the tree-stump scene; and Clift might also have come across as too young for the role, for Shane is a man who must seem to be carrying a certain world-weariness about him and whose past, although we learn little about it, weighs heavily on him. William Holden was first mentioned as a possibility for the role of Starrett and Katharine Hepburn for the part of his wife, but when all of these actors dropped out, Stevens looked at Paramount's roster of actors on contract and chose Alan Ladd, Van Heflin and Jean Arthur in less than ten minutes. It was a judicious selection, as was the supporting cast. As Jean Arthur was later, and rightly, to remark: "the heavies were wonderful."

Alan Ladd was an unconventional choice for a Western hero and his performance has perhaps been somewhat underestimated as a result, which in turn interestingly parallels both the homesteaders' and Chris Calloway's perception of the character. In Ladd's hands, Shane is certainly a less darkly dangerous and narcissistic figure than in the novel, but this makes his three explosions from passivity into action (the fight in the saloon, the shooting lesson, the final showdown) all the more powerful. Pointing out how different the film would have been if John Wayne, Gary Cooper or James Stewart had played the part, Philip French suggested of Ladd that "perhaps no other actor could have given the character quite that quality of blank, ethereal detachment which Ladd brought to the part. He is like an angel in an otherwise realistic medieval painting, and sets off the earthy realism of Van Heflin's father, Jean Arthur's unfulfilled pioneer mother and Brandon DeWilde's deprived, yearning child" (French: 60–1). He certainly has a different kind of screen presence from that of Van Heflin and Jean Arthur (whose performances will be dealt with in due course) and this suggestion that he is in a separate realm from those around him is totally appropriate to the character. Ladd is particularly good in the scenes with the boy, gently humorous in a way the boy appreciates, and always seeming to have time for him in a way that his father sometimes does not. It is beyond doubt Ladd's finest screen work.

The same is true for the then ten-year-old Brandon DeWilde, who, before his tragic death in a traffic accident at the age of 30, had never quite shaken off his role in *Shane.* His most memorable later screen performances were in *All Fall Down* (1961) for John Frankenheimer—who had once told the columnist Ezra Goodman that he thought *Shane* the greatest movie ever made (Goodman: 402)—and *Hud* (1963) for Martin Ritt. Both films allude to *Shane* in the way De Wilde once again extravagantly admires an elder hero figure whom he initially adopts as a role model but in whom (as will befit the more cynical 1960s) he will become progressively disenchanted. Prior to *Shane,* he had already proved his mettle on Broadway and later in Fred Zinnemann's film version of Carson McCullers' *The Member of the Wedding* (1953); and he was the only child actor ever considered for the role of Joey. He was at that time to become the youngest actor ever to be nominated for an acting Oscar; and his performance is one of the purest studies of hero worship in the history of the cinema. It is also pivotal, since much of the story is seen through the eyes of the boy, and this viewpoint permits Stevens to release what one might call the poet within himself, who, to borrow the words of the great Romantic poet, Samuel Taylor Coleridge "carries the simplicity of childhood into the powers of manhood, who, with a soul unsubdued by habit, unshackled by custom, contemplates all things with the freshness and wonder of a child." That extra poetic dimension is the film's biggest stylistic risk and has sometimes led to accusations of pretentiousness; but it is precisely that quality of heightened representation which Woody Allen thought lifted the film above other classics of the genre such as *The Oxbow Incident* (1943) and *High Noon* (1952), which, by comparison, remain at the level of first-class prose.

Intimations of grandeur are signaled at the start. After the Paramount logo, a brief four-note fanfare is heard, as if heralding a hero's arrival, and then Victor Young's majestic main theme unfolds over the credits (themselves strikingly bold, with suggestions of flecks of hay in the lettering) as we watch a lone rider dressed in buckskin descending into a Wyoming valley. Unlike other classic Western themes, such as the swirling excitement of Jerome Moross's theme for *The Big Country* (1958) or the pulsating rhythmic drive of Elmer Bernstein's music for *The Magnificent Seven* (1960), Young's title music has a measured tread, that simultaneously suggests spaciousness and a heroic nobility, and with a poignant undertow that will particularly come into its own at the finale. The tone and tempo seem just right for the film that is to follow, which has a steady rather than swift momentum and, unusually for a Western, only three scenes of action, that are carefully spaced and thrillingly staged.

As the credits end, an almost idyllic frontier scene is set before us: a father in the yard chopping wood; mother singing to herself in the kitchen as she prepares the evening meal; their son in the outdoors playing with his toy rifle and hiding in some reeds as he hunts a deer, which is sipping water from a stream and unconcerned by the boy's presence. Suddenly the animal looks up and turns its head, aware of something in the distance. The boy follows its gaze and sees a way off a horseman coming towards them, his approach momentarily framed by the deer's antlers. (This famous shot has sometimes been cited as evidence of Stevens' overdeliberate visual calculation, but, in fact, the director always claimed that he caught that image by a happy chance on only the third take.) Even from a distance boy and stranger seem to sense each other's presence. As the horseman draws nearer and spots the boy, a smile is exchanged; and a bond is immediately and wordlessly established. The boy runs to tell his father that somebody is coming.

The opening twenty minutes of *Shane* are a master class in scene-setting and concise storytelling, for they set up everything that is to follow in terms of theme, characterization and style. Explaining to Starrett that he is heading north and seeking Starrett's permission to cut through his place, the horseman turns to young Joey and comments on the boy's early observation of him. "You know," he says, "I like a man who watches things going on around him. It means he'll make his mark someday." It is one of those lines in the film that will resonate on several levels. By addressing Joey as a young adult, Shane seems immediately to gain the confidence of the boy, who blushes with pleasure at the compliment. At later stages in the film, Shane will have cause to be grateful for Joey's watchfulness: it will save his life. The line could further be taken as Stevens' credo as a filmmaker. After their first meeting, Katharine Hepburn was to describe Stevens as "a watcher" (Leaming: 300). When Kenneth Tynan interviewed him and enquired whether he had any hobbies, Stevens replied, affably: " I sure do…. Just looking around" (qtd in Moss: 188).

After their first encounter, Hepburn also called Stevens "taciturn" and "madly mysterious": it is a description that could easily be applied to Shane. Looking over the fence on which Joey is sitting, he says: "Been a long time since I've seen a Jersey cow." It is the most revealing thing he says about himself in the entire film. Indeed he seems to be speaking to himself more than to anyone around him; and Ladd imbues the line with a real feeling of nostalgia. Where has this character come from? Has he been brought up on a farm? It would explain his instinctive sympathy with the homesteaders and the ease with which he will later help Starrett as a hired hand. But if that has been his early life (we cannot be sure), what has he become since, and how?

A partial answer is offered to these questions in the very next moment. As Shane dismounts to accept Starrett's offer of a drink of water, Joey jumps off the fence and starts to cock his rifle. In an instant, the can has hit the ground with a crash and Shane has swung round, his hand by his holster, to face the boy, the gesture being so swift and decisive as to cause Joey to jump back in alarm. In the novel, Schaefer has described Shane as a man whose ostensible easiness has a sense of tension with it, "of a coiled spring of a trap set" (Schaefer: 3). In the film, this tension is conveyed by that single gesture, in which Shane signals an element of danger in his character and suggests a past in which such lightning-fast reactions are professionally tuned and a matter of life and death. There is an ominous echo of this moment at a later stage in the film, when the tinkle of a bell at Grafton's store signals the entry of Torrey into the saloon on Independence Day, and, on hearing the sound, the newly arrived gunfighter, Wilson (Jack Palance), swings round on his stool to face him, as if already scenting blood and anticipating that he is to be this man's nemesis. The soundtrack of *Shane*, incidentally, is one of the most sensitive and dramatic I have ever heard in a film, ranging from the softness of a dog's whimpering and scratching at a coffin to the deafening blast of a gunshot that hits you with the force of a declamatory outburst.

A voice from inside the cabin, gently rebuking Joey for pointing his gun at someone, alerts Shane for the first time to the presence of the boy's mother, Marian; and in a rather sheepish but friendly fashion, he acknowledges that Joey has caught him off guard. But Joe Starrett has been a little unnerved by the stranger's reaction ("A bit touchy, aren't you?"); and when the moment is followed by whoops in the distance that preface the unwelcome visit of Ryker and his men, he assumes that Shane must be part of Ryker's outfit. Taking Joey's rifle, he orders him at gunpoint to leave. "Would you mind putting that gun down first? Then I'll leave," says Shane. "What difference does it make? You're leaving anyway," says Starrett testily, to which Shane politely but pointedly replies: "I'd like it to be my idea." At this, the balance of power, as it were, shifts subtly over to Shane, as he lays claim to departure on his own terms; and his superiority is reinforced when Joey looks up at his father in silent support of Shane's request. Somewhat shamefacedly, Starrett lowers the rifle, before preparing himself to face the Rykers and clearly, as the stranger mounts his horse and departs, never expecting to see Shane again.

"Expecting trouble?" asks Morgan Ryker (John Dierkes), gesturing mockingly towards Starrett's rifle and laughing: Dierkes's sinister snigger will develop into one of the most ominous sounds in the film. Although assuring Starrett that he has not come here to cause trouble, Rufus Ryker (Emile Meyer) has come to inform him that he has a new beef contract and will need all his range. Significantly, it will not be the only time in the film when Ryker attempts to adopt a conciliatory tone towards Starrett until the latter's obstinacy goads him into making threats. On this occasion Marian comes outside in order to restrain her husband from losing his temper, when, unseen by both of them, Shane suddenly appears from the back of the cabin to stand alongside them. "Who are you, stranger?" asks Morgan. "I'm a friend of Starrett's," is Shane's reply. His appearance seems to effect a temporary cessation of hostilities, and, having issued his warning, Ryker and his men leave.

There is no precise equivalent in the novel for this scene and it is another example of the adapter's skill. In the novel, the Ryker character does not appear until the story is a third of the way through, whereas the film shrewdly introduces him near the beginning so that the main dramatic conflict can be established at the outset. Shane's coming to the aid of Starrett at this stage when he is being threatened by Ryker anticipates the story's culmination when he will do the same but this time decisively and finally. Indeed there is a further symmetry here, as Starrett's relationship with Shane will ironically begin and then end in enmity, as Starrett misreads their opening encounter and is overpowered in their final one. But why has Shane come back? We have seen him as he actually leans forward on his horse to open the gate prior to his departure: what has made him return? Has he scented trouble and knows where his sympathies lie? Has it been the sound of Marian's voice? It is noticeable that it is Marian who suggests to her husband that supper will be ready soon, implying that the stranger would be welcome to join them; it is also Marian who suggests that they should ask Shane to stay the night. When Joey visits Shane in the barn the next morning to tell him that they would like him to stay on, he says, "I bet you wouldn't leave just because it's too *dangerous* around here." On first viewing, one might assume that Shane's acceptance is in response to the danger (to show he is not afraid and to help the family). Yet, as Joey says this, he is being called back into the house by his mother, who is concerned that he is out in his nightshirt. It might be Marian's voice, as much as the call of danger, that motivates Shane's decision.

The supper scene is one of those Stevens' scenes which illustrates what Shelley Winters meant when she said that "George photographs what goes on in the air between people" (Ratcliffe: 39). It has a warmth and air of spontaneity about it that unobtrusively conveys the sense of people at ease in each other's company. At the same time the observant coverage and deft editing show that each of the four characters here is experiencing the occasion in a slightly different way. Moreover there are moments in the scene that add an undercurrent of tension to the ostensibly easy-going surface.

As we join them, the meal is almost over. While Marian is taking a pie from out of the stove and Joey is creeping behind Shane and staring in fascination at his holster and gun draped over the back of his chair, Joe is expatiating on his plans for the farm. One gets the impression that it is Joe who has been doing most of the talking and indeed that this opportunity for a man-to-man conversation about his plans for the future is something of a luxury for him. Shane listens politely; Marian joins them at the table. "We make out, don't we, Marian?" says Joe, with affection and enthusiasm; Marian's reply, "Of course" matches him in affection but not quite in enthusiasm, Jean Arthur's vocal intonation being at its most subtle there. Suddenly there is a noise from outside as a cow has wandered into the yard; and again Shane makes a sharp, almost involuntary movement towards his gun, once more causing Joey to start back in alarm. Alan Ladd's performance of that moment is very eloquent. His reaction to the scent of danger is lightning-fast and instinctive, but his face then reflects his discomfort and even dismay at this momentary disruption of decorum: it seems almost like a subliminal explosion of his past into the present. This time Starrett is discreet enough not to comment, but instead asks young Joey to chase the cow out of the yard. A fleeting moment of embarrassment, suggestive of their guest's mysterious past and hidden depths, is swiftly glossed over.

"I wouldn't ask you where you were bound," says Joe to Shane, indirectly asking Shane precisely that, while trying to give the impression that he is not aiming to pry. Shane's answer is as indirect at the question. "One place or another," he says. "Some place I've never been." Ladd invests the line with a quiet gravity and sadness, as if he has not yet found the place he is looking for. His sense of weary wanderlust is in stark contrast to that of Starrett, who is absolutely settled where he is and states emphatically that the only way that anyone will remove him from his home is in a pine box. When Joey asks him what he means, Marian intervenes and reproves Joe from talking that way in front of their son. Her sensitivity to the boy's feelings and fears contrasts with her husband's rather clumsy candor, and might also reflect her premonition of where the dispute with Ryker could lead: Joe's admirable doggedness and determination could also be the seeds of his destruction. It is perhaps the reason (almost subconscious) that her earlier "of course" in response to Joe's confidence and satisfaction about the way they are making out sounded a trifle perfunctory. Marian is a little more aware of, and anxious about, possible perilous consequences.

The most mysterious moment in the scene is yet to come and is an example of that subtlety of characterization that so bewitched Woody Allen. When Marian starts to lay out the plates for the pie, Joe comments in a jocular way, "Kinda fancy, aren't we?" When Joey asks what he means, he says, "Good plates, an extra fork." If he is attempting playfully to pull his wife's leg (giving herself airs?), it is clear that she does not appreciate the humor; and even Joe, who will admit he is a little slow sometimes, notices the change in her manner. "What's the matter, Marian?" he asks, to which she briskly replies, "Nothing." Van Heflin's expression catches Joe's restrained bafflement to perfection, the expression of a man who has inadvertently upset the woman he loves without quite grasping how. Shane says nothing at this stage, but, at the end of the meal and after looking out the window at the tree stump which Joe has been chopping when he first arrives, he turns and says, "That was an *elegant* [my emphasis] dinner, Mrs. Starrett."

That is a fine piece of screenwriting. "Elegant": one somehow knows that it is a word Joe Starrett has never used in his entire life. With that single adjective Shane discreetly discloses that he has recognized and appreciated Marian's endeavor to bring a touch of refinement to the rigors of frontier life. In an interview for the George Stevens, Jr., documentary on his father, Jean Arthur had said that Stevens had wanted her to play Marian as "a rather tired, faded figure, on whom ten years of pioneer marriage had taken their toll, and it was very difficult for me." (She also remarked that, in comparison with her previous collaborations with him, Stevens had become much more serious and withdrawn: the last ten years, including the war experience, had taken its toll on him also.) Intuitively Shane seems to have sensed something in Marian's character that Joe has never quite grasped, which foreshadows their growing feelings for each other. Also, and unknowingly perhaps, he has stirred a previously dormant dissatisfaction with her life that will explode into despair and desperation in her final scene.

Without anything being said, the connection between Shane and the Starretts is to take another step forward. Excusing himself from the table, Shane steps outside and a moment later, the Starretts find him chopping away at the tree-stump outside their cabin. (It is another demonstration of Shane's awareness of things going on around him: he will have noticed Joe Starrett hacking away at that stump when he first arrived.) In the novel, the incident occurs a little later (by then Shane is already working with Starrett) and is differently motivated, occurring after Starrett has taken Shane's side in an argument with a trader over the price of a cultivator. In the film, it is Shane's way of thanking both for their hospitality: the motivation includes Marian as well as Joe in his expression of gratitude. Also by placing the incident earlier than in the novel, the screenplay concisely, cleverly and convincingly incorporates the uprooting of the tree stump into part of the reason of why Starrett might want Shane to stay and why Shane might agree. For in this activity alone and again without anything being said, we see two men working together in a common cause and in close communication. Dynamically edited, and with Victor Young's joyous baroque counterpoint enhancing the scene's formal grandeur, the incident is molded into a cameo that celebrates frontier friendship and masculinity. As the men join together in a final endeavor to push the stump over, and with little Joey puffing out his chest and cheeks in his identification with their efforts, the camera moves forward and towards them as if representing the force they must overcome. When they succeed and then step away, Stevens dissolves to a shot of all four of them, tiny figures framed against the setting of the whole valley, and an image of idyllic tranquility after the previous exertions. And yet, in the overall context of the film, the scene has deeper dimensions than are immediately apparent. When the two men are straining every sinew to push the stump to the ground, Marian makes the eminently practical suggestion: "Why don't you hitch up a team?" Joe replies that to do so would cede victory to the tree stump and nullify all their physical effort: this is a contest of Man against Nature. Marian's failure to understand (or accept) the codes of honor that seem part of pioneer life seems gently humorous here, but will dominate her last scene with her husband, when she is insisting that his determination to face Ryker, even though he must know he is walking into a trap, is just foolish (and possibly fatal) masculine pride. What also links the uprooting of the tree stump sequence to the film's finale is that here, as at the end, Shane will be needed to finish a job that Starrett has started. Indeed in their ferocious final fight, Shane and Starrett will fall across that tree stump, in ironic contrast to the friendship it had sealed in the early scene but also as a reminder of this motif.

"I don't want my troubles to be none of yours," Starrett has told Shane, when the latter starts working for him: an unconsciously ironic comment in view of what will happen. While Shane is in Grafton's store to collect some wire for Starrett and also blanching at the cost of his store-bought work clothes (a nice touch: it seems one of the consequences of the coming of civilization to the West is inflation), Starrett is chopping wood in the yard and being quizzed about Shane by Joey. Although the conversation seems casual enough, an edge of exasperation begins to creep into Starrett's responses. "Don't you ask anything but questions?" he says. It's a finely written scene. Joe is trying to get on with his work and only half attending to his son's persistent queries or trying to deflect them with humor, but he might also, almost subconsciously, be finding the drift of the conversation a little unsettling. Joey is already trying to draw comparisons between his father and Shane, which could shade later into competitiveness and even conflict. "Could you whip him, pa?" he asks. "Could you whip Shane?" Starrett brushes the question aside, but the answer to that question will by the end have become literally a matter of life and death. During the conversation, one of the homesteaders, Ernie Wright (Leonard Strong) can be seen approaching in the distance in his buggy. Stevens keeps the camera still, encompassing the whole of the father/son dialogue which comes to a natural stop at the very moment Wright drives into the yard: the shot is a miracle of meticulous timing. Later in the film, when another of the homesteaders, Axel Shipstead (Douglas Spencer) approaches from a distance to tell Starrett of Torrey's death, Stevens will again film the incident in a single sustained shot, Shipstead's shouts from a distance being partially drowned out by the nervous whinnying of the horses in the foreground. It is a particularly effective dramatic moment, because, although we do not need to hear precisely what Shipstead is saying (we know what has happened), the agitation of the horses maintains the tense mood of the scene and ensures no loss of narrative momentum. "In one of those long takes," Stevens explained to Patrick McGilligan and Joseph McBride in his 1974 interview, "the camera gets rooted in one place, almost as if it has discovered something of extraordinary importance. It doesn't move in to examine it closely; it draws the audience in to make an effort to see more" (qtd in Cronin: 118).

By the time Ernie Wright has arrived at the Starretts' house, we have been given sufficient time to absorb some of the significance and subtle undercurrents of the conversation between father and son while experiencing a gathering curiosity about the reason for Wright's visit. One senses also that, as he nears the Starrett homestead, it has given Wright opportunity enough to gather up a head of indignant steam. Harassed overnight yet again by the Ryker boys whose horses have trampled over his crops, Wright is giving notice that he plans to move out and will not be talked out of it: he has listened to Starrett once too often. Marian again has to intervene when her husband (as in the scene with the Rykers) is on the point of losing his temper. Recovering his composure, Starrett proposes that they call a meeting at his place of all the other homesteaders to discuss a way forward. "If we're gonna have a meeting," Wright replies, partially pacified, "it better come to more than just poking holes in the air with your finger!" (Stevens particularly liked that line and credited it to his technical adviser Joe DeYong.)

The meeting with the homesteaders is one of those group scenes that Stevens does so well: expert deployment of space to indicate the relationships between people; natural unforced humor; and a convincing seeming spontaneity that arises from people who have known each other a long time and are at ease in each other's company. It is a concise way of introducing this community, both to Shane and to the audience; and the homesteaders are well characterized and well-cast, persuasively giving the impression of ordinary people going on with their lives. One can sense also why they would naturally gravitate towards Joe Starrett as the leader, who seems the most dedicated, determined and articulate of them all. By the end of the meeting they have reached a collective decision to go into town together to collect their supplies, both as a display of unity and a feeling that there is safety in numbers. However, there are two elements of disquiet beneath the ostensible agreement of purpose that are to have far-reaching consequences.

At the outset of the meeting, one of the homesteaders, Yank Potts (Will Somonds) is playing "Beautiful Dreamer" on his harmonica. (Somonds could actually play the harmonica, so Stevens used this to add to the atmosphere of the scene.) Marian and Joey are in Joey's bedroom reading a story and half-listening to the homesteaders' conversation in the other room, and the music forms a distant soft accompaniment that seems oddly applicable, for both Joey and Marian are, in their different ways, "beautiful dreamers." Suddenly there is a late arrival: the defiantly unaccompanied Stonewall Torrey (Elisha Cook, Jr.) who, as his nickname implies, is still carrying vestiges of the Civil War in his psychological make-up. "Howdy, Reb," says Potts, and launches into a sprightly rendering of "Marching to Georgia," announcing Stonewall's appearance by, as it were, playing his theme tune. There is some laughter at Torrey's expense; and when Torrey starts belligerently insisting that he needs no bodyguard to defend his claim, Potts again launches into a vigorous rendering of "Marching to Georgia," in mimicry (and mockery) of Torrey's bravado, before sliding back to "Beautiful Dreamer" to restore the more tranquil mood. Again the others laugh, as we do, for it is essentially good-natured in intention, musically pulling the Southerner's leg, as it were. However, it is also unwittingly striking at the man's Achilles heel—his fierce and hypersensitive Southern pride—which Torrey only just manages to rein in on this occasion, but which will be exploited to deadly effect when he comes face to face with the gunfighter Wilson. One of the most moving moments in the great funeral scene occurs when Potts will play "Dixie," but this time as a slow, sad lament as Torrey's coffin is being lowered into the ground. As he does so, Starrett looks across at him from the grave. At that moment one senses that both men are thinking back to that meeting in the Starretts' house and Torrey's arrival, where they playfully mocked his hot-tempered pride that has led tragically to his death.

If Torrey's spirit of independence undermined the "safety in numbers" cohesion of the homesteaders, the other element of disunity is Shane. One of the homesteaders, Lewis (Edgar Buchanan), has been at Grafton's when Shane has backed out of a confrontation with one of Ryker's men, Chris Calloway (Ben Johnson). Lewis thinks it has exposed the homesteaders to further ridicule and demonstrated that Shane could not be counted on to give them his support. Although Starrett rallies to his defense, saying how he had instructed him to stay out of trouble, Shane leaves the meeting so that they can talk more freely in his absence. It is an incident that can be seen to be a presentiment of the whole movement of the narrative towards its climax: namely, the failure of Shane to assimilate himself into this society. Stevens reinforces this by his subtle framing. In the scenes where the homesteaders are together (for example, in Grafton's, or at the Independence Day party or even at Torrey's funeral), Shane invariably is standing to one side or on the edge of the frame and never in a central position where he might be mistaken as one of the group. Overhearing Lewis's account of Shane's humiliation at Calloway's hands, Joey is shocked and cannot grasp why his hero would have acted in this way ("It's a long story, Joey," says Shane). Marian, on the other hand, seems instinctively to understand what was behind Shane's restraint ("I think we know," she says) and indeed to admire him all the more for it: there is an unusually long pause before she then says his name, quite softly, almost like a caress. It is a scene in which one can feel the emotional complexity of the film beginning to deepen. Also it is setting up, for maximum impact, the film's first carefully delayed, devastating action set piece, when Calloway makes the mistake of taunting Shane for a second time.

"The show starts," wrote Stevens in his production notes when Shane encounters Chris Calloway again. He understood that it is sometimes necessary to take an audience almost to the point of boredom to maximize a moment of shock. *Shane* has been proceeding at a measured, even leisurely pace, up to the moment when Calloway is standing behind Shane and clearly intent on a fight. His card-playing friend has scented trouble and thrown in his hand: "Just say I'm superstitious," he says. The bartender Will, who seems in a perpetual state of apprehension (in a definitive characterization by John Miller), starts fumbling the glasses in front of him as Calloway repeats his challenge. Shane orders two whiskeys and then turns. There are three quick cuts, as Shane throws whisky on Calloway's shirt; then in his face; and then punches him so hard that he will be sent careering backwards through the swing doors into Grafton's adjoining main store. A female customer promptly faints, one of three moments of comedy that Stevens typically inserts to vary the mood and punctuate the violence. The second occurs when Shane and Calloway have to pause in their hostilities to allow a cowboy to saunter nonchalantly into the saloon, serenely unaware of the mayhem going on inside. The third is a moment when Shane's final blow into Calloway's face is matched with a shot of the watching Joey as he bites off a piece of candy. It had been Joey who had told Shane of the fate of a previous farmhand of his father's after being roughed up by the Ryker boys ("They knocked his teeth out!"). Here the snap as he bites through his candy seems a comment on this fight's outcome and the fate of a cowboy who underestimates Shane: he will find he has bitten off more than he can chew.

For its time it was a remarkably brutal scene. Stevens was very insistent that, when Calloway rises to his feet after that that first blow, we should be shocked by the sight of his bloodied face. Punches hurt. The fight itself is an ugly, ill-matched affair, Shane seeming much more like an experienced streetfighter, moving his fists from side to side, looking for an opening, whereas the now dazed Calloway can only flail around in the hope that he can defeat an obviously more skillful opponent through brute strength. Furniture and glasses go flying; Stevens deploys multiple different camera positions (one even from under a staircase) to convey the dizzying sensation of a barroom brawl; the percussive soundtrack is augmented by shouts of encouragement from the sidelines to Calloway from Ryker's men (including, apparently from the director: "Knock him into that pigpen, Chris!" is Stevens' voice). It ends with Shane's punching Calloway while he is still on the floor and no longer able to defend himself.

At this point Ryker intervenes, saying he could use a man like Shane and offering to double the wages that Starrett is paying him. As a first reaction to what has happened, this is very striking. Those critics who find Calloway's later conversion implausible might consider what loyalty one would owe to an employer whose immediate response to your being beaten up is to offer a job at an increased salary to the person who has done it. It is noticeable that Calloway wanders off to lick his wounds and possibly reflect on what has happened rather than stick around to watch the punishment meted out to Shane by way of revenge. This punishment has been prompted not only by Shane's refusal of Ryker's offer, but by Shane's reaction to Ryker's suggestion of a surreptitious motive behind this refusal. "Pretty wife Starrett's got," Ryker says, provocatively, at which point Shane—for the first and only time in the film—loses his temper and in a loud voice calls Ryker "a dirty slinkin' old man!" At which point Ryker's men gather round Shane to teach him a lesson; and Shane, despite Joey's request that he must leave "because there are so many," must prepare to face the men alone.

Joe Starrett's intervention to rescue Shane from a savage beating will seal the bond of friendship between the two men. Unlike the other homesteaders, huddled together in a group on the porch and bewailing the absence of any law enforcement agency within a hundred miles, Starrett unhesitatingly plunges into the melee, having picked up an axe handle with which he will fell Ryker. The looming close-up of him as he then moves forward to attack Morgan is genuinely intimidating: when roused to anger, Starrett will clearly be a formidable opponent for anyone who stands in his way, even Shane. His action demonstrates how vital Starrett is to the homesteaders' cause; why he is naturally their leader; and why Ryker will come to think, rightly, that only Starrett is holding them together. I am surprised to find occasionally that some commentators criticize Stevens for "idealizing" the settlers as "all upstanding, hardy, pioneering types" (that from a review of the film's Blu-ray release on the website of Turner Classic Movies). In fact, they are all too human, with recognizable fears and frailties; and here their inactivity could be construed as both cowardly and hypocritical. For all their previous condemnation of Shane for initially backing down against Calloway, they are alarmed when the fight does actually occur and wring their hands in anxiety at the possible consequences. At this moment they seem a little like the townspeople of *High Noon*, ready to let someone else do their fighting for them and pointedly standing to one side when things get dangerous.

Although the fight sequence will develop towards the end into a conventional saloon brawl, it nevertheless represents a crucial point in the film. It has been an enactment in miniature of the conflict at the heart of the film—homesteaders versus cattlemen—and it has been a fight in which the homesteaders, against the odds, have emerged victorious. In finally bringing the fighting to a halt, the storekeeper Grafton (in a performance by Paul McVey that throughout eloquently suggests a man of decency and integrity) tells Starrett that "You've won"; and Grafton's voice is one that carries some weight and authority in that community, even influencing and reining in Ryker on occasion. As if to underline the victory, Starrett rashly insists that "Ryker ain't paying for the damages, not with a nickel he ain't. I'm paying for what's broke." Backing out of the saloon with Shane, he then cries out, "No, by Godfrey, *we'll* pay for what's broke. Me and Shane." With this impulsive, if impractical, declaration, Starrett is symbolically denying Ryker any claim on what has happened and relishing the totality of his victory. A grand gesture, but arguably an unwise and provocative one.

When Ivan Moffat identified a sensitivity to humiliation as a key aspect of Stevens' character and a key theme in his films, he related it particularly to their experience together in the war and the fear they witnessed in the eyes of the inmates of Dachau, directed at them even when they had come as liberators. "Humiliation on a small scale is comedy," Moffat reflected, " but humiliation on a larger scale, which George was in a position to observe in Europe at the end of World War Two, is no longer comic and becomes a tragedy" (Moffat: 218). At this particular point in *Shane*, the theme will be given an unusual twist, because at first we are invited to experience it from Ryker's point of view. His attempt to teach Shane and the homesteaders a lesson has disastrously back-fired. Grafton, whose opinion Ryker respects, has pronounced it a defeat; Starrett has had the last word, rubbing salt in the wounds. A line has now been crossed and, staggering to his feet and his patience now exhausted, Ryker has the air of a wounded animal about to strike back. He is through with fooling around, he tells Grafton. "From now on, when we fight with them," he says, "the air is gonna be filled with gun smoke." The heavy stress he places on the last word particularly emphasizes a harder line being taken and that he means business. Up to this point in the film, no gun has been fired, but the outcome of the barroom brawl—and Starrett's bragging over the victory—has unleashed the dogs of war and cued in the arrival of the gunfighter, Wilson. Ryker's humiliation will lead directly to the humiliation and gunning down of the homesteader Torrey.

Before Wilson's dramatic appearance, however (riding in from right to left of the frame, a sure sign of a character's villainy, and accompanied by Victor Young's strident horn motif, underlined by a heavy plodding rhythm, that seems a deliberate negation of the flowing main theme), we will have one of the most emotionally charged scenes of the whole film. How cleverly *Shane* negotiates the interaction between the external con-flict that drives the narrative and the internal conflict animating the characters. How simply Stevens places the intricacies of human motive before us in a way that seems nat-ural, but, in the precision of its tempo and composition, has a poetry of its own that is all the more affecting because there seems to be no straining after effect. The equivalent scene in the novel seems strident and unsubtle by comparison.

The Starretts and Shane have returned home. While Joey is now virtually head over heels with excitement at what he has witnessed, Marian is tending to the injuries of the two men. "Oh don't let's talk about Ryker anymore tonight," she says, forestalling an anx-iety she might feel about where all this will lead. She starts applying turpentine to a cut on Shane's forehead. "*Stings* like anything!" says Joey brightly, at which point Marian orders him to bed and his father follows suit. For a moment she and Shane are alone together; and, as he assures her he now feels fine, he calls her "Marian" for the first time. A slight pause; a momentary look is shared between them, lasting about a second; and then Joey appears at his bedroom door, motioning his mother towards him as he wants to tell her something, privately. The camera remains in medium shot, with Shane seated at the table, as he overhears Joey telling his mother that he loves Shane almost as much as he loves pa ("That's all right, isn't it?" he asks.) This declaration of love from behind closed doors has a delicate, melancholy resonance, for there is a sense that Joey is not only speaking *to* his mother, but also, unknowingly, speaking *for* her. Yet the sadness in the air is almost palpable: Shane has never looked more solitary, more alone. Like an inadvertent intruder on a private confidence, he rises carefully from his chair and quietly exits. When Marian returns a moment later, she stops momentarily as she sees that Shane has gone. Has he overheard what was said? Is that why he left? She goes to the door and looks out towards the barn where he sleeps, Victor Young's music at this point gently intertwining the Shane theme with the varsovienne theme particularly associated with Marian to suggest her confusion of feelings. Their bedroom door opens to the right of the frame and Joe appears. "What's the matter, honey?" he asks, for the second time in the film sensing that something is troubling her without knowing exactly what it is. And once again she does not answer him directly but just asks him to hold her. "Don't say anything," she says, "just hold me." He does so, and together they go into the bedroom and close the door. By keeping the camera still during all this, Stevens both respects the visual integrity of the scene while allowing the audience to register and reflect on the tangle of emotions going on under the surface. The scene is not quite over. In a beautiful and exquisitely timed coda, we hear Joey calling goodnight to each of his parents in turn; and then, after a slight pause, we hear him shout "'Night, Shane!" as if confirming Shane's place in the family. The shout is unheard; it is a call into the darkness to which there is no response; there is a fade to black. In the full context of the film, one can see that this scene foreshadows the finale, most notably when a call from Joey to his mother will curtail definitively a highly charged emotional moment between Marian and Shane; and when an unanswered call from Joey to Shane in the darkness will signify not "goodnight" but "goodbye."

Independence Day. While the cowboys are celebrating with a rodeo in the center of town, the Ryker brothers and Wilson are quietly conferring in the saloon. Grafton is standing by the swing doors, half attending to the celebrations taking place outside, but also taking in the conversation between the three men and clearly uneasy about Wilson's presence and at what he perceives is a worsening situation. Grafton's presence is shrewdly deployed by Stevens in this scene, not only adding to the tension but also pricking Ryker's conscience about possibly having to go further than he really wanted to go. The tension builds to the moment when there is a close-up of Grafton as he hears the tinkle of a bell that indicates that someone has come from the store into the saloon, for it is an entrance that portends the violence to come. Stonewall Torrey has entered, arriving to buy a jug to take to the Shipsteads' party, but also just having come from the homestead of Ernie Wright and witnessed the cattle stampede by the Ryker men over Wright's ploughed ground, which is the final act of intimidation that will drive him and his family out of their place for good.

As soon as Torrey has entered the saloon, Wilson has swung round on his stool to study him, like a hunter first scenting his prey. When Torrey proposes an ironic toast to Ryker for driving Ernie Wright off his claim, Wilson swings back to Ryker for confirmation that this is one of the homesteaders and a bit of a hot-head who might be easily provoked. Stevens' soundtrack is superb here. Torrey makes most of the noise, defiantly boasting that he cannot be scared away by Ryker's tactics any more than Joe Starrett; and then, equally defiantly, proposing a toast to what he calls the "the greatest state of the Union … the sovereign state of Alabama." More significant, however, is the whispered conversation in the foreground of the shot between three conspirators, debating and then agreeing to delay provoking a confrontation there and then. It is another example of the density of Stevens' compositional and dramatic sense, as he captures and contrasts foreground/background, soft/loud, seated/standing, cowboys/homesteader, conspiratorial trio/loudmouth individual in a single frame of quiet, controlled intensity. Even Torrey's whiskey-fueled courage contrasts with Wilson's coffee-fueled control: the impression given is that this gunfighter never drinks when on a job. When Torrey swaggers out of the saloon, kicking over a chair and deliberately smashing the louvres of the door with his elbow in a self-conscious display of bravado, the three men are seen staring through the gap after the departing figure. Wilson's expression at this point has been described as "leering," but that more accurately describes Morgan's response. As acted by Jack Palance, Wilson seems more contemplative and thoughtful, as if carefully assessing what he has seen. In his brash behavior, Torrey has unwittingly signed his own death warrant, for he has disclosed a temperament (careless volatility) and a topic (his Southern pride) that an experienced gunfighter can use to his advantage when inciting a desired quarrel.

Stevens dissolves from the broken saloon door to the American flag and the sound of a small cannon being fired. It concisely indicates a change of scene to the settlers' celebration at the Shipsteads'; it might be also be taken as an ironic conclusion to the preceding scene (Torrey is nothing if not a loose cannon). The music, the children, the animals are all woven into an affectionate evocation of frontier harmony. It is also the tenth wedding anniversary of Joe and Marian, who suddenly find themselves under a garland in their honor. After an embarrassed speech of thanks (done with endearing awkwardness by Heflin) and a kiss from husband to wife, the community join together to sing "Abide with Me," whose final notes are nicely merged with the opening of Wagner's "Wedding March" played by Mrs. Shipstead on the piano. In the glow of the moment, one might miss the fleeting expression of wistfulness that steals across Shane's face, as if reflecting on an emotional contentment that has eluded him. This scene makes an interest contrast to the preceding one, because, whereas the scene in the saloon has highlighted the external drama, this scene subtly explores the internal drama that is also taking place. When the dancing resumes, Starrett finds himself fenced out of the area (to his relief, one thinks) and Marian now dances with Shane, who is clearly a more elegant dancing partner than her husband. As Starrett watches them, and with just the slightest change of expression, Van Heflin conveys the character's flickering unease at what he sees. It is another of those moments where Starrett seems slightly bewildered and puzzled at something Marian has said or done, but cannot quite articulate what it is. Here it seems to trigger a feeling not as strong as jealousy nor as powerful as envy but something bemusedly in between. The moment is given particular piquancy because Marian is wearing her wedding dress, giving the dance between her and Shane an aura of courtship and love. For the first time, Starrett might have spotted a slight fissure in his marriage; and Shane and Marian might be enacting a wish that can never be fulfilled. Subtly but steadily, the film is moving towards the point when the exterior and the interior conflict in the drama will combine and collide.

"Howdy, Starrett." When the Starretts and Shane return to their homestead after the party, Ryker is waiting for them, along with Morgan and Wilson. The greeting is the same as that at the beginning of the film when Ryker and his men came to Starretts' place, but, in Emile Meyer's delivery, the tone is different; whereas at the beginning it was more threatening, here it seems more friendly. He has come to make Starrett an offer that he believes is fair and reasonable (two words that Ryker uses quite frequently in the film). If Starrett will come to work for him, he will pay him top wages; will allow him to run his cattle with Ryker's; and will meet any reasonable price that Starrett might ask for his homestead. He points out that it is an offer that will make him financially far better off than would be the case if he remained farming for himself.

Woody Allen thought this was one of the best scenes in the film, for, although it is presented in an unforced way, there is an enormous amount going on beneath the surface.

Part of its greatness is that it compels a reassessment of Ryker's character. Although he has formerly told Grafton that he is through with arguing, nevertheless he is still prepared to make one last pitch to Starrett in the hope that a confrontation can be avoided. The presence of Wilson at the scene is intriguing. One might surmise that Ryker is giving him the opportunity to appraise what he is dealing with, notably Starrett's stubbornness. It might also be a tactic of silent intimidation, indicating to Starrett that a new and dangerous factor has been brought into play. Nevertheless, there is no suggestion that the offer is not genuine; and if Starrett were to accept, then Wilson's services would no longer be required.

When Starrett begins to claim the moral high ground and ask what right Ryker has to harass the homesteaders in the way he has, Ryker is goaded into delivering a strong peroration about the hardships and dangers he and others before him have had to endure and survive in order to make the range safe for people like Starrett to live in, but who are now endangering his livelihood. It is the longest and most impassioned speech in the whole film; and it is characteristic of Stevens to allow the ostensible bad guy to have his say and invite us to see things from his point of view. Ryker is not a straightforward villain, but someone who is fighting to preserve what he believes is rightfully his and for which he and others have made huge sacrifices. Emile Meyer's performance has rarely been the credit it deserves, but he is at his finest here, providing an insight into the pain, passion and pride of the pioneers of the West, and respectfully framed by Stevens against a night sky in a way that, in Eugene Archer's eloquent phrase, "conjures evocative images of great achievement and forgotten glory" (Archer: 26). From his point of view, Ryker has made every attempt at conciliation, but, because he cannot make similar concessions to the other homesteaders, Starrett remains immovable. "You don't give a man much choice, do you, Starrett?" Ryker says, ominously, but also with a sense of regret, realizing that a showdown between them is looking increasingly inevitable. (Ironically, Shane will discover the same thing about Starrett's obstinacy.) Even then, Ryker has not finished, taking the trouble to dismount and make a personal pitch to young Joey, appealing for his support and claiming (convincingly) that he wants no trouble with his father.

Yet, through all this, Joey's attention has been elsewhere. A powerful scene in its own right is given an additional dimension and tension through Stevens' adroit cutting between the exchanges between Ryker and Starrett and the silent communication taking place between Shane and Wilson. During Ryker's speech, Shane has climbed down from the wagon to get a drink of water and at the same time get a closer look at Wilson. His action recalls the film's opening scene when he accepted Joe Starrett's offer of water, a connection emphasized still further when Shane stands at the side of the cabin in precisely the same spot when he returned to support Starrett against the Ryker boys. It is as if he is instinctively sensing that this is where that support has led him: to a meeting with a man like Wilson. At this point Wilson begins to dismount, with a calculated slow gracefulness that borders on narcissism. After also taking a drink of water, he mounts his horse and then backs it away rather than turn it, so that he can keep his gaze fixed on Shane. There is something ritualistic about the encounter, like two warriors sizing each other up in silent contemplation before what they recognize will be an inevitable duel to the death. It is played in striking visual contrast to the argument between Ryker and Starrett, but it also adds enormously to the suspense of the scene, because it suggests that a wholly different element has been brought into this conflict. "What do you make of him?" Starrett asks Shane of Wilson. "He's no cowpuncher," replies Shane. What he is will be made plain in the next scene, one of the most famous in the film.

Stevens dissolves from nighttime to the following day, as Shipstead and Torrey ride toward town, with Torrey's dog scampering alongside and Torrey himself looking almost comically small on his diminutive horse next to that of his companion. Inside the saloon, Ryker, Morgan and Wilson seem to be mulling over the previous evening's encounter with Starrett. Looking over to Sam Grafton, who now seems invariably to be hovering as Ryker's guilty conscience, Ryker turns to Wilson and says quietly but firmly, "I like Joe Starrett too, but I'll kill him if I have to." Sipping his coffee, Wilson corrects him with cool precision: " You mean *I'll* kill him if *you* have to." Ironically, these words are to be echoed at the later funeral scene, when Starrett vows to have it out with Ryker once and for all, "even if I have to kill him." As Marian protests, Stevens cuts to a large close-up of Shane's reaction, as if it has sounded a premonition of his own future role, when he will finally be drawn into a fight that Starrett cannot handle. What has brought things to a head by that time is the incident that has followed Wilson's comment. Sniggering at the gunfighter's remark, Morgan has drifted over to the saloon doors to look out over the street. "Well, looky here," he says, and then in a slightly lower voice, "looky here." The difference in tone is sufficient to alert Wilson, and he and Ryker move over to the doors to see what has caught Morgan's attention. The sight of Torrey is the opportunity they have been waiting for. Morgan looks expectantly at his brother for the go-ahead; Ryker whispers that any gunplay must look right to Grafton; Wilson half-smiles, in anticipation of a familiar situation. He needs no advice or guidelines from Ryker, for he knows exactly what he has to do.

He and Morgan step outside onto the porch, as if casually taking in the afternoon air; and Morgan seats himself in a chair while Wilson leans against the saloon wall. Stevens keeps the camera still as Torrey and Shipstead tether their horses outside the blacksmith's shop in the foreground of the shot, while in the background, we watch Wilson as he moves forward to the edge of the porch and onto the boardwalk. Victor Young's theme for Wilson at this point, deliberate and somber, seems rhythmically to match his menacing tread. There is the sound of thunder rumbling overhead; dark clouds intermittently pass over the sky; the air is heavy with foreboding.

"Hey … come here." Although Shipstead warns him not to go, Torrey cannot refuse to acknowledge Wilson's call from across the street, for, to do so, would be to emulate what he referred to as Ernie Wright's "cowardice" in the face of intimidation. As he crosses the street towards him, Wilson moves to the edge of the boardwalk, looking across at Shipstead as if to warn him not to interfere and compelling Torrey to change direction slightly, at which point he slithers in the mud and almost loses his footing. It is like a movement in a game of chess; Wilson has positioned himself very deliberately to place him at an advantage over his opponent. The mud is a masterstroke on Stevens' part, for it seems to underline the treacherous, uncertain path that Torrey is taking; and almost involuntarily, he takes two steps backwards as Wilson asks him where he thinks he is going. "For a whiskey," Torrey replies. The two walk parallel to each other towards the saloon, Wilson in the plainly superior position as he steps back onto the porch. Now seeming to tower above Torrey, he taunts him about his nickname "Stonewall" and about the man's Southern pride which he has witnessed in the earlier saloon scene. He stops in front of the saloon doors, making it clear, without needing to spell it out, that, if Torrey wants a whiskey from the saloon bar, he will have to pass Wilson to get it. "Who'd they name you after—or would you know?" says Torrey, his voice now carrying the dull defiance of a brave man suddenly seeming to realize that he is out of his depth and that he has been sucked into a situation from which there is no retreat. While speaking, Wilson has taken out a black glove and put it on his right hand. The calculated gesture seems part of Wilson's ritual of preparation for a gunfight (one fleetingly recalls Shane's comment to Joey that "most of them have tricks of their own"); and also part of his process of psychological intimidation, the donning of the glove signaling an imminent, fatal challenge. Stevens cuts to a shot from behind Wilson's gun holster, as if in anticipation of what is to happen; from that angle also, Torrey looks hopelessly vulnerable. It is a desperately unequal confrontation. When Wilson calls him "Southern trash," and Torrey cannot refrain from responding in kind ("You're a lowdown lying Yankee!"), the gauntlet has been tossed. "Prove it," Wilson says. We can just hear Shipstead call, "No, Torrey!" as if hoping even at this stage that his friend can be saved. The shout seems momentarily to distract Torrey, but it is too late; his gun has barely cleared the holster when he senses Wilson has beaten him.

When Wilson draws his gun, there is a startling pause of about three seconds, the two men seen almost from Shipstead's point of view; the pause suggests the viewpoint of someone holding his breath. It is just enough time for us to take in that Wilson has beaten Torrey to the draw and does not need to shoot; and for Wilson to relish the moment of having the power over another man's life or death. For his part, Torrey never looks up; it is as if his opponent has cruelly allowed him to stare into the abyss of what he has done and feel the full horror of its consequence before it happens. A single shot rings out, loud enough to cause us to start; and Torrey is knocked flat on his back and sent slithering backwards in the mud by the impact of the bullet. In an instant a life is over. The noise of the gunshot is followed by a close-up of Wilson with a half-smile on his face, as if savoring the moment of a job well done; and also by the sound of a bird singing softly in the distance, a sound Torrey will never hear and in poignant contrast to the brutality of what has just occurred.

"Killing used to be fun and games in Apacheland," said Sam Peckinpah, reflecting on pre–1950s Westerns. "Violence wasn't shown well. You fired a shot and three Indians fell down. But when Jack Palance shot Elisha Cook Jr. … things started to change" (qtd in Weddle: 108). The scene's shocking rendering of violence was undoubtedly to have a huge influence on Peckinpah's own revisionist reconstructions of the West and the Western, most notably in *The Wild Bunch* (1969) and *Pat Garrett and Billy the Kid* (1973). (Stevens might have recognized in Peckinpah something of his own perfectionism, for, on hearing that Peckinpah had fired fifteen people during the making of *Major Dundee* he commented thoughtfully: "Sounds like he wanted to make a good movie" (Weddle: 237). It is possible to surmise that, in addition to its presentation of violence, *Shane* might have also have been an influence on another key aspect of Peckinpah's Westerns; namely, the depiction of children as symbols of the future and possible inheritors of their predecessors' violent legacy. This has already been touched on in discussing the complex ramifications of Shane's shooting lesson for Joey, and it comes to the fore in the aftermath of Torrey's killing.

When Shipstead rides past the Lewis farm, the youngest of Lewis's girls waves uncomprehendingly at Torrey's body before an elder sister gently puts her hand down by her side. (It is a gentler anticipation of that famous moment in Arthur Penn's 1958 Western, *The Left-Handed Gun*, when the sheriff is shot by Billy the Kid, and a boy laughs uncomprehendingly at the incongruous sight of the sheriff's empty boot in the middle of the street until his mother slaps him across the face.) When Shipstead arrives at the

Starretts' homestead to tell them what had happened, Joey stares at Torrey's body sprawled across the saddle, his fascination with guns now given a much darker hue. One of the many remarkable things about the funeral sequence is the sensitivity Stevens brings to his direction of the children: the quick way Shipstead's older boy looks across at his brother to check that he has taken off his cap as a mark of respect; the way they huddle a little closer to their parents as if responding to the mood of mourning if not fully grasping its cause; the way Joey stares at a sobbing Mrs. Torrey as if seeing adult grief for the first time; or the moment when he wanders away from the huddled groups to stroke one of the horses and is watched by Lewis's youngest girl who gives a slight giggle when she thinks the horse might bite him. All of this is woven unobtrusively into the larger picture of the funeral service, but it is also moving the scene towards a crucial statement of its main theme: what the settlers are fighting for and why giving up now would be a betrayal of Torrey's courage. Starrett tries to articulate it but cannot find the words, and Shane has to finish the speech for him: that the struggle is really for the future and on behalf of their families and children, who have a right to live in the valley and grow up and raise families of their own in peace. It is the longest speech Shane makes in the film, his equivalent to Ryker's speech of self-justification at the Starretts' house; and it is all the more poignant and ironic because he is defining an ideal of which even then, one suspects, he knows he cannot be a part.

The sound of a coyote is heard, howling in the darkness; it is the night of reckoning. Stevens' build-up of suspense is unerring as he cuts between the Rykers and Wilson in Grafton's saloon and the Starrett homestead. Having seen the homesteaders returning to help the Lewises rebuild their home after the Rykers have set fire to it, Ryker now knows that no intimidation is going to work while Starrett is their leader; he will have to engineer a showdown. Sending Morgan out to the Starrett ranch with the message that his brother wants to see him, he says, "Tell him I'm a reasonable man, tell him I'm beat, tell him anything," and then, to emphasize the importance of the message, exclaims, "but, by Jupiter, get him here!" Jupiter was the Roman sky god particularly associated with lightning and the thunderbolt; the exclamation gives a sharp insight into Ryker's egotism and sense of righteous power. (Starrett's exclamations are the more prosaic "By Godfrey.") Significantly this exchange is overheard by Chris Calloway, which will affect the plot's development from this point.

In fact, Starrett is already preparing his horse in readiness for his ride into town. Marian looks over to Shane for support in trying to dissuade Joe from going, but he is demonstrating knots to Joey. "This is a false square knot, Joey, it can't hold," he says, possibly a coded reference to Starrett's mistaken bravado in thinking he can face up to Ryker and Wilson. But when Marian asks for a more direct intervention, Shane says: "I can't tell Joe what's right, Marian," and gets up and leaves the room, followed by little Joey who seems to be imitating Shane's walk back to the barn. (It is clear that Joey has no real understanding of what is at stake at this moment, which will be important later.) At this stage, it seems, Shane is prepared, or resigned, to let Starrett go into town, even though aware of the danger; and that remains the case, even after the visit of Morgan, for Shane at that point is still in his ordinary work clothes. What, then, is the deciding factor that convinces him that he must confront Ryker and Wilson in Starrett's place?

It is here that the intervention of Chris Calloway assumes great significance. Even admirers of the film have sometimes criticized this moment, Penelope Houston, for example, describing it as "a needless plot twist—one of Ryker's men comes to warn Shane, to announce a change of sides" (Houston: 72). As I argued earlier, Calloway's disillusionment with Ryker after the outcome of his saloon brawl with Shane is emotionally plausible; and it is reinforced by close-ups of him outside the saloon during Torrey's funeral, clasping his hands tightly together and subtly registering discomfort and disapproval at Morgan's laughter. Calloway might be a braggart who has met his match (rather like Torrey in this respect), but he is not a killer. And far from being "a needless plot twist," his intervention is dramatically crucial. In the novel, his conversion happens after Shane has left the valley and he offers to come to work for Starrett in his stead. In earlier drafts of the film script, he was to intercept Shane on his way into town to warn him of the situation in the saloon. By placing the scene earlier, Stevens tightens the dramatic screw. If Shane even up to this point had doubts about the right thing to do, this is the moment that clinches his decision. When Calloway calls out to him, Shane is still in his work clothes, indicating his reluctance to don his buckskin outfit (implicitly representing his former life). But when Calloway tells him that Starrett is "up against a stacked deck," Shane has no choice but to act. ("You don't give a man much choice, do you, Starrett?") Now knowing for certain that Starrett will be killed if he steps inside that saloon, Shane *has* to go in his place, for how could he ever face Marian and Joey (and himself) again, having been given that warning?

It is here that the psychology of the film deepens still further, for Starrett's explanation to his wife of the reasons he must face Ryker goes beyond the Westerner's usual justification of his behavior in terms of pride, courage, self-respect, self-justification and manhood. (Think of the Marshal in *High Noon*.) The conventional motives are there— the fear of appearing a coward to his wife and son, his obligation to the homesteaders in matching their courage in staying on—but there is something else. Van Heflin is particularly fine here, for he is conveying the sense of a man groping to articulate what he is almost afraid to say but knowing that it has to be said because he may not have another chance. "I know I'm kind of slow sometimes," he says hesitantly (one thinks of those moments when he senses Marian's distress without being able to grasp the cause), "but I see things" (subliminally we think back to that close-up as he watches the dance of Marian and Shane at the Independence Day party). "And I know that if anything ever happened to me, you and Joey would be taken care of, maybe even better than I could do it myself. I never thought I'd live to hear myself say that." The words are said entirely without rancor but with quiet understanding. There is an equivalent moment in the novel, but it takes place earlier on the evening after the saloon fight when Joe tells Marian he is "man enough to know a better when his trail meets mine" (Schaefer: 100). The placement of that sentiment in the film is much more poignant and powerful, because behind it is the implication that Shane and Marian might have fallen in love with each other, but, more particularly, it suggests why Starrett can face the possibility of his death with something approaching equanimity. The irony is that this emotional entanglement, on top of the "stacked deck" Starrett will face, is precisely the reason that Shane cannot allow him to go. Joey's idolization and Marian's adoration of Shane might afford Starrett some comfort in the event of his death, but it makes Shane's position impossible, for he would be taking advantage of a situation only he can prevent. Suddenly the inner emotional complexities of the film are pressing in on the external drama.

When Starrett is saying all this, Marian is sobbing, covering her eyes with her hands clenched like fists, and moaning, "Oh, Joe. Joe." The name of Shane is not mentioned between them, but they both understand what Joe is saying and, significantly, Marian neither protests nor denies. If Heflin is splendid in these final scenes, Jean Arthur is sublime. Eugene Archer thought that "as the wife, Jean Arthur seems sometimes out of place" (Archer: 27), but I have always felt that that she was in character in suggesting that. In some ways, the marital backstory of the Starretts is as mysterious as that of Shane's gunfighter past. Although Joe, and we, never doubt her loyalty and devotion to her husband, there is sometimes a hint of someone who has married beneath her (as suggested by her unspoken discomfort at her husband's behavior during that first supper with Shane), or as someone who occasionally craves for a more refined life (as suggested in that moment in Grafton's store, when she picks up the preserving jar and murmurs, "My, my, what will they think of next?"). Things come to a head when Shane enters the cabin wearing his gun and in his "combat clothes" (Blake: 135), and Marian seems equally appalled by that prospect. Her extraordinary outburst at this point—imploring Joe to leave their home, that she is sick of the work, that none of this is worth a life—carries such force because it comes not simply out of a present fear, but is surely the culmination of a frustration that been building up over a long time. It might be a final strategic ploy, but there feels a lot of genuine emotional anguish behind it. Starrett is clearly shocked and says he does not believe her, adding tellingly and perhaps provocatively, "Even if that were the truth, it wouldn't change things." (Perhaps it should.) Starrett's mind is made up, and, in the novel, it is at this point, that, before Starrett realizes what is happening, Shane has drawn his gun and knocked him out. By contrast, the equivalent moment in the film is dramatically heightened. If Starrett is going into town, he will have to get past Shane first.

When Starrett lunges at Shane's neck, he is doing more than just trying to get him out of the way. Behind the attack we sense Starrett's rage at the situation, shock at Marian's outburst, confused admiration and anger at Shane, dogged determination, innate farmer's strength, and perhaps even a desire to test whether Shane is quite the superior man everyone thinks he is. His ferocity seems to take Shane by surprise, in much the same way as he took Calloway by surprise in the saloon fight earlier. The fight is magnificently filmed, and the soundtrack is hair-raising. Marian's screams (wonderfully done by Jean Arthur) are like those of someone who is being tortured, and the sound merges with the terrified whinnying of Starrett's horse, the barking of the dog, the cattle in panic almost leaping and stampeding out of the corral. As two close friends are engaged in an ugly savage fight, Nature itself seems to share in the uproar. Sometimes we see the struggle from the window as Marian and Joey are rushing from side to side to get a sense of what is happening but seeming initially afraid to move outside and get too close to the horror unfolding before them, which seems worse than Marian's worst nightmare. Starrett is proving more than a match for Shane in this struggle, but, irrespective of honor, it is a struggle Shane cannot afford to lose. The two men fall across the tree stump, which has earlier symbolized their friendship; and it is here that Shane secretly draws out his gun and knocks Starrett out cold. As with the earlier incident with the tree stump, but this time more ominously, Shane must finish what Starrett has started.

"Shane, you hit him with your gun!" cries Joey, "I hate you!" That jars somewhat: the switch from hero worship to hate seems so swift and extreme. Yet Stevens has shown throughout this sequence that Joey has not grasped the life-and-death gravity of the situation. When he is playing with his gun and shouting "Bang! Bang!" inside the house, he is barely aware that his game is mimicking an impending scenario and shredding his mother's already frayed nerves, so that when she shouts at him, he is almost literally knocked off balance by her hysteria, to the point where she has to moderate her tone.

From the boy's point of view, in the fight Shane has cheated; moreover he seems to have hurt his father quite badly. In a night of high emotion, when all the people close to him are losing control, it is perhaps not surprising that Joey himself becomes caught up in the prevailing atmosphere. It is only when his father seems to be recovering and his mother tells him that Shane did what he had to do that Joey begins to understand the meaning of what has happened—and possibly too late. When he calls out an apology, Shane does not hear him. Once again we have an example of the film's enlarging and enhancing in dramatic terms a moment from the original. In the novel, the boy will follow Shane into town out of curiosity and excitement. In the film, there is that, but also a heart-aching apology to be delivered. As it turns out, this weight of immense sorrow will extend right through to the film's final shot.

If one might wish to modify Eugene Archer's contention that Jean Arthur sometimes seemed out of place as the farmer's wife, he is absolutely right to praise her performance in her farewell scene with Shane. "In her *unerringly timed* [my italics] final scene—bravely extending her hand in a friendly farewell to the man she will not admit she loves—she is superb" (Archer: 27). She has asked if Shane is doing this for her. "For you, Marian?" he says, and then smiles, adding, "and for Joe, and for little Joe." It is altogether a more appropriate and less pompous response than in the novel. ("Could I separate you in my mind and afterwards be a man?") "Then we'll never see you again," she says. Originally there was intended to be a prologue and epilogue to the film, with Joey now fourteen years old, and still hoping for Shane's return, but, probably wisely, the idea was dropped (Moffat: 269–71). It is the sense of finality that makes the scene so moving and Jean Arthur's control of the hesitations and pauses in her speech is wonderfully handled. " Please, Shane," she says, and then stops, as if the words will not come. "Mother..." Joey calls in the background, recalling her to her role in the family and perhaps also echoing the moment when it was Marian's voice calling to Joey that persuaded Shane to stay. "Please..." she says again, her eyes still on Shane after Joey has called for her. The words still obstinately refuse to form in her mind. She then extends a hand, rather stiffly and self-consciously, and simply says, "Take care of yourself." It is one of the most moving handshakes in movies.

Shane's ride to town is one of the film's visual highlights, formally majestic, and paced to perfection. It has the inevitability of classical drama, as if, without foreseeing it or willing it, Shane is now on the path he was destined to follow the moment he turned back to side with Joe Starrett in his first confrontation with the Rykers. Stevens gives us a magnificent long shot of him as a lone rider on a hill framed against a night sky, in every way the antithesis of Wilson's first entry in the film. Another shot of him, taken from a low angle and with the camera tracking in front of his chestnut horse, conveys an imposing sense of stature and determination. The ride is crosscut with Joey's pursuit, trying to keep Shane in view, and with Torrey's dog (which he seems to have adopted) panting alongside. (A lovely touch, that: the dog will see its late master avenged.) It is another example of Stevens' wide coverage of a sequence to add tension, heighten emotion, and give a different perspective to a situation. This is Joey's night of destiny too, and the turbulence of his emotional state, as well as the danger Shane is to face, is kept to the forefront of our consciousness. Because we have seen it earlier when the homesteaders have ridden into town and when Torrey has accompanied Shipstead to the blacksmith's prior to his fatal encounter with Wilson, the setting is now familiar to us; and we recognize signposts that indicate that Shane is nearing his destination. When he appears at the top of the hill and is framed between those three trees, we know the town is only a few minutes away. As Shane rides into town, there is a startling superimposition of Joey as he rushes across the cemetery, adding to the suspense of whether the boy will reach the town in time but also serving as a kind of premonition of an imminent encounter that can only end in death for one or other of the parties involved. For this sequence, incidentally, Stevens interpolated music from Franz Waxman's score for *Rope and Sand* (1949) in preference to Victor Young's scoring of the scene, an ironic reversal from *A Place in the Sun*, where some of Waxman's original score was replaced by Victor Young's music. The CD of the complete score (which, incidentally, reveals that future film composer Dominic Frontiere was one of the studio musicians on the recording session) allows a comparison of the two versions, and it does seem to me that in this instance, Stevens' instincts were correct, Waxman's harsher and more abrasive orchestration building the suspense more effectively.

"This was the Shane of the adventures I had dreamed for him," wrote the boy-narrator of the novel as Shane entered Grafton's saloon, "cool and competent, facing that room full of men, in the simple solitude of his own invincible completeness" (Schaefer: 134). The heightened prose emphasizes the boy's idealization of the hero as well as giving a hint as to the reason that some commentators have interpreted the tale as a dream-narrative. However, the tone of the film at this point is very different. For one thing there is no "room full of men"; the saloon is almost deserted. Ryker and Wilson are seated in their allotted places, awaiting Starrett's anticipated arrival; Morgan is concealed on the balcony. Two cowboys, who were playing cards, quickly leave on appraising the situation; the dog lopes away in seeming disapproval when Wilson makes a move; the ubiquitous Will is behind the bar; significantly there is no sign of Grafton. (From his anguished close-up at the sight of Torrey's body in the street, one might surmise that he has lapsed into resignation and despair at his failure to keep the peace in the territory.) Over the soundtrack we hear the dull rhythmic beat of a single bass drum, as if representing the scene's nervous pulse.

All this might seem like the preparation for an archetypal Western gunfight, but what is distinctive here is the unusual undertow of solemnity and even sadness. Shane is there only because there is no other choice of action open to him "Alan Ladd's gunfighter-saviour, Shane, is a reluctant dragon-slayer at best," wrote Frank D. McDonnell, adding that "his reluctance, as the film makes clear, is not the slow, deadly self-restraint in the William S. Hart tradition: rather it is a kind of existential ennui with the role itself, a disgust with the necessity of being a private bearer of justice" (McDonnell: 160). Perhaps "disgust" is too strong a word there, but it is undeniable that Shane has resisted returning to this role until all other avenues have been exhausted; and that his past has proved to be tragically inescapable. Equally striking, though, is the reluctance of the villains to face him. This is not because Shane represents a more formidable opponent than Starrett; it is because it is not his fight. "I've got no quarrel with you, Shane," says Ryker, and is prepared to let him leave with no hard feelings. Even Wilson, when he rises to his feet, is not about to issue a challenge. "Our fight ain't with you," he says, for this intervention has changed the nature of the confrontation, putting him on the defensive. (Jack Palance is particularly good in the moment when he sees Shane enter the saloon, carefully moving his coffee cup in readiness but also subtly conveying the sense of someone facing a somewhat unexpected and unwelcome development of events.) When Shane throws Torrey's words back in Wilson's face ("I've heard you're a lowdown Yankee liar"), the sound is unnaturally loud, as if the taunt is emanating from the bowels of the earth. Is this how Wilson hears it, as a voice from beyond the grave demanding vengeance? (It is intriguing that, when Shipstead is reporting Torrey's death to Starrett and Shane, he insists that he had not heard the exact words that Torrey had used but only the anger in their voices.) In a flurry of action, the two men draw; Wilson appears to get off a shot before collapsing backwards into some barrels behind him; Shane swivels quickly and kills Ryker before he has time to take in what has happened. A slight pause, as Shane moves over to look down sadly on the old man, recognizing a certain kinship with a pioneer whose days are now over. There is a curious moment when Shane then performs an elaborate flourish with his gun, spinning it forwards and backwards on his finger, before replacing it in his holster, which is perhaps his own personal signature as a gunfighter (like Wilson's black glove) and here given its final outing. If it seems an uncharacteristically flamboyant gesture, Stevens almost makes him pay for it, for, in relaxing his guard, Shane has not realized the danger is not yet over. It is Joey's shout of warning that alerts him to the presence of Morgan on the balcony, and an exchange of gunfire brings Morgan crashing to the floor.

The valley has now been made safe for the homesteaders, so it might appear odd that Henri Sadoul should describe the film as "structured like a modern tragedy" (Sadoul: 337); and yet he is right. For all that Shane has emerged victorious, the final scene has a mournful air of loss and sacrifice. (This is perhaps another aspect of *Shane* that Stevens had in mind when he described it as his "war movie.") Shane has applied his exceptional expertise in a worthy cause to bring about a desired outcome, but he himself has no place in the society he has saved nor can he ever enjoy the gratitude of the people whose future he has secured. He is an anachronism in the new West. He has done things he cannot live down or forget and therefore cannot settle into the future; and one wonders whether Stevens, after his war experience, identified with this also.

All of this is poignantly conveyed in the final scene between Shane and Joey, perfectly acted by Alan Ladd (gently speaking to Joey as he would to a young adult with new responsibilities) and Brandon de Wilde (his eyes widening and filling with tears as he begins to take in the enormity of what he is hearing). Joey has followed Shane into town to say sorry for what he said in a moment of anger at home; and, in tending to his injured father, he has probably not heard the final conversation between Shane and his mother. The sorrow he begins to feel now is on an altogether larger scale, for it signals the departure of a hero he has worshipped and marks the end of his childhood. Placing his hand on Joey's head as if anointing him for the onset of maturity, Shane tells Joey to run on home and assure his mother that everything is all right and that there are no more guns in the valley. "And Joey, take care of them," he says, perhaps consciously echoing Marian's last words to him, before adding as clarification, "both of them." (It is a subtle modification, recalling Shane's response to Marian about the real motivation for what he is doing: "For you, Marian? And for Joe, and little Joe.")

Stevens has a last masterstroke up his sleeve: the echoing hills. When Shane is riding away, Joey runs to the end of the porch and calls after him to return. Significantly, the echo begins on Joey's cry, "And mother wants you … wants you … wants you…. I know she does … she does … she does." Unwittingly he is giving voice to his mother's pain of separation as well as his own. But, as Shane has said, there is no going back. In a satisfying symmetrical structure, Joey has been the first to see him arrive in the valley and the last to see him leave. Indeed he might even be the last to see him alive, for Shane has been wounded in the final gunfight; does not answer Joey's anguished calls into the darkness;

and, in the final images, is a shadowy figure slumped on his horse and passing through the town's cemetery.

A classic Western, certainly, but also so much more: intimate as well as epic; real but also mythic. It is a densely characterized adult movie of repressed emotions, unrequited love, tragic sacrifice, and emotional epiphanies. It rises to the generic expectations of exciting action set against awesome landscapes as the pioneering America of the nineteenth century moves confidently towards a sense of its own identity, but it is also a psychological drama in which the characters experience what Alan Stanbrook has called "a series of self-awakenings" (Stanbrook: 40). Typifying the extent of Stevens' humanitarian reach, these self-awakenings involve not only the three main characters but extend to young Joey, Chris Calloway, and even to Ryker, whether proudly affirming his rightful claim to the land in his nighttime scene with Starrett or, in the scene in the saloon, sadly sensing a kinship with Shane as a man whose way of life is over. It shows the contamination of violence, recognizing it as part of the frontier legacy that lingers still in the American psyche, but exposing the toll it takes on both victims and perpetrators. It is a heroic film, but also a reflective one of great sadness; and a film of great maturity that nevertheless can accommodate a remarkably pure vision of a child-like assimilation of experience. In a letter to George Stevens, Jr. (21 August 2013) enthusing about the visual quality of the Blu-ray release of the film, Steven Spielberg mentioned he had seen *Shane* around a hundred times. A touch of hyperbole perhaps, though given Spielberg's credentials as a cineaste, you never know. He also referred to the film as "a masterpiece." In that regard, he was not exaggerating in the slightest.

Giant (1956)

> "Several people have said that he shot so much film from so many angles because he didn't know what he wanted. I've never thought that. I always thought that, if he's going to be a sculptor, he better have enough clay to make the bust, you know."—Rock Hudson, June 1982

JORDAN BENEDICT: "I run Reata at all times…. That's the way it is. Everything that's in it and on it is run by me…. That's the way it's always been too. Everything that has a Reata brand on it is run by me."

LESLIE, HIS WIFE: " Does that include me?"

The ending of *Giant* is anything but gigantic, but nothing short of magnificent. It concludes with a dialogue between two grandparents who are babysitting their grandchildren and reflecting on their lives. Epics are not usually given to understatement, but even Dimitri Tiomkin is becalmed over the soundtrack, resisting the temptation of a declamatory orchestral finale and instead transforming the march theme "The Eyes of Texas Are Upon You" into a lullaby as the film focuses finally on the elderly couple's infant grandson in his playpen.

At the beginning of this scene, Jordan Benedict (Rock Hudson) is stretched out on the couch at home with his wife, Leslie (Elizabeth Taylor). He is musing glumly on what he perceives as his failure as a rancher and parent. None of his children has taken the path he wanted for them, with one of them even trying her chances in Hollywood ("Good lord, an actress!" muses Jordan in horror). His status as a pillar of the Texas community as the owner of Reata ranch has been steadily usurped over the years by a former despised ranch-hand Jett Rink (James Dean) who has become an oil-rich tycoon. To add injury to insult, returning home from a gargantuan party in Rink's honor to celebrate the creation of a new hotel and airport, Benedict has become involved in a brawl with the owner of a diner and come off decidedly second-best, ending up flat on his back amid the salad and the dirty dishes, with a jukebox cheerily blaring out "The Yellow Rose of Texas" to accompany his fall from grace. His face is badly bruised; and, even more so, his pride.

As we have seen, humiliation plays a significant part in Stevens' films. Yet, in *Giant*, there is a nobility about this humiliation, because, although Jordan loses the fight, the motivation behind it is honorable. Marilyn Ann Moss suggested that Jordan has felt compelled to act because the owner has insulted his daughter-in-law Juana and by extension the entire Benedict family (Moss: 228). This is true, but Stevens takes the situation further than that because, after some awkwardness and discussion, the waitress has been instructed to serve the Benedict family. The more significant gesture occurs when Jordan moves into action on behalf of another Mexican family who are being refused service, sensing it is not right that his family should be tolerated because of who he is but the other family ejected. At the Rink party, Jordan had been accused of racism by his son, because, although he had confronted Rink after the latter had attacked Jordy, he had only done so out of family pride rather than rage at Rink's racial insult directed at Jordy's wife, Juana. Jordan had angrily rejected that accusation, insisting that he is "a fair man"; and it is that sense of fairness that surfaces now. For the first time in his life, racial prejudice has impinged on his own experience. However fleetingly, he has sensed what it must feel like to be at the receiving end of such hostility.

Still brooding over his shameful beating, Jordan is startled by his wife's reaction, so much so that he swivels round to face her, for she says that she had never felt more proud of him in her life. Stevens loved the irony of that. As he said at his 1973 American Film Institute seminar, it is "a reversal of how this kind of story would normally end—the hero is heroic. Here the hero is beaten, but his gal likes him. It's the first time she's ever really respected him because he's developed a kind of humility—not instinctive, but beaten into him" (Stevens Jr.: 230). Although deeply in love, Leslie has continually challenged her husband's principles, prejudices and presumed masculine superiority, so it is entirely logical that he only becomes a complete hero in her eyes when he has suffered defeat but in what she sees as a just stand against bigotry. As so often in Stevens's films, it is the heroine who is the agent of change and who drives the narrative engine of the film; and *Giant* is confirmation that no director in Hollywood ever made better films about marriage. Although it tends to be remembered first and foremost as the final film of James Dean before his tragically premature death in a car crash, the performances of Rock Hudson and Elizabeth Taylor form the emotional core of the film. Together they chart a stormy marital relationship in which a fiercely independent woman subtly brings about the progressive diminution of a patriarch's authority, which the film sees as part of his evolving humanity. It all prepares the way for that quietly devastating final shot, where the film's grand themes of generation conflict, racial intolerance and social change are compressed into a giant close-up of the brown eyes of the Mexican American child who will carry the family name forward into the next century. It must have seemed like a very bold ending in 1956. Over sixty years later, it looks both courageous and heart-rending.

First serialized in six consecutive issues of the *Ladies Home Journal*, the novel was published in 1952. Pulitzer Prize–winner for *So Big* in 1924, former member of the Algonquin Circle, author of such celebrated works as *Showboat* (1926) and *Cimarron* (1930) as well as co-author with George S. Kaufman of theatrical classics like *Dinner at Eight* (1932) and *Stage Door* (1937), Edna Ferber was one of the pre-eminent American authors of that time, and a new novel from her was a major literary event. In her introduction, she had written: "It is a novel peopled by imaginary characters who portray, I hope, the manners, mores, minds and emotions of part of that enormous and somewhat incredible commonwealth called Texas" (Ferber: 407–8). In fact, the "imaginary" characters were quite close to actual figures of Ferber's own acquaintance, notably the Kleberg family who owned the King ranch in Texas; and certainly the character of Jett Rink bore a strong resemblance to the Texas millionaire and oil tycoon Glenn McCarthy, even down to the vast party thrown by Rink to celebrate the launch of an airport in his name, which paralleled the legendary party thrown by McCarthy in 1949 (at a cost of $21 million) to celebrate the opening of his Shamrock Hotel in Houston. The novel got mixed reviews, partly because of its lopsided structure, but mainly for what some saw as its caricatured picture of Texans and Texas, which, in the words of Gordon Gow, was "denigrated as a vast breeding-ground for the materialist ethos" (Gow: 132). The *New York Times* loved the book, but noted wryly that "Miss Ferber makes it very clear that she doesn't like the Texas she writes about, and it's a cinch that when Texans read what she has written about them, they won't like Miss Ferber either" (Ferber: 408). This proved to be the case. The author professed to be saddened and hurt by their response, but when she writes about skyscraper office buildings rising "idiotically" out of the endless plain (p. 1); describes Rink's gigantic hotel as "majestically vulgar" (36); and is even ironical and dismissive about the Alamo (261), she surely could not have expected otherwise.

In adapting the novel for the screen, Stevens and his screenwriting partners Ivan Moffat and Fred Guiol took their time (between March and December of 1954), eventually reducing their initial draft from 370 pages to 240. At Stevens' request, Moffat wrote brief profiles of the three leading characters as guidelines for the actors (Moffat: 276–80). There were a number of changes made to the original, all of which are an improvement in terms of structure, incident and characterization. For example, the fight in the diner described above is an invention of the film. Also, whereas the novel begins with Rink's party and then goes into flashback, the film tells the story chronologically, beginning with the meeting between Jordan Benedict and Leslie at Leslie's home in Maryland, and then following the progress of their marriage to the present day. The film's structure is not only simpler because of this but actually crucial to its main theme, which is the development over time of the two main characters. It is one of the pleasing ironies of the film that, whereas the two central characters mature and grow, the man whose material circumstances change most drastically—i.e., Jett Rink—is the one whose character develops the least. The exteriors for the early scenes at Maryland were shot at Keswick near Charlottesville, Virginia, but most of the film was shot on location in Marta, Texas, which Mercedes McCambridge was to describe in her autobiography as "a large part of the ugliest landscape on the face of the earth" (McCambridge: 206). The physical demands of the location were intensified by the fact that the film went 44 days over its shooting schedule, although an anxious Jack Warner as head of Warner Bros. was eventually appeased by the fact that the film became the biggest money-maker in the history of the company up to that time.

"Doctor, that sure is a beautiful animal." The speaker is Jordan "Bick" Benedict, who has come to Maryland from his ranch in Texas to purchase the black stallion War Winds from its owner, Dr. Horace Lynnton (Paul Fix). His admiration is not limited to the stallion, however, for he is dazzled also by the dark-haired beauty who is riding it, the doctor's daughter, Leslie. It is curious to think now that Stevens was considering Audrey Hepburn, Grace Kelly and Eva Marie Saint for the female lead before settling on Elizabeth Taylor, because, as Susan Smith has noted in a fine account of the film, Taylor's screen persona, particularly in her association with horses, from *National Velvet* (1945) to *Reflections in a Golden Eye* (1967), could hardly seem a more perfect fit for the role of Leslie (Smith: 55–87). One of the features of the early part of the film is the way the future of both horse and heroine seems so closed entwined. Bick has come for a horse and will return with it by rail—before the camera pans left to reveal that he has acquired a wife also. It is a measure of the subtlety of Stevens' direction (and the excellence of the performances) that, although we never actually hear a romantic declaration or proposal or even see them touch or kiss, there is a pleasurable inevitability about the narrative revelation of their marriage. Their romance is conveyed entirely through looks and through the moment when the two stare across the field at War Winds on the morning of Benedict's departure, and the doctor, waiting patiently in his car to take Benedict to his train, realizes resignedly he may have to wait a little longer than envisaged and that, in all probability, he will be losing a daughter as well as a stallion.

During the dinner scene of the previous evening, Benedict has told Leslie's mother that he is here to buy the horse "if your daughter don't mind too much," and Leslie playfully joins in the conversation, saying she can list all its good and bad points in a manner that suggests a measure of identification. She is aware of her family's plans to sell her off, as it were, in an advantageous marriage to Sir David Karfrey (Rod Taylor), but says cheekily to her mother, "And you should see the greedy look on your face," when Benedict is reluctantly drawn into disclosing the sheer vastness of the ranch he owns. Not that Leslie will show any reluctance to marry Benedict, but the conversation over dinner about the horse gives a foretaste of what such a marriage might involve. "You know very well that horse is just too spirited for any woman to ride," her mother (Judith Evelyn) says, which becomes almost an inadvertent warning, for it implies that Leslie's exceptional spiritedness in being able to handle the horse might be too much for Benedict to handle in a wife, however much he is attracted to her. Similarly Leslie will underestimate Bick's pride in his Texas heritage, which is not to be ridiculed even in jest and which will be a major obstacle for her to overcome. Having decided overnight that she is in love with him and therefore studiously read up on Texan history, Leslie greets him at the breakfast table by saying, "We really stole Texas, didn't we, Mr. Benedict, away from the Mexicans." In the novel Benedict's startled reaction to that is described "as if he had touched a live wire" (Ferber: 74). That is not too dissimilar from the effect of Leslie on him generally, where antagonism and adoration will become close bedfellows. Leslie will learn to be more sensitive towards Bick's Texan sensibilities, but at the same time she will never be afraid of speaking out if they outrage her own values.

This will be foreshadowed in their first marital argument when they at last arrive at Reata after their honeymoon. In his interview for the George Stevens, Jr., documentary on his father, Alan J. Pakula vividly evoked this moment in the movie, describing the first shot of the Reata house as "one of the great American images ... that household in that endless, endless space. It is an absurdity, and yet there is something daring, misguided, outrageous and courageous about the very attempt to stick it there and defy the fates" (interview on 26 May 1983). Getting out of the car, Leslie is at first scarcely able to comprehend what she is seeing. She seems totally disorientated by the physical appearance of the place, so unlike the green pastures she has been used to: a vast isolated Victorian mansion incongruously planted in this wind-swept desert space with not a tree in sight and where the nearest neighbor is fifty miles away. This, then, is Texas. Significantly the argument takes place on the porch, as if there is a threshold of understanding as well as space she needs to cross before she can enter the house. Bick reprimands her for being polite to the house's Mexican staff, who have come to greet her, and which he says is inappropriate behavior towards her social inferiors. "You're a Texan now," he says, to which she replies: "Is that a state of mind? I'm still myself.... I still have a mind of my own. Elsewhere being gracious is acceptable." Battle lines, reflecting a conflict of cultures and gender expectations, have been instantly drawn.

Two other sources of conflict are also about to emerge: Bick's unmarried sister, Luz (the redoubtable Mercedes McCambridge in her most forbidding mode), who has run the ranch in Bick's absence; and the hired hand, Jett Rink, whom Bick dislikes but whom Luz has re-hired to help her and whom she holds in high regard as a good worker with something of her own truculent, irascible streak. Luz's displeasure at the new situation is quickly evident when she upbraids her brother for being away so long on his honeymoon. She has even allocated separate rooms for the newlyweds until Bick, with a sort of embarrassed amusement, has to remind her that, as husband and wife, he and Leslie will be sharing living quarters. It is clear that Luz intends to continue running the household in the way it has always been run, with Leslie as a barely tolerated presence in the background who obviously has no idea of the proper way of dealing with the Mexican household staff and who will prove unfit for the rigors of life at Reata. At first this assessment seems to have been confirmed, for at a lavish barbecue thrown in her honor, Leslie looks lost and forlorn; is sickened by the food on display (Stevens relishes his visual replication of Ferber's description of two fried eggs on top of a succulent steak "glaring at her with angry yellow eyes"); and faints dead away at the prospect of a rancher's glutinous consumption of the contents of a calf's skull. But if Luz sees this as a sign of Leslie's weakness and as a portent of her retreat into a pliant, subordinate role as an obedient wife, she has underestimated Leslie's resolve. The following morning Leslie awakens refreshed; emerges hale and hearty at the top of the stairs; vows never again to faint at Texan manners; prepares a breakfast for her husband, to his obvious surprise ("I'll never get the hang of you, Mrs. Benedict," he says, delightedly, a sentiment he will repeat 25 years later when they are surveying their grandchildren); and makes clear to Luz that from now on she will be running the house in her own way.

The simmering tensions between the two will climax in one of the most compelling stretches of the early part of the film and in which Leslie's horse will play a significant and tragic role. One morning Leslie has ridden out with Bick on War Winds to join him on a cattle roundup. Luz has arrived, being driven there by Jett Rink in his car. Worried that his wife might be tired in the heat, Bick instructs Jett to drive Leslie back to the house. After Leslie has said goodbye to her horse and she and Rink have departed, Bick attempts to reassure Luz about her importance to the ranch but that, now he has a wife, things will inevitably change and she will need to adjust to Leslie's management of the household arrangements. As he rides off to deal with his herd, Luz insists on mounting War Winds, against the advice of a Mexican worker, Angel Obregon (Victor Millan), whose son will later play an important role in the drama. "I suppose you came out here to show me how to run things too," she snaps; and Stevens cuts to a sudden close-up as she deliberately digs her spurs into the horse's flank, causing it to rear in fear and pain. The shock cut, which is repeated, is a real jolt. Behind it, one feels not only Luz's determination to master the animal in the same way she dominates through fear the Mexicans under her control, but also her retaliation against Leslie's challenging her pre-eminence at Reata. Her anger now finds an outlet in her mistreatment of Leslie's most prized possession.

The theme of mistreatment will be extended in the scene of Leslie's journey home with Jett Rink. At first the two seem to strike up a tentative friendship, as Leslie's sympathy finds a chink in Jett's defensive armor, particularly over his lowly status at the ranch. Also his rebellious, even disrespectful, streak might subconsciously strike a chord with Leslie, who has already shown a disinclination to take the Benedicts at their own evaluation and unthinkingly replicate their values. His waspish comments about how the Benedicts acquired so much land at the expense of the Mexicans, which he might have expected to prompt a wifely rebuke from Leslie, go unchallenged because they are not that different from the observation she herself had made over the breakfast table to Bick before their marriage. Now, in passing through the Mexican quarter, Vientecito, Leslie is brought up short by the sight of the squalid living conditions, which expose her to the huge gap between rich and poor on her husband's land. Appalled, she insists that Rink stops the car. Against Jett's advice (for his antipathy towards the Benedicts does not extend to feeling any sympathy for the Mexican workers and their families), she enters the house of one of the inhabitants and discovers a newborn child who is seriously ill. In defiance of what is deemed appropriate in such circumstances, where the Mexicans are left to fend for themselves, she promises to return later with a doctor.

While this is happening, Luz is engaged elsewhere in a contest of wills with War Winds that she is determined to win. There is a magnificent long shot of a lone rider on a bucking horse against a beautiful landscape in a straight horizontal line, that is followed by an abrupt sickening close-up of spurs once again being dug into a horse's flesh and drawing blood. Stevens' own description in his 1973 American Film Institute interview of what he intended in these two shots cannot be bettered: "In two cuts there's a story—how we contribute to our own undoing" (Stevens Jr.: 232)

We are not actually shown Luz's fatal fall. Instead Stevens allows the audience to infer what has occurred from a shot of War Winds as it limps back to the porch at Reata and the consternation of the servants as they run out to inspect the riderless horse. Stevens will frame the next few minutes around the shots of War Winds as the mute injured survivor of the affair. When Leslie eventually returns in the evening, she is first alerted to the crisis by her sight of the distressed horse outside the house, but she hurries inside before she can examine the extent of the horse's injuries and she never does learn of Luz's cruelty that has brought about the death. "If only I hadn't bought that horse," murmurs Bick amid the mourners around Luz's body, and Leslie is quick to defend him from any self-reproach, although not picking up the darker implications of what he has said, particularly relating to the close connection we have seen in the early scenes between acquiring a horse and acquiring a wife. Leslie might have missed the undercurrents of the remark, because, even amid the grief, she has other things on her mind, notably that she can take advantage of the doctor's presence by insisting that he accompanies her to Vientecito to treat the sick child. "He doesn't tend to those people," she is told, but she refuses to be swayed; and in her determination to take the doctor to the village with all possible speed, her farewell to War Winds is cursory, not realizing that it will be final. At this point Stevens lingers momentarily on a shot of War Winds as it turns its head towards the departing figure of Leslie, as if in mute admonition of the callousness of humans and the imminent injustice of its fate. As he demonstrated in *Shane*, Stevens directs animals brilliantly as well as humans.

There is another connection with *Shane* in the scene which follows when Leslie returns home later that night to find Bick in darkness standing despondently by the window. It is similar to the scene at the Starretts' home after the barroom brawl in *Shane*, when Joey and Shane have gone to bed and Marian is standing alone in the room before Joe appears at the bedroom door and she asks him simply to hold her without saying anything. In both scenes, there are layers of undisclosed emotion beneath the surface and what is left unspoken is as important as what is said. In medium shot we are shown Leslie as she joins her husband by the window and they put their arms round each other. For a moment there is no dialogue until Leslie asks hesitantly (the slight pause suggests she is already fearing the worst): "Where's my ... horse?" "I shot him," replies Bick quietly. "Bone was broken. Somebody had to do it. I thought it'd be better if it was me." Leslie's head sinks deeper into Bick's chest. After a slight pause, Bick asks: "The baby?" "Alive, thanks to Dr. Walker," replies Leslie. (The baby will grow up to be Angel, as played by Sal Mineo in the second half of the film.) "Good," replies Bick. It is a sensitively written, acted and directed scene, suggesting a complex of feelings in delicate balance: the shooting of the horse sensed as a kind of revenge killing for the death of Luz but also a merciful relief for a suffering animal; the saving of the Mexican child an act of defiance on Leslie's part, but with a worthwhile outcome; and a marital relationship being tested by the differences of background, values, and codes of conduct between husband and wife who nevertheless still cling lovingly to each other in the dark.

The marriage will move into a new phase after the deaths of Bick's sister and Leslie's horse, but the changes will be gradual and subtle. After the death of War Winds, Marilyn Moss wrote about the character of Leslie that "whereas her sexuality drew Bick to her—and to War Winds—that sexuality has no place in the domestic life Leslie now takes" (Moss: 227). The impression given there of a retreat into submissive domesticity is not really supported by the development of the character, who retains her independence of mind and indeed her sexuality. This is particularly evident in the scene shortly afterwards when Bick has accused her of being rude to his friends and of failing to understand Texan ways but is appeased when she tells him to take off his hat and coaxes him into bed. The hat is still in the place he left it the following morning, the implication being that it is Bick who has proved to be the more sexually submissive of the two. And the incident of which Bick has been complaining has shown Leslie at her most fiercely outspoken as well as Elizabeth Taylor at her most commanding, never better than on those occasions when she can pour sarcastic scorn on assumptions of male supremacy.

The men are assembled on one side of the room, with their womenfolk dutifully exchanging small talk in the background. They are clearly discomfited when Leslie joins them and invites them to continue while she listens. When it is made clear that her presence is unwelcome and even unladylike, for their conversation is dealing with "men's stuff," such as politics and business, Leslie explodes in fury. "Men's stuff!" she cries. "Lord have mercy! Set up my spinning wheel, girls, I'll join the harem section in a minute!" In front of the aghast gathering (male and female), she goes on: "If I may say so before retiring, you gentlemen date back one hundred thousand years. You ought to be wearing leopard skins and carrying clubs. Politics! Business! What is so masculine about a conversation that a woman cannot enter into it?"

When her most sympathetic ally in the household, Uncle Bawley (Chill Wills in the most beguilingly benign performance of his career), tries to pacify her by offering to get her a cup of coffee, she says, "You too, Uncle Brutus?" pointedly interpreting his act of diplomacy as a stab in the back. Even when she later apologizes to Bick if she has offended his friends and is trying to worm her way back into his affections (it does not take long), she does so without giving ground. Gently but firmly, she insists: "But in principle I was absolutely right."

Leslie's outburst is magnificent. In the context of '50s American cinema, I cannot think of anything quite like it in its pre-feminist derision at assumed masculine superiority in matters of business and politics—or anything, come to that. In Stevens' cinema, it is one of the strongest moments in a career that continually dramatized and insisted on female equality, the importance of the role of women, and their fearlessness when pointing up the absurdities of masculine pomp and pride. It is an extension and development of the great scene in *Shane* when Marian rails against what she calls a "foolish kind of pride" as her husband is being fatally drawn into a confrontation with a professional gunfighter. In *Giant*, the issues at this point are less life-and-death, but the prevailing ideology is similar. In the context of the film, Leslie's challenge to masculine values is crucial, because we shall see that, over the years of her turbulent marriage to Bick, she never compromises on her own values nor shrinks from expressing them; and it is he who, in due course, must shift his prejudices to become more in accord with the feelings of his wife.

Inevitably the marital differences will sharpen and intensify when they have children, for they will have different ideas about their upbringing, particularly that of their son, Jordan. A crisis occurs at Jordan's fourth birthday party, when the gift of a pony from his father seems much less attractive to him than a doctor's set, presumably a gift from his mother. The boy becomes hysterical when placed unwillingly on the pony and, in a display of anger, his father will mount behind him, and gallop the pony a distance from and to the house, with the boy screaming in protest. Clearly desiring his son to behave in his own image, Bick is furious at his son's discomfort and seeming timidity, which are shown to be in stark contrast to the ease with which young Angel will now ride the pony. (This is a motif that will recur later in the film, when, unnoticed and unacknowledged by Benedict until too late, Angel will grow up to be the kind of man Bick desired his own son to be.) In the meantime, Leslie has been appalled by her husband's behavior and the distress caused; and during the stormy evening that follows and in a dimly lit room that seems to accentuate the gloomy mood, a quiet argument develops between them, in which Leslie will suggest that they need some time apart and that it would be better, she says, "if I took the children home for a visit." The word "home" is particularly pointed in that context, for it will underline how Leslie still feels something of a stranger in Bick's world. When the word "home" recurs in the last scene of the film, it will have completely different connotations.

We are building towards another of those wedding scenes so characteristic of Stevens and which always carry in his films substantial thematic and emotional weight. Leslie has taken their children back to her parents' house for Thanksgiving, but even this has not gone entirely to plan, for when the children discover that the turkey they are invited to eat is actually the family pet Pedro whom they have come to love, they burst into tears and are not to be consoled. (Rather daring of Stevens, I have always thought, to undercut one of America's most sacred anniversaries in this way; but also highly typical in the way he makes the scene funny and sad at the same time.) The other big event at the house is the marriage of Leslie's sister, Lacey (Carolyn Craig), to Leslie's former beau, Sir David Karfrey. One might initially see parallels between this scene and the one in *Woman of the Year,* when a wife, as bridesmaid at a wedding, is drawn silently into contemplating the state of her own marriage on hearing the words of the ceremony. Stevens amplifies the sound slightly at this point to convey Leslie's heightened sensitivity to what she is hearing, as if it is reverberating in her mind. What she does not know is that her husband has arrived at the house and has carefully made his way through the congregation to stand behind her at the point of her sister's formal betrothal. It is a visually imaginative way of re-affirming the lifelong devotion of Bick and Leslie to each other, for she senses his presence even before looking around; but the parallel with *Woman of the Year* also highlights a key difference between the two scenes. Whereas the response of Katharine Hepburn's heroine in the earlier film was to try and change and become a model housewife, which would involve a denial of her true personality, Leslie's reconciliation with Bick involves no such submission. "I haven't changed," she tells him. "I'm just the same now as when I went away."

It seems to me that Stevens makes no bones about where his sympathies lie here. I would venture to suggest that Elizabeth Taylor's uncompromising Leslie could be seen as a surrogate of Stevens himself, and that Rock Hudson's Benedict is the equivalent of studio head, Jack Warner, the man ostensibly in control and holding the purse strings but who is often being outmaneuvered by the person who has different ideas about how his vision can be achieved and indeed what it should be. Later in the film there is an important scene when Bick's Texan friends are purring over the government's oil depletion allowance during wartime which favored oil companies. Not for the first time, Leslie startles them by voicing a strong contrary opinion, suggesting that the allowance should be for first-class brains instead, pointing to her doctor father as a much more deserving case than they are for special financial favors. According to Ivan Moffat, the sentiment infuriated oil interests and bankers, one of whom threatened to transfer his account if the line remained, but when Jack Warner wanted it removed, Stevens steadfastly refused (Moffat: 272). George Stevens, Jr., told me that Jack Warner had all kinds of qualms about the film's ending not on a note of epic grandeur but with two grandparents talking quietly about their life and addressing the theme of race, but again Stevens was not to be swayed or intimidated, and Leslie (i.e., Stevens) is allowed the film's final statement and sentiment, while Bick (i.e., Warner) looks on bemused, but with evident admiration.

"I thought I'd fired him off this place." Bick's first comment on seeing Rink when he and Leslie have returned to Reata after their honeymoon establishes an instant antagonism which is only going to intensify as Rink will encroach on his status in the Texan community and indeed on his family life. At this stage Rink has been reinstated by Luz to help run the ranch in Bick's absence, but Bick's hostility seems to have something to do with Rink's demeanor, which oozes surly insolence. "Nobody is king in this country," he mutters to himself. Stevens' original idea for the role was Alan Ladd, who might have caught the character's outsider status (he was a very good Gatsby in the otherwise unremarkable 1948 film version) but would have perhaps lacked the venom of Rink's resentment. As played by Dean, Rink has an arrogance behind his ostensible subservience and also a strong streak of narcissism (as in those stylized poses, when he occupies the whole of the wide-screen as he stretches his legs across the bonnet of his car or when he threads a rifle between his arms and behind his lowered head in what looks like a self-conscious crucifixion pose). Although Rink is pointedly excluded from the outdoor banquet to welcome Bick's new wife, Stevens makes us aware of his presence in the distance, as someone on the outside looking in perhaps, but also (because of the visual prominence given to that presence) as someone biding his time.

Expecting to be dismissed from the ranch after the death of his sole ally, Luz, Rink has been summoned into Benedict's office to be told that she had bequeathed him a small piece of land in her will. The lawyers present presume that Rink would prefer a generous cash settlement, but Rink sits obstinately silent, as if barely listening to what is being said, instead fiddling with his rope, and, as it were, almost literally stringing them along. Commenting on this scene, Stevens said of Dean: "He's like a magnet. You watch him. Even when he's not doing anything, you watch him and not the others" (Moffat: 274). The lawyers might have all the words and all the arguments, but it is Rink who takes control, spurning the cash offer and taking the land instead, giving a curt wave of farewell before leaving the room. This gesture (which will become one of his trademarks) combines the message of goodbye with a sort of tacit signal that he has seen through the effort to buy him off and is treating it with all the disdain he can muster. The lure of the money might be a powerful one, but more powerful still is the opportunity to continue being a thorn in Benedict's side.

Yet there is something more to this than a desire to spite Benedict, and it becomes apparent when he takes possession of the land. It is a scene which, according to some reports, led to a degree of friction between Dean and Stevens, because the director had something specific in mind when Rink starts pacing out the territory and apparently was putting down specific markers as to where Dean's feet should land. According to the film's dialect coach, Robert Hinkle, who was present when the scene was being shot, the rumor that director and actor had a big argument was nothing more than "George ticking Jimmy off so that a ticked off Jett Rink would give the performance he needed to" (Hinkle: 97). It is one of the great moments of the film, when Rink measures out step by step every inch of this minuscule piece of land in an almost exaggerated movement, with the strides suggesting fierce pride and angry defiance as well as simple ownership. Dmitri Tiomkin's music catches the tone perfectly, with the jaunty impudence of Rink's theme on accordion and banjo (quite different in character from the grandeur of the film's main theme) gradually swelling into a full orchestral statement as Rink climbs to the top of a windmill to survey his domain and to suggest the character's rising ambition.

Progress will initially be slow. On her way home from visiting Vienticento after the birth of her children, Leslie has passed Little Reata and, seeing her in the distance, Jett has fired a shot into the air to attract her attention and to invite her into his home. Dean is particularly good in this scene, as he scuttles round the house to make Leslie some tea and seems at once proud, surprised and a little self-conscious at the unexpected pleasure of this visit. Leslie notices a book on self-improvement on the table, a detail which would link Jett's character with other outsiders in Stevens' world who are yearning to better themselves; Alice Adams, Montgomery Clift's George Eastman in *A Place in the Sun*. She also notices an old newspaper photo of her wedding on his wall (significantly Bick is not present on the photo), which suggests that his infatuation with Leslie might have begun even before they have met; and perhaps even more than that, what he aspires to by way of marriage partner. On reflection, it is a detail which will gather extra resonance when he breaks down at his grand celebratory party and starts murmuring Leslie's name. Similarly, when Leslie asks him when he is going to get married, that too will gather ironic overtones later at the party, particularly when he asks Leslie's daughter, Luz, the same question: is he recalling the conversation he has had with Leslie all those years ago? He says that he could hardly expect anyone to marry him in his current circumstances, to which Leslie comments: "Money isn't all, you know, Jett." He chuckles at this, before countering, "Not when you got it." In a scene full of subtle hints, ironies and portents about Jett's future (and superbly acted by Dean and Taylor), that is a particularly potent exchange because it presages the whole of the second half of the film, where Jett will find that "money isn't all" even when "you got it." As Leslie leaves the house, and unnoticed by her, the slight squelching sound made by her footprint seems to suggest the presence of something under the surface of the land: the answer to Rink's prayer or the beginning of his downfall? Once again it is Leslie's action which will set a chain of events in motion.

"My well came in, Bick." When he strikes oil, Rink's first instinct is not simply to rejoice in his good fortune; it is also to revel in what he knows will be Benedict's dismay. Driving round to the Reata house at high speed and interrupting a quiet family get-together on the porch, he springs out of the car and lurches towards them like an ungainly beast, with oil still dripping from his face and clothes. His address of Benedict as "Bick" is a calculated impudence, a cheeky way of declaring that he is now on equal footing with his former employer, and indeed will soon surpass him in terms of fortune. In one of the most telling images of the film, he puts his oily hand on one of the white columns of the porch, leaving a dark thumbprint on what Ferber in the novel called the "anachronistic white-pillared mansions" (Ferber: 2). It is an image which symbolizes the coming displacement of the old landed gentry by the upcoming *nouveau riche*. (Visually it could also be said to anticipate the racial theme which will come more to the fore in the second half of the film.) Leslie attempts to defuse a tense and embarrassing situation by saying sincerely how pleased they are for him, but this only emboldens Rink to take his outrageous behavior a step further. "My, you sure do look pretty," he says to her, "good enough to eat." Previously his compliments have been between the two of them and within the bounds of decorum, but this overt sexual overture is a step too far and Bick goes for him. In the melee that follows, Bick is restrained, but this allows Rink, on point of leaving, suddenly to turn and punch Bick in the groin before jumping into his car and making his getaway. (It anticipates a similar struggle in the second half of the film when Bick's son, Jordy, confronts Rink for insulting his Mexican wife). Stevens is playing interesting variations on traditional western fistfights here. Rink never fights fair; and, in a rather daring subversion of the conventional American hero, Stevens has Bick involved in three fights during the course of the film, not one of which he wins. As Rink drives away in triumph, one senses at that point that Bick might be ruefully recalling those words of his of years ago ("I thought I'd fired him off this place"); and Uncle Bawley gives the sentiment a more literal twist. "You should have shot that fella a long time ago," he muses. "Now he's too rich to kill."

The second half of *Giant* boldly defies the laws of epic movie-making. There is a lot of humor and some spectacle but hardly any action. It builds not towards a crashing crescendo but to an exquisite diminuendo. Its two main antagonists square up to each other finally in a much anticipated hostile confrontation, but the fight never materializes, because Rink can barely stand upright, so the climactic conflict ends almost comically in inconclusive frustration. Both men will end up later and separately on the floor, with the character who has risen spectacularly up the social ladder (Rink) last seen alone in a drunken unconscious heap in a lavish but deserted conference hall; and the character whose community status has fallen (Benedict) ending up flattened ignominiously in a fight in a local diner. Yet the fall has diametrically opposite implications: in Rink's case, an embarrassing decline; in Benedict's a moral elevation. Stevens's favorite theme of the outsider is unusually handled here, because, as the film develops, it shifts from one character to another: first, it has been Bick, in unfamiliar Maryland surroundings; then Leslie, in barren windswept Texas; then Jett Rink, a peripheral rancher hovering on the outskirts of the story before the discovery of oil transforms his fortunes; and finally to Jordy and Juana, outcasts at the gargantuan celebration of Rink's wealth. The theme of racial prejudice, which has originally seemed a relatively minor subtext in this story of the growth of modern Texas, will rise imperceptibly into becoming the film's major concern. The film's earlier suggestion of expansiveness, anticipated by the way its title is emblazoned in huge lettering on the credits, will narrow its focus finally and wonderfully to the tiniest of details: a huge close-up of a child's eyes symbolizing a hope for future social harmony.

Years have passed since Rink's outrageous behavior on the Benedict porch and his grubby oil print on those anachronistic white pillars. How well Stevens handles the passage of time in the film. Through a series of dissolves and brief sequences, we see the transformation of Little Reata into Jettexas Co. The cattle country which earlier Bick showed off so proudly to his young wife is growing more and more to look like an oil field. The Benedict children are now grown and striking off in their own direction, which is directly opposite to the one envisaged for them by their parents, Jordy pursuing his ambition as a doctor rather than a rancher in opposition to his father, Judy (Fran Bennett) wishing to study animal husbandry rather than follow the educational ambitions her mother has for her. Luz (Carroll Baker) will be the most rebellious of all, striking up a romantic relationship with Rink that could not be further from her parents' wishes. (Carroll Baker's performance is one of the particular delights of the film's second half, an enlivening presence that gives impulse to the narrative every time she appears.) There is a finely sustained, often funny, bedroom conversation (Bick is actually reading a comic) between husband and wife about their children's future and the sacrifice of their own ambitions for them. At first Stevens has Bick in profile at the foreground of the frame as he slyly tries to win over his wife about Judy's ambitions. He then reverses the angle with Leslie in the foreground as she sits up on her bed ("Brace yourself") and broaches the subject of Jordy's plan to be a doctor. Both are initially outraged but then the mood subsides. Acknowledging their mutual acquiescence to the fact that times are changing, Stevens cuts finally to a medium shot of them both as they conclude that the children will probably decide for themselves anyway, and Leslie's realization that she and Bick have suddenly become the older generation.

The Christmas morning scene is a particularly fine example of Stevens's cinematic mastery. The family's get-together is conveyed with a seemingly artless spontaneity and yet there is a profusion of visual detail that adds both variety of mood and important narrative progression, for it will contain the seeds of everything that is to come. It is 1941, a fortnight after the bombing of Pearl Harbor. Newlyweds Judy and her husband Bob Dace (Earl Holliman) have stolen quietly into the house at 3 a.m. and emerge later to the sound of Christmas carols and the greetings of a houseful of guests. (As if to emphasize the importance of the marriage theme, incidentally, Judy's is one of five—I am including that of Vashti Smythe (Jane Withers) who was at one time expected to be Bick's wife—

that occur in the film.) There will be two late arrivals that will be given some prominence. The chief foreman Old Polo (Alexander Scourby) will arrive with his family, and his grandson, Angel (Sal Mineo), who is in army uniform and, as Old Polo proudly announces, "the first soldier from Rieta." Stevens announces Angel's appearance with a striking close-up, as if emphasizing the old man's pride; also suggesting the impact of his entrance on Leslie, who saved his life when a baby and who is noticeably the first to move forward to greet him; but also presaging his significance as the sequence unfolds. The second important entrance at this juncture is that of Dr. Guerra (Maurice Jara) and a young nurse Juana who is working with him in the Mexican village. The immediate attraction between Jordy and Juana could hardly be more apparent, for, in trying to shake her hand, he gives himself a mild electric shock. (Was David Lean thinking of that moment when he does something similar when Zhivago and Lara fleetingly first touch in *Doctor Zhivago*?) When the two say goodbye later that morning, there is a brief shot of Leslie as she watches her son staring after the departing Juana. She misses nothing and might be divining his feelings before he is aware of them himself. This contrasts humorously, but also pointedly, with an earlier moment when Jordy has opened his father's Christmas present, which is a Stetson hat several sizes too large for him and as incongruous as the present of a pony all those years ago. Leslie might be able to intuit her son's feelings, but Bick is no nearer to understanding him now than he was then. Noticing the laughter of the guests when Jordy tries on the hat, Bick spins round and turns his back on the scene very sharply (finely acted by Hudson here), as if mortified at what he has seen.

Later that morning, and by this time very drunk, Bick attempts to have a heart-to-heart talk about the future of Reata with Jordy and his new son-in-law, Bob. A significant presence in the background of the frame is Angel, who has been asked to stay behind after his family has left by Bob, who wants to talk to him about his Army experience. Angel never says anything and stays as a barely glimpsed figure in the background, but one could argue that he is the most important character in this whole scene: as its conscience; and as the answer to Reata's succession problem which Benedict literally does not see. Jordy makes clear that he is set on a medical career, wishing to work with Dr. Guerra; and even has the audacity to advise his father to go easy on the bourbon on account of his blood pressure. (It is a nice touch that years later, in the final scene, Bick will offer the same advice to Uncle Bawley, as if he is now taking more notice of his son's medical recommendations.) But he makes clear that there are numerous men better qualified than him to take over Reata when the time comes, before saying how sorry he is that Angel has to go. "That boy is the best dang man on the place," Bick says firmly. "Anyone at Reata could do it better than me," says Jordy and then takes a quick look to his left, almost as if trying to prompt his father to look in Angel's direction and make the connection, but it is too subtle for him. "Work with Guerra!" Bick scoffs, as his son leaves the room, and Angel continues to sits obediently and unnoticed in the background. When Bick then tries to enlist his son-in-law to take over, Bob has to tell him he has already been called up for military service by President Roosevelt, and, in any case, when he returns, he and Judy want to have a small place of their own rather than take on Reata. "Big stuff is old stuff," Bob tells him. Bick can hardly believe his ears and has to repeat it to make sure he has heard right. (It is indeed a remarkable line for a film of epic length about the growth of Texas.) How anyone can pass up the chance of running a ranch on the scale of Reata is quite beyond his comprehension and, muttering to himself in disbelief, is again blind to the presence in the background of Angel, who has been listening to all this but exits unobtrusively when Bob and Judy leave the room. Stevens's mise-en-scène is at its most exact there and gathers particular poignancy in retrospect, when we realize that it is the last time we will see Angel in the film. The scene's capacity to surprise has one final twist. While grumbling to himself and petulantly declaring that he might just as well give the land back to the Comanches, Luz pipes up smartly, "That's the Christmas spirit, Dad, give it back to the Indians!" The sentiment has something of the audacity of Leslie's suggestion all those years ago that Texas had been stolen from the Mexicans.

While tossing out her advice to her dad, Luz has gone to answer the front door and there for the first time she meets Jett Rink. The attraction is immediate. An odd time to call, but then, when he says he did not realize it was Christmas, one is not entirely sure that he is joking. He has come on business and is on his way to Washington, for, in these times of war, "the country needs petroleum" and he knows that Benedict cannot hold out any longer against Rink's purchase of the land. He has Bick, so to speak, over a barrel. The former ranch hand, whom Bick had wanted to fire off the place, has now conclusively usurped the empire of his former employer. From this time forward, Reata and the Benedict name will diminish in importance.

In this Christmas morning sequence, as elsewhere, Rock Hudson's performance cannot be faulted. Edna Ferber had indicated that she would have liked Burt Lancaster to play the role, but Stevens had been impressed by Hudson's performance in Douglas Sirk's *Magnificent Obsession* (1954) and thought he had the quality he was looking for. Hard to see how the Burt Lancaster of that period could have conveyed the requisite vulnerability and gathering submissiveness of the character with quite the conviction that Hudson achieves. Nor can one imagine Lancaster's being so willing to cede prominence (and top billing) to his leading actress in the way that Hudson did to Jane Wyman in Sirk's *All That Heaven Allows* (1955) and to Elizabeth Taylor in *Giant*, a concession absolutely crucial to the film, for it is Leslie who will be seen as the film's main driving force. Hudson handles the humor expertly, in a way that will anticipate his successful series of romantic comedies with Doris Day; and not until John Frankenheimer's *Seconds* (1966) will he deliver a drunken scene as felicitously. Yet, more than that, it seems to me a performance at the service of the director and unselfishly shorn of protective professional ego. He is not afraid of looking foolish in some scenes or indeed of looking weak. He is often the butt of Leslie's wit. There is a daring rebuff to Hudson's romantic irresistibility in a lovely moment when Luz is saying there was a rumor that every woman in the territory was after him and Leslie answers, nonchalantly: "I'm sure it's quite true, darling. It took me two whole days to land him." When Bob tells his father-in-law that he has made a commitment to serve his country in the war before resuming his life as a rancher, Bick says sulkily: "Have it your own way. You might as well. Everyone else does around here." It is a moment that completes the character's relinquishing of parental and patriarchal authority; and the sensitivity with which Hudson conveys this suggests that he recognized and was not afraid to abet Stevens in this rather startling deconstruction (even destruction) of the traditional American hero in a Hollywood movie.

What Stevens called the film's "excellent structural design" is particularly evident in the following scenes. The two main narrative events are the marriage of Jordy to Juana and the celebration of Bob's return to Reata after the war, yet they are handled in an unusual and original way. Unlike the marriage of Judy to Bob (or, for that matter, of Bick to Leslie), Stevens actually shows the wedding ceremony of Jordy and Juana, as if to give it maximum importance. This is all the more striking because he could have saved the revelation of the marriage until the celebration party for Bob's return home, when we see (but cannot hear) Jordy's breaking the news to his mother before announcing it to the whole gathering. To judge from his reaction. Jordy's father, unlike Leslie, seems dismayed by the news; and the fact that all this has taken place without his consent and that he is the last to know only further undercuts his position of influence. Earlier we have seen Bob's return as he has been greeted jubilantly from the train by the Reata community, so that when Stevens shows a newspaper headline proclaiming "Angel Obregon Comes Home Today," he seems to be setting up the expectation of a similar celebration. It is therefore a devastating dramatic blow when the train pulls away to reveal a coffin, draped with the American flag, on the stationary baggage cart, with a group of silent black-clad mourners silhouetted against an afternoon sky. Stevens holds the shot for a moment to give an audience the opportunity to pause and think about its significance: how it contains in a single image the destruction and sacrifice of war not through action and spectacle but through quiet contemplation of a situation which at that time was being replayed to countless families across the country. The subsequent funeral is framed around the shot of a young boy playing on his own in the churchyard that adjoins the cemetery, childhood games juxtaposed with adult rituals of death in a manner that fleetingly recalls René Clément's great anti-war film, *Jeux Interdits* (*Forbidden Games*, 1952). Angel's grieving parents are presented with an American flag in recognition of their son's sacrifice. From the back of the group, Benedict will step forward to give Polo the flag of Texas he has kept in his cabinet. It is a gesture intended to comfort the family in their grief, but one could sense behind it a desire to honor the memory of a young man whom Bick might have belatedly recognized could—and probably should—have been his successor. (This will give an added dimension to the film's ending, as if young Jordan Benedict IV will in some way be the ghost of Angel Obregon.) As the service proceeds and a choir of children sing the American national anthem, Stevens cuts back to the shot of the boy playing, too young to comprehend fully the significance of what is taking place in the adjoining cemetery and for whom a recognition of the reality of death is still some way off. It is a sequence that seems concisely to take in the whole cycle of life and death; and the kind of scene that reminds me why John Ford called Stevens "an artist."

The film dissolves from burial to birth: a daughter to Judy and Bob, observed by smiling grandparents; a son to Jordy and Juana, observed by grandparents whose reaction (as noticed by Jordy) is flecked with anxiety. The racial theme is to rise to the surface now and will be intertwined with the staging of Jett Rink's vast party, to which the whole of Texas aristocracy has been invited. Jett's flagrant display of racial prejudice here will be one of the factors that will progressively lead to his public humiliation on a grand scale and on a stage that has been prepared in his honor. Jordy has confronted him after Juana has been refused service in the beauty parlor. After sneering "Aren't you the one who married the squaw?" Jett has taken advantage of Jordy's defenselessness when restrained by Rink's bodyguards and punched him in the groin, as if revisiting a similar scene all those years ago on the Benedict porch. As if wanting to repay that old score, Bick will challenge him again now. However, when they move to the wine cellar to settle the argument (a black cat scuttles across their path in alarm at their approach), Rink is in no fit state even to defend himself and Bick concludes he is not worth hitting, avenging himself instead by causing row after row of the wine racks to collapse with an almighty crash that can be heard by the distinguished gathering outside the room. It will presage the shattering of what was to be Jett's evening of triumph. His speech, due to be broadcast across the nation, remains undelivered for, to the sound of rapturous applause and celebratory music in anticipation of his peroration, he will pass out where he sits in a drunken stupor.

Prior to all this, there has been a private scene between Jett and Luz, who, much to her parents' astonishment and disapproval, has been the Carnival Queen at the center of the street parade in Rink's honor. Now they are having a quiet conversation in the Bottle Club prior to the big party, a scene which is not in the novel but which Ivan Moffat thought was one of the best scenes in the movie, because it showed James Dean at his most creative. In terms of the writing, the scene was left deliberately indecisive and was partly improvised; and, as Moffat wrote: "Dean improvised it even more, he threw in more hesitations and laughs.... He never proposed directly because he doesn't want to be rejected. She's not sure what she wants" (Moffat: 274). As always, Stevens frames the conversation very precisely. They are seated slightly to one side of each other and rarely look at each other directly, so that, even without any dialogue, one can deduce from their body language not only attraction but wariness. "If I was you, I'd start thinking about getting married," Rink says to Luz, possibly even distantly remembering the occasion when Leslie has said the same thing to him. He then starts speculating what a sensation it would cause if he announced his own engagement tonight. "Is that a proposal?" Luz asks. Rink does not answer the question directly but says, "Sure would blow the roof off, wouldn't it?" He chuckles, but the mood is more tense than relaxed, and a shadow falls across his face when Luz gently advises him to go easy on the alcohol and leaves without giving him a definite sign of encouragement. Is that a rejection? As Moffat wrote, she is not sure she wants; but there is a feeling also that there is more to Rink's evasiveness than simply a fear of being turned down. Is he in love with Luz? Is he thinking of proposing marriage at that function simply in order to astound the assembled gathering? Is the deeper motivation to spite Benedict? Or is the real attraction of Luz to Jett the fact she is Leslie's daughter? What is clever in the performance and the writing in this scene is that, for all Rink's wealth and power, one can still spy behind the facade the insecure and resentful former ranch hand. In his nervousness around Luz, one can still detect the same personality of the young Rink bustling around in his tiny house in Little Reata as he looks for some tea to impress his precious guest, Leslie. "Money isn't all, you know, Jett," she has told him. At this banquet in his honor, those words will come back to haunt him.

Later that night the waiters are all assembled outside the banquet room and waiting to be allowed in so that they can tidy up. When someone asks if they can enter yet, one of Rink's bodyguards (who has rather contemptuously addressed his boss as "doll face" as he has attempted to rouse him) waves them away and says, before exiting: "He owns the place, let him enjoy it." Accompanied by Uncle Bawley, Luz has arrived at the door, having heard of Jett's disgrace at the banquet, and we are given a shot of Rink from her point of view: a long shot of a small figure almost invisible in a large deserted room. There are few more resounding images in American cinema of the hollowness of material wealth when unaccompanied by human warmth or generosity. Jett rises unsteadily to his feet and begins the speech that has been written for him by Governor Whitside (Charles Watts); and on the phrase "distinguished guests," Stevens cuts ironically to a shot of the rows of empty tables, for all the guests by now have gone home. Whether Rink actually realizes he is addressing a speech to an empty hall is left open to question; what is more notable is the drift from the prepared platitudes of his official address to the core disillusionment that is eating away at his soul. "Mother Texas, what did she give to me?" he wails about his so-called proud heritage, before moaning that "you've got to work and sweat and steal it from her." The speech is now deteriorating into virtual incoherence. "*Poor* Jet," moans the rich tycoon, and drunkenly bewails the past as "flunky to Bick Benedict." "Poor boy," he goes on; and then, with his emotional defenses down, howls: "Rich Mrs. Benedict … pretty Leslie … beautiful girl bride … the woman a man wants." By this time a tearful Luz has seen enough and quietly closes the door to return to her family. It is a damning piece of self-disclosure, but perhaps the most touching moment in the film as regards Rink, because he is seen at his most isolated and vulnerable. "Governor," he says, turning to an empty chair, "if you want to know what you can do," but, alas, we never hear the ending of that ominous sentence before he falls forward over the table and onto the floor. It is a tormented outpouring of sorrow and self-pity and arguably one of Dean's finest screen moments, taking the darkness of his character to its furthest point. Most extraordinary, though, is the shadow it casts across the American Dream. Of the three Stevens protagonists in his great trilogy who come to recognize that their ultimate dream is unattainable (George Eastman in *A Place in the Sun,* and Shane), Jett Rink is at once the most socially successful and at the end the most utterly bereft. An occasion to celebrate the height of his success has instead sounded the depth of his solitude.

Bick Benedict is also to have a moment of self-realization when he gets involved in that fight in Sarge's Diner, but the revelation will be salutary and in complete contrast to Rink's feelings of isolation and despair. Interceding on the Mexican family's behalf as they are being roughly ejected by Sarge (Mickey Simpson), he has introduced himself, clearly expecting his name to carry some weight and influence in these parts; and it is an illustration of how far his standing in the community has fallen when Sarge does not recognize the name or feel it gives him special privileges. "The name Benedict meant something to people round here for a considerable time," Bick persists, to which Sarge responds sarcastically by pointing towards the cubicle where Bick has been sitting. "That here papoose down there, is his name Benedict too?" he sneers. There is a slight pause as Stevens cuts to a reverse angle shot from the cubicle, before Bick turns and replies: "Yes, come to think of it, it is." There is a momentary sense that he literally has never thought of that before, and for the first time embraces the idea. It is typical of Stevens' genius that he is not afraid to follow one of the most moving moments of the film with a slapstick brawl, which will simultaneously cut Bick down to size but elevate him in his wife's eyes as the true hero she always wanted him to be. The scene might end to the strident strains of "The Yellow Rose of Texas," but it has been preceded by a scene in the car with the family singing together "South of the border/Down Mexico way," a song whose sentiments of love between an American and a Mexican will feed into the beauty of the film's extraordinary last shot.

In spite of (or maybe because of) its huge commercial success and multiple Oscar nominations, *Giant* has tended to be underrated over the years. Influential critics have tended to prefer the melodramatic flair and Brechtian aesthetics of another splendid, though very different, Texas oil saga of that year, Douglas Sirk's *Written on the Wind*, also starring Rock Hudson. Also the film has often been assessed primarily in relation to the legend and legacy of James Dean, which has tended to overshadow other more important aspects of the movie. Recently, however, there has been a shift in critical sensibilities, and critics such as Gail Solnit and Peter Tonguette (see bibliography) have astutely reappraised the film in terms of its masterful and progressive insights into themes of race, gender and class which seem to have more relevance than ever in today's America. All the major Stevens' themes are there—marital trials and tribulations, the gauntlet that the liberated woman throws at the feet of a patriarchal society, the yearnings of the outsider—but what is even more apparent now is the ingenuity of the film's construction, which turns the epic form on its head, and the originality of its narrative progression, which ends finally on an image that dissolves the physical, cultural and psychological boundaries that divide Mexico and America, and, implicitly, one nation from another. For an epic, it might seem deceptively modest. What is gigantic in the film is not the scale of its setting and action but the breadth of its humanity.

SIX

The Final Years,
1959–1969

The Diary of Anne Frank (1959)

> "I see the eight of us in the Annexe as if we were a patch of blue sky sur-rounded by menacing black clouds. The perfectly rounded spot on which we're standing is still safe, but the clouds are moving in on us, and the ring between us and the approaching danger is being pulled tighter and tighter.… I can only cry out and implore, 'Oh, ring, ring, open wide and let us out!'"—Anne Frank, 8 November 1943

> "I wanted to make a film about a human being who knew how to conduct herself in a time of overwhelming misfortune, even though the audience knows from the outset what Anne doesn't know, her ultimate fate.… By having written down her experiences, Anne mystically discovered the secret of how to make mankind think."—George Stevens, 1963

Anne Frank is World War II's most famous teenager and her diary one of the most powerful indictments of Nazism ever published. From July 1942 until August 1944, she lived in hiding in an annex of an office building in Amsterdam, alongside her family (father, mother and elder sister, Margot), another family to whom she gave the pseudonym of the Van Daans (mother, father and son, Peter) and an elderly dentist whom she called Mr. Dussel. In one of her last diary entries on 15 July 1944, she wrote: "It's difficult in times like these: ideals, dreams and cherished hopes rise within us, only to be crushed by grim reality. It's a wonder I haven't abandoned all my ideals, they seem so absurd and impractical. Yet I cling to them because I still believe, in spite of everything, that people are really good at heart" (Frank: 330). Less than three weeks later on 4 August, their hiding place was discovered and the occupants dispatched to concentration camps. Only Otto Frank was to survive. Anne's mother was murdered when she went to the aid of her daughter, Margot, who was being assaulted by an SS guard. Both Margot and Anne died of typhus in the hellish conditions at Belsen. Anne was three months short of her sixteenth birthday.

When published as *The Diary of a Young Girl* in 1952 and then adapted for the stage by the distinguished writing team of Frances Goodrich and Albert Hackett, the impact of Anne Frank's testimony was immediate and, in some cases, devastating. Writing about a production he attended in Berlin in 1956, Kenneth Tynan said the experience went beyond that of being moved by a theatrical performance. The audience, wrote Tynan, were left "drained and ashen, some staring straight ahead, others staring at the ground for a full half-minute. Then, as if awakening from a nightmare, they rose and filed out in total silence" (Tynan: 451). For Stevens, the diary expressed the kind of precarious affirmation of humanity at the heart of his own romantic humanism. Moreover the message it held was timely, particularly when, after a decade of Cold War paranoia in America, Stevens feared that the Nazi atrocities were in danger of being forgotten, underplayed or even forgiven. This feeling might have been reinforced by a film of the previous year, Edward Dmytryk's *The Young Lions,* adapted from the novel by one of Stevens's "Irregulars," Irwin Shaw, where at the insistence of the film's star Marlon Brando, but to the dismay of the author, the main German character's Nazism had been softened to make him more sympathetic. Nevertheless, if Stevens was now ready to make his war picture, and researched the material and the settings with his customary thoroughness, his intention was not to replicate visually the horror he had encountered and felt at Dachau but to record the hope and heroism of which humanity at its finest is capable under almost inconceivable duress.

Even without the war context, one could see why Stevens might have been drawn to the material. Like Alice Adams and so many other of his main protagonists, Anne is a classic Stevens outsider, at odds with the community in which she moves. She is frequently at loggerheads with her mother and argues constantly with the Van Daans and Mr. Dussel. They all compare her unfavorably with her sister, Margot, whose docility is in stark contrast to Anne's volatility and much prized when people are compelled to live together in constant close proximity. The observation of daily domestic routine might even prompt a fleeting recollection of the more overtly comic morning sequences of *The More the Merrier,* as when Anne has to duck between Peter, his cat and Margot, to move inside the room or the occasion when Mr. Dussel pointedly retreats to the toilet as the only room in which he can find peace and solitude. Above all, anyone who had seen *I Remember Mama* would probably suspect the same directorial hand at work on *The Diary of Anne Frank,* for the dramatic framework is very similar. Both works deal with the situation and privations of an immigrant family in a foreign land. (The Franks were German, but, being Jewish, had emigrated to Holland when the Nazis came to power.) Both are structured around the written testimony of a young woman with aspirations of a literary or journalistic career but who finds her artistic voice through writing about herself and her family. Coincidentally, both have a scene which features a reading of *A Tale of Two Cities,* in each case dwelling on the ending where the hero's sacrifice and execution are seen as more triumphant than tragic. Both works even feature a significant role for a cat, a source of comedy in the earlier film and a source of suspense in the later.

Nevertheless, the surrounding context (economically and evocatively filmed by George Stevens, Jr., and photographed by Jack Cardiff) casts a constant pall of fear across the domestic routine inside. Long periods of silence must be endured and not even a curtain must be touched for fear of betraying their presence. The sounds of sirens outside or footsteps approaching the concealed doorway can stop a conversation in midflow and add a chill of dread to the pervading atmosphere. Moments of celebration have to be carefully regulated and confined to certain times of the day so as not to alert anyone in the downstairs office or factory. Allied bombing raids might bring comfort but also add to the danger of their situation. (In one such scene Stevens had the set shaken violently without warning the actors beforehand to give an additional realism to their enactment of fear.) The sounds of marching soldiers, of explosions at night, of gunshots in the street, can summon up nightmares. Their courageous helpers, Mr. Kraler (Douglas Spencer) and Miep (Dody Heath), bring them news from outside that can only confirm that they are safer where they are, whatever the privations; and from their vantage point in the loft, they can see shops being closed and people down below herded into trucks that will transport them to the death camps. From here they can also see the sky, which reminds them of the fresh air which they are not allowed to breathe, but also gives Anne some sense of hope and the will to carry on. "As long as you can look fearlessly at the sky," she will write on 23 February 1944, "you'll know that you're pure within and will find happiness once more" (Frank: 196). The film will open and close with shots of the sky, symbol of the freedom that Anne has been denied but of a spirit that has not been defeated.

For the most part Stevens has adhered closely to the theatrical text, with minimal deletions or revision, and resisted any temptation to open out the material in any appreciable way, since a sense of claustrophobia is essential to the theme. He takes advantage of the camera's proximity to the action to pick out nuances of performance, such as Millie Perkins' quizzically raised eyebrow as Anne registers another example of adult absurdity, or Joseph Schildkraut's secret look of anxiety as Otto Frank tries to persuade Anne of some of the advantages of their current hiding place while being all-too-aware of the difficulties ahead. At key moments the camera explores the layout of the premises, moving down from the hiding place in the annex, to the office where Mr. Kraler and Miep attend to the business, and then down to the spice factory itself where the men are busying themselves with their jobs and quite unaware of the anxious silent drama being played out above them. At the beginning of the film, when Otto Frank returns to the building after the war, there is a complicated travelling shot from the upstairs to the front door which will be recalled later at moments of heightened danger to the secret occupants. Close-ups are used sparingly (Cinemascope was not a process that was kind to the close-up of a human face), but when they are used—as in the close-ups of Anne and Peter (Richard Beymer), when they are becoming aware of their deep feelings for each other—they are very telling. There is a particularly lovely moment when they are saying goodnight in Peter's room, silhouetted in profile in the shadows, and Peter kisses her lightly on the forehead, so that when Anne opens the door to leave, the light that floods the room seems like a sudden illumination occurring inside her that she has never experienced before. ("Hm…" growls Mrs. Van Daan suspiciously, as Anne proceeds dreamily—and uncharacteristically—to kiss everyone in her family before retiring to bed.) As always, when Stevens uses a dissolve, it is rarely simply to suggest a transition from one time and/or place to another; it is more often to suggest an association of ideas. Marilyn Moss has noted one particularly expressive dissolve after Mr. Dussel (Ed Wynn) has joined the others in hiding and told the group what is happening outside before he leaves the room to unpack his meager belongings. From a medium shot of an anxious Mr. Frank, Stevens dissolves to a street of marching soldiers, with the soundtrack echoing to German patriotic music, but then to a dissolve of a map of the world which is above the bookcase concealing the entrance to the Franks' hiding place. Then the camera moves down to the bookcase, "having," as Moss writes, "come full circle from inside the hiding place, going outside to the street, to the world of danger, and then to an even larger world, signified by the map" (Moss: 254). In just one dissolve is contained the specific situation of the Franks, the immediate context of the street outside which harbors terrors, and the larger context of the global conflict itself, whose outcome might determine their future. Equally powerful and ominous is the dissolve which accompanies Anne's nightmare about her friend Sanni, who has been taken by the Nazis. She seems to see her swaying among a group of other women in line in a concentration camp (the implication is that they are leaning unsteadily together to avoid falling over through weakness) and it is both a terrifying vision of the imagined fate of her friend and an equally frightening premonition of her own destiny.

The film proceeds slowly, appropriately enough to reflect the situation of trapped people on whom time weighs heavily. The somber tread of Alfred Newman's music eloquently accompanies the group as day after day, and with little sign of hope, they settle down to their separate routines, their nerves always jangling at the slightest unexpected sound, and with their characters beginning to crack under the continual constraint. Stevens is unable to force the pace for that would be inappropriate, and sometimes one might feel that the film itself becomes weighed down by the monotony and the sadness it depicts.

Yet there are moments that suddenly move the film to an added level of intensity. In the midst of their Hanukkah celebrations, they hear a faint rattling at the front door and realize that someone is burgling the premises in the office below. Candles are quickly extinguished; and shoes are removed to minimize any noise of movement. Peter inadvertently knocks over an object and, hearing the crash above, the burglar hurriedly exits the building, leaving them in a paroxysm of anxiety about whether his attempted burglary will deter him from going to the police with his suspicions. As Mr. Frank, followed by Anne and Peter, makes his way quickly down the stairs to close the front door, he hears a night watchman approaching and has to hide as the man looks inside and then is momentarily called away by two passing German soldiers. In the time it takes them to return to the building and search for intruders, Anne has fainted and is caught by Peter, who carries her back to the annex, followed swiftly by Mr. Frank, who manages to get inside and conceal the entrance to their hiding place before the night watchman and the soldiers have reached the office. The editing of the sequence maximizes the tension, as Stevens cuts between the various planes of action (annex, stairs, doorway) in a choreographed motion of hide and seek. There is the added agonizing twist of the behavior of Peter's cat, which wanders onto the kitchen ledge, pushing over a funnel, but somehow getting its head stuck so that the funnel does not immediately crash to the floor. In trying to shake itself free, will the cat cause the funnel to fall and alert the soldiers below that there might be someone in the building? Somehow the cat pulls back and manages to get its head out of the funnel without allowing it to fall. For David Mamet it is "one of the best suspense sequences in movies," to the extent that, having worked out that it could not possibly have been achieved by a trick shot, he felt compelled to contact the director's son to explain to him how it was done. Apparently, there were a number of cats and Stevens, in his son's words, "shot an *unbelievable* amount of film, waiting for *some* cat to do something 'uncatlike'" (Mamet: 100).

After the excitement of that scene (which was followed by a brief intermission on the film's roadshow screenings), the next hour might seem something of a dramatic anticlimax. Anne blossoms into young womanhood and feels the first stirrings of love for Peter. This is a test for the film's debutant Millie Perkins, whose acting inexperience is arguably exposed in her rather flat narration of Anne's diary entries, which never quite rises to the idealism of the sentiments. Although they have great charm, her scenes with Beymer tend to sag a little through a certain slowness of tempo. Nonetheless, she does catch a lot of the humor of the character; holds her own in her interchanges with the older members of the cast; and at key moments can be very moving (as in her shocked reaction to Mr. Dussel's account of the disappearance of her friend, or the smile of gratitude she flashes towards her father as he utters a quick final word of comfort to the others prior to their imminent capture). The other members of the cast are flawless. Diane Baker subtly conveys Margot's loneliness behind her patient demeanor; and Ed Wynn expertly catches Mr. Dussel's quirkiness (which can be irritating as well as entertaining), sometimes lightening the tone but never at the expense of the character or the drama. As Mr. and Mrs. Van Daan, Lou Jacobi and Shelley Winters are not afraid to convey weakness as well as endurance, the unlikeable traits as well as the positive ones, the relentless pessimism of the latter, the selfish greed of the former. Joseph Schildkraut and Gusti Huber were repeating the roles of Mr. and Mrs. Frank which they had played on stage and they perform impeccably, particularly Schildkraut, making his first screen appearance for a decade (older cinemagoers might well have remembered his Oscar-winning performance as Dreyfuss in William Dieterle's classic 1937 bio-pic, *The Life of Emile Zola*) and investing the role with a dignity and moral integrity that avoid any trace of pomposity. The main events of this second half involve the discovery that Mr. Van Daan has been stealing some of the bread, occasioning Mrs. Frank's outrage and her demand that the Van Daans be ordered to leave their place of hiding. The mood of recrimination changes when news is brought that the Allies have landed in Normandy, an event which causes Mr. Van Daan to break down in tears of shame at his behavior and Mrs. Frank to apologize for her outburst, both actions symptomatic of the intolerable strain under which they have been living. Now maybe their ordeal is coming to an end and liberation is at hand. Their joy will be short-lived. If the film has had its patches of boredom in this second half, Stevens's handling of the ending is masterly.

It is the morning of 4 August 1944; and it is as if there is something in the air that tells them that this will be the day of discovery. (Louis Malle's 1987 autobiographical masterpiece about his childhood memories of the war, *Au Revoir les Enfants,* has a similar sense of foreboding that one particular day, even before anything has happened, will turn out to be like no other.) The phone has been ringing intermittently downstairs, although the office is closed. Mr. Dussel thinks they must answer it; it might be a warning. Mr. Frank insists they must not; it would reveal that someone is in the building. When the phone rings again, Mr. Dussel makes a dash towards the phone and has to be forcibly restrained. The attention of all of them is now directed towards the door of their hideaway, and Stevens's low-angle shot gives the impression of their staring into an abyss which they had long feared. There is a temporary respite as the phone stops ringing. Anne and Peter retire to the loft and stare at the open sky, with the melted snow dripping onto Anne's eyelashes and face and with birds flying past the window. It is here where she expresses her belief in the essential goodness of people and her hope for the future, and where she realizes she is in love with Peter. As she speaks, we hear sirens in the distance become ever louder and then the screeching of brakes as the trucks come to a halt. In discussing Alfred Newman's beautiful score, Christopher Palmer wrote of this moment: "The revelation [of adolescent love] comes only seconds before the Gestapo arrives to arrest them, and the music evokes the wonder and tenderness of their feelings, rising in one of Newman's most moving passages to an agonised, ecstatic climax as the dreaded knocking on the door prompts them to a first and last passionate kiss" (Palmer: 88). Like the agonizing farewells that conclude *A Place in the Sun* and *Shane*, it is a goodbye shared between people who love each other but who are recognizing with full clarity that they are seeing each other for the last time. As they all quietly gather their things together and await the inevitable, the sound rises to a crescendo of shouts, persistent ringing of the doorbell, a pounding on the door, and then the sound of wood being smashed. We do not see the actual moment of entry, for we do not need to; it is already in the imagination of the eight people who had occupied that place and indeed in the minds of everyone who has watched the film. It is the inevitable and inexorable confrontation with one's worst nightmare.

The Greatest Story Ever Told (1965)

> "The basic theme of the story is one which, unfortunately, has not always been associated with it in the past. It relates to the universality of men and how they must learn to live together. I think it is a theme of great earnestness and utmost simplicity."—George Stevens, 1965

> "Everybody should do a biblical picture—once."—Robert Aldrich

On 5 May 1945, Stevens attended a religious service held at Dachau concentration camp attended by former prisoners and in memory of those who had perished. He found little comfort in the occasion. Raised as a Protestant, Stevens was not a particularly religious man, and what he had seen at Dachau turned him decisively away from any religious belief for a number of years. In an unpublished interview with Robert Hughes twenty years later, Stevens recalled that what he felt then was "the better the Christian, the better the anti–Semite…. It justified the whole goddamned terror" (qtd in Harris: 375). As George Stevens, Jr., was later to observe: "He saw *The Greatest Story Ever Told* as an opportunity to take the 'mischief' out of the story of Jesus, by which he meant the anti–Semitism that had long been attached to it" (Stevens Jr.: 220). The solemn and patient dignity with which the ancient story is told does not derive from someone who has seen a lot of religious epics: it derives from the vision of someone who has seen a modern hell on earth.

In one sense the film's title might be somewhat misleading. It promises a celebratory interpretation of the story of Christ whereas the tone of the film is more cautionary. Much of the dialogue is whispered more than declaimed, partially out of reverence but sometimes out of fear, because not everyone who hears such talk can be trusted. The color is subdued, and indeed a large part of the second half of the film is played out in darkness, deliberately so on the part of Christ's accusers who wish to bring Him to trial under cover of night before substantial support can be assembled in His defense. The depiction of the miracles is visually retrained and emotionally complex, emphasizing Christ's unease and apprehension more than joy at what they might portend; and the reporting of them mainly serves the purpose of mounting incriminating evidence of sedition and sorcery. One of the film's most perceptive commentators, Derek Elley, has written of what he called its "dark brooding atmosphere of stylised tragedy" (Elley: 50). Stevens said his aim was a very simple one: to tell the story of someone who wanted to unite people. Yet it is a story being told against a background of recent history that includes the horrors of the Holocaust and Hiroshima, and the fallout from a Cold War that could lead to global annihilation. It is an inspiring story of a Savior whose example will live on after death, but as the biblical events unfold, we become all the more aware not of its remoteness but of its relevance, for it also a story that involves the power and ruthlessness of the state against the individual; the easy manipulation of mob morality; the persecution of an outsider who will be put to death, having committed no crime; the injustice that stems from misunderstanding; a show trial in which a political verdict has already been reached; and a pervasive motif of spying and betrayal where brother will betray brother. It would not be difficult to find parallel defining events of the twentieth century. Even the Nativity scene ends on a note of foreboding, with a long shot of shadowy cloaked figures on a hill, framed against a dark night sky, who are preparing to ride back and report to King Herod on what they have seen.

"There are enormous aspects of responsibility related to telling this story," Stevens told James Silke in 1964. "This is just the most fascinating adventure in film making that I could possibly contemplate" (qtd in Cronin: 48). He had never wanted for courage nor balked at a challenge at any stage of his career, but one wonders if, by this time, he was putting a brave face on things, for he had set himself an almost superhuman task. The project was a huge undertaking, and Stevens was not only the director but also the producer of the film, as well as being its co-screenwriter. The original financiers, Twentieth Century–Fox, overwhelmed by the mounting costs of their production, *Cleopatra* (1963), had withdrawn from the film, to be replaced by United Artists. The logistics of the film were daunting, to say the least. Having done a vast amount of research in preparation of the script and in the choice of locations, Stevens finally chose to use the Glen Canyon area of Utah for most of the outdoor scenes, with other scenes shot in Arizona. The weather conditions hampered production. A heavy downfall of snow delayed the filming of Christ's entry into Jerusalem on Palm Sunday. The Colorado River stood in for the River Jordan for the John the Baptist scenes, prompting Charlton Heston to observe that, if the Jordan had been as cold as the Colorado, Christianity might never have got off the ground. Executive producer Frank Davis had his work cut out just attending to the animal requirements on the film, let alone everything else, and where a typical day might involve the purchase of four camels and ordering gallons upon gallons of yellow paint for the lilies of the field sequence.

Small wonder that the production took its toll. Stevens' trusted cameraman William Mellor died in 1963 and was replaced by Loyal Griggs. Stevens himself suffered with a stomach ulcer during the shooting of the film. When he was getting seriously behind schedule because of the arduous shooting on location, David Lean was asked and willingly agreed to shoot the scenes with King Herod (played by Claude Rains, whom Lean suggested for the role) and similarly Jean Negulesco stepped in to direct the Nativity sequence. Stevens was deeply grateful for the assistance of such esteemed colleagues, but it reflected in turn the regard with which Stevens was held in the industry and particularly by fellow directors, who were acknowledging the many battles that Stevens, as president of the Screen Directors Guild, had fought on their behalf.

While coping with the physical ardors of the film, which were extreme enough, Stevens also had to keep the artistic and aesthetic vision uppermost in his mind. There were 117 speaking parts. He was telling a story that was familiar to audiences, and unlike other biblical films, such as *The Robe* (1953), *Ben-Hur* (1959) or even *King of Kings* (1961), where the character of Barabbas is given as much attention as that of Christ, he had no subplot or subtext to provide narrative variety or contrast. It was a story in which every scene seemed to represent a fresh challenge. As Derek Elley has noted, the way other artists over the centuries had interpreted the story was built into Stevens' approach, with the film, as he put it, "saturated by the influence of Renaissance models, most notably Titian and (in the dramatic use of chiaroscuro) Tintoretto" (Elley: 43). This is plainly evident in his staging of the Last Supper in the manner of da Vinci's painting. His awareness and incorporation of how other artists had interpreted the story might also have been behind his thinking in using parts of Handel's *Messiah* and Verdi's *Requiem* over the soundtrack at crucial points, a decision that aroused much negative criticism.

When Charlton Heston saw the completed film at a preview screening on 15 January 1965, he was overwhelmed. "It knocked me out," he wrote in his journal, *The Actor's Life*. "It has the formless irresistible momentum of a river and the same inevitability too. Von Sydow gives surely one of the best performances I've seen as Christ.... I'm proud to be in it" (Heston: 214). When he later read the reviews after the New York premiere in February, he wrote: "I've never so ill-estimated a critical reaction" (Heston: 216). The critics were mostly disdainful, accusing the film of, among other things, serene vulgarity, ponderous pacing, and reverential tedium. Typical of the patronizing response was the derogatory review by the esteemed cultural commentator Dwight McDonald (*Esquire*, July 1965), who began by laying down rules for a successful film about Christ before testing Stevens's film against them, a dubious critical strategy, since he was pre-judging the film before seeing it according to criteria of his own devising. (Henry James would have been horrified by such critical presumption.) He then boasted that he left the film halfway through, a shameful abrogation of journalistic responsibility. This review was later to be included in its entirety in a film studies textbook for students, Lee R. Bobker's *Elements of Film* as exemplary of good film critical practice, whereas it could more plausibly be used to demonstrate the opposite, grounded as it is in condescension and inadequate film knowledge (qtd in Bobker: 258). Much more recommendable as a contemporary assessment of the film would have been Raymond Durgnat's review in *Films and Filming* (July 1965), which, although overall unfavorable, was much more thoughtful, closely argued and cinematically informed. In their book on biblical epics (see bibliography), Bruce Babington and Peter Evans also offered a careful and sensitive reading of the film's intention and achievement.

Reflecting later on the critical hostility, Heston held to his high esteem of the film and of von Sydow's performance, but wondered whether Stevens had been wise "to use so many American stars in bit parts, most of them uneasy in period costumes and incapable of handling new testament syntax" (Heston: 216). Jay Gould suggested that "Stevens seems purposely to have chosen the stars for the archetypal natures of their screen persona" and called the film "a miracle of casting" (Gould: 36–7), but most critics were so distracted by the plethora of familiar faces (John Wayne's appearance at the foot of the Cross as a Roman centurion seems to have been the last straw) that they overlooked the quality of some of the performances. Jose Ferrer as Herod Antipas suggests a man whose weariness of spirit (not even Salome's dance seems to arouse much erotic feeling in him) is at the root of his distrust of John the Baptist's fervor as well as his fear of the political danger he might represent. His palace seems an expressive extension of his personality: gloomy, run down, and going to seed. He shares a finely conceived scene with Telly Savalas's Pontius Pilate, where they both laugh disbelievingly at the Savior's idea that one "should love thine enemies"; and Savalas broods effectively in the trial scene, powerfully conveying the sense of a weak politician out of his depth in dealing with a dilemma he has no idea how to resolve. Van Heflin as Bar Amand is excellent in two of the film's most powerful moments: the disbelief that then swells to awed excitement at the raising of

Lazarus; and the moment when, after being struck across the face by a Roman soldier, he then very deliberately (and, in the event, forlornly) turns the other cheek. Donald Pleasence as the Devil in hermit's clothing only has to appear in a scene to chill the atmosphere; and his presence is an embodiment of the forces of cruelty, duplicity, treachery and hostility of that society that will ultimately condemn Christ to death.

Of the disciples, David McCallum is an interestingly conceived Judas, seeming from the outset an outsider who is seething with a lifelong sense of ill-usage or from some suspected or imaginary slight. His envy at others' preferment wrestles with a self-hatred which could always put him in danger of acting against his better instincts. His precise motivation for betrayal is left open, but one is reminded of Graham Greene's essay "The Lost Childhood," and the quotation which concludes it: "In the lost boyhood of Judas, Christ was betrayed" (Greene: 18). There are moments when one senses through a quick close-up a flare of jealousy towards Peter (Gary Raymond) among the disciples, as if Peter is being singled out as a favorite over him. When he peevishly admonishes Mary Magdalene for buying oil to anoint Jesus's feet with money that could have been donated to the poor, Jesus responds firmly: "Do you care so much for the poor, Judas? The poor we have with us always. She is preparing me for my burial." That admonition seems double-edged: not only casting doubt on the real reason for Judas's anger but possibly even looking ahead to His ultimate betrayal and knowing in His heart from whom it will come.

The critics were broadly in agreement with one aspect of the film's achievement and it could hardly be a more fundamental one: namely, the performance of Max von Sydow as Christ. It was an inspired piece of casting, in a sense making the best of both worlds. For the serious cinemagoer, he would bring a wealth of association from his performances in the religious dramas of Ingmar Bergman, most notably perhaps as the Knight confronting Death in *The Seventh Seal* (1957). For the average cinemagoer, he would be a relative unknown, making his American film debut and (in contrast to the cameo roles) unencumbered by associations from previous films. He is an actor with a commanding physical presence and he seems effortlessly charismatic, virile, strong, compassionate, with an aura of mysticism that sets him apart from the people around him. It is a flawless performance, dignified without being sanctimonious and almost hypnotic in its concentration. (It has been noted that he never seems to blink.) In his interview for the George Stevens, Jr., documentary, von Sydow explained that, although he saw Christ as the son of God, he also wanted to portray the role as that of a man with human shortcomings and that he did not wish to portray Christ as any form of superman. Accordingly he gives the familiar a sense of spontaneity as if these things are occurring to Christ for the first time. The Lord's Prayer comes at a moment when he is sensing that his disciples need some sort of spiritual resurgence and it is only when halfway through that they begin to repeat His words. There will be no anger directed at Judas for his betrayal or at Peter for his denial nor at the disciples for falling asleep on their watch prior to the arrest; more sadness at human frailty where "the spirit is willing but the flesh is weak." His one outburst of anger is directed at the money lenders in the Temple for their sacrilege but one senses also that it might be a calculated act of provocation to bring matters to a head. All of this is in line with von Sydow's conception of the human dimensions of the man. The miracles are presented with visual restraint and are achieved not through some supernatural agency but through a tremendous effort of faith. When Jesus insists that Uriah (Sal Mineo) can walk, the subsequent miracle could be as much psychosomatic as supernatural ("It is your faith that has made you well"). Von Sydow's reaction after the event is noticeably more troubled than triumphant. It is a confirmation of the exceptional powers with which Christ is endowed but with it comes the certainty of a predestined fate He cannot avoid. This is taken ever further in what is surely the film's finest scene; the raising of Lazarus.

As Christ is reproached for returning too late to save Lazarus's life, Stevens holds a medium shot for some moments so that the full force of accusation can be registered. He then cuts to a close-up and we see that Christ has tears in His eyes; von Sydow wanted to convey the sense of someone in great pain. The supreme test has come. Stevens cuts to a long shot of the figures in mourning arrayed around the landscape as the lone figure of Christ walks up the hill towards the tomb. A heavy expectant silence fills the air. When He reaches the tomb, He pauses, then looks up to the heavens and prays to God for strength. Stevens cuts to a remarkable shot from inside the tomb as the doorway is eased open and darkness becomes light. There is a long shot of the people absolutely still; an echo and a rumble of thunder; a small figure appears at the doorway of the tomb; and then a gradual bustle of movement as the excitement swells and people begin running to tell others of what they have witnessed. It is noticeable that Judas's reaction is different from the reverential awe of the other disciples; he seems to be wandering around in a haze of puzzled disbelief. The news is shouted up to the Roman soldiers at the gate that a man has been brought back to life; a cripple can now walk; a blind man can see. Significantly, amid the jubilation, there is no reaction shot of von Sydow's Christ. The celebration is tempered by a sense of what it must mean. The miracle is a confirmation of Christ the Messiah; but it is also a death sentence.

Stevens' use of music in this scene proved controversial. As the joy rises, Alfred Newman's alleluias over the soundtrack are joined, and then displaced, by the "Hallelujah Chorus" from Handel's *Messiah*. Christopher Palmer thought the Handelian substitutions were out of keeping and "their over-familiarity distracting" (86), although it might have been their very familiarity that prompted their usage, Stevens feeling that it enlarged and universalized the moment. In his review of the music in *Films in Review* (April 1965), Page Cook, who thought Newman's score "the most esthetic and subtly integrated of all Biblical film scores," described the introduction of Handel at this point as "vulgar theatricality" and its reintroduction in the finale for Christ's resurrection as "inexcusable" (Karlin: 15). There is no doubt that Newman himself was unhappy at this, and arguably it does overshadow the other parts of his score, which have a restrained lyricism. One can see why, if Handel is used to celebrate the raising of Lazarus, he would logically have to be called into play later to salute the miracle of the Resurrection, but its jubilant outburst seems by that time quite at odds with the film's quiet pessimism and indeed its final message: "Do not fret over tomorrow; leave it to fret over its own needs. For today, today's troubles are enough."

In addition to arguable flaws in the casting, pacing and music, the failure of the film might have occurred simply because it missed its historical moment. By the time it was released, both critics and public seemed to have had a surfeit of films of epic length on biblical themes. There was no way in which Stevens could force the pace (the only shock cut in the film—and a very effective one—is the moment when a shot of a nail's being driven into Christ's hand is crosscut with Judas's self-immolation by throwing himself on a pyre);and it is a film whose intelligence and pictorial beauty compete with an absence of narrative energy as it treads solemnly to its conclusion. Nevertheless, Max von Sydow told George Stevens, Jr., that he thought it " was a wonderful failure; a beautiful and very moving failure in some ways." I wonder if Stevens by this time, even unconsciously, thought the same of Christianity itself. It is a magnificent ideal, but humanity had so far either fallen short of its aspirations or perverted its teachings for its own ends. Over this greatest ever story still hangs the shadow of the concentration camps..

The Only Game in Town (1970)

> "There is no director whose films I like better than George's—he had that peculiar blend of the ironic and a sense of the tragic and a sense of what was funny."—Warren Beatty

> "I'm going to make it the way I used to make comedies at RKO; I'm going to get in and shoot it and get it done."—George Stevens

The story behind the making of *The Only Game in Town* had more twists and turns than the film itself. It was based on a play by Frank D. Gilroy (author of the Pulitzer Prize–winning *The Subject Was Roses*), which was impulsively purchased for filming before it had actually been tried out on stage. According to Gilroy, it had been spotted at Studio Duplicating, where multiple copies of play manuscripts were typed up by unemployed actors prior to binding and sending off to agents and production companies. As sometimes happened, a typist alerted a major Hollywood studio—in this case, Twentieth Century-Fox—of a property which might have movie potential. Fox promptly bought the script, seeing it as a vehicle for Elizabeth Taylor and Frank Sinatra, with George Stevens as director. Unfortunately, by the time the play reached Broadway, it had proved a resounding flop during its tryouts in Baltimore, New Haven and Boston. It opened on May 20, 1968, at the Broadhurst Theatre, New York City, with Barry Nelson, Tammy Grimes, and Leo Genn as the cast; and closed after a fortnight. In his acerbic survey of the Broadway theater scene between 1967 and 1968, *The Season,* William Goldman cited five reasons for the play's failure: the film sale, which irritated the critics before they had even seen it; knowledge of its disastrous showings on the road; the fact that it was the last play of the season, and audiences and critics were suffering from theater fatigue; the venue, which was too large for a one-set play; and disappointment with the author after the success of *The Subject Was Roses* (Goldman: 63). Goldman liked the play, calling it a "tough and touching story of two losers backing into a commitment," but felt it was essentially a "charm show," with "no galvanizing power; you either went with the people or you didn't" (63). The same was to be true of the film.

While the play was suffering these setbacks, Sinatra had withdrawn from the projected film because of conflicting concert engagements, and the leading male part had been offered to Warren Beatty, who accepted it in preference to a starring role in *Butch Cassidy and the Sundance Kid* (1969). It was a decision he never regretted, even though the critical and commercial fortunes of the two films could hardly have been more different. For Beatty, however, the opportunity to be directed by Stevens was not to be missed, for he was one of his directing heroes. He had hoped to persuade him to cast him as Judas in *The Greatest Story Ever Told*; and Stevens had been his first choice to direct his production of *Bonnie and Clyde* (1967). Although that film was to be directed subsequently (and superbly) by Arthur Penn, Stevens' influence on it can still be felt, particularly on the soundtrack, where the sound of the gunshots was very much in the style of what Stevens had done in *Shane*. What drew Beatty to *The Only Game in Town* was not the role, then, but the experience, which he thought would be educational.

For better or worse, the casting of Beatty significantly altered the dynamic of the play's central relationship. In the play, the showgirl heroine, Fran Walker is younger than the pianist/gambler hero, Joe Grady, and considerably younger than the married businessman Tom Lockwood with whom she is having an affair and who is old enough to be her father. Stevens did consider re-casting the role of Fran for Mia Farrow, until an irate Elizabeth Taylor (who had only just finished playing a mother role to Mia Farrow in Joseph Losey's *Secret Ceremony*) thought he was trying to get her sacked and quickly put a stop to that. The script required a little maneuvering to accommodate the new pairing, with the minimizing of the age difference between hero and heroine sometimes working to the material's advantage. For example, when Joe is predicting a lonely old age for Fran if she rejects his offer of marriage ("which is worse—the heart abused or the heart unused?"), one could argue that the casting of Elizabeth Taylor works in the film's favor. For a character supposedly in her late twenties, as in the play, the hero's prophecy could seem just whimsical and excessively pessimistic. For a character in her thirties, as in the film, the argument might just strike a more sympathetic chord. Praising Taylor's performance, Peter Tonguette thought she seemed "poignantly middle-aged" and "more authentically 'discontent' than in *Who's Afraid of Virginia Woolf*" (Tonguette: 99). Certainly Fran's occasional mothering of Joe seems more in the nature of an older woman. As handled by the film, even the romantic resolution seems as much a flight from loneliness as a declaration of love; and has the air of two people who are not so much giving way to sentiment as weighing up the attraction of stability.

A further complication occurred when, despite the Las Vegas setting which is essential to the story, Taylor insisted that the film be shot in Paris, so that she could be near her husband, Richard Burton, who at the time was in Paris co-starring with Rex Harrison in Stanley Donen's film *Staircase* (1969), adapted from Charles Dyer's play and also incongruously being filmed in Paris though its setting was actually London. In the case of Stevens's film, the expense of re-creating Las Vegas and its casinos on a Paris soundstage, plus the huge salary commanded by its star, pushed the budget of what had started out as a light romantic comedy to a hefty $11 million. Beatty was later to describe the film to George Stevens, Jr., as "a gigantic soufflé."

Having gone to the trouble of recreating Vegas on French territory, the film was necessarily obliged to make use of the setting. Stevens duly complies. There is an elegantly shot opening, when the heroine, Fran is on the way home after her chorus-line routine on stage, and her walk develops into a little visual poem on the theme of wistful longing, as she stares at wedding dresses in a shop window and at an empty phone box. As we will learn later, the telephone is her main means of connection with a lover who has kept her dangling on a string. There are also two spectacularly shot casino sequences, which, in their visual excitement, powerfully convey the gambling fever which possesses Joe and could always lead to his downfall. These sequences could take attention away from the main relationship and elongate the film to its detriment as a light romantic comedy. Yet it would be fair to say that Stevens's comedies were never that funny, because they tended to be rooted in reality and invariably had serious undertones. Even Fran finds Joe's banter more irritating than amusing; and it becomes clear that his wisecracks reflect not so much a gaiety of spirit as an instinctive defense-mechanism to ward off commitment or self-disclosure. One of the most powerful scenes in the film is not funny at all, as Joe starts smashing some of Fran's precious ornaments in her flat in his search for a gambling stake and Fran, who has been hiding his savings precisely to guard against such temptation, finally throws the money at him.

In a letter to Fred Zinneman on September 30, 1968, Stevens had called his new project "a very nice little story mostly in two rooms of a small apartment.... I present the possibilities in this dull fashion so, if the film proves interesting, you will think generously, as you do, how remarkable are the fellows of my craft" (Quoted in Moss: 289). After the rigors of *The Greatest Story Ever Told,* the modesty of this new project no doubt appealed; and the material might have reminded him of *Swing Time* and *Vivacious Lady,* because it seems something of an amalgam of both (the gambler and the showgirl). There is even a touch of *The More the Merrier,* as two strangers agree out of convenience to share apartment space, but find themselves falling in love, even though the heroine is romantically involved with another man.

At the beginning, Fran is in love with Tom Lockwood (Charles Brasswell), a wealthy businessman based in San Francisco who, during the five years of their relationship, has been promising to obtain a divorce. She drifts into a relationship with Joe, who is a compulsive gambler awaiting the lucky streak that will enable him to leave Las Vegas and make a new career for himself in New York. After a one-night stand with Fran, Joe has won a lot of money in the casino and, thinking she must have brought him luck, has returned to take her out on the town. However, she goes home alone when he starts gambling again (nicely filmed here: just the sound of the noise around the tables is enough to trigger Joe's compulsion and he becomes so caught up in the excitement that he does not even notice when Fran leaves). He will later call shamefacedly at her apartment in the early morning to ask for a loan of twenty bucks, for he has lost all his money at the gambling tables. Not even the attempt at levity can disguise his feeling of humiliation and self-loathing. (It adds some piquancy to that exchange earlier when they are in bed together and Fran has said, "I'm not sure I like you," and he replies, "I knew we had something in common.") Is it convincing that, out of sympathy and with no strings attached, Fran will offer him a place to stay while he raises enough money to leave for New York? The film makes it so. The loneliness of both characters is palpable. Fran can certainly empathize with Joe's feelings of failure; she will later tell Tom that "I was sick and tired of winners." Joe's tears might even bring to mind her last memory of her father before his desertion of his family when she was still a child. And one emotion that Elizabeth Taylor could always act with complete conviction was warm-heartedness.

The arrangement is thrown into confusion when Lockwood unexpectedly shows up in her apartment, having obtained his divorce papers and now offering marriage and a European honeymoon. To his—and her—surprise, Fran turns him down, for she has fallen for Joe, but without telling him, or informing him that Tom's departure signals the end of their affair. The final act sees Joe once again going on a gambling binge, after which he and Fran come to a resolution about their relationship, with Joe offering her marriage. "Granted that marriage is a most faulty, pitiful and wheezing institution," he tells her, "right now it's the only game in town." Typically he tosses in a more utilitarian reason also: it will avoid embarrassment when booking into hotels.

The action of the play takes place entirely in Fran's apartment, so, in adapting his text for the screen, Gilroy took the opportunity to open out the setting; to fill in the action which occurs in the spaces between the scenes; and to show those incidents which the play can only narrate. We are shown how Fran and Joe first meet. Their growing intimacy is indicated by a shot of Fran's watching him from a booth next to the piano, then a shot of his hands as he moves onto another tune, and then a shot of Fran as she sits next to him on the piano stool: not quite a jump cut, but a concise way of suggesting both time passing and passion growing. The fishing expedition the two share is perfunctorily filmed, but it heightens the comic suspense when they arrive back at the apartment in high spirits only to find Fran's lover there, Joe blithely introducing himself as a casual friend and Fran deftly maneuvering his departure in a quick bit of improvisation ("Thanks for bringing me home"). The most elaborate opening out covers Joe's gambling spree, observed by a woman with a purple wig (Olga Valery) whose strange appearance and insistent presence grow increasingly disconcerting: is she an omen of good fortune or of impending doom? Perhaps the most imaginative stroke in the adaptation occurs in the incident after Joe has left the casino in the early hours and is sitting by a fountain, at which point he folds a $100 bill he has taken from his pocket into the shape of a boat and then watches as it floats down a stream and into a sewer. In the play Joe will tell us of this incident after he has revealed that he has won $22,000. In the film, we do not yet know that; and, because his mood seems so serious, we are invited to assume that he has lost again and that this gesture might be that of someone surrendering to his fate.

Reviewing the film in the *New York Times,* Vincent Canby thought that assigning talents of the magnitude of Stevens, Taylor and Beatty to what he called a "small, sentimental Broadway flop" was "rather like trying to outfit a leaky Central Park rowboat for a celebrity cruise through the Greek islands" (qtd in Biskind: 148). Admittedly it requires a stretch of the imagination to conceive of Elizabeth Taylor and Warren Beatty as two of life's losers; and the incongruity is heightened when Hollywood's most eligible and elusive bachelor at that time (Beatty) is required to make a pitch on behalf of marriage, and when Hollywood's most bejeweled leading lady (Taylor) exclaims "Holy cow!" when given a ten-carat diamond ring by her lover. Nonetheless, the two stars display expert comedy timing and an interesting contrast in styles, with Taylor's vocal intonations between whisper, shout, snarl and screech playing against Beatty's smooth, steady drizzle of ostensible wit that is but a wobbly carapace over Joe's insecurity and sense of failure. Beatty is particularly good in the final stretch of the film at conveying the bemusement of someone whose self-perception as a failure has been upset by a streak of good fortune and who has now to reassess both himself and his future. Taylor is equally good and poignant in her character's major moment of self-realization, when, after Tom's proposal and, dithering around packing and hastily putting Tom's framed photo back on her dressing table before he notices its absence, Fran suddenly wonders whether this is what she wants after all. Stevens saves his nimblest piece of filming for the scene when Fran, preparing to leave her apartment with Tom, calls Joe at the club to say goodbye. At the other end of the phone, Joe starts to pick up Fran's unease more from her pauses and her tone of voice than from anything she says. Half-hidden from view, Tom is blithely calling out endearments from an adjoining room, utterly unaware of an alternative drama unfolding that could scuttle all his plans; while Fran, in the middle, is suddenly stricken with confusion and doubt about a long-desired future whose appeal seems to be diminishing before her eyes. Stevens's crosscutting between the three of them, where rhythmic editing and close framing combine with the performances to catch subtle nuances of expression and shifts of emotion, is the film's cinematic highlight, with an intimacy of detail that would be hard to replicate on stage.

Although the film bombed at the box office and was indifferently received by the majority of critics, it should be said that some welcomed Stevens' return to the mood and style of his earlier films. Bruce Beresford thought it had "wit" and "doesn't deserve the neglect critics have heaped upon it" (Beresford: 14). Edguardo Cozarinski thought it was "graced by a certain pervading charm" (qtd in Roud: 961). David Shipman thought it was his best film since *Something to Live For* and found it "pleasing to see an old master return to such form in his last film" (Shipman: 856). Reviewing it in *Films and Filming* (June 1970), Gordon Gow was so fulsome in his praise that he deserves citing in some detail. "The shifts from humour to tenderness could scarcely be managed better … the interplay between [Taylor] and Beatty is delightful…. Stevens makes compulsive viewing of faces and even of backs as he manoeuvres Elizabeth Taylor and Warren Beatty through confined spaces." He mentions the "intrusion" of "nostalgic old tunes"—it is significant in terms of the characters that Fran chooses the melancholy "But Not for Me" when Joe asks her for a tune to play, while he launches into the hopeful "Some Enchanted Evening" outside her door when he calls back at her apartment—but argues that sentimentality is avoided through the skill of the acting and direction. "In his occasional movies that were dependent chiefly upon dialogue, like *Woman of the Year* and *The Talk of the Town*," Gow wrote, "the merriment was considerable but a good less subtle than here" (Gow: 81–2). At that point one is tempted to part company with Gow's otherwise refreshing enthusiasm. For all the film's virtues that he eloquently elucidates, one still misses the sheer abundance of suspense, character, and thematic substance of a film like *The Talk of the Town,* which, although only five minutes longer, seems altogether on a different scale of ambition and achievement. When placed alongside *Woman of the Year* in terms of comic depth and character development, *The Only Game in Town* looks somewhat threadbare. In the absence of the kind of supporting characterization that gave such richness and variety to the early comedies (unhappily, Fran and Joe seem like the ultimate Stevens' outsiders in that they have no friends), Stevens strives to occupy the corridor outside Fran's apartment with charming vignettes of neighbors and pets scurrying about their business, but nothing quite develops into a sustainable running joke.

Frank D. Gilroy at least had little cause for complaint He had received a substantial advance payment for the movie rights for a play which subsequently flopped; and, although the movie also failed, "as a life experience," he wrote, "I profited enormously" (Gilroy: 157). He was in Paris for three months working on pre-production, during which time Stevens kept encouraging him to look through his viewfinder. When Gilroy asked why, Stevens replied: "You're going to be a director one day." Two years later, and galvanized by Stevens' encouragement, Gilroy was to direct his first film, *Desperate Characters* (1971); and later in the decade, he was to make the comedy *Once in Paris* (1978), partly inspired by his experience on working on *The Only Game in Town,* and a sort of genial counterpart to Stevens' film. They would make an enterprising double feature.

If the film was indirectly to inspire Gilroy's future career as a director, it was also to prove Stevens's swansong. As Julie Kirgo noted in her booklet essay for the 2013 Blu-ray release, there is something curiously fitting about the film's last shot, a close-up of Elizabeth Taylor in the arms of a man she loves, which reminded Kirgo of the final shot of *A Place in the Sun.* Stevens has a last card up his sleeve. Joe has suggested to Fran that they close their eyes so that, when they are old, they will always remember the details of this moment when they declared their love. "They close their eyes" is the final direction of the play as the curtain comes down; but, in the film, as Stevens frames their embrace in close-up, Fran opens them again. Hopefully? Fearfully? It is the cold light of day; and Fran was always more of a realist than Joe. It is a nice twist on the conventional romantic comedy ending, with its optimism qualified and mature and with no illusions about the problematic path ahead.

Conclusion:
Anything Else?

George Stevens retired from filmmaking after *The Only Game in Town*. He died in Lancaster, California, following a sudden heart attack, on 8 March 1975. He was 70 years old.

In an interview at the American Film Institute on 23 May 1973, when asked about his directing technique, he succinctly summed up his credo as follows: "Cinema, at its most effective, is one scene effectively superseded by the next. Isn't that it?" (Stevens Jr.: 232)

Reflecting on this, screenwriter and director David Mamet (one of Stevens' staunchest admirers) concluded thoughtfully: "I don't think he left anything out" (Mamet: 60).

Looking back on Stevens' magnificent career which spanned five decades of cinematic evolution, I don't think he left anything out either.

Filmography

As an apprentice and assistant cameraman, Stevens worked on the following films: *Heroes of the Street, The Flaming Arrow, Devil's Ghost, Destroying Angel* (all 1922); *Michael O'Halloran, The Virginian* (1923). For Hal Roach studios, he worked as assistant cameraman and cameraman between 1924 and 1932 on: *The White Sheep, The Battling Oriole* (1924), *Black Cyclone, Are Husbands Human?* (1925); *The Desert's Toll, The Devil's Horse, Be Your Age* (1926), *Are Brunettes Safe?, Bigger and Better Blondes, The Valley of Hell, No Man's Law, Lightning, The Girl from Paree* (1927). He photographed many of the Laurel and Hardy silents, including: *Slipping Wives* (1926), *Putting Pants on Philip, The Second Hundred Years, The Battle of the Century, Sugar Daddies* (1927), *Leave 'em Laughing, The Finishing Touch* (1928); *Big Business* (1929). He also photographed some of Laurel and Hardy's most famous early talkies, including: *Men o' War, The Hoose Gow, Perfect Day* (1929); *Night Owls, Blotto, Brats, Below Zero, Hog Wild, The Laurel and Hardy Murder Case, Another Fine Mess* (1930); *Pardon Us* (1931). He also photographed some shorts for Harry Langdon in 1930. A full listing of his photographic credits are contained in Marilyn Ann Moss's biography.

He directed the following shorts for Hal Roach studios: *Ladies Last, Blood and Thunder* (1930); *High Gear, Air Tight, Call a Cop, Mama Loves Papa, The Kick Off* (1931). He then directed the following shorts for producer Warren Doane at Universal studios: *Who, Me?, The Finishing Touch, Boys Will Be Boys, Family Troubles* (1932); *Rock-A-Bye Cowboy, Should Crooners Marry?, Room Mates, Quiet, Please!* (1932). For producer Lou Brock at RKO, he directed *Grin and Bear It* (1932), *What Fur, Flirting in the Park, A Divorce Courtship, Walking Back Home* (1933); *Bridal Bait, Rough Necking, The Undie-World, Cracked Shots, Strictly Fresh Yeggs* (1934). He also directed the RKO shorts *Ocean Swells* (1934), *Pickled Peppers, Hunger Pains* (1935).

Stevens discussed his early career as cameraman and as director of short film comedies before his move into features in an interview with Leonard Maltin in 1970, published in *Directors in Action,* edited by Bob Thomas (1973, pp. 66–71).

In addition to the features listed below, Stevens directed the Laurel and Hardy segment of *Hollywood Party* (1934). At Pandro S. Berman's request, he also re-shot sequences from an ill-fated Ginger Rogers and Douglas Fairbanks, Jr., vehicle, *Having Wonderful Time* (1939) after a disastrous sneak preview, an experience which accelerated his decision to leave RKO. The sequence he directed in *On Our Merry Way* (1948), starring James Stewart and Henry Fonda, is discussed in Chapter Four.

Features

The Cohens and the Kellys in Trouble (Universal, 1933)

Producer: Carl Laemmle, Jr.; *Screenplay*: Albert Austin, Homer Croy, Fred Guiol, Jack Jungmeyer, Vernon Smith; *Cinematography*: Len Powers; *Editor*: Robert Carlisle.

Cast: George Sidney (Nathan Cohen), Charles Murray (Patrick Kelly), Maureen O'Sullivan (Molly Kelly), Andy Devine (Andy Anderson), Jobyna Howland (Queenie Truelove), Maude Fulton (Miss Fern), Frank Albertson (Bob Graham), Henry Armetta (Captain Silva). 68 minutes.

Kentucky Kernels (RKO, 1934)

Producers: Lee S. Marcus, H.N. Swanson; *Screenplay*: Fred Guiol, Bert Kalmar, Harry Ruby; *Cinematography*: Edward Cronjager; *Music*: Bert Kalmar and Harry Ruby; *Editor*: James B. Morley.

Cast: Bert Wheeler (Willie Doyle), Robert Woolsey (Elmer Dugan), Mary Carlisle (Gloria Wakefield), George McFarland (Spanky Milford), Noah Beery (Colonel Wakefield), Lucille La Verne (Aunt Hannah). 75 minutes.

Bachelor Bait (RKO, 1934)

Producers: Pandro S. Berman, Lou Brock; *Screenplay*: Edward Halperin, Victor Halperin, Glenn Tryon; *Cinematography*: David Abel; *Music*: Max Steiner; *Editor*: James B. Morley; *Art Direction*: Van Nest Polglase and Carroll Clark.

Cast: Stuart Erwin (Mr. William Watts), Rochelle Hudson (Cynthia Douglas), Pert Kelton (Allie Summers), Richard Gallagher (Bramwell Van Dusen), Berton Churchill (Barney Nolan), Grady Sutton (Don Belden), Clarence Wilson (Clement). 74 minutes.

Laddie (RKO, 1935)

Producer: Pandro S. Berman; *Screenplay*: Ray Harris, Dorothy Yost, from the novel by Gene Stratton Porter; *Cinematography*: Harold Wenstrom; *Music*: Roy Webb; *Editor*: James B. Morley; *Art Direction*: Van Nest Polglase and Perry Ferguson.

Cast: John Beal (Laddie Stanton), Gloria Stuart (Pamela Pryor), Virginia Weidler ("Little Sister" Stanton), Donald Crisp (Mr. Pryor), Dorothy Peterson (Mrs. Stanton), Willard Robertson (Mr. John Stanton), William Bakewell (Robert Pryor). 70 minutes.

The Nitwits (RKO, 1935)

Producer: Lee S. Marcus; *Screenplay*: Al Boasberg, Fred Guiol, from an original story by Stuart Palmer; *Cinematography*: Edward Cronjager; *Music*: Dorothy Fields, Jimmy McHugh, L. Wolfe Gilbert and Felix Bernard; *Editor*: John Lockert; *Art Direction*: Van Nest Polglase and Perry Ferguson.

Cast: Bert Wheeler (Johnnie), Robert Woolsey (Newton), Fred Keating (William Darrell), Betty Grable (Mary Roberts), Evelyn Brent (Mrs. Alice Lake) Erik Rhodes (George Clark), Hale Hamilton (Lake). 81 minutes.

Alice Adams (RKO, 1935)

Producer: Pandro S. Berman; *Screenplay*: Dorothy Yost, Mortimer Offner, Jane Murfin, from the novel by Booth Tarkington; *Cinematography*: Robert De Grasse; *Music:* Roy Webb; *Editor*: Jane Loring; *Art Direction*: Van Nest Polglase.

Cast: Katharine Hepburn (Alice Adams), Fred MacMurray (Arthur Russell), Fred Stone (Mr. Virgil Adams), Evelyn Venable (Mildred Palmer), Frank Albertson (Walter Adams), Ann Shoemaker (Mrs. Adams), Charley Grapewin (J.A. Lamb), Grady Sutton (Frank Dowling), Hedda Hopper (Mrs. Palmer), Jonathan Hale (Mr. Palmer), Janet McLead (Henrietta Lamb), Virginia Howell (Mrs. Dowling), Zeffie Tilbury (Mrs. Dresser), Ella McKenzie (Ella Dowling), Hattie McDaniel (Malena). 99 minutes.

Oscar nominations: Best Picture; Best Actress (Katharine Hepburn).

Annie Oakley (RKO, 1935)

Producer: Cliff Reid; *Screenplay*: Joel Sayre and John Twist; from an original story by Joseph A. Fields and Ewart Adamson; *Cinematography*: J. Roy Hunt; *Music*: Alberto Colombo; *Editor*: George Hiveley; *Art Direction*: Van Nest Polglase and Perry Ferguson.

Cast: Barbara Stanwyck (Annie Oakley), Preston Foster (Toby Walker), Melvyn Douglas (Jeff Hogarth), Moroni Olsen (Colonel William Cody), Pert Kelton (Vera Delmar), Andy Clyde (James MacIvor), Chief Thunderbird (Sitting Bull), Margaret Armstrong (Mrs. Oakley), Delmar Watson (Wesley Oakley), Adeline Craig (Susan Oakley). 88 minutes.

Swing Time (RKO, 1936)

Producer: Pandro S. Berman; *Screenplay*: Howard Lindsay and Allan Scott, after an original story by Erwin Gelsey; *Cinematography*: David Abel; *Music*: Jerome Kern and Dorothy Fields; *Editor*: Henry Berman; *Art Direction*: Van Nest Polglase, Carroll Clark, John Harkrider, and Darrell Silvera; *Choreography*: Hermes Pan.

Cast: Fred Astaire (Lucky), Ginger Rogers (Penelope Carroll), Victor Moore (Pop Everett), Helen Broderick (Mabel Anderson), Eric Blore (Gordon), Betty Furness (Margaret Watson), George Metaxa (Ricardo Romero), John Harrington (Raymond), Pierre Watkin (Simpson), Landers Stevens (Judge Watson), Gerald Homer (Eric), Abe Reynolds (Tailor) Fern Emmett (Maid), Howard Hickman (First Minister), Edgar Dearing (Policeman), Ferdinand Minuer (Second Minister), Olin Francis (Tough Mug). 103 minutes.

Oscar: Best Song ("The Way You Look Tonight")

Quality Street (RKO, 1937)

Producer: Pandro S. Berman; *Screenplay*: Allan Scott, Mortimer Offner, Jack Townley, based on the play by J.M. Barrie; *Music*: Roy Webb; *Photography*: Robert De Grasse; *Editor*: Henry Berman; *Art Direction*: Hobe Erwin and Darrell Silvera.

Cast: Katharine Hepburn (Phoebe Throssel), Franchot Tone (Valentine Brown), Fay Bainter (Susan Throssel), Eric Blore (Recruiting Sergeant), Cora Witherspoon (Patty), Estelle Winwood (Mary Willoughby), Florence Lake (Henrietta Turnbull), Helena Grant (Fanny Willoughby), Bonita Granville (Isabella), Clifford Severn (Arthur), Sherwood Bailey (William Smith), Roland Varno (Ensign Blades), Joan Fontaine (Charlotte Parrett), William Blakewell (Lt. Spicer), York Sherwood (Postman). 84 minutes.

Oscar nomination: Best Music Score.

A Damsel in Distress (RKO, 1937)

Producer: Pandro S. Berman; *Screenplay*: P.G. Wodehouse, Ernest Pagano, S.K. Lauren, from the novel by P.G. Wodehouse; *Cinematography*: Joseph August; *Music*: George and Ira Gershwin; *Editor*: Henry Berman; *Art Direction*: Van Nest Polglase and Carroll Clark; *Choreography*: Hermes Pan.

Cast: Fred Astaire (Jerry Halliday), Joan Fontaine (Lady Alyce Marshmorton), George Burns (himself), Gracie Allen (herself), Reginald Gardiner (Keggs), Ray Noble (Reggie), Constance Collier (Lady Caroline), Montagu Love (Lord John Marshmorton), Harry Watson (Albert), Jan Duggan (Mrs. Ruggles). 100 minutes.

Oscar: Best Dance Direction (Hermes Pan for "Fun House" number)
Oscar nomination: Best Art Direction.

Vivacious Lady (RKO, 1938)

Producer: George Stevens; *Screenplay*: P.J. Wolfson, Ernest Pagano, from a story by I.A.R. Wylie; *Cinematography*: Robery De Grasse; *Music*: Roy Webb; *Editor*: Henry Berman; *Art Direction*: Van Nest Polglase, Robert De Grasse.

Cast: Ginger Rogers (Francy), James Stewart (Peter), James Ellison (Keith), Beulah Bondi (Mrs. Morgan), Charles Coburn (Mr. Morgan), Frances Mercer (Helen), Phyllis Kennedy (Jenny), Grady Sutton (Culpepper), Alec Craig (Joseph), Franklin Pangborn (Apartment Manager), Jack Carson (Waiter Captain), Willie Best (Porter). 90 minutes.

Oscar nominations: Best Art Direction; Best Sound (James Wilkinson).

Gunga Din (RKO, 1939)

Producer: George Stevens; *Screenplay*: Joel Sayre and Fred Guiol, from an original story by Ben Hecht and Charles McArthur, as suggested by the Rudyard Kipling poem; *Cinematography*: Joseph August; *Music*: Alfred Newman; *Editors*: Henry Berman and John Lockert; *Art Direction*: Van Nest Polglase, Perry Ferguson and Darrell Silvera.

Cast: Cary Grant (Sergeant Archibald Cutter); Victor McLaglen (Sergeant MacChesney), Douglas Fairbanks, Jr. (Sergeant Thomas Ballantine), Sam Jaffe (Gunga Din), Eduardo Ciannelli (Sufi Khan), Joan Fontaine (Emaline Stebbins), Montagu Love (Colonel Weeks), Robert Coote (Bertie Higginbotham), Abner Biberman (Chota), Lumsden Hare (Major Mitchell). 117 minutes.

Vigil in the Night (RKO, 1940)

Producer: George Stevens; *Screenplay*: Fred Guiol, P.J. Wolfson, Rowland Leigh, from the novel by A.J. Cronin; *Cinematography*: Robert De Grasse; *Music*: Alfred Newman; *Editor*: Henry Berman; *Art Direction*: Van Nest Polglase.

Cast: Carole Lombard (Anne Lee), Brian Aherne (Dr. Prescott), Anne Shirley (Lucy Lee), Julien Mitchell (Matthew Bowley), Robert Coote (Dr. Caley), Brenda Forbes (Nora), Rita Page (Glennie), Peter Cushing (Joe Shand), Ethel Griffies (Matron East), Doris Lloyd (Mrs. Bowley), Emily Fitzroy (Sister Gilson). 96 minutes.

Penny Serenade (Columbia, 1941)

Producer: George Stevens; *Screenplay*: Morrie Ryskind, from a story by Martha Cheavens; *Cinematography*: Joseph August; *Music*: W. Franke Harling; *Editor*: Otto Meyer.

Cast: Cary Grant (Roger Adams), Irene Dunne (Julie Gardiner Adams), Beulah Bondi (Miss Oliver), Edgar Buchanan (Applejack Carney), Ann Doran (Dotty), Eva Lee Kuney (Trina, age 6), Leonard Willey (Dr. Hartley), Wallis Clark (Judge), Walter Soderling (Billings), Baby Biffle (Trina, age 1). 125 minutes.

Oscar nomination: Best Actor (Cary Grant).

Woman of the Year (MGM, 1942)

Producer: Joseph L. Mankiewicz; *Screenplay*: Ring Lardner, Jr., Michael Kanin; *Cinematography*: Joseph Ruttenberg; *Music* Franz Waxman; *Editor*: Frank Sullivan;

Art Direction: Cedric Gibbons, Edwin B. Willis.

Cast: Spencer Tracy (Sam Craig), Katharine Hepburn (Tess Harding), Fay Bainter (Ellen Whitcomb), Reginald Owen (Clayton), Minor Watson (William Harding), William Bendix (Pinkie Peters), Gladys Blake (Flo Peters), Dan Tobin (Gerald Howe), Roscoe Karns (Phil Whittaker), William Tannen (Ellis), Ludwig Stossel (Dr. Lubeck), Sara Haden (Matron), Edith Evanson (Alma), George Kezas (Chris). 114 minutes.

Oscar: Best Original Screenplay.

Oscar nomination: Best Actress (Katharine Hepburn).

The Talk of the Town (Columbia, 1942)

Producer: George Stevens; *Screenplay*: Irwin Shaw, Sidney Buchman; *Music*: Frederick Hollander, Morris Stoloff; *Cinematography*: Ted Tetzlaff; *Editor*: Otto Meyer; *Art Direction*: Lionel Banks and Rudolph Sternad.

Cast: Cary Grant (Leopold Dilg), Jean Arthur (Nora Shelley), Ronald Colman (Michael Lightcap), Edgar Buchanan (Sam Yates), Glenda Farrell (Regina Bush), Charles Dingle (Andrew Holmes), Emma Dunn (Mrs. Shelley), Rex Ingram (Tilney), Leonid Kinskey (Jan Pulaski), Tom Tyler (Clyde Bracken), Don Beddoe (Chief of Police), George Watts (Judge Grunstadt), Clyde Fillimore (Senator James Boyd), Frank M. Thomas (District Attorney). 118 minutes.

Oscar nominations: Best Film; Best Original Story (Sidney Harmon); Best Screenplay; Best Black and White Cinematography; Best Editing; Best Music Score; Best Art Direction.

The More the Merrier (Columbia, 1943)

Producer: George Stevens; *Screenplay*: Richard Flournoy, Lewis R. Foster, Frank Ross, Robert

Russell; *Cinematography*: Ted Tetzlaff; *Music*: Leigh Harline; *Editor*: Otto Meyer; *Art Direction*: Lionel Banks and Rudolph Sternad.

Cast: Jean Arthur (Connie Milligan), Joel McCrea (Joe Carter), Charles Coburn (Benjamin Dingle), Richard Gaines (Charles J. Prendergast), Bruce Bennett (Evans), Frank Sully (Pike), Clyde Fillmore (Senator Noonan), Stanley Clements (Morton Rodakiewicz), Don Douglas (Harding). 104 minutes.

Oscar: Best Supporting Actor (Charles Coburn).

Oscar nominations: Best Picture; Best Actress (Jean Arthur); Best Director; Best Original Story (Frank Ross and Robert Russell); Best Screenplay.

I Remember Mama (RKO, 1948)

Producer: George Stevens; *Screenplay*: DeWitt Bodeen, from the play by John Van Druten; *Cinematography*: Nicholas Musaraca; *Music*: Roy Webb; *Editors*: Robert Swink and Tholen Gladden; *Art Direction*: Albert D'Agostino, Carroll Clark, Darrell Silvera and Emile Kuri.

Cast: Irene Dunne (Mama), Barbara Bel Geddes (Katrin), Oskar Homolka (Uncle Chris), Philip Dorn (Papa), Cedrick Hardwicke (Mr. Hyde), Edgar Bergen (Mr. Thorkelson), Rudy Vallee (Dr. Johnson), Peggy McIntyre (Christine), June Hedin (Dagmar), Steve Brown (Nels), Ellen Corby (Aunt Trina), Hope Landin (Aunt Jenny), Edith Evanson (Aunt Sigrid), Tommy Ivo (Cousin Arne), Barbara O'Neil (Jessie Brown), Florence Bates (Florence Dana Moorhead). 134 minutes.

Oscar nominations: Best Actress (Irene Dunne); Best Supporting Actor (Oscar Homolka); Best Supporting Actress (Barbara Bel Geddes, Ellen Corby); Best Black and White Cinematography.

A Place in the Sun (Paramount, 1951)

Producer: George Stevens; *Screenplay*: Harry Brown, Michael Wilson, after the Patrick Kearney play based on the novel *An American Tragedy* by Theodore Dreiser; *Cinematography*: William Mellor; *Music*: Franz Waxman; *Editor*: William Hornbeck;

Art Direction: Hans Dreier and Walter Tyler.

Cast: Montgomery Clift (George Eastman), Elizabeth Taylor (Angela Vickers), Shelley Winters (Alice Tripp), Anne Revere (Hannah Eastman), Keefe Brasselle (Earl Eastman), Herbert Heyes (Charles Eastman), Shepperd Strudwick (Anthony Vickers), Frieda Inescort (Mrs. Vickers), Kathryn Givney (Louise Eastman), Raymond Burr (Frank Marlowe), Fred Clark (Bellows), Walter Sande (Jansen), Ian Wolfe (Dr. Wyeland), Lois Charttrand (Martha Eastman), Douglas Spencer (Boatkeeper), John Ridgely (Coroner), Ted de Corsia (Judge), Charles Dayton (Kelly), Paul Frees (the Reverend Morrison). 122 minutes.

Oscars: Best Direction; Best Black and White Cinematography; Best Music Score; Best Editing; Best Costume Design (Edith Head).

Oscar nominations: Best Film; Best Actor (Montgomery Clift); Best Actress (Shelley Winters).

Something to Live For (Paramount, 1952)

Producer: George Stevens; *Screenplay*: Dwight Taylor; *Cinematography*: George Barnes; *Music*: Victor Young; *Editors*: William Hornbeck and Tom McAdoo; *Art Direction*: Hal Percira, Walter Tyley and Emile Kuri.

Cast: Ray Milland (Alan Miller), Joan Fontaine (Jenny Carey), Teresa Wright (Edna Miller), Richard Derr (Tony Collins), Douglas Dick (Baker), Herbert Heyes (Crawley), Harry Bellaver (Billy), Paul Valentine (Albert), Frank Orth (Waiter), Robert Cornthwaite (Young Man), Helen Spring (Mrs. Crawley), Rudy Lee (Chris), Patric Mitchell (Johnny), Joey (Douglas Spencer). 89 minutes.

Shane (Paramount, 1953)

Producer: George Stevens; *Screenplay*: A.B. Guthrie, Jr., with additional dialogue by Jack Sher, based on the novel by Jack Schaefer; *Cinematography*: Loyal Griggs; *Music*: Victor Young; *Editors*: William Hornbeck, Tom McAdoo; *Art Direction*: Hal Pereira, Walter Tyler, Emile Kuri; *Sound*: Harry Lindgren, Gene Garvin.

Cast: Alan Ladd (Shane), Jean Arthur (Marian Starrett), Van Heflin (Joe Starrett), Brandon de Wilde (Joey), Walter Jack Palance (Jack Wilson), Emile Meyer (Rufus Ryker), John Dierkes (Morgan Ryker), Ben Johnson (Chris Calloway), Paul McVey (Sam Grafton),Edgar Buchanan (Fred Lewis), Elisha Cook, Jr. ("Stonewall" Torrey), Ellen Corby (Mrs. Torrey), Douglas Spencer (Axel Shipstead), Edith Evanson (Mrs. Shipstead), John Miller (Atkey), Leonard Strong (Ernie Wright), Ray Spiker (Johnson), Janice Carroll (Susan Lewis), Martin Mason (Howells), Nancy Culp (Mrs. Howells), Helen Brown (Mrs. Lewis). 118 minutes.

Oscar: Best Color Cinematography.

Oscar nominations: Best Picture; Best Supporting Actor (Brandon de Wilde, Walter Jack Palance); Best Director; Best Adapted Screenplay.

Giant (Warner Bros, 1956)

Producers: George Stevens, Harry Ginsberg; *Screenplay*: Fred Guiol, Ivan Moffat, based on the novel by Edna Ferber; *Cinematography*: William Mellor; *Music*: Dimitri Tiomkin; *Editor*: William Hornbeck; *Art Direction*: Boris Leven, Ralph Hurst

Cast: Elizabeth Taylor (Leslie Benedict), Rock Hudson (Bick Benedict), James Dean (Jett Rink), Mercedes McCambridge (Luz Benedict), Chill Wills(Uncle Bawley), Jane Withers (Vashti Synthe), Carroll Baker (Luz Benedict II), Sal Mineo (Angel Obregon), Dennis Hopper (Jordan Benedict), Judith Evelyn (Mrs. Horace Lynnton), Paul Fix (Dr. Horace Lynnton), Rod Taylor (Sir David Karfrey), Earl Holliman (Bob Dace), Robert Nichols (Pinky Snythe), Alexander Scourby (Old Polo), Fran Bennett (Judy Benedict), Charles Watts (Whitside), Elsa Cardenas (Juana), Carolyn Craig (Lacey Lynnton), Mary Ann Edwards (Adarene Clinch), Sheb Wooley (Gabe Target), Monte Hale (Bale Clinch), Victor Millan (Angel Obregon I), Mickey Simpson (Sarge), Pilar del Rey (Mrs. Obregon), Maurice Jara (Dr. Guerra), Noreen Nash (Lorna Lane), Napoleon Whiting (Swazey), Tina Menard (Lupe), Ray Whitley (Watts). 198 minutes.

Oscar: Best Director.

Oscar nominations: Best Picture; Best Actor (Rock Hudson, James Dean); Best Supporting Actress (Mercedes McCambridge); Best Adapted Screenplay; Best Music Score; Best Editing; Best Art Direction; Best Costume Design (Moss Mabry, Marjorie Best).

The Diary of Anne Frank (Twentieth Century–Fox, 1959)

Producer: George Stevens; *Screenplay*: Frances Goodrich, Albert Hackett, based on their play adapted from Anne Frank's *Diary* and writings; *Cinematography*: William Mellor; *Music*: Alfred Newman; *Editors*: David Bretherton, William Mace; Robert Swink; *Art Direction*: Lyle Wheeler and George W. Davis, with Walter Scott and Stuart Reiss.

Cast: Millie Perkins (Anne Frank), Joseph Schildkraut (Otto Frank), Shelley Winters (Mrs. Van Daan), Lou Jacobi (Mr. Van Daan), Richard Beymer (Peter Van Daan), Gusti Huber (Mrs. Frank), Diane Baker (Margot Frank), Douglas Spencer (Kraler), Dody Heath (Miep), Ed Wynn (Mr. Dussel). 170 minutes.

Oscars: Best Supporting Actress (Shelley Winters); Best Cinematography (Black and White); Best Art Direction (Black and White).

Oscar nominations: Best Picture; Best Supporting actor (Ed Wynn); Best Director; Best Music Score; Best Costume Design (Charles Lemair, Mary Wills).

The Greatest Story Ever Told (United Artists, 1965)

Producer: George Stevens; *Screenplay*: James Lee Barrett and George Stevens, after the Bible and the writings of Fulton Oursler and Henry Denker, in creative association with Carl Sandburg; *Cinematography*: William Mellor and Loyal Griggs; *Music*: Alfred Newman; *Editors*: Harold F. Kress, Art J. Nelson, Frank O'Neill; *Art Direction*: Richard Day, William Creber and David Hall.

Cast: Max von Sydow (Jesus), Charlton Heston (John the Baptist), Dorothy McGuire (Mary), Robert Loggia (Joseph), Rodolfo Acosta (Captain of Lancers), Michael Anderson, Jr. (James the Younger), Carroll Baker (Veronica), Ina Balin (Martha of Bethany), Robert Blake (Simon the Zealot), Pat Boone (Young Man at the Tomb), Victor Buono (Sorak), Richard Conte (Barabbas), Joanna Dunham (Mary Magdalene), Jose Ferrer (Herod Antipas), Van Heflin (Bar Amand), Martin

Landau (Caiaphas), Angela Lansbury (Claudia), Mark Leonard (Balthazar), Janet Margolin (Mary of Bethany), David McCallum (Judas Iscariot), Roddy McDowall (Matthew), Sal Mineo (Uriah), Nehemiah Persoff (Shemiah), Donald Pleasence (The Dark Hermit), Sidney Poitier (Simon of Cyrene), Claude Rains (King Herod), Gary Raymond (Peter), Telly Savalas (Pontius Pilate), Joseph Schildkraut (Nicodemus), Frank Silvera (Caspar), John Wayne (Roman Centurion), Shelley Winters (Woman of No Name), Ed Wynn (Old Aram). 199 minutes.

Oscar nominations: Best Color Cinematography; Best Music Score; Best Art Direction; Best Costume Design (Vittorio Nino Novarese, Marjorie Best); Best Special Visual Effects (J. McMillan Johnson).

The Only Game in Town (Twentieth Century–Fox, 1970)

Producer: Fred Kohlmar; *Screenplay*: Frank D. Gilroy, based on his play; *Cinematography*: Henri Decae; *Music*: Maurice Jarre; *Editors*: John W. Holmes, William Sands and Pat Shade; *Art Direction*: Herman Blumenthal and August Capelier.

Cast: Elizabeth Taylor (Fran Walker), Warren Beatty (Joe Grady), Charles Braswell (Thomas J. Lockwood), Hank Henry (Tony), Olga Valery (Strange Lady at Casino). 112 minutes

Special Awards

Directors Guild Award, *A Place in the Sun,* 1951.
Directors Guild Award, *Shane,* 1953.
Irving Thalberg Award, Academy of Motion Picture Arts and Sciences, 1953.
D.W. Griffith Award, The Directors Guild, 1960.

Discography

The following CD soundtrack releases are particularly valuable because they contain not only the complete music scores but also alternate and rejected cues, much material that did not make it into the final film, and documentation about the recordings. The material relating to the controversies about the music for *A Place in the Sun* and *The Greatest Story Ever Told* is of especial interest.

A Place in the Sun (Kritzerland). Music by Franz Waxman, with additional material by Daniele Amfitheatrof and Victor Young.
Shane (La-La Land). Music by Victor Young, with additional material ("Ride to Town") by Franz Waxman.
Giant, two CDs (La-La Land). Music by Dimitri Tiomkin.
The Greatest Story Ever Told, three CDs. (Varese Sarabande). Music by Alfred Newman (plus Handel and Verdi).

Bibliography

Adair, Gilbert. 1983. "Directors of the Decade: George Stevens," *Films and Filming,* June, pp. 6–9.

Agee, James. 1967. *Agee on Film,* London: Peter Owen.

Als, Hilton. 2016. "Better with Age: *I Remember Mama,*" *The New Yorker,* 20 June.

Archer, Eugene. 1957. "George Stevens and the American Dream," *Film Culture,* Volume 3, No. 1, pp. 3–32.

Babington, Bruce, and Evans, Peter William. 1993. *Biblical Epics: Sacred Narrative in the Hollywood Cinema,* Manchester University Press.

Barrie, J.M. 1918. *Quality Street,* London: Hodder and Stoughton.

Bartlett, Nicholas. 1965. "Sentiment and Humanism: A Note on the Films of George Stevens," *Film,* Volume 38, Summer, pp. 26–9.

Bazin, Andre. 1971. "The Evolution of the Western," in *What Is Cinema,* Volume 2, edited by Hugh Gray, University of California Press, pp. 149–57.

Behlmer, Rudy (editor). 1972. *Memo from David O. Selznick,* London: Macmillan.

Beresford, Bruce. 1970. "George Stevens," *Film,* Volume 59, pp. 13–15.

Biskind, Peter. 2010. *Star: The Life and Wild Times of Warren Beatty,* London: Simon & Schuster.

Blake, Michael F. 2003. *Code of Honor,* Oxford: Taylor Trad.

Bobker, Lee R. 1979. *Elements of Film,* 3rd edition, New York: Harcourt, Brace and Jovanovich.

Bosworth, Patricia. 1978. *Montgomery Clift,* New York: Harcourt, Brace and Jovanovich.

Bradshaw, Peter. 2013. "Review: *A Place in the Sun,*" *The Guardian* (UK), 1 February.

Brownlow, Kevin. 1996. *David Lean: A Biography,* London: Richard Cohen.

_____. 1979. *The War, the West, and the Wilderness,* London: Secker & Warburg.

Capra, Frank. 1971. *The Name Above the Title: An Autobiography,* New York: Macmillan.

Cardiff, Jack. 1996. *Magic Hour.* Faber & Faber.

Casper, Drew. 2007. *Post-War Hollywood, 1946–62.* Oxford: Blackwell.

Chandler, Charlotte. 2010. *The Real Kate: A Personal Biography of Katharine Hepburn,* London: J.R.

Chandler, Raymond. 1962. *Raymond Chandler Speaking,* edited by Dorothy Gardiner and Kathrine Sorley Walker, London: Hamish Hamilton.

Ciment, Michel (editor). 2017. "Dossier on George Stevens," *Positif,* February, pp. 92–112.

Collins, Jim. 1981 "Towards Defining a Matrix of the Musical Comedy: The Place of the Spectator Within the Textual Mechanisms" in *Genre: The Musical,* edited by Rick Altman, London: Routledge& Kegan Paul, pp. 134–46.

Corliss, Richard. 1975. *Talking Pictures,* London: David & Charles.

Countryman, Edward, and von-Heussen Countryman, Yvonne. 1999. *Shane,* Palgrave: British Film Institute Classics.

Cronin, A.J. 1939. *Vigil in the Night,* New York: A.J. Cornell.

Cronin, Paul (editor). 2004. *George Stevens Interviews,* University Press of Mississippi.

Dewey, Donald. 1997. *James Stewart: A Biography,* London: Little, Brown.

Dick, Bernard F. 2002. *Anatomy of Film,* 4th edition, New York: Bedford/St Martin's.

Dixon, Wheeler Winston, 2002. "Budd Boetticher: The Last Interview," *Film Criticism,* Spring, pp. 52–72.

Doherty, Thomas. 1993. *Projections of War: Hollywood, American Culture and World War II,* New York: Columbia University Press.

Dreiser, Theodore. 1925. *An American Tragedy,* New York: Signet, 1964.

Durgnat, Raymond. 1969. *The Crazy Mirror: Hollywood Comedy and the American Image,* London: Faber & Faber.

Eisenstein, Sergei. 1963. *The Film Sense,* London: Faber & Faber.

Eliot, T.S. 1963. "A Prediction" (1924), in *Henry James: A Collection of Critical Essays,* edited by Leon Edel, Prentice Hall, pp. 55–6.

Elley, Derek. 1984. *The Epic Film,* London: Routledge.

Elley, Derek (editor). 1991. *Variety Movie Guide,* London: Hamlyn.

Eyles, Allen. 1967. *The Western: An Illustrated Guide,* London: A. Zwemmer.

Eyre, Richard. 2003. *National Service,* London: Bloomsbury.

Ferber, Edna. 1952. *Giant,* New York: Perennial Classics, 2000.

Frank, Anne. 1944. *The Diary of a Young Girl,* edited by Otto H. Frank and Mirjam Pressler, London: Viking, 1997.

Fuller, Graham. 2016. "Top Gun: *Shane,*" *Sight and Sound,* January, pp. 94–5.

Geist, Kenneth L. 1978. *Pictures Will Talk: The Life and Films of Joseph L. Mankiewicz,* New York: Charles Scribner's Sons.

Gilroy, Frank D. 2000. *Complete Full Length Plays, 1962–1999: Volume 1,* Smith and Kraus.

Goldman, William. 1969. *The Season: A Candid Look at Broadway,* New York: Limelight, 1984.

Goodman, Ezra. 1962. *The Fifty Year Decline and Fall of Hollywood,* New York: Macfadden.

Goodrich, Frances, and Hackett, Albert. 1956. *The Diary of Anne Frank,* London and Glasgow: Blackie.

Gow, Gordon. 1970. "The Only Game in Town," *Films and Filming,* June, pp. 81–2.

Greene, Graham. 1969. *Collected Essays,* London: Bodley Head.

Guinness, Alec. 2001. *A Commonplace Book,* London: Hamish Hamilton.

Halliday, Jon. 1971. *Sirk on Sirk,* London: Secker & Warburg.

Harris, Mark. 2014. *Five Came Back,* London: Canongate.

Haskell, Molly. 1973. *From Reverence to Rape,* New York: Holt, Rinehart and Winston.

Hastings, Max. 1985. *Victory in Europe: D-Day to V-E Day,* London: Weidenfeld & Nicholson.

Hertog, Susan. 2011. *Dangerous Ambition: Rebecca West and Dorothy Thompson,* New York: Ballantine.

Heston, Charlton. 1980. *The Actor's Life: Journals 1956–1976,* London: Penguin.

_____. 1995. *In the Arena: The Autobiography,* London: HarperCollins.

Hinkle, Robert. 2009. *Call Me Lucky: A Texan in Hollywood,* University of Oklahoma Press.

Houston, Penelope. 1953. "*Shane* and George Stevens," *Sight and Sound,* October, pp. 71–6.

_____. 1963. *The Contemporary Cinema,* London: Penguin.

Hubai, Gergely. 2012. *Torn Music: Rejected Film Scores,* Los Angeles: Silman James.

Jewell, Richard B. 2007. *The Golden Age of Cinema: Hollywood 1929–1945,* London: Blackwell.

Jewell, Richard B., and Harbin, Vernon, 1982. *The RKO Story,* London: Octopus.

Kael, Pauline. 1968. *Kiss Kiss Bang Bang,* New York: Bantam.

Kanin, Garson. 1972. *Tracy and Hepburn: An Intimate Memoir,* London: Angus & Robertson.

Kirgo, Julie. 2013. " Booklet: *The Only Game in Town,*" Twilight Time, BluRay.

Knight, Arthur. 1957. *The Liveliest Art,* New York: Mentor.

Koszarski, Richard (editor). 1977. *Hollywood Directors, 1941–1976,* Oxford.

Lavender, David. 1969. *The Penguin Book of the American West.* London: Penguin.

Leaming, Barbara. 1995. *Katharine Hepburn,* New York: Crown.

Lyman, Richard. 2001. " Coming Back to *Shane*: Watching Movies with Woody Allen," *New York Times,* 3 August.

Maltin, Leonard. 2008. *Leonard Maltin's 2009 Movie Guide,* Plume.

Mamet, David. 2007. *Bambi vs Godzilla: On the Nature, Purpose and Practice of the Movie Business,* London: Simon & Schuster.

Marsh, Clive, and Ortiz, Gaye (editors). 1997. *Explorations in Theology and Film,* London: Blackwell.

McBride, Joseph. 1992. *Frank Capra: The Catastrophe of Success,* New York: Simon & Schuster.

McCambridge, Mercedes. 1981. *The Quality of Mercy: An Autobiography,* New York: Times.

McKee, Robert. 1993. " *Shane*" in *Filmworks,* BBC Publications, pp. 32–5.

McVay, Douglas. 1965. "George Stevens," *Films and Filming,* May and June, pp. 10–14; pp. 16–19.

Merck, Mandy. 2007. *Hollywood's American Tragedies,* Berg: New York.

Moffat, Ivan. 2004. *The Ivan Moffat File,* edited by Gavin Lambert, New York; Pantheon.

Moss, Marilyn Ann. 2004. *Giant: George Stevens, A Life on Film,* University of Wisconsin Press.

Oller, John. 1997. *Jean Arthur: The Actress Nobody Knew,* New York: Limelight.

Parrish, Robert. 1976. *Growing Up in Hollywood,* London: Bodley Head.

Phillips, Gene D. 1973. "George Stevens," in *The Movie Makers: Artists in an Industry,* Chicago: Nelson Hall, pp. 83–98.

Ratcliffe, Michael. 1964. "The Sentimentalist," *Films and Filming,* February, p. 39.

Redfield, William. 1967. *Letters from an Actor,* London: Cassell.

Richie, Donald. 1970. *George Stevens: An American Romantic,* New York: Museum of Modern Art.

Roud, Richard (editor), 1980. *Cinema: A Critical Dictionary,* Volumes One and Two, London: Secker & Warburg.

Sarris, Andrew. 1968. *The American Cinema: Directors and Directions, 1929-1968,* New York: Dutton.

———. 1998. *You Ain't Heard Nothing Yet,* Oxford University Press.

Schaefer, Jack. 1949. *Shane,* Houghton Mifflin.

Schickel, Richard. 1985. *Cary Grant: A Celebration,* London: Bloomsbury.

Schindler, Colin. 1979. *Hollywood Goes to War,* London: Routledge & Kegan Paul.

Schwartz, Nancy L. 1977. "*Alice Adams*: From American Tragedy to Small-Town Dream-Come-True," in *The Classic American Novel and The Movies,* edited by Gerald Peary and Roger Schatzkin, New York: Frederick Ungar, pp. 218–25.

Sennett, Ted. 1989. "Men Will be Boys: *Gunga Din,*" in *Hollywood's Golden Year, 1939,* New York: St. Martins, pp. 3–17.

Shaw, Irwin. 1949. *The Young Lions,* London: Jonathan Cape.

Shipman, David. 1982; 1984. *The Story of Cinema,* Volumes 1 and 2, London: Hodder and Stoughton.

Silvester, Christopher (editor). 1998. *The Grove Book of Hollywood,* New York: Grove.

Sinyard, Neil. 1992. *Children in the Movies,* London: Batsford.

———. 1984. "George Stevens: A Fine Romantic: Parts 1 and 2," *National Film Theatre Programme,* August and September, pp. 8–10, 9–11.

Smith, Henry Nash. 1950. *Virgin Land: The American West as Symbol and Myth.* New York: Vintage.

Smith, Susan. 2012. *Elizabeth Taylor,* London: British Film Institute.

Solnit, Rebecca. 2015. "Giantess," *Harper's Magazine,* September.

Spoto, Donald. 1996. *Rebel: The Life and Legend of James Dean,* London: HarperCollins.

Stanbrook, Alan. 1966. "The Return of *Shane,*" *Films and Filming,* June, pp. 37–41.

Stang, Joanne. 1959. "Hollywood Romantic: George Stevens," *Films and Filming,* pp. 9–11, 33.

Steen, Mike (editor). 1974. *Hollywood Speaks,* New York: G.P. Putnam.

Stevens, George, Jr. 2006. *Conversations with the Great Moviemakers of Hollywood's Golden Age,* New York: Vintage.

Taylor, C. 1967. "Blacklist: Horror Role for Anne Revere," 20 June, *Los Angeles Times,* p. 20.

Thomas, Bob. 1967. *King Cohn,* London: Barrie and Rockliff.

Tibbetts, John C., and Welsh, James M. 2005. *The Encyclopedia of Novels into Film,* 2nd edition, New York: Facts on File.

Tonguette, Peter. 2013. "Review: *The Only Game in Town,*" *Sight and Sound,* August.

———. 2016 "*Giant* at 60," *Sight and Sound* online, 13 December.

Truffaut, Francois. 1989. *Letters,* translated by Gilbert Adair, London: Faber & Faber.

Tyler, Parker. 1947; 1971. *Magic and Myth of the Movies,* London: Secker & Warburg.

Tynan, Kenneth. 1954. " Days in the Dream Factory," *Punch,* 12 and 19 May, in *The Grove Book of Hollywood,* edited by Christopher Sylvester, New York: Grove, 1998, pp. 434–41.

———. 1961. *Curtains,* Longmans: London.

Van Druten, John. 1944. *I Remember Mama,* New York: Samuel French.

Vidor, King. 1972. *King Vidor on Film Making,* London: W.H. Allen.

Warshow, Robert. 1970. "Movie Chronicle: The Westerner," in *The Immediate Experience,* New York: Atheneum, pp. 135–54.

Weddle, David. 1996. *Sam Peckinpah: "If They Move, Kill 'Em!,"* London: Faber.

Winters, Shelley. 1989. *Best of Times, Worst of Times.* London: Muller.

Yeck, Joanne L., and Jewell, Richard. 1987. "Interview with Pandro S. Berman," *Magill's Cinema Annual 1987,* edited by Frank C. Magill, Pasadena: Salem, pp. 15–22.

Zinnemann, Fred. 1992. *An Autobiography,* London: Bloomsbury.

Index